Expanding Class

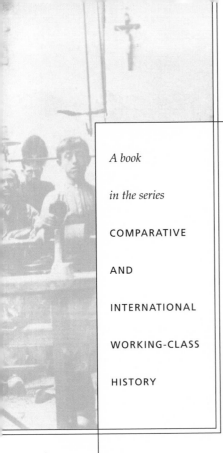

A book

in the series

COMPARATIVE

AND

INTERNATIONAL

WORKING-CLASS

HISTORY

General Editors

Andrew Gordon *Harvard University*

Daniel James *Duke University*

Alexander Keyssar *Duke University*

EXPANDING CLASS

Power and Everyday Politics in Industrial

Communities, The Netherlands, 1850 – 1950

Don Kalb

Duke University Press

Durham and London

1997

HD
8519
.N67
K 35
1997

Designed by Cherie Westmoreland   Typeset in Palatino with Frutiger display by Keystone Typesetting, Inc.

Library of Congress Cataloging-in-Publication Data appear on the last printed page of this book.

Portions of an article by Don Kalb, "Moral Production, Class Capacities, and Communal Commotion: An Illustration from Central Brabant Shoemaking," *Social History* 16 (1991): 279–99, have been included in this book, by permission of the publisher, Routledge Ltd.

Contents

Preface

This book originated from three engagements: the history of working class culture, in particular in the Dutch province of North Brabant; the theory and methodology of the encounter between anthropology and history; and the current apparently wholesale substitution for marxian, political-economy approaches of a postmodern quest for identity, discourse, and culture research.

The historical studies presented here were started in the late eighties. As I entered the final phase of writing and revising, I became increasingly aware that over the years, while responding to theoretical debate in the field, I had in fact been developing a rather particular approach to popular culture and class formation. This approach seemed to represent a methodology that made definite choices both within the wider interdisciplinary field of anthropology and history and within the current debates on marxism, materialism, and its more or less postmodern opponents. I realized I needed to try to spell out these methodological considerations in order to fully clarify the point of what I was trying to do in the historical case studies.

What resulted is the present book. It oscillates, sometimes perhaps somewhat uneasily, between global arguments in "high" theory and local reports from "low" on the North Brabant ground. But whatever its shortcomings, I do believe that it sharpens our understanding of North Brabant popular history, industrial class formation, and the methodological issues at stake in wider debates in social science history and historical anthropology.

I have received crucial support from Professor Gerrit Jansen and Professor Hans Righart, both of Utrecht University, who provided me in various ways with a decisive measure of trust and encouragement. I am particularly grateful to Dr. Jack Burgers, who brought me to Utrecht University in 1990 and has remained a nearby source of inspiration, support, and joy since then. I was fortunate to become engaged with the Amsterdam School of Social Science Research in 1989; its broad, inter-disciplinary, internationally oriented, and historically interested social science environment has certainly left its mark on the present text. The interdisciplinary orientation of the urban studies group and the depart-ment of general social sciences of Utrecht University, being much less historical and much more focused on contemporary social problems, pro-vided me with new subjects and insights while my colleagues seemed to appreciate my own particular contributions; it is a good place to work. Apart from Jack Burgers, I thank in particular Godfried Engbersen for support and conversations. Nico Wilterdink, from both Utrecht Univer-sity and the Amsterdam School, carefully read and commented on an earlier version of the text. Bonno Thoden van Velsen (Utrecht and Am-sterdam) asked incisive questions. NWO, the Dutch organization for scientific research, as well as Utrecht University, enabled me to travel to the United States on a yearly basis. I thank Gerald Sider of the City University of New York graduate center for some very wise words; Gus Carbonella of the graduate center at CUNY, for continuing conversations, great insights, and much humor and friendship; Ron Aminzade and Mary Joe Maynes of the University of Minnesota, for friendship, impor-tant help, and welcome comments on chapter 1; Mike Hanagan of the Center for the Study of Social Change of the New School for Social Re-search, for support and comments; Charles Tilly of Columbia, for encour-agement and comments on chapter 2; Alf Lüdtke of the Max Planck Institut für Geschichte at Göttingen, for friendship, conversations, and encouragement; and finally Svend Aage Andersen of the Center for Cul-tural Studies at Aarhus University, for his friendship and conversations. Three anonymous reviewers for Duke University Press had very percep-tive remarks. They helped me to organize my argument better and to see the loose ends. Valerie Millholland, my editor at Duke, kept me on track during the editorial process.

Ann Long edited and corrected my broken American-English. Hen-riëtte van de Graaf gave important secretarial support when I needed this.

In Eindhoven I have incurred debts with Ad Otten of the Philips Company Archives, local historian Jan van Oorschot, and Jan Spooren-berg and Jan Hagen, both of the municipal archive. I thank Toon Ververs for support in Kaatsheuvel. Dr. Sjef Stoop kindly provided me with a draft version of his dissertation.

My co-editors of *Focaal* were a continuing source of comradeship without which the final decade would have been very different. I thank in particular Herman Tak and Hans Marks, and no less so Bart Vink, for simply being there all the time, and for some special times in particular. Although she doesn't want to be thanked, this really is the place to express my unending love and gratitude to Ellen. My father and mother, Jo Kalb and Dinie Kalb-van Grimbergen, have been essential sources of inspiration and support. I dedicate the book to my mother, who died four years ago at the age of fifty-nine. I want Zep and Lois to know that their grandma's spirit inhabits this text.

Historical explanation discloses not how history must have eventuated but why it eventuated, in this way and not in other ways. . . .

What concerned Marx most closely was not "economics" nor even . . . epistemology but power. It was to understand power in society that he entered that lifelong detour into economic theory.

E. P. THOMPSON *The Poverty of Theory*

Arbeit war weit mehr als instrumentelles Handeln. Arbeit stand vielmehr für eine vielschichtige Praxis, in der ökonomische, soziale und kulturelle Momente gleichermassen bedeutsam waren.

ALF LÜDTKE *Eigen-Sinn*

Empirical observation must in each separate instance bring out empirically, and without mystification and speculation, the connection of the social and political structure with production.

MARX *German Ideology*

There is an economic logic and a moral logic and it is futile to argue as to which we give priority since they are different expressions of the same "kernel" of human relationship.

E. P. THOMPSON *The Long Revolution*

A class does not necessarily speak with one voice, nor even a clear voice.

GERALD SIDER *Culture and Class in Anthropology and History*

Why make things simple when one can make them complicated?

JACQUES REVEL *Le Pouvoir au Village*

After so many failed prophecies, is it not in the interest of social science to embrace complexity, be it at some sacrifice of its claim to predictive power?

ALBERT O. HIRSCHMAN, *Rival Views of Market Society*

Introduction

For some, this book will be out of place. It studies an unfashionable subject, the formation and reformation of industrial working classes, and elaborates an unpopular approach, a specific version of class analysis. It does so self-consciously and refuses to partake in contemporary currents of intellectual deforestation, as Eric Wolf once called those elusive trends that variously appear under the banner of "the literary turn," postmaterialism, poststructuralism, discourse analysis, language, consumption.

The book presents studies of industrial class formation in the Dutch province of North Brabant between about 1880 and 1950. This region is situated in the south of the Netherlands, below the great rivers and bordering Belgium. Peripherally located vis-à-vis the political, economic, and cultural centers of the nation, it combined small-scale commercial and peasant agriculture with extensive industrialization. However, despite a high degree of industrial wage dependency, by 1910 its local population did not bring forth a strong labor movement popularizing the language of class. Here we have a case that seems perfectly suited to foster the current dismay with class-oriented social and historical analysis. Living in one of the industrial heartlands of the Netherlands, people in this region never appear to have understood themselves as essentially class divided. Rather, they embraced Catholic "solidarism," seem to have put their trust in forms of company paternalism, or expressed politically inarticulate versions of populism. On first glance, Brabant provides excellent reasons to join the choir of contemporary class skeptics in social science.

It is my contention that contemporary disillusionment with class, as a research program and as an analytic category, is primarily caused by unnecessary reductionism, reification, and essentialism in conventional materialist methodologies. Instead of subscribing to probably short-lived postmodernist, poststructuralist, and postmaterialist intellectual fads, I propose to remedy materialist traditions from within. I will do so by taking steps in two contrary, albeit complementary, directions: firstly, by developing a more ambitious, encompassing, relational, dynamic, and comprehensive class concept; and secondly, by elaborating a more open, less deductive, and more contingent form of social class analysis. By expanding the scope of class, while giving room to the nondeductible, contingent, but nevertheless systematic influences of time and place, these moves will, I hope, recover the ground for culturally sensitive versions of materialist research. These are needed, not so much because class analysis should become an interpretive endeavor, as Mike Savage has recently suggested,[1] but rather because it is utterly mystifying to study culture, discourse, meaning, or even hegemony as sui generis, as possessing a force and directionality of their own. The current shift away from social history and historical sociology to the popular fields of cultural history, cultural studies, and communication studies is misleading.

My case studies of class formation in subregions of industrializing Brabant tend to illustrate that an anthropological interest in popular culture, discourse, and everyday life can, and indeed should, be wedded to a class-oriented analysis of the sources, operation, and mechanisms of social power and social process. This is so not only because power, change, and inequality are central aspects of social life that ought not be missed by any serious analyst of human affairs (that is, unless he or she accepts political irrelevance), but more importantly because class-oriented analysis can reveal crucial ambiguities, contradictions, divisions, limits, obstacles, and dynamics of culture that cannot be uncovered in other ways. In short, by consciously elaborating an approach based on a materialist idea of class with the intention to study social power and social process, I claim a more penetrating methodology for explaining and understanding culture.

This program immediately suggests three principal methodological concerns: a concern with culture as social process; with power as integral to culture and culture to power; and consequently with the social processes that lead to the forging and unforging of hegemonies. In contrast to what recent texts seem to imply,[2] this triplet precisely requires an engagement with class, because class, of all the key concepts of social analysis, has been the most specific tool for describing and analyzing the "fields of force" that produce, at the same moment, both social alignments and social cleavages, as well as the vector of change therein. The concept of class, therefore, enables an understanding of culture that is at the same time dynamic and relational, since it is rooted in the basic and never frictionless ties and interdependencies between sets of people as arising from their efforts to survive and maintain themselves. Departing from the concrete, diverging, and contradictory interests (in the broad sense) of groups of people rather than from the supposed sharing of abstract meaning, it prevents the static, holistic, billiard-ball-like notions of culture and society that so often plague anthropology and sociology.[3]

The concept of class, moreover, hosts the most comprehensive efforts to deal with social power. It informs a conceptualization of power not simply as a mere attribute of particular agents or institutions as in functionalist treatments, but rather as an integral property of the patterns of relationships between sets of people, as the work of scholars such as Edward Thompson and Eric Wolf amply illustrates.[4] Class presupposes that human interests (broadly conceived) simply and realistically begin with the ways in which people (of both sexes) try to secure their livelihoods by performing their daily work. It emphatically claims that work is never just the act of earning a living, but rather the social and cultural crux around which whole ways of life become organized and maintained. Class, in addition, assumes that work, survival, and reproduction are what bring people together in the first place. It argues that from the daily necessity to secure a living arise specific and complex patterns of social labor, which in turn underpin—and are maintained by—specific forms of civilization and appropriation. It finally holds that human needs for orientation and meaning are part and parcel of the problems and complexities of these basic practices and key relationships.

Without an idea of class so deployed, an engagement with culture as process and with the social dynamics undergirding the making, unmaking, and limits of cultural dominance is ultimately vacuous, because inherently static and sui generis. Class points, at the same moment, to people's intentional efforts to make the best of their world as well as to their unchosen need to find the friction-ridden alignments to do so. Thus, it dynamizes culture and deinstitutionalizes power.

EXPANDING CLASS

Among the fallacies that plague class-oriented approaches, economistic reductions reign prominent. They come in various disciplinary guises, ranging from analytic philosophy to stratification sociology and, of course, neoclassical economy.[5] Economic reductionism is, among other things, expressed in teleological philosophies of history and positivist theories about the determination of action by purported class position.

What distinguishes these argumentative misconceptions in the first place is a very flat, abbreviated, hardly relational, essentialist, and instrumentalist reading of central materialist concepts such as "production," "interest," and "materiality." They consequently tend to attach much weight to the observable behavior of, by definition, profit-maximizing individuals.

This is not the place to prove that such fallacies might as well be supported as be rejected by the canonical texts of historical materialism. Karl Marx was not the person to sit down quietly and work out his ideas according to the rigorous standards of twentieth-century analytical philosophy. But particularly among what can be called "relational marxists" (who have generally and rather confusingly been called "cultural materialists") a strong and persuasive case has been made against economistic and essentialist readings of materialism.[6] Variously building on marxist authors such as E. P. Thompson and Raymond Williams, or seeking support in anthropology and comparative historical sociology, scholars such as Derek Sayer, Jorge Larrain, Richard Miller, Arthur Stinchcombe, and Maurice Godelier, as well as Eric Wolf and David Harvey, have shown the way out of such fallacies without immediately throwing away the baby with the bathwater.[7]

Part of the problem might have originated with Marx's politically inspired exaggerations of untrammeled capitalist dominance, while another part is certainly due to reification by subsequent authors. Marx, like other scholars such as Adam Smith and Karl Polanyi, believed that modern capitalist society was marked by a separation of the sphere of the (market)-economy from the political and cultural spheres of society. This created an "unfettered economy" which then caused an unprecedented unleashing of productive and technological powers. Marx envisioned that before long society itself would become dominated by capital in the same way as textile production had become dominated by steam power. This, however, was an unwarranted exaggeration. Firstly, only some branches would ever become so concentrated and automated as the nineteenth-century textile manufacturing that Marx and others believed to become paradigmatic. Moreover, as sociologists, historical demographers, and social historians have shown, even in the most advanced textile localities in Lancashire at the time there obtained, instead of a growing separation between family, community, and capital, close and functionally necessary mutual interdependencies.[8]

Though Marx obviously reasoned by analogy rather than by strict definition, his sensitizing notion of a separation of the economy from other spheres was subsequently reified by more rigorous authors. The "economy" was increasingly taken to be a real, observable, clearly de-marcated, independent thing. From here it was but a short step to class as a purely economic fact and to interest as purely economically defined. That this is a fatally flawed reification of the original use of concepts by Marx has often been claimed by such British marxists as Rodney Hilton, Edward Thompson, and Raymond Williams.[9] Derek Sayer has recently pointed out that their reading was certainly justified.[10] Marx, Sayer shows, in accordance with his epistemology, had a fully relational and historical notion of economy, production, materiality. Marx was, maintains Sayer, "precisely redefining 'economic' relations—and thus the 'economic sphere', or 'economic structure', or 'economic base' of society—as comprising the totality of social relations . . . which make particular forms of production . . . possible."[11] Human values, systems of law, family practices, community relationships, and urban forms enter regularly into the fact and definition of production, because production simply cannot do without them. Marx, therefore, held that a mode of production was not just a mode of physical survival but rather a "definite mode of life."[12] Indeed, his consistent use of the distinction between the social and the material was not meant to indicate observably distinct and separate spheres, or things, or phenomena, but only to analytically dis-tinguish between different functions of one and the same phenomenon.

Reductionist approaches to class and economy, therefore, seem to have originated more with the a priori assumptions of ahistorical neo-classical economy (which is, of course, also a form of materialism) and its attendant positivist methodologies than with historical materialism per se. And the same is true with essentialist visions of the modern subject as homo-economicus, as per definition displaying the dominant drive to profit maximization. The problem is, as Derek Sayer has eloquently ar-gued, that such methodologies mistake appearances for essential facts. They are victims of the same fetishism that Marx indeed spent a lifetime arguing against.

An expanded concept of class, searching for the interconnections be-tween relationships in (and of) production, narrowly conceived, and social and cultural practices beyond the immediate point of production, albeit supportive of it, thus is really nothing new. It has been well estab-lished among historical materialists as diverse as Maurice Godelier, Rod-ney Hilton, Edward Thompson, Raymond Williams, and Eric Wolf. By pointing to the dynamic, and sometimes even contradictory intersections of culture, society, and production, and by directing attention to their mutual determinations and conflictual interdependencies in reproducing a whole way of life, I hold that such an expanded, historical, and relational class concept offers the best possibilities for escaping the intellectual errors of reductionism, reification, and essentialism. An expanded idea of class should describe the whole "field of force"[13] that emerges when unequal, divided, sometimes even antagonist sets of people, with differential access to different sets of resources, try to survive, understand, and reproduce their mutually connected ways of life. As a means of concentrating on the respective sources, limits, and purposes of their social power, and on the ways their interaction produces process and change, both inadvertently and intentionally, engendering opportunities as well as setbacks, class so conceived is an essential tool for understanding human action, including its preconditions and consequences. It is my contention that it will better serve a nonreductionist account of human life than any version of poststructuralism or postmaterialism that professes to do so, simply because it seeks to ground human meaning and signification in real inequalities and contradictory interdependencies, and does not conceive of it as a largely free-floating and autonomous phenomenon.

Marx's wild and multifaceted writing permits many different readings. Relational marxists tend to concentrate on his historical and methodological pieces and less on the deductive parts of *Capital* or on his more straightforwardly political texts. But, of course, other readings might equally well summon the support of the master, so it will remain necessary to clear my road a bit in order to clarify the further implications of a relational reading.

The brand of historical materialism I tend to adopt has important consequences for the Marxist theory of history and the idea of determination. Again, this is not the place to work this out at length. For a more extensive and persuasive treatment the reader is referred to the above-mentioned authors. But, both in general and for my own studies of industrial class formation in Brabant, it should be emphasized that the marxist teleological theory of history is a corpse that must be buried. Society has not become the sort of appendage to market-based steam power that Marx envisioned, nor have classes polarized the way he predicted, and neither has social revolution established socialism in the advanced West. Such teleology has been abundantly falsified.

But more fundamentally, the methodology of a relational materialism necessarily leaves the trajectory of capitalist development open and contingent. Though relational marxists hold that particular capitalist societies do display systematic tendencies of development as a function of their particular internal and external relationships, their overall direction can never be deduced as in "capital-logic" explanations. Rather, patterns and directions of development should be established by empirical study of concrete societies delimited in space and time. Such studies should focus on the relative capacities of (local) capitalist classes, on their insertion into global networks of accumulation and exchange, on the power of other classes, the effects of coalition formation, as well as on the forms and functions of the state. Instead of being deductible from the imputed logic of capital "set free," these contingent (though systematically related) conditions vary with place and time. Teleological history, therefore, gives way to close and historically grounded study.

An expanded class concept, then, implies a more limited role for "pure capitalism" in history, as well as a more open and contingent form of social class analysis. If capitalist production and its tendencies of development are conceived of as being fundamentally connected with the particular social systems in which they become established, specific local histories and particular social and cultural properties will necessarily help to shape possible local futures. In addition, as capitalism spread from the cores of the world system, compromised its antagonists at home, and engendered commercialization, industrialization, protest, and accommodation in other parts of the globe, it created multiple and interlinked local and regional trajectories of development. These trajectories were dependent on local conditions and relationships and on the moment and nature of their insertion into increasingly global patterns of accumulation. Class, therefore, implies a close consideration of the interaction between global and local histories; it directs attention to the particularities of place, as well as to the interlinkages in space. Class presumes a double vision: on geographical as well as on historical relationships; and above all on their continuous interaction.

Instead of deducing local histories from an imputed global and internal capitalist logic, then, one cannot but acknowledge, to paraphrase Charles Tilly, that when and where things happen within a sequence (like capitalist development) affects how they happen and what their outcome will be.[14] Or as Peter Worsley has written: "Capitalism works on existing cultural materials and often introduces new ones, but the dialectical synthesis is always culturally specific."[15] In sum: Localized and observable processes of capitalist change tend to be "path dependent" and not (pre)determined by any abstract capital-logic.[16]

Both the contingency and "path dependency" of local process, as well as the expanded and relational notion of class itself, have devastating consequences for the conventional sociological idea of determination. The canonical assumption in class theory of the determination of action and consciousness by structure rested in fact on a mild version of base/superstructure thinking. But since the "superstructure" happens to be heavily implicated in the "base" and vice versa, this chain of unproductive reasoning loses its very foundation.

However, this does not necessarily suggest the need for a poststructuralist or postmaterialist way out. In fact, if we take the argument to its logical conclusion, the structure-action polarity should leave its place in the methodological hierarchy to the dialectic between the local and the global. In the recent intriguing discussion of "structurist" approaches by Christopher Lloyd we can indeed find signs that the eighties' fascination with nonspatial, nonprocessual structure-action dilemmas, as expressed in the work of such eminent authors as Anthony Giddens and Pierre Bourdieu, has reached its end and is giving way to the spatial and processual problems of local-global linkages and their social consequences, in particular their effects on the relative power of social groups.[17] Instead of increasingly sophisticated schemes of neologisms to circumvent the never-ending problems of structure-action determinations, we may apparently expect in the near future a seminal, historically grounded interest in the opportunities and fates of localities and spatially defined and interlinked groups and classes in the light of global and national capital flows. Such a program coalesces neatly with the methodological starting points of a relational materialist class analysis.

Authors such as Andrew Abbott and Ron Aminzade have gone so far as to suggest that, if spatial and temporal relationships become so prominent in tracing trajectories of class, the chronology of spatially defined sequences in time (such as collective conflicts, the forging of alliances, the start of social programs, the nature and timing of industrial class formation, industrial restructuring) will take the place of the conventional positivist idea of determination.[18] They infer from this that narrativist methodologies, because providing the best vehicle for representing the different chronological chains of relevant spatial scales, have to take the place of the "variables paradigm." Variables presuppose fixed relations between fixed entities. They cannot deal with dynamic processual relationships in time and over space that constantly shape and reshape the effective nature of the constituent entities. Indeed, there can no longer be a conception of entities as entities, since clear boundaries turn out not to exist. Class analysis, then, becomes a narrative strategy, focusing on the historically embedded, shifting relationships between social groups as they are linked through production and reproduction, alternating between micro and macro levels, and accounting for the complex social processes in which they become entwined—processes which structure their chances and resources and which are perpetually kept going by their actions and interactions. The fascination with variables truly seems on the wane.

Relational materialist studies of class have in diverse ways been promoted by political-economy-minded anthropologists,[19] by the practitioners of the new urban sociology and critical geography,[20] and above all by protagonists of the new social history (including like-minded historical sociologists).[21] While anthropologists and new urban sociologists variously connected space, time, social organization, culture, political process, and urban environments to the study of class, the new social history turned the relational study of class virtually into its raison d'être. Here is the characterization of the new social history by Sean Wilentz:

In place of a static, instrumentalist economic determinism, they have treated class as a dynamic social relation, a form of social domination, determined largely by changing relations of production but shaped by cultural and political factors (including ethnicity and religion) without any apparent logic of economic interest. They take for granted the inescapable fact that class relations order power and social relationships; they have examined the numerous conflicts and accommodations that give rise to and accompany these relations as a complex series of social encounters, fusing culture and politics as well as economics. In short, they insist that the history of class relations cannot be deduced by some "economic" or sociological calculus and imposed on the past.... It must be examined as part of a human achievement in which men and women struggle to comprehend the social relations into which they were born ... (and in which) they sustain or challenge those relations in every phase of social life. (Wilentz 1984, 10)

Given such antireductionist endeavors, it comes as a surprise that contemporary dismay with class generally sets up a straw man of an economistic marxism that has been rare of late (except in some quarters of positivist inquiry such as stratification sociology and neoclassical economy). And it is true, critics are not just concentrating on some unsolved conceptual and methodological problems in order to build further on recent advances, but often propose the abandonment of the whole paradigm. Efforts at relational, historical, and expansive approaches to class, from E. P. Thompson to Michael Burawoy or Sharon Zukin, are thrown on a heap with straightforward economisms. They are dismissed for tenaciously hanging on to materialist premises that lead to demonstrably wrong empirical assumptions and deduce class consciousness where nothing even faintly resembling it can be found. Whether in such innovative strands of class-oriented research as the new social history or the new urban sociology, critics consistently point at the ultimate failure of empirical researchers to "connect structural position to class identity in a straightforward manner" (Berlanstein 1993, 10), or to find the "missing links in the chain of (class) structure, consciousness and action" (Pahl, 1989, 710), as if that were the single and exclusive raison d'être of class-oriented research. They often commence to embrace language, discourse, culture, or consumption as the largely independent intervening variable.

From a relational materialist point of view, however, class would never simply be this interest or that interest, to paraphrase E. P. Thompson, but rather the friction of interests. It is not this or that relation to the means of production, but the whole "field of force" that makes a particular mode of production in its totality possible, including its attendant modes of life. It is the "setting of limits and exerting of pressures"[22] that people become confronted with when they try to hold on to their own, or strive to become what seems legitimate and desirable to them. Class is, in short, an analytic, relational, and dynamic construct that sensitizes one to basic social mechanisms and key social relationships.[23] One cannot simply hope to find it out there in any unmediated way, just as there is no passe-partout for establishing its character.

Talking about a class, therefore, is always problematic and provisional (just like the idea of a group or a category). It is a shorthand for designating loosely defined sets of people who are affected by dynamic processes of capitalist change in comparable ways, ways that bear a family resemblance to each other. But we can never be certain which social and cultural processes are operating within a class so conceived to make collective styles, awareness, and action likely or unlikely. Repertoires of local knowledge as well as differential access to differently structured social, cultural, and material resources may diverge so much within a class that calling such people a class can appear utterly nonsensical to them. These are empirical questions of segmentation that are contingent to any study of class. But they cannot be a reason for abandoning the analysis of the whole wider context of shifting relationships, power, and action that class entails, especially since such segmentations are often the result of differences in timing and start positions of households and groups in their encounter with processes of capitalist industrialization. They therefore tend to be part and parcel of the patterned social and spatial unevenness of the process. They may be logically contingent, then, but are not necessarily external to class in history.

To the extent, however, that still lingering traces of reductionism, reification, essentialism, and teleology in the new materialisms are being criticized, the critique should not be dismissed. Instead of synchronically inquiring into the occupational backgrounds or relations to the means of production of people (households or individuals?) at one point in time, it appears less reductionistic, because more dynamic and contextual, to study the consequences of change in capitalist relationships over the long or medium run for "class identities" and collective action. Indeed, Thompson has powerfully shown that the theater of class can only be watched in the medium of time. By far the most illuminating research on class has been done by processual researchers, in particular by practitioners of the new social history. Concepts such as proletarianization and working class formation have been coined to designate the nature and direction of social change during the "long" nineteenth century. But though helping to prevent crude, mechanistic, and synchronic versions of reductionism, these processual concepts are now also questioned for carrying overly reductionist assumptions.

Craig Calhoun, for example, has highlighted the teleological and imprecise nature of some of the uses of the concept of class formation.[24] Both class formation and proletarianization can in fact only be used in a "thin" sense, describing the process by which ever larger percentages of populations come to depend on (industrial) wage labor of some kind.[25] But both are often deployed in more specific senses. Proletarianization is repeatedly conceived as a process of ever greater domination of capital over labor and as an always more complete subsumption of labor by capital. Working class formation, moreover, is often held to relate to proletarianization in the same way as action and consciousness in reductionist arguments are held to spring from occupational position. The concept therefore tends to harvest skepsis for being teleological. At the end of the process we should expect to find a working class "fully formed," with a mature and politically correct class consciousness. Both the finalism of increasing capitalist domination during the "long" nineteenth century as well as the assumption of increasingly "purified" class consciousness are untenable.

Historical research has shown that capitalists rarely chose the most capital-intensive route to competitiveness and labor control. Raphael Samuel emphasized the multiplication of menial and physical labor during industrialization.[26] Patrick Joyce pointed to the widespread practice of subcontracting among English entrepreneurs, as well as to the function of the working class family in internal labor markets.[27] The importance of paternalist practices among advanced employers has been stressed by Joyce and by Burawoy.[28] Alf Lüdtke emphasized the prevalence of "Kolonnenarbeit," that is, the internal subcontracting to self-regulating groups of more or less skilled workers in German metalware and engineering industries.[29] Sabel and Zeitlin have shown the importance of weakly capitalized, skill-intensive, and flexible forms of regional industrialization throughout Europe.[30] Wood and others have reminded us of recurrent processes of reskilling and the introduction of new categories of technology-oriented jobs in European industrialization.[31] Though there is no doubt about the general growth of unskilled, dominated, fully market dependent, and restrictive labor in industry up to the mid-twentieth century, there is also no reason to conclude that increasing capitalist control and ever sharper proletarian subsumption to technology as well as subjection to unstable markets was the only relevant trend. And to the extent that growing subordination was prevalent in certain trades, cities, or regions, it often affected young starting workers more than those habituated to older practices. Proletarianization, in the demanding sense of increased subjection, need not necessarily have been so predominant and inescapable an experience in the life of individual workers.

As industrialization took different social and technical paths in different regions and nations, forms of working class consciousness and organization differed accordingly. Though working class formation, understood as the growth of organization (and collective consciousness) among workers, occurred in all industrial regions of Europe, its social form and ideological content varied greatly. England, the most advanced country, gave birth to a large and activist trade union movement, whereas the labor party appeared rather late on the scene and remained relatively weak.[32] By the end of the century, on the other hand, France knew a notoriously weak and fragmented, albeit radical, labor movement in combination with strong republican-socialist politics. Germany became the quintessential example of a popular, unified, and centralized labor movement, where party and union were closely coordinated and widely supported, albeit in a remarkably uneven regional pattern. Other industrializing countries, with the exception of Belgium, had not yet witnessed strong national movements at the end of the century. This comparative variety warns against teleological and essentialist ideas of working class formation. Moreover, the variety of routes to an industrial world multiplies when we take different regional and urban patterns into account, when we start to include workers' organization within Catholic and other non-left-wing frameworks, and begin looking for systematic differences in everyday life, patterns of household formation, family practices, relationships with other classes, urban and regional political cultures and public life, and the consequences of different histories of state formation.

Thus, while the stronger, synchronic forms of economic reductionism have been thoroughly discredited by the new materialisms (the new social history, new urban sociology, the political economy school in U.S. anthropology, marxist cultural studies), weaker, processual forms of essentialism and finalism, embodied in such concepts as working class formation and proletarianization, do linger on.

Serious criticism of essentialism and finalism in processual approaches to class, such as the working class formation and proletarianization approach, seems to fall into at least two clusters of scientific work. The first I will call the historical anthropology critique, which is primarily concerned with the problem of nonreducible working class "identities."[33] The second consists of the macro-comparativists' effort to deal with the problem of nonteleological and diverging national paths of class formation.[34] Characteristically, as we will see, both tend to dismember what, from the point of view of a relational materialist methodology, operating with an expanded class concept, appears to be the unity of spatially and temporally delimited processes of working class formation (in the "thin" sense of the term). My alternative to these alternatives is sketched later.

Approaches within historical anthropology to working class identities take their nonreducibility to "the base," the "structure," or the "system" as their methodological point of departure. Patrick Joyce, for example, sets out to show that "the consciousness of a class need not be the consciousness of class."[35] With a wealth of material from popular culture, leisure, and formalized discourses about work, the union, and politics, he successfully persuades his readers that nineteenth-century English workers did not entertain highly conflictual and dichotomous notions of production-based, essential conflict between classes. Their worldviews, on the contrary, were consistently conciliatory and populist. Their imagined utopias, likewise, never touched on anything like the colllectivization of the means of production, nor even on disobedience. The a priori emphasis on class formation as the master process in nineteenth-century England, propounded by Eric Hobsbawm and Edward Thompson, is therefore misleading, argues Joyce. Working people up to the end of the century and after held to "traditional" notions of society and morality. Such notions were derived more from the world of the independent cottage laborer than from the urban landscape of factory industry.

Likewise, William Reddy has dismissed the concept of class as utterly incapable of capturing popular mentalities.[36] The concept, he maintains, is hopelessly tainted with assumptions about the equivalent meaning of money and markets to differentially positioned people. Exchange between employers and workers, however, is not so much uneven, as marxists hold, but fundamentally dissimilar ("asymmetrical"). The poor need to sell their labor power in order to survive, while the rich can employ them or not, just as they please. Markets, therefore, instead of being liberating, can be very coercive to those with little means. This coerciveness has consistently been overlooked by left-wing theorists, says Reddy. The left has been fully distracted by the "liberal illusion" of general progress by universal exchange and has only parted way with their liberal confreres to the extent that they thought people were getting too small a piece of the growing cake. Both the assumption of the spread of markets and of market-based grievances, on closer scrutiny, turn out to be wrong. His detailed historical research on textile workers in northern France richly demonstrates that the fact and experience of unjust factory discipline and political domination of communities by large entrepreneurs was much more widespread among dependent wage workers than were complaints about money and markets. It was unjust discipline and the violation of honor rather than the feeling of getting too little that animated their recurrent rebellions. Reddy, therefore, proposes to put the whole materialist tradition aside for being obsessed with numerical inequality instead of with asymmetries of culture and power. We need a new theory of history, he says, that does not make any a priori assumption about either the direction of historical change (like the spread of markets), the formation of organized collectivities such as classes, or the motives of people. He finds these requisites in a micro-level "interpretive theory of history." He argues that people are, by definition, constrained by any social order and that meanings based in public discourses always tend to rationalize the enforced disciplines. At the moment coercion dwindles, such as in revolutionary situations, repressed individual desires are set free and lead to "crises of meaning."

Historical anthropologies such as those of Reddy and Joyce have their strong points. Their methods of systematic interpretation of disparate evidence on working class identities sensitizes us to the discrepancies between the assumptions of received theories and actual historical popular outlooks and forms of experience. This is a genuine gain. But their weaknesses are also evident. They tend to search for essentials of identity and often generalize over wide, dissimilar populations and broad epochs. Thus Joyce notes the great differences between workers' culture in London, Lancashire, and Yorkshire, as well as the substantial gap between skilled and unskilled workers, respectable and less respectable. Nevertheless, the sources of his discourse analysis, typically produced for a national public, do not allow him to address the consequences of such differences in regional modes of production and cleavages between class segments for the popular reception of these formal discourses. The picture he paints of working class outlooks, consequently, is static and global. More importantly, working class experience appears as coherent and unified, truly amounting to a system of conceptions and beliefs. The dynamics of experience that class released underneath the Victorian cloak of respectability, and its moralizing dreams of social integration, are not studied or theorized. Anthropologists have often warned against such coherent and essentialist ideas of culture, and it is precisely here that a relational concept of class is needed.[37]

Reddy's "interpretive theory of history" similarly externalizes contradiction, tension, and ambivalence of human experience by relegating its source to historical "accidents" such as revolutions (indeed, that is what revolutions become in his micro-level theory). He disconnects experiential dynamics from the real everyday frictions and cleavages of social life. His emphasis on workers' condemnation of unjust discipline and violated honor is evidently salutary and empirically well established, but he fails to connect such feelings to the particular mechanisms, resources, and traditions that classes were able to mobilize on their behalf. Nor is he particularly interested in the collective resources needed by dependent populations for collectively nourishing and voicing their complaints in the first place. While his empirical research is very seminal and suggestive, his theoretical statements consciously abdicate any attempt to link identities and the occurrence of collective protest to wider patterns of class power and social change.

Though their point of critique is well taken, historical anthropologies of working class identities tend to evade history by failing to address the patterned interplay of social, material, and experiential processes that gives direction to history. Their concern with reading the texts of popular identity tends to distract them from analyzing the real, material, and context-bound processes and relationships that underlie the formation of such identities in action and practice. These processes and relationships generate important variations between localities, regions, class segments, and countries, and should therefore be internal to any concern with the production of culture and identity.

The comparativist critique of teleological assumptions connected with the concept of working class formation centers on the reality of different national paths and patterns of workers' organization and collective action. In order to escape the essentialist assumption that a class in itself will necessarily and naturally "act for itself," Ira Katznelson proposes to dissect the concept of class into four "levels."[38] The first level describes "the structure of capitalist economic development," the extent of proletarianization of a given national population, the degree of capital accumulation and concentration. The second level refers to "the social organization of society lived by actual people in real social formations." It concerns the organization of work, labor markets, cities, etc. But it does not contain "consciousness, culture, and politics." Katznelson insists that this level tells us "how workers exist . . . in certain circumstances, but not how they will think or act" (Katznelson 1986, 17). At the third level, classes "are formed as groups," sharing certain dispositions and understandings. And at the fourth level we finally encounter organization and "self-conscious" collective action. It is the variation in the "content and form" of the fourth level that he and others set out to explain by relating it to variations in levels one, two, and, above all, level three.

The problem with Katznelson's scheme is his nominalist distinction between "levels" which subsequently tend to be treated as really existing distinct and separate things. Consequently, and in spite of his intent to prevent just that, there is an inevitable progressive logic in his scheme that leads to the suggestion that level four should somehow be the crown on the accomplishments of class formation in the earlier levels. It is actually the reification of levels—the apparent empirical separation of capitalist logic (level one), structure (level two), consciousness (level three), and action (level four)—that produces this unfortunate result. The levels transform into "stages."

While discussing the content of the levels, Katznelson feels forced to add that "in reality" each level's content is systematically affected by the content of other levels. Thus he acknowledges the presence of the state and organized class forces in the sphere of production, just as he recognizes that production enters demography and urbanization. But if that is the case, as it certainly is, it should also be said that the "dispositions" residing in level three are by definition part and parcel of any other level.

Even so abstract a concept as capital accumulation cannot be empirically conceived of without a whole world of necessary "dispositions," and indeed, thoughts, actions, convictions, and the power of persuasion and coercion to back them. But the unintended effect of sharply distinguishing between the supposed empirical contents of the levels is that they become treated as empirically distinct phenomena, neatly separated both in reality and description. This nominalist reification also leads him to argue that on levels one and two his cases for comparison are relatively similar, while they would precisely start to diverge on higher levels. His account fatally echoes the base-superstructure distinction that relational marxist historiography had set out to dismantle, including an attribution of more than mere "relative autonomy" to his superstructure.

Historical anthropology approaches and macro-comparativists have correctly stressed the nonreducibility and nonfinalism of working class identities and national patterns of working class formation. However, by seeking solutions for reductionism and teleology in the particular historical weight to be attributed to culture, they have parted from the more basic question of how culture, class, and production are, in each empirical case, interwoven. The road they took could not but lead them away from clarifying the specific dialectical, mutually constitutive relations between Marx's "modes of production" and "modes of life." Accordingly, their work suffers respectively from essentialist notions of identity and from a reified opposition between the mental and the material. Though their points of critique were seminal, their proposed methodological alternatives, in the end, were dissatisfying. It cannot be a question of how much culture we have to glue onto class before we arrive at persuasive treatments. It is a question of how to identify and describe their dynamic intersections. Theoretical concepts are not empirical variables.

POWER, HEGEMONY, EVERYDAY POLITICS

Trajectories of class and industrial class formation should not be explained by recourse to a supposed economic base, nor to any unilinear process such as labor's subjection to capital through technology and markets. Instead of longing for reduction, I think we should finally embrace complexity by confronting head-on the enormous variability of the processes at stake. There is the obvious fact of multiple and highly diverging local, regional, and national paths of industrialization and industrial class formation. There are the differences in starting points and timing, in particular in relation to other "master processes." There are variations in the interconnections with other master processes, and variations in spatial interlinkages. In addition, there is the surprising variability of power and resource distribution among classes and class segments in different times, places, and contexts. And there is the remarkable but as yet weakly captured variety of culturally distinct outcomes between groups, localities, regions, and nations. Within the encompassing process of industrial class formation, it is with this variability, its causes, consequences, and bases in real life, that our methodologies must come to grips.

What I propose is a return from abstract, reified visions and macrocomparisons to grounded theory. The approach should in some ways resemble the earlier anthropology of peasant societies as embodied, for example, in the famous Puerto Rican project[39] but be directed at industrial working class formation, and should follow the example set by local working class formation studies[40] but with a much greater anthropological eye for everyday life and cultural processes,[41] as well as a geographer's instinct for space and spatial linkages. It is my contention that, in order to do so, we need a methodology that aims, in each particular case, to explore the specific interconnections between what Marx called "mode of production" and "mode of life," as inspired by a relational and expanded idea of class. This means that we will have to clarify how family, locality, public life, and the linkages with higher societal levels like the national state and the world system relate to the nature and vicissitudes of everyday work and survival, and how the particular pattern and timing of such connections produce particular *couleurs locales* within the encompassing process of class formation.

In order to describe and theorize succinctly the particular nature of specific local configurations, I believe we need to part with all a priori determinations, directionalities, and relative autonomies. Instead, we must start by elaborating the conceptual tools of power and hegemony, and introduce the notion of everyday politics.

It seems symptomatic of the methodological weakness of both the macro-comparativist and the historical anthropology alternatives to proletarianization and working class formation approaches that detailed, small-scale, and ethnographic analyses of localized cases are abandoned for increasingly macroscopic and transhistorical visions. Arguably, anthropological miniatures, by bringing together actions, agents, and contexts (and the inflated dilemma's of structure-agency / micro-macro etc.), are the most realistic methodological tool to prevent precisely the unsatisfactory reductions and reifications that these approaches originally set out to counter.[42] Though people are always incorporated into higher levels of spatial and systemic coordination, it is the particular strength of views from below, as Michael Burawoy, Alf Lüdtke, James Scott, and others have recently been reminding us, that they facilitate an idea of how such differentiated and abstract large-scale structures come together, and are appropriated, in concrete human lives and everyday conjunctures.[43] Micro perspectives can show how large-scale structures shape the specific "fields of force" and "webs of significance" within which common daily lives are led. They can enable us to see how such "fields" and "webs" motivate people and become in turn motivated by them, how people try to make use of them and adapt them to their needs, and how they become appropriated in specific forms of daily life, local knowledge, and survival.

Most importantly, when wedded to a relational and expanded concept of class, the view from below enables a dynamic approach to culture and a deinstitutionalized analysis of power. Culture, indeed, is not primarily the "shared beliefs, attitudes, and systems of meaning" that conventional anthropology has presented to us.[44] Culture, certainly, is shared. And there is no doubt that it is a public process in the first place. But by excluding the prior issue of how exactly meanings become shared, what the limits are to the sharing, how public meanings relate to events in more private spheres, how culture is produced, used by different people in different positions and contexts, and sometimes contested, such conventional anthropological conceptions of culture bear an irreparably conservative stamp and make them a hopelessly inappropriate tool for the study of complex and dynamic societies.[45]

From the point of view of relational materialism, however, the most important issue here is not the currently celebrated fact that complex societies generally provide multiple sources of knowing and tend to generate divergent and competing discourses, styles, and ideologies. Although this basic premise of contemporary cultural studies forms a welcome and necessary denial of the notion of a unitary and coherent cultural universe, a class-oriented approach seeks to enter the debate somewhere else.

Anthropologists have taught us that the essential importance of an approach from below is that it may provide a keen sense of the ways in which common knowledge, inscribed in the real and routinizing everyday practices of keeping life going, diverges, relativizes, hesitantly questions, or sometimes outrightly denies the tenets of wider, official, ritualized, and often state-sanctioned cultural systems. This is exactly the point at which the methodology of interpreting or reading culture is transformed into studying culture as a dynamic hegemonic process. Anthropologists such as Robert Redfield and Robert Lowie have long pointed to the discrepancy and interconnections between respectively "little traditions" and "great traditions," "matter-of-fact usage" and "rationalizations."[46] But it was Antonio Gramsci who turned the dialectic between "common sense" or "folklore" and hegemony into the central fact of cultural process and thus started to link the study of culture to the analysis of social power.[47]

A relational concept of class becomes relevant to the study of hegemony and cultural dominance, not because it supposedly describes clearly demarcated and homogeneous collectivities with clearly discernible and coherent conflictive interests which then become projected in ideological class struggle, as Gramsci and other marxists sometimes seem to imply. Classes are simply not the transcendent, coherent, and empirically well delineated things they are too often taken to be. Nor do they generally represent themselves in such a way. Rather, a relational concept of class can be used to specify the mechanisms, processes, and shifts in basic social relationships that constantly generate frictions between current repertoires of "matter-of-fact" knowledge, daily work, and reproductive routines on the one hand, and the more abstract rationalizations and legitimations (ritualized in official public life and institutionalized in great traditions and state politics) on the other.

Culture and hegemony, then, are an active material force. They are inscribed in the very structures of daily life, work, and appropriation; they are embodied in work rules, technological knowledge, relationships between equals and unequals, and between sexes, generations, and within households. Hegemony is acted out on the street and in public life. And it becomes generally expressed in the freedoms and obligations that sets of people may claim vis-à-vis each other, and that seem desirable, respectable, just, and rightful to them. Moreover, its terms are not just inscribed in the social routines pertaining to these spheres and places; they are also the object of constant negotiations, appropriations, and sometimes outright contestations *in situ.*

Negotiations, renegotiations, abrogations, and contestations, indeed, inevitably recur because capitalism, by definition, always tends to "creatively destroy" the terms of an earlier compromise and steadily proceeds to introduce new ones. Capitalists, private or collective, are forced to do so either because of changes in the order of competitiveness among themselves and the competitive advantage of their regions, restructuring of technology and work organization, shifts in the balance of power between classes and regions, and changes in the arrangements between wage work and reproduction.

Thus, while a micro-perspective may register these scattered fragments of cultural power all over the spheres and spots of daily life, a relational concept of class may suggest their common base in the shifting social balances of industrial capitalism as a mode of production, accumulation, and everyday life. These shifting relational balances should be thought of as possessing a force and directionality of their own. They develop a momentum that is felt throughout the whole chain of interdependent actors, setting limits and exerting pressures on the motives and actions of widely scattered sets of people who can often hardly be aware of the origins and implications of the process, nor of their actual interdependencies, or are aware of them in thoroughly different terms. In combination, then, hegemony and class amount to a radical deinstitutionalizing and dynamizing of the concept of power. However, they do so without granting it the transcendental and sui generis character it has acquired through the work of Michel Foucault and other radical poststructuralists such as Jacques Derrida. Power is never simply anywhere. It is embodied in the specific interdependencies between sets of people as described by the concept of class, and derives its direction and impact therefrom. Power, in my view, becomes fully internal to the dynamic study of culture only when it is wedded to the expanded study of class and class formation.

Hegemony, to recapitulate, designates a whole dynamic "field of force," both cultural and material, that exerts pressures and sets limits on the motivations and actions of people, while never encompassing all genres of action and experience. In order to become relational, dynamic, and directional, this "field of force" requires the notion of class to specify its sources, limits, and mechanisms, and demands a strategy from below to explore its concrete, contextual, and conflictive dimensions. This relational vision of class and cultural process amounts to a radically deinstitutionalized idea of power, because power is studied as the inseparable property of the shifting relationships that both class and hegemony entail.

These insights can now be brought to bear on Alf Lüdtke's idea of "everyday politics." Lüdtke developed the concept in order to direct attention away from large-scale social movements, formal politics, and historical instances of outright popular rebellion or explicit class protest.[48] The concept should highlight the small acts by which common people, habitually rather than incidentally, appropriate time, space, autonomy, and opportunities for themselves and their own. I embrace the concept against the methodological background sketched above. The notion of everyday politics conveniently circumvents the problems of reductionism and economism associated with the concept of interest. But in contrast to the opposite of interest, which in this context would be "meaning," it wisely sticks to the idea that people entertain visions of what is best and most advantageous for themselves and look for ways to realize that. I therefore hold that everyday politics describes the whole spectrum of motivations, from short-term instrumental interests to longer-term emotional needs, projects, affections, and belongings.

Everyday politics, moreover, should not be seen as the opposite of state politics or class politics. Indeed, the small-scale private or collective resources needed to realize social opportunities, from pride and satisfaction to wealth and leisure, are closely intertwined with the patterned fields of force that are specified by class, organized by states and formal collectivities, and manifested in current hegemonies.[49] Indeed, I believe that much of the inspiration (though not all) behind the effort at self-realization by enlarging one's room for maneuver is derived from existing (class structured) cultural repertoires, not unlike Bourdieu's idea of habitus.[50] It is a question of levels of abstraction and aggregation. I hold everyday politics to be a very intimate approximation of real human beings trying to make the best of their world. However, they necessarily do so within a wider field of force, shaped by relations not of their own making. These relations are marked by systematic social divisions and conflicting interests, which are expressed in formalized structures and hegemonic regimes (and sometimes by open rivalry and rebellion) that can be constraining as well as enabling and at the same time display determinate tendencies for change.

The concept of everyday politics, as I define it, designates the practical encounter of common actors with existing cultural expectations and social power. It is, as it were, negotiation from below, and not only with one's superiors but also with one's self or with significant others. Moreover, it need not necessarily deny or shore up reigning cultural claims. It may certainly be the silent act of deviance, the exaggeration and ridiculing of deference, the momentary inversion of social roles, but it may also describe the ability to sneak through mazes, to withstand distractions, or to keep up respectable appearances in times of adversity, since what everyday politics is depends upon context. But it is never just arbitrary or incidental. On the contrary, I use the concept to designate the exemplary ways in which differentially positioned common people deal with the specific key relationships and cultural themes that shape the local industrial capitalist settings under study. It is the common experience and appropriation of, accommodation to, and struggle with existing hegemonies as they are grounded in specific, territorially delineated regimes of industrial production and capitalist accumulation that I seek to probe.

Finally, the concept of everyday politics is not limited to the world of work and wages, just as class should not be restricted to labor. Since practices and relationships outside production proper, such as family, community, and leisure, and formal structures like those of the state and civil life are, in general, closely and specifically interwoven with the everyday reality of work, they also become the terrain of everyday politics. Everyday politics thus relates to the whole dynamic field of force in which the specific properties of a whole pattern of industrialization and class formation are rooted.

To conclude: Each trajectory of industrial class formation implies a complex and characteristic conjunction of work, everyday life, appropriation, accumulation, and hegemony. The enormous variety of ensuing cultures of manifest protest and consent is therefore in the nature of things. Instead of elevating any one pattern (local, national, or ideological) to the status of paradigm, we would do better to face the fact of divergence, as Katzelson and Zolberg have insisted.

Historical divergence, however, is only part of a larger problem. More fundamentally, we need to establish a methodology that prevents the misleading reductions, reifications, and essentialisms that have stood in the way of sensitive class analysis. We really have to embrace complexity. Instead of bothering about abstract and timeless definitions and determinations, as sociologists, philosophers, and economists have so often tended to do, we need to describe and explain, in each empirical case, precisely those complex and characteristic conjunctions of work, everyday life, appropriation, accumulation, and hegemony that class informs. We need an understanding of class as it is lived and produced in specific temporal and spatial relationships.

It is my contention, therefore, that instead of abandoning the supposedly dead corpus of class and opting for the charms of culture, postmaterialism, or poststructuralism, we would do better to confront the very idols that have caused its collapse. I propose to do so by expanding its scope and developing a less rigid, less deductive, more dynamic, and contextualized methodology along the lines set out above. In other words, we need a relational approach to class, expressed through a concern for power, hegemony, and everyday politics, searching for the nature and social consequences of determinate historical and spatial relationships of capital accumulation.

THE RELEVANCE AND PECULIARITY OF NORTH BRABANT

The relevance of North Brabant to the general history and theory of industrial class formation in Europe resides in a paradox. During the late nineteenth and early twentieth centuries Brabant became one of the most extensively industrialized regions in the Netherlands, but its working population never broadly supported large-scale social movements employing the language of class. North Brabant thus is an anomaly to the classical theories of modernization and modernity.

The shoemaking district of central Brabant and the central industrial district of southeast Brabant, the particular settings studied here, both contained communities where industry accounted for over 70 percent of local jobs. Indeed, Kaatsheuvel, a central Brabant shoemaking village, and Eindhoven, the electrical boomtown of the southeast, were the two localities in the late 1920s with the most industrialized employment structures in the country at large. But instead of producing socialism or any other form of organized and interest-based popular dissent, they became typical cases of popular social Catholicism and paternalism / deference. Although independent labor union formation and a local social democratic party did occur in both settings, they remained either isolated phenomena or were based on groups of educated migrants. Even a weak correlation between the reified categories of "class position" and "class consciousness" would not easily have been established in Brabant.

The relevance of my expanded, contingent, and relational approach to industrial class formation in North Brabant also lies in a paradox. This paradox consists in the capacity of relational class analysis to clarify precisely the causes for the absence of class as political consciousness and explicit discourse, while at the same time exploring the local meanings that class acquired.

My approach can accomplish this because it does not treat the sense of anomaly, and the exceptionalist theories to which it has given rise (and which we shall discuss below), as accurate empirical descriptions of the region's key properties, let alone as adequate historical explanations. Instead, it helps us to see such exceptionalist visions as reflecting, and refracting, the crucial divergences in timing, position, and subsequent trajectory of the region's insertion in wider networks of capitalist exchange, relative to other places. The historical and spatial contingency of this approach, urging a dialectical grasp of the interaction between local and global histories, does not allow one to explain the absence of "modern" class protest by simply pointing at the co-presence of other anomalous traits from the point of view of modernization theory, such as a persevering and activist Catholicism. If we accept the foregoing methodological arguments on class and class formation, we have to describe and explain the whole of any region's multifaceted deviation from expected would-be universalist patterns of development as an integral consequence of its particular trajectory to capitalist modernity, being principally the combined effect of its precapitalist properties and its place and capacities in wider networks of capitalist exchange.

In the case of North Brabant, as we will see in a moment, this means that we have to try to grasp religion and an activist clergy, as well as a late and prolonged demographic expansion, not as external coincidences but as integral properties of the region's path to industrial class formation. Consequently, in the case studies that follow we will explore the problems and possibilities of groups of workers as they lived within particular configurations of industry, family, and church. This is the key triangular relationship that gave proletarian life in the region its peculiar, and little charted, stamp. While my case studies of shoemakers in central Brabant and electrical workers at Eindhoven are unified by this combined and characteristic problematic, they specialize respectively on the interplay between Catholicism and small-scale industrial development in central Brabant, and between proletarian family relationships and the growth of the electronics giant of Philips in Eindhoven. Together, then, these studies are exemplary for the range of experiences of the region as a whole.

Novelists, journalists, sociologists, and historians have painted an ambivalent, incomplete, even incoherent picture of the province of North Brabant, and its authorities have generally joined them in this. On the one hand, we have the folkloric and culturalist assertion that the proverbial North Brabanter is cordial, naive, and obedient, but not very serious, nor very punctual, a bit careless, and lacking strong will. Authors variously point to Catholicism, poverty, peripherality, and backwardness in the region, as well as to small peasant agriculture and life in large families, as giving ground to such visions. On the other hand, reformists and modernists emphasize the violence and criminality in the region, the high rate of public drunkenness, and the lack of trustworthiness. At the same time, there is a remarkable popular indeterminacy as to whether the region should be seen as industrial or agricultural. And when it is seen as industrial, there is a characteristic ambivalence about the degree to which modernism or traditionalism should be attributed to its methods of production.[51] In addition, the region may be seen as either spontaneously and devotionally Catholic, or thoroughly dominated by Catholic clergy. At the same time, however, authors tend to argue that local people are often likely to spurn clerical advice and draw on their own plans.[52] Clearly, there is disagreement about the nature, extent, and effects of dominance, in particular Catholic dominance. There is related uncertainty about the nature of personality, agency, autonomy, and will. And there is a problem with time, expressed in the hesitations about traditionalism or modernity, industry or agriculture. Among outside commentators, the region produced a pervasive sense of exceptionalism.

But, as argued, North Brabant, like any region, took its own path to modernity and did not adhere to the supposed blueprints delivered by more advanced others. This path displayed its own characteristic conjunctions of work, everyday life, appropriation, accumulation, and hegemony. In addition to Catholicism/clerical activism and the region's continued demographic expansion deep into the twentieth century, a third feature of this path was its remarkable bias in its economic structures, which were generally highly labor intensive, low value added, and dependent on external markets.

While these three parameters have certainly been recognized, they have generally been treated in isolation from each other; second, they have been approached at a rather high level of aggregation; and third, there has been no serious attempt to see them not just as conditions but as combining to produce a very particular dynamic in local people's lives, in local cultures, and in the wider regional society. Beyond studying their interconnections, my analysis should enable us to see how this matrix made up the specific grid of power through which the identities of local working people were formed and through which they acted upon the world and became dedicated to their projects.[53] Let us, in very general terms, sketch the outline of these three basic ingredients of regional transition to industrial capitalism and examine the discussions that they have provoked.

In general, the rulers of North Brabant had remained loyal to Catholicism during the Reformation and the region had subsequently endured official discrimination under the Protestant Dutch Republic. Within the Dutch state it functioned primarily as a military buffer against Continental powers. Locally rooted elites felt they provided the central state with far more revenues in taxes than were returned to them in provisions and opportunities. Indeed they generally sensed that domination by the Dutch Republic prevented North Brabant from taking its natural course of economic development and social differentiation. Prior to the Dutch revolt and reformation, as part of the unified fiefdom of Brabant under Burgundian rulers, North Brabant had experienced a golden age of economic progress and urbanization. It had been closely linked to the thriving urban centers of Antwerp and Brussels and it became a center of civilization in northwestern Europe. The achievements of this period were impressive and are probably best expressed in the magnificent cathedral of the city of Den Bosch and the powerful paintings of Hieronymus Bosch. But after the revolt, the region became dominated by a maritime, mercantilist, and Protestant power and was cut off from its Spanish-ruled and partly devastated southern partners. The region sharply declined. Seen from the riches of Amsterdam in the seventeenth century, it had devolved into a sparsely populated and underdeveloped peasant backwater.

Catholicism, in this context, became the principal expresson of regional self-consciousness. Regional representatives mobilized in the eighteenth and nineteenth century to acquire formal minority rights for Catholics. They became finally successful in the aftermath of the parliamentary victory against post-Napoleonic autocracy in 1848, and the Catholic hierarchy was reinstalled in 1853. Being the cement of Catholic (proto)parties and regional political networks, Catholicism gradually climbed its way to ascendancy in an increasingly less Protestant Dutch polity, with North Brabant as a main stronghold.

Thus a rising tide of political Catholicism, expressing regional emancipation, was the background against which local industrialization took place. In this context it is relevant that the main impetus to concentration and factory formation in industry, both in Brabant and in the Netherlands at large, came after 1890.[54] Developing industrial classes found Catholics well prepared to implant Catholic "solidaristic" and "corporatist" structures in the political economy. The new social climate in the church, expressed in such encyclicals as *Rerum Novarum*, condemning both socialist and liberal doctrines of materialism and modernism, legitimized social interventionism by the Catholic Church. Though certainly not without its internal contradictions, as we shall see, social Catholic practices and discourses were consequently implanted in many industries and localities in Brabant and elsewhere.

As social Catholicism became a powerful and well-organized bloc, before long placing itself in the center of Dutch politics, it provoked fierce discussion.[55] Dutch society in the twentieth century became segmented into four "pillars": Catholicism and Protestantism did so intentionally; socialism and liberalism had to follow against their own universalist programs (the "pillars" received this name only after the Second World War). These pillars tended to organize the whole of the life of their members, from the cradle to the grave, from work to leisure, from broadcasting and schools to gardening. The Catholic pillar was held to be the quintessential example of this tendency to self-containment.

As pillarization, after the war, was increasingly seen as a fundamental obstacle to social and political change, reformist socialists and liberals began to question whether it actually functioned as a system for the emancipation of cultural minorities, as it was held to do by the grand narratives of Dutch nation-state formation, or whether it primarily served the ideological control of its constituents.[56] The Catholic pillar, being central to any large-scale political change, was a prime target of these discussions. And since the province of North Brabant was one of its bulwarks, criticism of pillarization hit at the heart of its social system.

The Catholic labor movement was widely perceived as the mainstay of the Catholic pillar. Discussions about pillarization, therefore, inevitably arrived at the question of whether Catholic labor unions had actually been created from below, from among workers, or been ordered from above. Left-wing social historians such as Floor van Gelder, Jos Perry, Bob Reinalda, and Ger Harmsen have shown that Catholic union formation was generally ordered by the clergy after Catholic workers began to join socialist initiatives.[57] Thus Catholic union formation turned out to be a defensive act by an embattled clerical hierarchy. Such research led to the reappraisal of the original legitimizing text of C. Kuiper, who had emphasized the movement's roots in the solid antimaterialist convictions of Catholic workers.[58]

Later research, however, again refined this picture. It shows that in some places, like the shoemaking district of central Brabant, Catholic union formation was largely pushed through by an alliance of workers and *petits vicaires* against a conservative bloc of established clergy and local entrepreneurs. In such local political contexts Catholic unions became very popular.[59] In other places, like Eindhoven, Catholic unions could, after a hesitant start initiated by the clerical hierarchy and its lay supporters, quickly gain broad support from local populations when the balance between workers and clerics within the organization shifted in favor of the former.

Thus social Catholicism was a tension-ridden field of force that mediated between diverging and conflicting interests. It shaped the terrain of class in North Brabant in important ways. But while social Catholicism became rooted everywhere, its particular dynamic and hegemonic power can only be understood as part of particular local trajectories of class formation. Indeed, it was class formation (whether agricultural or industrial) to which it responded, in which it aimed to intervene, and of which it sought to shape the political and cultural outcome. The real histories of social Catholicism, therefore, were part and parcel of the diverse local trajectories of class formation.

Questions of Catholicism have been intimately associated with the remarkable demographic expansion of the province, in particular of the Eindhoven region. The demographic transition in the Netherlands at large had a distinct timing, and this was to some degree caused by the patterns of procreation in the Catholic territories. While other countries like England, Belgium, and Germany witnessed declining rates of population growth in the period between 1900 and 1950, the Dutch population in these years began to grow faster than ever. Statistically this was caused by a quick decrease in the mortality rate after 1870 in combination with a retarded decline in the rate of fertility. This was the same pattern of demographic change that had occurred in the early industrializing countries of Europe in the nineteenth century. But it took place half a century later.[60]

The Catholic population was central to this demographic outcome of social change. Whereas their numbers had been relatively stagnant up to 1870, they rose quickly thereafter. Although Catholic fertility was declining, it declined much slower than that of Protestants, and for a short period was even twice as high as the figure for nonconfessionals.[61] Dutch twentieth-century demographic expansion was more due to Catholics than other denominations. In Dutch discussions, Catholic procreation patterns have generally been related to their minority status in the Netherlands and the consequent clerical attempts to enlarge the Catholic population by disseminating the holy ideal of the large family.[62] Thus, here again, ideas of clerical dominance and devotion turn up.

However, the picture became more complicated when social research showed that industrial workers as well as peasants were the most fertile categories, and that it was precisely these classes that were overrepresented in the Catholic industrializing periphery. As in other regions of industrializing Europe, expanding opportunities to earn cash incomes led to a decrease in marriage age and to a steep rise in the number of marriages as couples succeeded in establishing themselves independently. While marriage fertility was declining slowly, the combination of these trends nevertheless led to steady population growth.[63] It was therefore no coincidence that the most salient demographic expansion as well as the most powerful process of industrialization and urbanization in the Netherlands after 1910 occurred at one place and time, that is, in the Eindhoven region.

This sheds a different light on the question of clerical dominance and Catholic procreation. Surely, it would be nonsense to deny the importance of Catholic ideologies of the family or the influence of priests over households in relatively small and underdeveloped communities. But the close interweaving of demographic growth with a particular pattern of industrialization in the Catholic periphery at least suggests that those ideologies, instead of being the independent factor earlier researchers have statistically mistaken them to be, have acted within a particular, spatially delimited and temporally defined, comprehensive pattern of class formation. Indeed, I would contend that it was precisely from this specific pattern of class formation in the (proto)industrializing periphery that Catholic ideologies of procreation derived their force and function. Instead of indicating clerical dominance or internalized religious beliefs *tout court*, demographic growth was part and parcel of the particular conjunctions of work, family, accumulation, and hegemony that marked the formation of industrial classes in North Brabant.

Recently, the historical anthropologist Peter Meurkens has proposed a variant of the clerical dominance thesis.[64] He presents evidence from an isolated rural locality in North Brabant that shows a significant shortening of the time interval between subsequent births, leading to a rise in marriage fertility in the later nineteenth century. He relates this process to a successful cultural campaign by the church. Objecting to breast feeding for considerations of hygiene, prudishness, and fear of the body, and therefore strongly advocating bottle-feeding, the church would have been the unintended initiator of this change in reproductive patterns. The consequent spread of bottle-feeding led to an increase of marriage fertility because women, after having given birth, became fertile more rapidly than when breast-feeding.

Although Meurkens's thesis is interesting in its own right, it is probably not directly relevant to the question of demographic expansion in the

Catholic territories at large. Indeed, for the general process it was not so much an increase in marriage fertility that was central (in fact fertility on a higher level of aggregation steadily declined), as the decline of the age of marriage and the rise in the number of marriages. This path out of the old European reproductive pattern occurred everywhere in Europe and is associated with (proto)industrialization.[65] There seems, therefore, no need for exceptionalist theories to explain the demographic transition in the Catholic and industrializing Dutch periphery.

Both social Catholicism and demographic growth were basic aspects of class formation in North Brabant. In their everyday interactions, however, both were again intimately interwoven with a third "factor." This was the region's very particular pattern of economic expansion and capitalist accumulation.[66] Observers of Brabant manufacturing were often hardly able to judge whether it was backward or dynamic.[67] The fact was that industry in North Brabant, from the late eighteenth century onward, specialized in the large-scale production of highly labor intensive consumer commodities for extraregional markets, which were often dominated by more advanced foreign producers, thereby paying surprisingly low wages and increasingly employing a uniquely large number of adolescent girls.

But while its generally low level of capital intensity and its "immature" labor force may have given it the appearance of backwardness, this industry was definitely successful. As a location for labor-intensive manufacturing, North Brabant had concentrated about half the nation's textile industry within its confines by 1910, as well as the greater part of shoemaking and cigarmaking, and almost all of the new branch of electrical manufacturing.[68] Its locational advantages within the national and international economic system were clear: its low wages, which for males amounted to 60 percent of the national average, allowed it to outcompete many manufacturers of low-value-added, labor-intensive, mass-produced consumer commodities. Entrepreneurs in such old and urban textile centers as Leiden and Haarlem were already in the eighteenth century putting out the more labor-intensive parts of their production to households in Brabant. This led to poverty in their urban centers and to the spread of cash incomes in the Brabant countryside. Originally functioning as a protoindustrial putting out system to peasant households, such textile production subsequently gave rise to new processes of urbanization as industry gradually became more capitalized and started to centralize around new or renewed cores such as Tilburg and Helmond. In the later nineteenth and early twentieth centuries, the cluster of shoemaking villages around Waalwijk in central Brabant and the dispersed urban region of Eindhoven came into being in a similar way. The different degrees of population concentration and the varied spatial morphologies of these manufacturing landscapes were largely a function of the amounts and sorts of capital that became centralized and the sorts of local labor which it deployed. Labor-intensive mass manufacturing in North Brabant was dynamic enough to change fundamentally the face of the region within a few decades.

However, it is not sufficient to say that North Brabant mass manufacturing was labor intensive and low value added. For the lives of workers it was of more immediate relevance that it was also highly feminized.[69] In shoemaking some 35 percent of the labor force consisted of girls and unmarried women. In Eindhoven, in textiles and cigarmaking the percentage of girls and unmarried women amounted to about 50 percent, while the Philips labor force in the large lamp factory around 1910 consisted of 75 percent adolescent girls. In contrast, the average percentage of working females in the overall labor force of the Netherlands never exceeded 20 percent before the 1960s.[70] It becomes clear, then, that production structures in North Brabant were quite particular and bore little resemblance to national patterns.

Why did the industries of North Brabant employ so many young women? Certainly it was profitable for entrepreneurs in little-skilled branches of industry with low profit margins to employ categories of labor, such as girls, who were used to earning very low wages. Moreover, in the highly volatile and permanently fluctuating markets for cheap consumer products it was very convenient for entrepreneurs to have recourse to categories of workers who could temporarily do without (full) incomes. Girls, in fact, functioned as a labor reserve and a turnover pool, providing industry with a degree of labor flexibility that could never have been realized on the basis of male labor alone. In particular, for industrial producers in a small, open, and trade-oriented country such as the Netherlands, which in the later nineteenth and twentieth centuries maintained a hard currency policy without protecting its industry against foreign dumping, this labor policy was a good way to stay in capricious markets that were mostly dominated by more advanced foreign producers.

But why did males accept such high degrees of feminization? The answer lies in the origin of local industries. The typical mass production of North Brabant grew in the countryside, initially using the labor input of underemployed members of peasant and peasant-worker families, as suggested by the original protoindustrial model put forward by Mendels, Braun, Kriedte, Medick, and Schlumbohm.[71] There was no link with urban artisans or skilled workers who could uphold traditions of guild-like regulation of their male-centered trades. Instead, as is best shown in the Eindhoven case, semiproletarian families, maintaining access to some land while seeking alternative sources of income, made use of the opportunity to let their daughters perform industrial jobs. The industrialization of North Brabant did not so much lead to gradual male wage increases as to an expansion of income opportunities for members of peasant-worker families, in particular for daughters.[72]

Within Brabant there is variation in the degree to which manufacturing actually developed in conjunction with young female labor and small-scale agriculture. The southeast, being the less developed and more isolated part of the region, experienced a somewhat later and more feminized industrialization as well as a more protracted decline of peasant agriculture than central Brabant. In the shoemaking district, bordering on the great rivers but situated on one of the most barren soils in Europe, the link with agriculture seems to have been feeble. Nonetheless, families did try to raise livestock and, if possible, secure access to useful land. However, in this particular conjunction of household, industry, and agriculture, the family everywhere functioned as a permanent and accessible labor reserve, whose daughters in particular were in high demand. Children were assets in everyday survival, to employers as well as to parents.[73]

In general terms this is the specific configuration within which class formation in North Brabant took place. Having lost its original urban bases and being devalued to the status of rural periphery during the early modern period, the region regained momentum in the nineteenth century. It embraced Catholicism as the political and cultural vehicle for ascent within a seaborne, Protestant polity, while developing a new urban system as older protoindustries were restructured into concentrations of highly labor intensive mass manufacturing. Rising opportunities to earn cash led to firm population growth after 1870, as more couples felt secure enough to marry and to do so much earlier in their lives.

These developments combined in creating a muted and complex pattern of industrial class formation in North Brabant. It was a pattern in which the income of households became highly dependent on the labor of teenage children, while at the same time featuring the implantation of practices of social Catholicism in work and production. This particular intersection of Catholicism, labor-intensive mass manufacturing, and children as a source of income both for employers and for parents made up the particular field of force within which common lives in North Brabant were led and social classes were made.

Taken together, in their specific mutual interconnections, these three features serve as the general starting point for explaining the absence of organized popular dissent in the industrial nuclei of North Brabant. In the subsequent case studies, which will be compared in the epilogue, I explore more closely the origins, nature, and above all the dynamics of these specific conjunctions of work, family, industry, and hegemony. Besides essays in relational class analysis, these case studies are "thick" descriptions of what happens between and within people, and with regions and local cultures, when they modernize along the apparently anomalous and still little understood route exemplified by North Brabant.

PART ONE

The Limits of Dominance and Deference:

Power and Culture in Shoemaking Villages,

1900–1920

1 Communal Commotion:

The Complexities of the Shoemakers Conflict in 1910

In the summer of 1910 the Dutch town of Waalwijk, on the river Meuse, in the shoe-producing district of barren central Brabant, flourished. Wages were relatively high, unemployment was negligible, so it was perfectly legitimate for the municipal secretary to show some modest signs of pride in his yearly report to the queen.[1] Social relations appeared to be harmonious, and in a sense Waalwijk stood as a symbol for the better times to come in this backward region. As in all central Brabant municipalities, a Catholic Shoemakers Union existed in this town but, as could be expected in a place where living conditions by any standard were substantially better than in the mainly protoindustrial neighboring villages, it was rather passive.[2] In the hinterland, the earnings of the home-working population were substantially lower, the working day much longer, and, as a consequence of the truck system, prices of primary products 10 to 20 percent higher.[3] In comparison, workers and factory owners in Waalwijk had established relations of reciprocity and seemed apparently agreed on creating economic and social progress.

Against all expectations, however, this town experienced an explosive labor conflict.[4] In the early morning of 24 August 1910 a strange and severe dispute broke out in the factory of the van Schijndel family. This factory, the largest and most advanced workplace in the Netherlands, was famous locally for its technical and social achievements. It was even permitted to carry a royal *predicat*. In its stitching department, where some forty-five girls were employed on sewing machines to produce the uppers of high-class ladies' shoes, a young teenage girl asked a friend, who was working next to her, to be so friendly as to pass a glass of water. She was brutally reprimanded by her employer, whereupon the chairwoman of the local girls' branch of the Catholic Shoemakers Union, who happened to work on the same line, intervened, showed herself to be

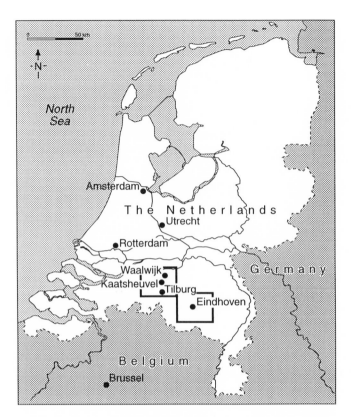

The Netherlands, with North Brabant industrial communities high-lighted.

very upset about old van Schijndel's behavior, and judged that social relations in the factory were too bad for them to continue working in it. She demonstratively left the work floor, to be followed immediately by the stitching girls, who were all members of the girls' branch of the union. On hearing what had happened, more than half the male workers in the factory, about fifty men, who in many cases were probably the fathers and brothers of the striking girls, followed suit.[5] Thus a super-ficially trivial event had occasioned a collective walkout.

For the second time that year, the strikers reported to the committee of the Catholic Shoemakers Union, which met in the nearby village of Kaats-heuvel, that the van Schijndel family refused to recognize the union and used constant minor threats, in the form of fines and restrictions, against its members. In the local and Catholic press the legitimacy of such an irregular and wildcat strike was fiercely disputed, but the committee

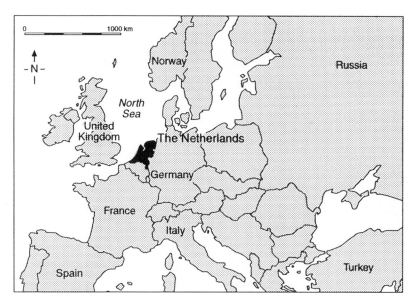

Central Brabant, ca. 1930.

unanimously stood behind its members, and declared that van Schijndel had waged an underground war against the Catholic workers' organizations. The strike, it maintained, was legitimate, as it was a struggle for union recognition.[6]

Present-day Dutch historians with left-wing and humanist inclinations have reproduced this explanation for the strike at the Royal Steam Shoefactory of van Schijndel.[7] But, as I will try to show, they have thereby reproduced an articulate discourse, mainly in the Catholic press and that of the Catholic Shoemakers Union, that obscured more fundamental causes. This, indeed, alludes to a more general problem of historical research on the working classes. Documentary sources tend to represent dominant meanings, and this in principle is also true of the sources from established labor unions, where divisions between functionaries and workers have developed, and certainly for those unions in continental Europe that embodied cross-class alliances as did the Catholic labor movements in the Netherlands.

Here a claim is made for a very different interpretation, one that is anthropologically stronger and sheds new light on the course and dynamics of Catholic union formation in the Dutch periphery. It will be argued that central Brabant's shoemakers, instead of defending the Catholic union, were actually motivated by deeply felt distresses concerning their place and prospects in the social relationships of shoe production. Such anxieties were totally ignored by this union. The event therefore showed the fracturing of a Catholic union rather than its popularity.

Moreover, I want to take this conflict and the interpretations that have sought to explain it then and now as an opportunity to criticize two main tendencies in contemporary historical sociology and social history. The first tendency, which is associated with the work of E. P. Thompson, Eric Hobsbawm, and Charles Tilly, stresses the rationality and strategic nature of working class responses to capitalist development. The second, stemming from the work of Gareth Stedman Jones, among others, maintains that class interests do not just speak for themselves but should be first produced in political languages of class, conflict, and reciprocity. I will argue that both approaches are in need of a more anthropological understanding of participants in hegemonic processes. We must leave the human capacity to experience the materialities of life intact and at the same time recognize the problematic nature of articulate sociopolitical languages. For any analyst of class both the conceptual distinction and problematic relation between articulate languages and practical experiences is of vital importance. A better understanding of participants in hegemonic processes can be developed empirically by paying due attention to the details of routine-breaking events.

CLUES TO CLASS AND CONFLICT

Collective action always produces unfocused and inconclusive messages in the contemporary press, which often, because of their character, are not properly handled by historical researchers who strive to build a coherent narrative. This is certainly true in this case. Thus the persistent denials of the employer that he was trying to tackle the Catholic Shoemakers Union has for all practical purposes been seen as merely a rationalized self-defense. In his letters to the press and to the union he was, however, very careful to stress that he had only been opposing "a spirit of discontent" that had, in his view, particularly arisen in the stitching department. He insisted that by fining people he had only been reasserting control in the factory. "We declare," he wrote, "that the control we exercise in the factory is not yet sharp enough to counter the slowing down of work and the pointless chattering." He was convinced of the noncooperative attitude of the stitching girls. "That the girls don't work as regularly as they should is proven by the fact that their production was substantially higher during the week before the Waalwijk Fair. Why don't they always work like this?" The employer felt it was perfectly legitimate to exercise authority on the shop floor and therefore against his honor to start negotiations with the union leadership. In his opinion it was they who were fundamentally at fault.[8]

His stance is to a certain extent confirmed by journalists of the Catholic daily press, who did not take at face value the union's claim that Van Schijndel's workers were denied the right to organize. On the basis of an inquiry on the spot it was concluded that the whole conflict was very "subjective." If there was an offensive against union rights it was not waged openly or directly. Considering all the information, the rather neutral *Dagblad van Noord-Brabant* concluded: "There seems to be no reason for following the logic of the conflict to its extreme, because it is all very subjective. It is not possible to make an ultimate judgment."[9]

Though many comments from the press were strongly criticized by the Catholic Shoemakers Union for their bourgeois misunderstanding of proletarian life, the union committee, in a published letter to Van Schijndel, surprisingly supported this purported "subjective" nature of the protest. "The organized stitchers and shoemakers seem *instinctively* to have understood the intention to destroy the Catholic Union," it said (my emphasis). Maybe there were no facts to be shown, it said, but there was surely a problem of psychology. The letter made much of the maltreatment and extensive control of the workers in this factory. This is important because it confirms the picture painted in the above-mentioned remarks about strained relationships.[10] This picture is strengthened, moreover, by other information. For example, we learn that the shop floor regime was not only restrictive but also highly arbitrary. One worker reported that one day he was fined for throwing shoes to the next colleague on the line, while on another day he had been ordered to do so. Finally he was fired for being a troublemaker.[11] Taken together, such messages point to the existence of a rather despotic work regime.

Other bits of information suggest that this despotism was not limited to Van Schijndel's factory. On the contrary it seemed to be typical of modern shoemaking factories in central Brabant. This is shown by an earlier instance of collective protest in the nearby village of Kaatsheuvel. In 1909, when the government, in a half-hearted effort to regulate labor relations, required the signing of individual labor contracts and the framing of factory rules, the workers at van Dortmond's factory went on strike after reading the bad arrangements for overtime and the generally restrictive spirit of the factory rules. As was mentioned by the Catholic shoemakers' press, the stitching girls were even scared to work under such regulations. After two days of negotiations, Van Dortmond changed the text about overtime and promised not to take the regulations too literally. This was accepted as a compromise. It is interesting, however, that Van Dortmond, like Van Schijndel, was known locally as a very good "patron," someone who was in the forefront of social-minded employers in this municipality.[12] Nevertheless, as at Van Schijndel's in 1910, it was only "his" workers who went on strike. These two conflicts in the most advanced and respected factories of central Brabant were, moreover, the only ones to occur in the region after 1905. Other potential conflicts used to be resolved quickly by the retreat of the employers.[13] Paradoxically both these "progressive patrons" stubbornly clung to their positions. This suggests that their stance was not just coincidental.

Stubbornness was especially true of Van Schijndel in 1910: he flatly refused to talk to Catholic labor representatives or even the clergy, and thus did nothing to reinstitute daily routines. This sternness caused a completely unexpected situation in Waalwijk. In fact it featured a couple of events that, more clearly than anything else, contained hints of unreported but widespread dissatisfaction over the nature of social relationships in shoemaking in general. In the first week after the strike began the clergy and Catholic union officials had succeeded in "Catholicizing" the strike. Striking workers were asked to remain indoors and to visit church every morning for prayers. They were also told not to drink any kind of alcohol.[14] This was obviously part of an effort to turn the conflict into a ritual of solemnity, devotion, and loyalty to the church. In the face of a fierce criticism of the union's leadership in the press, the strikers were willing to demonstrate their utmost respectability.

But nothing of this demonstration of Catholic respectability was continued in the next weeks. Instead, a kind of spontaneous mass mobilization erupted that ultimately forced the mayor of Waalwijk to call in extra forces from the military police. Already, in the first week of September, a big fight broke out in the public square in Waalwijk when someone had dared to criticize the Catholic union. More than five hundred people threw lumps of earth at the man, who was lucky to escape. In the second week a blackleg was attacked by a crowd of people. He was knocked about, and consequently suffered a nervous breakdown. Set free by the police, he was brought home, but this again led to a large crowd surrounding his house. The police resorted to armed action to disperse the mob. On the morning of Thursday, 15 September, a male scab escorted by the police was welcomed by a crowd of more than a thousand people, many of them not belonging to the Catholic union. That same evening, someone who was reported to be a dealer in blackleg labor was attacked by another crowd and could only save himself by fleeing into a nearby house. On the next Friday a permanent threat of violent escalation which the police did not seem able to cope with led the mayor to forbid any further public gatherings. The Catholic union leadership immediately, but uncomfortably, felt itself obliged to ask its members not to participate in crowd actions any more. It is not certain whether this really happened. Though further incidents were only vaguely reported in the press, it is clear that minor disturbances, and their potential escalation, went on for much longer. Special police measures were only canceled the following spring.[15]

It is evident from the mass unrest in the town of Waalwijk that, above all, grievances were in no way limited to Van Schijndel's factory. Rather, the strike created an opportunity for the expression of discontent that was widely felt throughout the working population. Moreover, the crowd activities that led to the calling of the military police were rather uncoordinated, "unpolitical" in the narrow sense of the word, and potentially violent. There was clearly widely felt indignation at Van Schijndel's policy and at blackleg practices, but it was not channeled into concerted action. Rather, it was aimed in the main at defenseless common people, who could only be accused of having broken the front of spontaneous and inarticulate popular solidarity in the town. Thus it seems that only public fractures of working class solidarity sparked off violent mass action.

However, there also emerged more effective acts of solidarity with the strikers. The industrial communities of central Brabant raised substantial amounts of money to support them. Some people began playing music to raise money, others sold handmade shoes. Many people turned the tradition of improvised oral verses to the cause of the union, poetically condemning blackleg practices and glorifying the union and its priests.[16]

The conflict, though, was eventually won by Van Schijndel. After some months he was able to contract a sufficient number of scabs to run his factory. The strikers, moreover, all found jobs elsewhere. But the Catholic Union of Shoemakers never canceled the sanctions against working for this employer. Time and again moderate leaders tried to place the issue on the agenda, but it always aroused the membership's fierce condemnation. Interviewers in the 1970s were struck by the emotions which still hung around the strike of 1910. Old shoemakers were still moved to tears by the memory of Van Schijndel's victory.[17]

It must be emphasized, however, that we have various information that does not fit easily into the neat picture of threatened union rights at Van Schijndel. Rather, we have a set of hints that relationships on the shop floor were quite strained, and that the phenomenon was not limited to this one factory, as there are indications that things also occurred in other "advanced" factories in central Brabant. Also the nature of the collective commotion that emerged in the aftermath of the strike suggests that grievances were not limited to just this employer. Rather, they point to problems of legitimacy in the wider community, concerning the development of relations in shoemaking in general. It should be stressed that neither in the local press nor in the Catholic shoemakers' press was there any sign that literate elites or the shoemakers' leadership in the unions in fact understood this development and its social consequences, at least not on a public or analytical level. Thus, contemporary discourses did not recognize changes in daily life. Therefore attention must now be given to the social bases, the development, structure, and ideology of the Catholic shoemakers' unions.

SOCIAL CATHOLICISM, CLASS, AND ECONOMY IN CENTRAL BRABANT

The formation of a large Catholic workers' movement in the Netherlands has been one of the central issues of social and historical thought in this country. The Catholic workers' movement not only almost equaled socialist unions in number, it was simultaneously one of the major institutions of the Catholic bloc, and thus a central phenomenon in the religious-political segmentation of the Dutch population in the twentieth century.[18] This was particularly true in the southern provinces, which, though extensively industrialized, remained peripheral and underdeveloped up to 1950. The Catholic workers' movement and the Catholic bloc as a whole developed a strong position, unrivaled by left-wing organizations.

One of the central subjects of debate in the Netherlands has been the question to what extent the Catholic labor movement actually came from below. By 1980 a consensus developed among left-wing historians, who were the only genuine social historians at the time, that the whole Catholic organization was essentially a defensive attempt on the part of clerical functionaries to fence off social penetration in Catholic working class communities.[19] Thus the emphatic striving for class cooperation that marked Catholic unions has been seen as ordered from above rather than coming from below. Moreover, local research has shown that clerics only became interested in organizing workers after socialists challenged established Catholic positions.[20] In the absence of such challenges, local clerics never inclined to new approaches to the "social question."

Central Brabant's shoemakers, however, have been presented as a case against the social-control argument by Harmsen and others. Here we have an illustration of a working class striving to build Catholic unions in the face of repression from both local entrepreneurs and the clerical hierarchy. Van Meeuwen and Mandemakers concluded that central Brabant's shoemakers built "their own (Catholic) unions." The strike at Van Schijndel is then understood as a major instance of workers clinging to "their own" Catholic union when attacked by a strong employer.[21] Accordingly, Mandemakers and Van Meeuwen reproduced contemporary arguments for the strike.

The idea of workers building and defending "their own" Catholic unions, however, creates new problems. How is the religious aspect to be interpreted? What about the language of class cooperation? Why did shoemakers build Catholic unions—why not secular ones? Not surprisingly, these authors tend to give uncertain answers to such questions. On the one hand they hold that shoemakers were interested in "improving their poor living and working conditions," and not in issues of ideology and religion, while on the other they treat Catholicism as "a strong influence [that] structured the minds of the shoemakers and the ideology of the union."[22] Clearly it is one or the other; it cannot be both, at least not in this way of stating the problem. Although their work has been seminal in stressing varieties of experience, it did not offer a strong analysis of the particular reception of Catholic ideology and its social bases in central Brabant. In fact, it tends to treat Catholic ideology as an invention of the shoemaking population itself. Van Meeuwen and Mandemakers thereby overlooked the important fact that Catholic shoemakers' unions were part of the Catholic bloc, of a grand modern hegemonic project, in which social gatherings were constantly infused with Catholic ideological discourses. All local clubs, for example, were assisted by a "clerical adviser." And the Catholic shoemakers' press was censored and consisted in the main of ideological messages by learned Catholics.[23] The weekly meetings of the local unions, besides facilitating mutual talk on strategy and working life, always featured a lecture by Catholic organizers.

It follows that the crucial task of analyzing the nature, structure, and content of social Catholicism as a hegemonic process has been all but neglected. The vertical and horizontal axes of communication within the Catholic shoemakers' union have not been set in relation to each other.

That task has been argued away by overstressing the spontaneous character of Catholic union formation among shoemakers. The undeniable fact that shoemakers participated actively in the making of Catholic unions, consequently, has been made to carry too much weight. As a result, social Catholicism has been made too flat, too simple, and too innocent.

There are no extensive studies of the reception of Catholic ideology among early-twentieth-century clerically organized workers in the Netherlands. There are no analyses of social Catholicism as a hegemonic project. So to begin to address that question in the particular case of central Brabant's shoemakers, we need an analysis of the wider context of power and proletarianization during that particular conjunction in which Catholic unions came into being. This should be the proper ground on which to build an understanding of the relationships between workers' problems, class practices, and Catholic discourse.[24]

The class problems that gave rise to the formation of unions in central Brabant after 1900 were initially related to the pattern of economic development that occurred there. Up to that time shoemaking in central Brabant had been almost exclusively protoindustrial. Since 1800 extensive but unstable chains of protoindustrial shoemaking households had been formed. Due to an abundant supply of proletarianized and half-proletarianized labor, very low wages and low costs of living, combined with entrepreneurial initiatives of local petty bourgeois households, the greater part of Dutch shoemaking became concentrated in this barren rural area.[25] The region was favorably situated near sources of raw materials and its principal market on the urban Dutch west coast. By 1900, however, increasing foreign competition, internal overcrowding, and the rising cost of leather forced local entrepreneurs to pursue new strategies in order to maintain levels of profitability. Although some began using imported machinery like the MacKay Stitcher in centralized workshops and others tried to improve product quality, the majority developed new means of appropriating surpluses from their dependent households by means of the truck system. By 1900 this form of "superexploitation" had created a world in which many households worked fifteen hours a day for wages that amounted to no more than half the country's average. Widespread embezzlement of materials and an exceptionally high rate of minor criminality and public drunkenness suggest serious problems of legitimacy in the region, while horizontal solidarities between home-working families apparently were not easily established. The formation of Catholic unions in central Brabant was one answer to the particular difficulties created by this pattern of development.[26]

In the villages and towns of central Brabant, Catholic shoemakers' unions were built after 1900 by a coalition between the best skilled workers of the most advanced factories and the lower local clergy. They were explicitly directed toward two goals: first, organizing the home-working families of "superexploiting" entrepreneurs in an effort to counter their declining standards of living and, second, thereby facilitating regulation of the labor market in order to provide collective agreements for the whole industry. Crucial in this endeavor was the active participation of highly skilled factory workers, enjoying good incomes and great local prestige. They were encouraged and supported by *petits vicaires*, who had received their education in the "progressive" climate of opinion expressed by the encyclical of *Rerum Novarum* (1891). No less important was the support they received from the biggest entrepreneurs in the region. This need not surprise us. The forging of solidarity bonds between different segments of this working class was made possible in part by the inflexibility of big entrepreneurs, who had made investments in fixed capital, to maintain levels of prices and profits in the face of competition from protoindustrialists. The failure of their earlier efforts to regulate prices by collective agreements between sellers of shoes led them to envisage a protected labor market, in order to make price competition by reduction of wages through truck systems impossible. Consequently, it was the labor aristocrats who, protected by the lower clergy, ventured to organize home workers. These labor aristocrats became the first officers of the official Catholic shoemakers' union around 1905.[27]

In accordance with their policy, the focal point of union formation was not Waalwijk, which by 1905 consisted mainly of advanced factories, but the hinterland village of Kaatsheuvel, where four factories with a total of about a hundred workers existed in the middle of numerous protoindustrial chains, employing almost two thousand home workers.[28] From 1900 onward cells of Catholic activists tried to organize these home workers. Their efforts, however, only succeeded after the bishop had instituted a clear procedure for establishing clerically protected workers' organizations in 1905. Before that date solidarity was too fragile, and home workers preferred to play a waiting game. By 1908 these efforts had been moderately successful, as shown by an organizational rate of about 50 percent of heads of households and a developing campaign against the truck system and other forms of "nonmarket" exploitation.[29]

What about Catholic ideology and its reception among the shoemaking population? Social Catholicism was an ingenious ideological system for criticizing some aspects of capitalism while preserving others. The market was looked at with suspicion, but private property per se was considered fundamental to any moral order. Property, moreover, was imbued with propriety, which, above all, meant the proper care of dependents. The idea of noblesse oblige and the stress on the obedience of the lower orders were closely connected. Ideally it substituted a hierarchy with an emphasis on social duty for the possessive individualism of the capitalist market.

By 1900 social Catholicism had developed a special historical theory of politico-economic development in the modern age. Society in the Middle Ages was seen as well ordered and reciprocal, where all estates, bound together by the church, still obediently contributed their properties and skills to the social organism. Subsequent enlightenment, and especially the French Revolution, had culminated in liberal societies, in which greed and egoism were admired and institutionalized in the market. The liberal market seduced patrons to neglect their social duties and to engage in all forms of competition. Some of these forms of competition were considered "dishonest," because they had negative effects on social cohesion. "Dishonest competition" referred to all those entrepreneurial practices which led to excessive working hours, impoverishment, female and child labor, and consequently the disintegration of the working class family. Thus "dishonest competition" was the main Catholic explanation of the "social question." Catholic intellectuals, therefore, proposed a nonliberal and nonsocialist strategy of building a hierarchically ordered corporatism.[30]

Contemporary left-wing observers have tended to laugh at social theories that came from the womb of a theocratic conservative moloch like the Catholic Church. Thus its particular properties, strengths, and weaknesses have not been properly understood. In the case of the shoemakers, however, it is easy to see how applicable this historical theory was to their condition around 1900. The theme of "dishonest competition" delivered a useful description and explanation of shoemakers' experiences. Small protoindustrial entrepreneurs used a couple of "dishonest" devices to remain in the market, devices that evidently led to excessive working hours, pressure on wages, truck systems, etc. At the same time there did exist some examples of "good patrons" in the factory sector. Against Marxist predictions, shoemakers found that "paternalism" still existed. Social problems did not primarily spring from the actions of big local owners. On the contrary, it was the industrial petty bourgeoisie with their "dishonest" practices like the truck system that lay at the roots of local misery.

Given the plausibility of social Catholic discourse in the conditions of central Brabant, the important role played by some lower clerics in the formation of shoemakers' union, and of course the absence of a viable ideological alternative, it is understandable why social Catholicism found a warm welcome among shoemakers. Local labor aristocracies participated actively in clerically administered events. Thus in 1908, for example, almost 20 percent of the members of the Kaatsheuvel branch of the union, a figure close to the total number of factory workers in the village, participated in Catholic "sociological courses." "Dishonest" practices were fiercely condemned in the Catholic shoemakers' press and also by shoemakers-authors, whereas big industrialists were treated with much respect, and each new machine placed in their factories was proudly mentioned. Their factories were represented as a higher order of production and cooperation, pointing to a future in which protoindustry and its miseries would be overcome. Shoemakers had dreams of regulation, discipline, and the "decent living" which could surely arise if the union collaborated with factory owners in order to do away with protoindustry. Morally acceptable relations of production, both in social Catholicism and among the shoemakers, lay firmly in the factory system.[31]

As may be clear by now, the general nature of social problems in central Brabant around 1900, the class coalition between lower clerics and labor aristocrats that made union formation possible, and the union's explicit objectives as coined by Catholic ideologues all supported a heavy concentration upon the urban hinterland and upon protoindustry. Built into the Catholic union, therefore, was a static theory of the "honest" and paternalist relations supposedly existing in the advanced shoe industry, a vision that perhaps contained some truth around 1900, but was not necessarily accurate in the world of 1910. Though local working class leaders clearly noticed changing structures in the advanced sector from 1907 onwards, and reported on this in their newspaper, these fragments of information did not lead to any kind of theoretical reflection, ideological revision, or public discussion of the issue. As a consequence, the strike at Van Dortmond in 1909 was considered only an unhappy incident, and the explosive conflict at Van Schijndel in 1910 was consistently held to be caused by the "unwillingness" to recognize the union of this one employer. Accordingly, in the case of Waalwijk in 1910, much was made of the fact that Van Schijndel happened to be a liberal Protestant, and that one of his foremen was a member of a small social democratic group.[32] In this way, by calling upon the "we-feelings" of Catholics and re-creating historical images of enemy groups, shoemakers' leaders chose to help ignite violent popular protest rather than analyze its causes. The evolving nature of relationships in advanced industry thus turned out to be the ideological blind spot of the Catholic shoemakers' union. In fact, the class coalition that was formalized in the Catholic unions effectively prohibited the public articulation of a discourse on the development of the factory sector and the pattern of its social relationships. The moment in which the nature of class relationships in factory production was changing was exactly the moment when shoemakers lost out against clerics. Right at that time the organizational structures of the Catholic hegemonic project presided over the spontaneous social movement of a working class.

But what, then, were the hidden motives behind the spontaneous strike in 1910 and the potentially violent unrest that followed? A key to this problem might lie in the actual form and sequence in which collective action emerged among van Schijndel's labor force.

HIDDEN FEELINGS, MATERIAL FORCES, AND CLASS CAPACITIES

Spontaneous collective action in 1910 was initiated by female workers. It was only after their walkout that male shoemakers showed both their readiness to strike and their cross-sex solidarity. What motivated girls to play this central role and why were they capable of acting collectively at that moment? And—what was the most astonishing fact—what motivated male workers to follow suit and join them?

As daughters of shoemakers, stitchers' interests diverged from those of their parents. Indeed, relationships in shoemaking were organized in such a way as to make them contradictory. Girls were sent to the factory to contribute to household incomes. Generally speaking, it was in the interests of fathers to maintain their daughters' obedience as workers. That was not easy, because the process of the labor market ran counter to a stable gender hierarchy. As the use of machines in shoe factories increased, the productivity of the male-dominated part of the production process increased enormously, while the productivity of the stitching departments did not keep up. As a consequence, the demand for stitching girls was steadily rising, and the market practically reached a point of saturation by 1910. In the relationships of shoemaking, however, this situation was mainly expressed through the increasing market value of fathers who could bring in several daughters. Girls therefore had great bargaining power with their fathers. Contradictions in production were therefore re-created as contradictions between the sexes and the generations.

Because of gradual market saturation, pressure on stitching girls to raise individual productivity was constantly growing. This process lay at the roots of the worsening relations between large employers and their stitching departments. It was a process, moreover, with complex consequences for the relations between fathers and daughters as well as for class politics in the region. Now and then, stitchers had expressed their discontent in short collective actions. In 1903, for example, the stitching personnel at Van Schijndel's factory had struck and their demands had been quickly acknowledged.[33] But in 1909 other aspects of the process came to the surface. Together with male workers, and on their initiative, stitching girls in the village of Kaatsheuvel had struck for shorter working hours and a softening of factory regulations. Contradictions between fathers and daughters became evident here for the first time, as girls were no longer willing to return to work after a compromise had been made between male workers and the employer. Only after a collective meeting of strikers, in which fathers had forcefully reminded stitchers that their "irresponsible behavior" was threatening household incomes, did the girls feel obliged to return to work. Immediately after this incident male shoemakers came up with the idea of developing Catholic girls' unions, with the explicit objective of disciplining stitchers in case of conflict.

It is a measure of the contradictory qualities of the hegemonic process that it was actually at Van Schijndel's factory in Waalwijk that a Catholic girls' union had been most successful in recruiting stitchers. Elsewhere, in more backward conditions, girls' unions never effectively came into being. Yet at Van Schijndel's it was this formal association which played a crucial role in the collective walkout in 1910. Without the duties and moral significance of formal leadership of a Catholic organization, the chairwoman of the girls' branch could not possibly have taken action when her colleague was fined. Without the girls' union, stitchers might have acted with less solidarity, and the collective discontent would never have come to the fore in 1910. Thus while the causes of the girls' discontent lay in their increasing exploitation by employers and parents, their capacity to act collectively was crucially and paradoxically reinforced by the Catholic girls' organization itself. Though Catholicism heavily stressed the inferiority of women as producers, the girls' manifest complaints during the strike seem to imply that, at the same time, social Catholicism's claim for "humane treatment" and "community" in labor relations may have legitimized and sharpened the girls' perceptions of their dissatisfactions. The sheer fact of collective organization facilitated communication among the stitchers. Ideology and organizational structure, however contradictory and ambiguous, seem to have enhanced the capacity for structured collective action among the female stitchers.

Given the centrality of male domination over girls' work for their families in central Brabant, the cross-sex solidarity that developed after the girls' walkout in 1910 is perhaps surprising. What made male workers willing to join in this female-initiated action? How had male perceptions changed to account for cross-generation solidarity? What was the nature of male grievances? Between 1900 and 1910 a completely new kind of labor process had developed in the advanced Waalwijk sector of shoe production. The typical factory shoemaker of 1900 was a highly skilled handworker, a laster, or a skilled worker who operated a couple of machines. The former received relatively high piece rates, the latter a comparable wage. The foreman, and sometimes even the employer, was a blue-collar worker. Apart from differences between lasters, cutters, and other machine workers, and more fundamentally between the ages and the sexes, there had been little subdivision of each task, and scarcely any formalized hierarchies. These relationships were the basis of a relatively paternalist work regime for the adult male labor force. This moral community of the adult males was expressed by collective participation in the Catholic union, with the foreman as its spokesman.[34]

After 1905, however, Good-Year-Welt technology was introduced in the most advanced factories. This created a far-reaching subdivision of male tasks. By 1910, at Van Schijndel's factory, around sixty different tasks existed in a workforce of one hundred males. New processes resulted in serious deskilling of much male work. Whereas in 1900 all factory shoemakers belonged to a highly skilled labor aristocracy, in the biggest factories in 1910 around eighty percent of male jobs could be performed by more or less untrained boys, who began to appear in ever larger numbers on the shop floor. Of the one hundred men's jobs at Van Schijndel's only ten demanded a practical training of more than a year.[35] A division therefore developed between a small number of key workers who still earned good wages and had relatively guaranteed employment and a majority of less well treated machine operators.

Mechanization in shoemaking had profound effects on daily working conditions. Shoemaking machines are largely monofunctional motorized tools. Workers all have their own individual tasks. High production speed, therefore, was not a function of the machine, nor the central driving system, as in textiles, but came exclusively down to the individual worker. As a consequence, high production quotas were realized through elaborate systems of individual and collective fines and bonuses. At the same time detailed supervision was needed to prevent low-quality work. Around 1910 the shoe factories of central Brabant witnessed the emergence of formal hierarchies, aimed primarily at strict supervision. This produced very restrictive conditions on the workshop floor.[36]

Deskilling, segmentation, and individualization of the male labor force had serious implications around 1910 not only for the everyday quality of work but also for life outside the factory. The majority of unskilled workers tended to be victims of seasonal and other fluctuations for which the mass-production shoe industry became notorious. As a result, their annual earnings were never as high as their nominal weekly wages suggested.[37] At the same time, their work was intensified, with work tempos and demands for accuracy constantly rising.[38] Growing uncertainties combined with magnified duties. More than ever, deskilled workers directly and individually faced the whip of the market. Reciprocal relationships in industry were increasingly limited to a very small part of the working population. This served to develop a hidden critique of the entrepreneurial stance.[39]

In these same years, however, because of changes in the political economy of shoemaking, the big entrepreneurs lost interest in maintaining close relationships with workers and their organizations. Around 1900 shoe factories could only flourish in the middle-quality sector. The very best shoes were still made by hand, while simpler footwear was largely made in the protoindustrial sector, at least in the Netherlands. Moreover, factory systems could only be developed on the basis of substantial investment in fixed capital. By 1910, however, the best equipment, Good-Year-Welt technology, could be leased, and large steam engines were replaced by small gas and electric motors. There was thus a very substantial lowering of levels of capital intensity. As a result, the number of shoe factories in central Brabant was rapidly increasing by 1910, and the market for middle-quality shoes became quickly overcrowded. This again had its consequences for entrepreneurial strategies. Around 1900 the larger industrialists had an interest in curbing protoindustrial "superexploitation." This could only be done, though, by "sociopolitical" means, so they pleaded for moderate, clerically controlled workers "organizations," in order to facilitate the regulation of the labor market. By 1910, however, their interests moved more and more in the direction of mechanized economies of scale and increased productivity levels in order to cope with a diminishing rate of profit. Whatever truth there was in the old paternalism, big entrepreneurs now lost their habit of keeping up paternalist appearances.[40]

These developments in the relationships of production combined to diminish informal male workers' capacities to regulate production among themselves, a power based both on the importance of their skills for the factory labor process and on the relative absence of differentiation and segmentation among them.[41] Confronted with the informal power of solidarity, employers had consistently been willing to negotiate and to accept workers' demands during the sporadic and small-scale conflicts in the factory sector around 1900. After 1905 conflicts no longer occurred in the factory sector. But when open struggle and disagreement suddenly emerged on an unprecedented scale in 1910, the largest factory owner was in a position simply to push aside workers' criticisms of harsh work regimes. He could even consciously risk a confrontation. Within two months he turned out to be able to contract enough blackleg labor to man his machines. This was indeed a dramatic signal of the waning of informal workers' power during the preceding years.[42]

Neither spontaneous solidarity in August 1910 nor the potentially violent communal commotion to which it gave rise can reasonably be explained by reproducing complaints about union recognition. The Catholic union, of course, played some part, but that role, as already indicated for the emergence of female protest, was rather diffuse and symbolic, and its relation to the events was highly contradictory. On the one hand, the "wild" character of the action was certainly an effect of the inadequacies of Catholic discourse on factory production. While pointing to workers' problems in protoindustrial settings, Catholic discourse was utterly insensitive to shoemakers' problems in the context of "machinofacture." This blind spot was reinforced by the Catholic discourse on women and by gender contradictions in working class reproduction. Young female factory workers already had long-term experience of despotic production regimes. Their problems, however, were kept from collective awareness, and indeed were effectively repressed by male workers, together with the Catholic girls' organization formed explicitly for that purpose. In sum: Catholic discourse did not contribute anything to an explanation of collective distress, and it did not point to collective solutions. At the very same time that those male factory workers who had been its most explicit supporters were in need of formal organizations to counter the diminution of informal power, the Catholic movement turned out to be a dead end.

Moreover, the convulsive and potentially violent character of crowd action in Waalwijk was intimately related to the union's incapacity to deal with the conflict. Shoemakers' leaders were effectively isolated from their following by being part of the Catholic hegemonic project. In the process of criticizing protoindustrial exploitative practices, important links had been forged between local intellectuals like the *petits vicaires* and the union core and its followers. But those links were not revived during the conflict. On the contrary, the incorporation of the shoemakers' leadership into the Catholic structure disarmed them decisively and did not seem to leave them any alternative but to stimulate crowd anger by invoking Catholic "we-feelings." The local population consequently turned out to be incapable of translating widely felt frustrations into politically effective action.

In this context it makes sense to consider what actually happened within the Catholic Shoemakers Union itself. As mentioned, the shoemakers' leadership was seriously paralyzed and did nothing but ask for negotiations and collect money to support the strikers. Their clerical "advisers," however, were accused by the clerical hierarchy of failing to prevent an "unorganizational" strike. They were finally dismissed by the bishop after the conflict had ebbed away. One of them was removed to an agrarian community where, as shoemakers' legend says, he soon died in bitterness. Thus the clerical apparatus showed the limits of the workers' space in the Catholic structure. The shoemakers on the union board took this lesson to heart and would never again be willing either to announce a strike in a large factory or to support a wildcat action. While shoemakers' power in the factories was destroyed by a particular form of mechanization, in the Catholic union movement it was annihilated by Catholic officialdom and hierarchy.

In the Catholic movement, however, there eventually emerged some resistance to clerical hegemony from the shoemakers' leadership itself. But again, it was largely a symbolic and contradictory affair. It consisted of efforts to redirect the theme of "dishonest competition," the accepted cause of workers' problems in official Catholic discourse, to relationships in mechanized mass production. During the next decade, and up to the early 1920s, the semiofficial language of shoemakers' Catholicism as developed in its journal expressed strong feelings against modern, mechanized mass production. Resigning from effective industrial action, the union in fact advocated the development of small, artisanal, and paternalist family enterprises as the only way of re-creating the paternalist ideal. Thus while incorporating "indigenous" feelings toward morally acceptable relations of production and deviating from official discursive meanings, the union simultaneously expressed its powerlessness in the context of modern industry and clericalism.[43]

There is yet another interesting relationship to be studied in the nature of events in 1910: that between the hidden shoemakers' critique of the new morality of factory production and the Catholic labor union. In this relationship, the union acted not so much as a politico-economic force but rather as a powerful affective symbol in the communal commotion that emerged. This symbolic value was epitomized in the shoemakers' leadership's declaration that Van Schijndel's workers had "instinctively" understood the decline of factory paternalism and the emergence of intensified despotic regimes as an attack on the union.[44] The politically accepted and current vocabulary of threatened union rights evidently gave expression to the facts and fears of a jeopardized reciprocity between the classes and threatened working class collectivity. Discussed by intellectuals in the press, this vocabulary was again reduced to purely legal meanings, and these commentaries therefore missed the point shoemakers were making. Shoemakers themselves actually cared about the waning of "social union." As Catholic discourse did not facilitate a more precise and discursive articulation of their concerns, shoemakers themselves proved incapable of raising them to the level of public discussion and theoretical reflection.

In this light, finally, it is interesting to recall that violence during the conflict was mainly directed toward common and powerless persons. Shoemakers were intent on preventing public signs of working class disagreement. In the face of the insensitivity of official Catholicism, the paralysis of their own leaders, and the disappearance of workers' collectivity on the shop floor, a closed working class public front was the last ritual performance of "union" that could be enacted. Essentially this was a final and dramatic effort to keep their social identity and moral integrity intact. This being at stake, the diffuse violence of crowd action at Waalwijk is more comprehensible. It carried a dramatic moral meaning and was closely related to the subordination and powerlessness produced by the processes of proletarianization. Though it paradoxically emerged in the name and language of Catholicism, it was certainly inspired by the unarticulated but nonetheless collective criticism of social and industrial change.

By the middle of the nineteenth century the shoemakers of northwestern Europe were still the revolutionary philosophers of the urban working classes as painted for us by Eric Hobsbawm and Joan Scott.[45] Later, the ruralization of this industry in all the countries of Europe and the subsequent formation of factory systems forced this group from the political scene. Shoemakers did not, however, become the model civilians of a socially better integrated twentieth century. It is true, though, that the dynamics of industrial development and the market forced them to channel the greater part of their efforts into economic rather than political affairs. The struggle between small independent proprietors, who employed family and friends, and large, vertically integrated, mass-producing enterprises became a more central concern in the shoemakers' social critique than the struggle between workers and employers. In this respect central Brabant was no exception.[46] The events in Waalwijk in 1910, in fact, nicely illustrated one transition in this developmental chain.

The collective commotion in Waalwijk in 1910 contained other elements of theoretical importance. The potentially violent protest, which some would certainly call "archaic" or "primitive," points to shortcomings in theories of working class action. Recent authors have stressed the rationality of workers' responses to capitalist development, as expressed by the gradual disappearance of violence, the increased use of "industrial muscle" and the strike weapon, and the general shortening of labor conflicts.[47] Though this research contains important arguments against an older Durkheimian conservative sociology that proclaimed the irrationality, anomie, and "loss of tradition" of new urban laborers, it removed from view some important elements of the life and notions of the dominated classes, elements that have to do with the ways in which power and knowledge, the hegemonic process and collective understanding are related to each other.[48]

This tendency is reinforced, moreover, by the bias in this body of research toward the solidary strategies of relatively privileged and well-integrated artisanal workers.[49] Weaker proletarians, either in big industry or in unskilled peripheral branches, tended to be only faintly present in these studies. There are reasons to assume, however—and this is certainly illustrated by the shoemakers of central Brabant—that their weapons largely remained "primitive," that is, weakly organized, potentially violent, mostly individualistic, and often scarcely legitimate.[50]

In the course of the twentieth century, moreover, with increasing bu-reaucratization and institutionalization of labor organizations, an expansion of state intervention in production and redistribution, and the emergence of several varieties of conservative hegemonic projects, "primitive" forms of labor protest actually gained new currency.[51] Approaches that give due attention to "strange," "unsystematic," and unexpected details, like the excessive crowd anger in Waalwijk, sensitize researchers to the ambiguous nature of "normal" relations. Workers of the twentieth century, therefore, seem at once less "modern" and less "integrated."[52]

By emphasizing the rationality of working class protest, recent theories tend to remove from view the possibility of more fundamental motivations beyond articulate protest. It should be stressed that people do not simply try to realize neatly defined goals by advancing deliberate claims and mobilizing resources. That is often a game played only by relatively integrated and privileged groups, who know the accepted rules of action and the effects that can reasonably be calculated. Those more fundamental motivations that spring from historical and class-structured visions of the good, just, and honorable life can, however, inspire very different forms of both working class political intransigence and working class political apathy, especially among the less powerful.[53] In cases where the legitimacy of evolving relationships is questioned, and where established moralities of production are transgressed, such feelings can very well lead to explosive popular action or to deafening resignation, depending on context. They doubtless figured in the crowd actions of shoemakers, who found themselves proletarianized, their work intensified, claims on their energy increased, and the respectful paternalism to which they were traditionally entitled withdrawn.

Violence in Waalwijk should alert us to an important aspect of class experience and class action in hegemonic processes. If the forging of new hegemonies in twentieth-century Europe primarily consisted of the creation of a new regulating apparatus and its cultural justification in production and reproduction, the extent to which working populations were capable of having their problems, anxieties, and desires articulated in and by them becomes in its turn a central structuring condition for working class culture and action. The actual nature and extent of working class participation in the making of new languages and apparatuses of moral production is therefore of crucial importance to the understanding of hegemony, class experience, and protest.[54] And its historical legacy fundamentally structures the affective, cognitive, and practical capacities of subordinate people to counter and criticize the direction of development of productive relationships. Shoemakers in central Brabant apparently did not have the capability to revise Catholic discourse so as to make it meaningful to the new conditions of machinofacture. This created collective but individually experienced stresses that could only come to the surface when the routines of daily practice were broken, for example by the convulsions at Van Schijndel. Rationality does not reside exclusively in the mind. Rather, it is one possible outcome of the public and discursive forging of definitions, explanations, and justifications. And it is precisely on this level that hegemony operates, by prescribing certain languages and precluding others. The capacities of classes to intervene in such processes of closure and disclosure are a crucial condition for rational, that is, effective politics.

2 Solidary Logic or Civilizing Process? Workers, Priests, and Alcohol in Shoemaking Villages

Class is certainly a key concept of social history just as civilization is for the figurational sociology of Norbert Elias and his followers.[1] Each of these traditions needs to come to terms with the other. Notwithstanding fundamentally divergent assumptions, interests, and styles, both traditions would gain from a closer examination of each other's concepts, subjects, and methods. Norbert Elias's work, which centers on state formation and the growth of monopolies of violence in building its theory of the collectivizing and civilizing process, is notoriously silent on "economies" and their social and cultural implications. In fact it consciously neutralizes the vicissitudes of markets, class, and accumulation through the abstract and quite teleological notions of differentiation and integration. Thus, figurational sociology is rather weak "on the ground" of everyday existence, struggle, and survival, persistently tending toward global and more or less smoothly enveloping long-term processes, and not delivering much insight into the social and cultural dynamics of concrete historical localities and their working populations.[2]

Marxist social history, on the other hand, though certainly more varied, has tended to focus on the labor process and the contradictory interests it presumably generates. By so doing it tends to isolate its version of "economy" from "superstructures," often deriving the latter from the former, or, paradoxically, when studying those "superstructures," tending to disconnect them from production, appropriation, accumulation.[3] While the theory of the civilizing process would gain from a materialist understanding of capitalist accumulation and the contradictions it generates, marxist analysis could be strengthened by more closely attending to civilizational processes and to changes in those volatile standards of public and private conduct that occupy a silent and uncertain "cultural" place between the narrowly economic and the purely political.

Addressing problems of the civilizing process from a materialist standpoint not only demonstrates the usefulness of materialist approaches to this question but also helps to develop appropriate materialist concepts for areas not usually associated with them. The central Brabant shoemaking communities between 1900 and 1920 can be seen to illustrate the fate and development of a concrete historical "civilizing" campaign in its micro context. This campaign, organized by Catholic labor unions, explicitly aimed at the cultural "refinement" of local working classes.

An explicit civilizing effort by labor organizations in Europe, though at first sight perhaps a bit surprising, is in fact not at all exceptional. Though labor unions have only quite recently been studied with respect to their cultural allegiances and visions of leisure and pleasure, their civilizing mission was historically quite general and evident. Historical research has shown how union movements intervened in the free time of industrial workers in order to "refine" them, to civilize them, and to give them more affinity with bourgeois culture.[4] Since labor movements, by definition, gave expression to new visions of social order and individual conduct, and since they were the most practical institutions for bourgeois reformers and intellectuals seeking contact with workers, these civilizing aspirations should not be surprising. Catholic labor unions were no exception to this general pattern, though in a sense they merely presented new versions of an old vision and substituted the clerical "adviser" in black cassock for the enlightened and dissenting intellectual. To some extent Catholic unions tended to be even stronger civilizers, since the moral aspects of their actions were the ultimate motive for engagement of the clergy.[5]

This case study spans a period of fundamental discontinuity in the local forms of production, accumulation, and class relationships and, as will be shown, in the related local civilizing repertoires. The case is therefore highly useful as an illustration of the ways in which processes of class impinge upon processes of civilization. Central Brabant lends itself well to the effort to highlight the "economic" shortcomings of figurational sociology and forms a good test case for a materialist approach to questions of culture. About 1910 the regional economy entered a period of restructuring implying a substantial rearrangement of social relations and social problems. These societal shifts turned out to have had profound effects on the fate of the civilizing offensive that had been launched in earlier years and under different social and economic conditions. The campaign, accordingly, became seriously discredited and eventually almost disappeared from public life. Before turning to central Brabant, however, I will first elaborate some crucial considerations that shape the theoretical approach and its central concepts.

STATES AND MARKETS:
COMPETING PARADIGMS OF CULTURE CHANGE?

The civilizing process, according to Norbert Elias, is grounded in a process of collectivization, of increasing interdependencies between actors in society as a result of processes of differentiation and integration. In particular, Elias attributes great weight to the centralization and monopolization of the means of violence and coercion under the control of the state. On the level of the management of individual emotions and affects as displayed in public conduct, these civilizing processes would strengthen the disposition toward restraint. Elias thus made a connection between the sociology of societal differentiation and the sociology of emotions.

What is unsatisfactory from the viewpoint of a more materialist theory of history, however, is Elias's persistent tendency toward very long-term visions and his consequent depiction of a relatively smooth and rather teleologic process in which phases of societal integration always seem to follow phases of differentiation. His concentration on the level of the state and his confidence in its claims and mechanisms seem to have made him less concerned with the consequences of the interplay between states and markets. Moreover, the sociology of the civilizing process positively disclaims the theoretical relevance of the workings and the effects of the formation of markets for labor and capital, treating the overt emergence of class in the nineteenth century as a historical exception soon to be displaced by new forms of integration.[6]

From the vantage point of the late twentieth century, Elias seems to have been unduly impressed by the integrative capacities of the state. Indeed, capitalism, markets, and class place important limits on the relevance of the theory of the civilizing process, as markets and capitalism ("All that is solid melts into air") by definition create less stable and less integrated societies than state-building models suggest. Capitalist processes, even regulated by state action, are fundamentally contradictory, uneven, and now and then outright revolutionizing. The teleologic assumption of an ultimately unidirectional and rather smoothly operating collectivizing process, and the related assumption of a permanent dissemination of new and more civilized—that is, more restrained—standards of behavior from high to low in society are therefore doubtful, to say the least.[7]

Since the integrative force and forms of state formation are dependent on the social nature of the economies from which the state takes its material and organizational resources, a materialist theory of the civilizing process would probably focus on the specific ties, solidarities, and contradictions between classes and segments of classes as they arise in the forms of social production. Such ties and cleavages are perpetually generated and regenerated by the particularities of "economic" process, while at the very same moment this particular process is in turn shaped by them. Here the notion of solidary logic as coined by Michael Hanagan and Charles Tilly can be a welcome instrument for alternative analyses.[8] Substituting a specific and materially grounded relationship between classes in a given "economic" space for the abstract and teleological collectivizing process à la Elias, the idea of a logic of solidarity seems to offer a solid materialist tool for addressing questions that have not often been systematically explored by marxist researchers.

In order to apply the idea of solidary logic, originally developed to analyze labor processes, to the problem of public behavioral standards, there is need for an intermediary and derivative concept that enables a better grasp of processes in the sphere of the public politico-cultural domain. It is, of course, a very useful Gramscian assumption that this indeed is the terrain on which class hegemonies are established, negotiated, and confronted. But we need, first, to connect (counter)hegemonic processes in the public sphere directly to the changing social forms of the labor process and the solidary logics that grow out of it. Then, we must extend the notion of hegemony to the rather elusive domain of public behavioral standards. Therefore it is necessary to supplement the concept of solidary logic with the idea of a local civilizing coalition.[9]

Locally entrenched civilizing coalitions are a necessary precondition for any civilizing campaign to get a footing among local working populations. Civilizing coalitions, therefore, are based on an alliance between central segments of local working classes, local power holders, and civilizing agencies like the church, political parties, and bourgeois-led associations, which often have supralocal origins and commitments. The main thesis of this case study is that the chances for such a civilizing coalition to emerge and be successful are fundamentally structured by social relations of production, and of course by their logic of development.

It should be pointed out, however, that the analysis in terms of solidarity logics and civilizing coalitions is not meant as a complete substitute for the civilizing consequences of state formation. Rather, by introducing notions of socially and materially grounded agency, these concepts should span the gap left open by Elias between the moral heights of the state and the vicissitudes of down-to-earth production and daily life. In conjunction with a materialist conception of history this enables us to envision the civilizing capabilities of a whole regime of accumulation.

THE LOGIC OF SOLIDARITY IN CENTRAL BRABANT

Central Brabant, south of the river Meuse, was at the turn of the century a peripheral, underdeveloped, barren, and predominantly Catholic area. The country between the Meuse and the cities of Tilburg (textiles) and Den Bosch (old provincial capital, with diverse small-scale industries) had by 1900 become the heartland of Dutch protoindustrial shoemaking, engaging some seven thousand households scattered over several towns and villages and the hamlets in between.[10]

Although sources suggest rising social tensions, strikes, and efforts at union building by 1900, only around 1905 did stable and formalized unions emerge in shoemakers villages. These Catholic unions, "assisted" by members of the lesser local clergy (*geestelijk adviseurs*), succeeded in organizing more than half the male heads of shoemaking households. Catholic shoemakers unions in those years were not the hierarchical and centralized institutions of clerical control that have been painted by left-wing criticism. On the contrary, these unions were rather decentralized grassroots organizations, forming an interesting amalgamation of clerical and shoemakers' projects. The activist core was relatively large and extended through a system of "neighborhood commissars" into the heart of the village communities. The weekly meetings were obligatory for all members, and they were attended by hundreds of men. Once in a while, the gathered membership did show its determination not to accept far-reaching claims to this-worldly authority by the clergy. The unions thus were platforms of constant negotiation between clerical objectives and workers' opinions.[11]

The process of union formation in these backward shoemaking communities created almost a kind of organization euphoria and a revolution of rising expectations. Sources suggest that hopes for real improvements in living conditions were rising quickly. In fact a virtual communications revolution was going on, expressed not only in these sometimes turbulent weekly gatherings but also in the biweekly journal *De Leerbewerker*

(The leatherworker) published by the Catholic unions. This journal might well have been the first printed medium (except for religious illustrations) to penetrate this industrial countryside and find its way to proletarian households. And of course, alongside these new forms of mass communication, a whole new culture of committees, informal contacts, and collective actions developed, which created the public space for many to try to name collective problems and aspirations. Tightly knit as these communities were, a collective sense of purpose quickly gathered force.

The popular character of Catholic shoemakers' unions needs some explanation since it is not representative of the Catholic labor movement as a whole, nor does it correspond to the image of the movement as painted in recent historical research in the Netherlands. Left-wing social historians have taken the position that the Catholic labor movement was not a genuine social movement since in reality it was simply ordered from above by a conservative and defensive clergy in response to socialist penetration in Catholic industrial regions. These historians countered the apologetic thesis that the Catholic workers' movement was brought into being by Catholic workers not willing to support the "marxist doctrine of violence." Recent studies indeed confirmed that Catholic unions emerged only after intervention by clergy prepared to risk local confrontations by denying workers the holy sacraments if they did not quit secular and socialist organizations. Nevertheless, recent historians of central Brabant have maintained that Catholic labor organizations in this region were a genuine creation from below, created by popular action and against a bloc of local entrepreneurs and higher local clergy. Catholic shoemakers thus appear as an interesting case that needs explanation.

The cause of this particular and diverging development should be sought in the specific problems of industrial growth in central Brabant, and more particularly in the capacities of, and the coalitions and cleavages between, classes and segments of classes. Throughout the nineteenth century central Brabant shoemaking featured a large-scale protoindustrial development. Here a considerable part of Dutch shoe production was concentrated. An active class of local entrepreneurs, taking advantage of cheap, abundant, and experienced protoindustrial labor and relatively cheap access to raw materials, made this region into one of the most densely industrialized districts of the country.

The last quarter of the century saw growing foreign competition on the Dutch market for ready-made shoes and an increasing internal overcrowding as well. Though some entrepreneurs tried to build factory systems as a response, protoindustry could adapt by enlarging and modernizing central workshops under entrepreneurial supervision and control. The stitching of underparts became more and more concentrated while lasting and often also the female job of stitching of upperparts were put out. For years, these and similar arrangements competed successfully with full-fledged factories. Indeed most new factories were quickly restructured after their start into combined factory/home-working arrangements.

The problems with the development of factories in central Brabant were in fact anchored in the nature of the protoindustrial relationship. Home workers were dependent on entrepreneurs for both their successful access to the market in the summer season and especially for credit and food supplies in the winter. This, indeed, was the material basis of paternalism. It was the entrepreneur's duty to deliver winter goods on credit, and in turn the obligation of the household to stay with this patron in the summer. Thus almost all owners of shoe enterprises simultaneously operated formal or informal shops for basic foodstuffs as a guarantee of the delivery of household production in the high season. As response to a detrimental overcrowding of the market by 1900, numerous entrepreneurs began to pass the problems of falling profits on to "their" households by cutting wages and increasing the profits made on food delivery.

Paternalism and the truck system gave small entrepreneurs the opportunity to stay in the market by creating a kind of "superexploited debt proletariat." And indeed, of all Dutch industries, shoemaking became the most notorious example of this more general rural phenomenon.[12] Not surprisingly, it also became one of the best examples of an industry in which small proprietors succeeded in constantly underselling larger entrepreneurs with fixed capital outlays (buildings, machinery) and in undermining their attempts at market regulation.

The expansion of what Marx referred to as "absolute surplus labor" resulted not only in lower incomes but also in longer work hours. Around 1900, in the high season, workdays of more than fifteen hours, six days a week, were not uncommon. And contributions of wife and children became ever more necessary.[13] This logic could only unfold in the powerless protoindustrial households. Though complaints about increasing embezzlement and deceit indicate a rising tide of discontent, home workers did not develop the kind of solidarities that would have enabled them to collectively set limits to hours and wages.

In the years after 1900 an alliance developed between highly skilled labor aristocrats and their large employers to counter this process in the name of general and regional interest. It sought to organize home workers in labor unions in order to specify and implement a set of minimal labor conditions as to ban competition on wages. Especially after large manufacturers' efforts at market regulation by mutual price agreements failed, they publicly advocated the formation of labor unions in order to enforce higher wage levels for home workers and to limit the opportunities for competition by wage reduction. In the regional press they declared their support for any such efforts.

The core of the labor unions emerging after 1905 in shoemaking communities consisted of locally rooted, respected, and highly skilled labor aristocrats. All of them earned relatively high wages at the best factories and workshops of the region, many of them owned their own houses, and several of them were mutually related through ties of kinship. Even around 1900 their knowledge and skills were essential for the daily routine of labor processes in shoemaking. They included workers but also supervisors and controllers of factories and workshops.[14]

Years before the actual formation of labor unions, this blue-collar elite had been maintaining intensive contacts with those members of the local lower clergy who felt inspired by the new "progressive" climate in the Catholic Church after the encyclical of *Rerum Novarum* (1891). Encouraged by their employers and supported by parts of the clergy and several paid officials of the Catholic social reform campaign in Tilburg, these labor aristocrats made an attempt to bring together the larger part of protoindustrial workers in formal unions, against the determined resistance of a bloc of petty entrepreneurs and the conservative sector of the village higher clergy. Their attempts were successful only after the bishop of Den Bosch established a clear procedure for the recognition of Catholic labor unions in 1905. Local priests then lost their capacity to sabotage the social endeavors of their *petits vicaires*. After 1905, central Brabant witnessed the mushrooming of Catholic shoemakers unions for which the groundwork had already been laid by small local groups of labor aristocrats.

In sum, solidary logics in central Brabant shoemaking communities originated in "progressive coalitions" between labor aristocrats, larger entrepreneurs, and a dissenting lower clergy. These coalitions aimed at uniting "superexploited" protoindustrial families in formal and clerically protected labor unions in order to counter unlimited pressures on wages that threatened to draw the whole region into crisis. Conservative counterforces, however, were so firmly entrenched that this solidary logic could only become effective after the centralization of clerical social policies under the authority of the bishop.

A COALITION AGAINST ALCOHOL

The alliance between labor elites, large employers, and "social priests" was, in addition to its economic aims, an explicit civilizing coalition. In terms of prestige and material well-being the distance between its labor representatives and the protoindustrial proletariat on which its activities became focused was wide. The coalition behind the labor unions implied a frontal attack on several practices of popular culture. Central to this civilizing mission was its campaign against the use of alcoholic beverages and against public drunkenness. Alcohol symbolized irregular and dysfunctional popular culture out of place in the civilized mass manufacturing society which the coalition envisioned.

Its civilizing mission was clearly expressed in the Catholic union's biweekly newspaper *De Leerbewerker.* In 1908, about half its messages consisted of arguments for more civilized and respectable behavior. Many were concerned with alcohol. These articles were written mainly by members of a national lay group for Catholic social intervention, *De Katholieke Sociale Actie.* But of all articles apparently written by local shoemakers, more than half also concerned alcohol consumption. Local correspondents to the paper regularly complained about public drunkenness. And it happened more than once that the union's local boards announced that the names of notorious drinkers were known and that disciplinary measures could be taken.[15]

What motivated lower priests, capitalists, and members of labor aristocracies to participate in this civilizing campaign? And is it possible to draw conclusions about its effects? To what extent can we explain the outcomes of this campaign in terms of the specific class structuring and class logic of central Brabant shoemaking?

During the nineteenth century, the Dutch Catholic church and its political representatives were hesitant about involvement in antialcohol activism. Protestants and liberals from the urbanized western part of the country had taken the lead in the temperance movement, and for the largely conservative Catholic leadership this fact alone was enough to keep them at a distance. In parliamentary discussions on a new law concerning the sale and use of alcohol (1878), a central Catholic spokesman like Schaepman could still confidently assert that alcohol "was necessary for healthy brains and nervous system."[16] Moreover, the production and consumption of alcoholic beverages was notoriously higher in the Catholic south than in the Protestant north. The Catholic Church was quite literally identified with alcohol through its association with popular wines like *Liebfraumilch* and the profitable trade in monastery beers.

With the rise of a socially engaged Catholicism, the "social question" was put on the clerical agenda. Temperance became a central part of its "social action." For some Catholic protagonists "social action" and temperance even became identical. Thus the struggles within the church and Catholic communities between a conservative and a "social" Catholicism automatically led to conflicts about alcohol. In the conservative diocese of eastern Brabant, with its seat in the old city of Den Bosch, this struggle was particularly fierce. And the domination of its administration by staunch conservatives led "social" priests in the industrial villages to take the theme of temperance very seriously.

Industrial capitalists had their own motives for underwriting the temperance campaign of Catholic shoemakers' unions, motives that were derived from their everyday experience with managing a gradually changing labor process. After 1900, work in factories was being transformed from a rather rough and barely skilled process aimed at the lesser grades of product quality, into a much more precise and high-quality affair. In the years before, the use of alcohol on the shop floor had still been quite common, and the observance of saint Monday had been widespread. As local folklore insists, on a sunny day shoemakers would rather go fishing than spend their day working. Musical instruments and collective singing had been an accepted and normal part of factory work.[17] But by 1910 labor processes in some factories were fundamentally transformed. The division of labor deepened substantially and led to the development of meticulous systems of piecework with elaborate fines and bonuses. Management of larger factories devolved to white-collar workers within formalized hierarchies completely new for the region. Workers were confronted with a drastic increase in the need for attentiveness and accuracy in the performance of their tasks and were forced to submit to a speedup. Moments of relaxation and sociability were quickly disappearing from the shop floor in the larger factories. Against this background of an increasingly restrictive labor process, it is understandable that larger employers no longer wished to tolerate alcohol or the male sociability and uncontrollable shifts of status and solidarity which often were its accompaniment.[18]

As blue-collar foremen, cutters, and controllers, the core of union activists were well informed about the necessity to raise the quality of labor and the speed. They were therefore supporters of the ban on alcohol and its associated customs from the factories. As blue-collar supervisors they shared the anxieties of their employers. But, at the same time, as protagonists of a new social order in the region, they certainly had other kinds of objections against alcohol, objections that were not limited to problems of the factory labor process narrowly conceived.

The deterioration of living standards in protoindustrial shoemaking had not resulted in explicit and collective protest. This did not mean, however, that people were blindly and obediently consenting to their deepening exploitation. In fact, numerous individual strategies for the maintenance of family incomes had been developed that could not be made public but were nevertheless felt to be quite legitimate. Embezzlement of leather by home workers had become a widespread phenomenon, even leading to a black market drawing salesmen secretly from the neighboring town. In the evening and on weekends people silently worked for such traveling merchants, thus risking dismissal by local employers who feared further pressure on prices in the urban markets. In looking back to those days, an older activist shoemaker recalled that such activities had contributed 10 percent or more to family incomes.[19]

In this context, village pubs were not only places where people enjoyed their customary sociability; in fact, pubs increasingly became the local center for information about and contacts with this lively informal economy. Employers tried to counter the effects of such informal practices by strictly controlling "their" home workers. The local pubs were the place where you could earn some additional money, or where you could boast your success with illegal practices; you could also be betrayed there. Both mutual dependence and respect and mutual suspicion and physical violence were interwoven with the customs of the pub. The development problems of shoe-producing villages thus led to a spread of "minor criminality," in which alcohol, public drunkenness, and physical violence were central elements.[20]

The workers' elites of the Catholic shoemakers unions who were advancing collective regulation of hours and wages were well informed about such practices and about their causes and effects. By campaigning against alcohol and the customs of the pub, they believed they addressed a core element of local social problems. If competition over wages had to be stopped, the whole associated complex of the informal economy had to be attacked. Therefore, civilizing the regional economy seemed possible only by simultaneously civilizing the individual producers. In the eyes of shoemaker activists, the struggle against alcohol was a vital symbol of their struggle for a new regulation of social production.

In the circles of shoemaker activists one could hear the same general objections against alcohol that circulated everywhere in the growing labor movements of industrializing Europe. They saw a contradiction in principle between their fundamental social project and the use of alcohol. The latter, it was argued, was just a temporary and individual amelioration of deprivation, whereas the former was a collective solution to its structural causes. Unionists everywhere were against stupor, because they strove to enlighten; they were skeptical of individual solutions, because they were seen as part of the problem. The most convinced shoemaker activists were teetotalers, which in central Brabant was expressed by their membership in the Catholic "Union of the Cross." These men were praised by the shoemakers' press as the "soldiers of the union." In the frequent ceremonial marches of the Catholic unions through the towns and villages of central Brabant, these men walked at the head of the column, in military rhythm, proudly gathered around the banner of Saint Crispin, displaying their "Union of the Cross" insignia on the breast.[21]

But questions of principle aside, shoemaker activists also had more prosaic objections against the pub. Because of the long working hours, Sundays were the only day available for the male sociability of the café. But on Sunday mornings people were expected to attend church, after which there was a customary drink at home with the family. Showing up at the pub was possible only later in the afternoon. However, this was also the only available time for weekly and obligatory union meetings. The union and the pub, in short, were direct competitors in the leisure time of male shoemakers.

To what extent was this civilizational offensive successful? A first indication is the popularity of the Catholic labor unions. By 1910 the unions were capable of organizing some 50 percent of male workers in the villages. Old shoemakers stayed out of the movement, as did less skilled categories of factory workers. Apparently, the less skilled and more peripheral workers were too dependent on vertical ties with small entrepreneurs to be able to choose horizontal solidarities and new civilizational models.[22]

This division between central and peripheral workers was reproduced within the labor unions themselves. Many members seemed to approach union life quite pragmatically, for example as a convenient way of coming into contact with a foreman or a cutter who had job opportunities to distribute among his friends, or as an assurance against unemployment.

Such people did participate in the organization but seemed to keep distance from the cultural inspiration of its leadership.

On the other side of the social divide, there was a substantial number of members who seemed to embody the new behavioral requirements. Thus, in 1908 about 15 percent of the members of the Kaatsheuvel branch participated in courses on Catholic social theory.[23] Together with their supporters, and applauded by large and respected employers and the local clergy, the labor action did to some extent succeed in creating a public culture in which the open use of alcohol, frequent pub attendance, some traditional forms of male sociability, and the wholehearted participation in customary popular festivities became less and less appropriate for ambitious shoemakers. In some quarters this did lead to new relationships. On New Year's Eve 1908, for example, many occasions of public drunkenness were recorded at Kaatsheuvel. But the union leadership could proudly point to the neighborhood of "Vaartkant," where there was no trouble and where the percentage of organized workers and teetotalers was high. This neighborhood was presented as a model for civilized living, respectable families, and indeed advanced factory production.[24]

But all in all, the consequences of the emergence of Catholic shoemakers' unions, both as actors on the local labor market and as promoters of a civilizing offensive, were ambivalent. Their primary aims, the integration and civilization of protoindustrial workers, were not realized since this particular group remained out of its sphere of influence. The segmentation of the work force in shoemaking, and accordingly the gap in power, resources, and reproductive strategies, was greater than solidary logics could bridge. However, this was not caused just by the inherent cultural distance between segments of the working class. It was probably based as well on an accurate estimation on the part of the less privileged of their chances of material improvement through collective strategies. Effective intervention on the labor market would certainly have resulted in the bankruptcy of numerous small and backward entrepreneurs, who would not have been able to compete without truck systems and pressure on hours and wages. A "healthy" and regulated market would have meant widespread unemployment and starvation of peripheral and less skilled workers. Therefore, it is reasonable to assume that the civilizing effort of Catholic shoemakers' unions resonated mainly among respectable, highly skilled, and relatively well paid factory workers. Thus it contributed to a deepening of the social and cultural gap between central and peripheral households in shoemaking villages.

Between 1900 and 1910 the overcrowded market and ensuing survival problems of a mechanizing shoemaking industry had formed the material basis of a logic of solidarity. After 1910, however, restructuring of the shoe industry implied a rearrangement of class relations, social problems, and strategies for power. In particular, this later development brought an end to local solidary logics and eventually culminated in the dissolution of existing alliances. Thus the Catholic labor project lost its popular attraction among shoemakers.

This restructuring of economic relations in shoemaking after 1910 was caused by an interrelated set of developments which had deep repercussions for the relations between classes and segments of classes in central Brabant. For one, work in the bigger factories was largely deskilled as a consequence of the further introduction of new production techniques, accompanied by further substitution of white-collar management hierarchies for blue-collar supervision. Secondly, access to the new techniques was facilitated by the spread of lease contracts. Families with a little capital and a good reputation could substantially enlarge their operations and transform their putting-out business into factory production. This development of factory systems was even further stimulated by the quick spread of small gas and electrical engines. As a result, after 1910 small factories proliferated all over central Brabant. Finally, and most decisively, the First World War abruptly reversed market forces by creating a suppliers' market with high prices.[25] In sum, the strong market-induced pressures on shoe-producing populations which had formed the basis of logics of solidarity in central Brabant were fundamentally relaxed, creating space for completely different strategies.

This restructuring of the shoe economy meant the disintegration of the "old" labor aristocracies who had formed the backbone of Catholic labor union formation in central Brabant. This leading working class segment was dissolved into two new groups, the first of which became part of the new and relatively numerous class of small factory owners, the second of which took over the new white-collar supervisory functions in the large and fully mechanized factories. At the same time, at the lower end of shoemakers' society, many new opportunities emerged as employment widened, both in large factories and in the quickly increasing number of small factories, as well as in a newly vitalized home-working sector where the former problems of truck systems, indebtedness, and long work hours had largely disappeared. Particularly visible was a new and numerous class of teenage boys and girls working at low-skilled jobs in the larger factories.

In these same years after 1910, large central Brabant shoe manufacturers gradually became uninterested in the alliance with labor elites they once had helped to forge. Those sales and labor-market problems which had motivated them toward this alliance had now disappeared. In the new suppliers' market after 1914, their competition with small and backward manufacturers was not much of a problem. And in the years between 1910 and 1914 new competition emerged from the side of the smaller factory sector. Since these smaller manufacturers did not resemble "superexploiting" protoindustrialists, the alliance with organized labor no longer seemed to alleviate their problems. This new market structure required wholly different strategies. Further mechanization, economies of scale, steps toward vertical integration, and new marketing techniques like advertising and fashion were called for. Cross-class collective strategies no longer suited larger capitalists. Though inequality probably increased, as indicated by the numerous complaints about "undeserved wealth" among the largest employers, about their newly built country homes and their conspicuous consumption, market pressures for everyone seemed to be alleviated to such an extent that observers in the twenties could somewhat uneasily remark that there had been a considerable "enrichment for all."[26]

Catholic shoemakers' unions lost their original social, ideological, and cultural character. Some of those members of the former union elite who succeeded in acquiring their own enterprises left the union while others remained loyal, sometimes holding an honorary membership. Thus the union tended toward an alliance with the newly emerging small factory sector, giving it a decidedly populist and petty bourgeois outlook. Those former labor aristocrats who took upon themselves the new management positions in the largest factories generally left the union. After 1910 their loyalty toward their employers increased, while their intimacy with lower-status workers decreased. Finally, there are good indications that young unskilled workers at large mechanized factories tended to stay out of union life.

Whereas Catholic shoemakers' unions before 1910 had found themselves in an alliance with large employers and against small entrepreneurs and protoindustry, united in a utopian vision of a well-regulated and disciplined factory economy, they now tended toward an idealized world of small, paternalist, and family-based producers. Social peace, they now held, was primarily threatened by large "monopolistic" manufacturers enjoying "unacceptable profits," realized over the backs of workers and consumers alike.

However, the hierarchic framework of the Catholic "pillar," to whose authority and organizational capacities local Catholic shoemakers' unions were increasingly submitted, also dampened organized collective protest. In a time of growing individual opportunity, the shoemakers' leadership showed an incapacity for concerted action and constantly avoided conflict.[27] Its antimonopolistic diagnosis of social problems dissolved into a glorification of small paternalist and "good Catholic" employers. Instead of organizing collective action, union leadership encouraged workers to leave large factories and find work in the small-scale sector. Expansion of small-scale manufacturing, the union now believed, was the best way to "break and curb the power . . . of big industry."[28] The union even pledged governmental support for the "middenstandsbedrijf."

In this context the stress on civilization disappeared from the shoemakers' press. While in 1908 they consisted of some fifty percent of "civilizing messages," by 1918 this was reduced to a meagre six percent.[29] The campaign against alcohol and popular pleasures seemed to lose credit among the shoemakers' leadership as well as among its followers and the wider working class population. In 1910 the union board still publicly prided itself on demanding that local authorities limit the number of days for the annual fair. But already by 1912, the whole Kaatsheuvel union membership rallied against the board's decision to support the bishop's plan to reduce the number of yearly Catholic holy days and even forced its leadership to demand that local employers not implement this diocesan order. In the neighboring village of Oisterwijk a similar event took place in 1915 when the board proposed to continue work during the days of the local fair so as not to spend too much money while the world was at war. At the Sunday meeting, union members showed deep indignation and forced the board to immediately withdraw this proposal.[30]

It is remarkable that the rare civilizing messages that did appear in the shoemakers' press in these years hardly ever mentioned alcohol. Moreover, the ceremonial marches with banners, brass bands, and a prestigious position for teetotalers also disappeared. Evidently after 1910 teetotalism and temperance were losing their semblance of manly and purposeful respectability in the villages. Evidence from oral history indicates that those shoemakers who still dared to wear "Union of the Cross" insignia by the twenties had become the object of pranks and mockery.

To judge from the small percentage of civilizing messages, the union board apparently no longer attached great interest anymore to this once central cultural theme. Nevertheless, it is interesting to note that scattered comments in the paper suggest a new and quite different civilizational problem was emerging. Workers were reported to be less and less interested in their work and hardly willing to respect the authority of employers.[31] In negotiations with employers the union board painfully had to confess that "cafés and cinemas were generally attended to by workers." They also felt embarrassed by the fact that ordinary girls and mothers frequently dressed as ladies of the court.[32] The local youth was not held in high esteem by the union board. Teenagers were hardly concerned with union affairs. Still worse, union leaders thought that the local youth was running wild and busy with all kinds of debauchery. They were only interested in playing cards and football. In the shoemakers' press they were fiercely reprimanded for not spending time on further formal schooling in the trade, the accessibility to which was now a major union demand. The local youth needed to understand that "an ordinary worker's son could reasonably aspire to become a manufacturer."[33]

The disappearance of nineteenth-century development problems in shoemaking thus led to the related phenomena of the transformation of class relations, the ending of a specific logic of solidarity, the dissolution of existing alliances and coalitions, and the discrediting of the original civilizational discourses. This discrediting of the civilizing campaign was not just the effect of a diminishing willingness among local people to pay attention to it. More fundamentally, it was the effect of the erosion of the logic of solidarity between large employers, "social" priests, and labor aristocracies, implied by structural transformations of the social and economic base on which it was grounded. The "old" cultural polarity between organized, civilized, and highly skilled labor aristocrats working in the best factories of the region versus the marginal, alcoholic, pub-attending, and barely skilled home worker lost its social and cultural centrality. In its place a new but less compelling polarity developed, opposing serious, ambitious, skilled shoemakers, working for high wages or even managing their own business, to a class of unskilled, young operators, employed at large, mechanized factories, who spent their free time together, out on the street, with football, cinema, and forms of reportedly "uncomplicated" pleasure.

Except for the language in which it was expressed, the ideology of shoemakers' unions in these years began to diverge from the official discourses of social Catholicism. Instead of a Catholic trade union consciousness, union leaderships began to carefully formulate a small producers' ideology which was in some respects closer to Proudhon than to twentieth-century Catholic "solidaristic" corporatism. Closely related to this ideological shift, Catholic union activists developed a vision of work and leisure which could have been derived from sober Protestant ethics. Finally, both these idiosyncratic ideological themes came together in a cultural critique almost foreshadowing the later preoccupations of critical theory: accusing big capital of alienating ordinary workers from the political culture of work and duty corresponding with their class position by offering them the devilish mass pleasures of sport and cinema.

The persistent reiteration of these themes in the late teens and early twenties does however point to the fact that the larger part of the local population, and in particular the industrial youth, became less and less attracted to these cultural ideals, which is also indicated by their diminishing engagement with union affairs. Thus the Catholic civilizing project lost its social foundations and its popular appeal. Only with the introduction in the later twenties of modern, clerically organized leisure practices for young workers, like Catholic football clubs and scouting associations, could Catholicism regain some of the cultural initiative it had lost between 1910 and 1920. Catholic labor unions never again developed the same degree of civilizing fervor as in their early years.

CONCLUSION

This case study illustrates the ways in which local civilizing coalitions are fundamentally structured by patterns of solidarity, segmentation, and fragmentation that are based on the development of labor processes and market relations. Understanding the force and direction of the civilizing process requires more than is offered by Elias's work; it requires systematic attention to the ties and cleavages of class both "on the ground" and in the higher abstractions of world system and market relationships.

On the other side of the theoretical divide, however, there seems to be a need for materialist analysis to become more sensitive to the intricate but systematic interdependencies that arise between the worlds of production and reproduction, between work, leisure, and the public sphere in general. In particular, we need a firmer theoretical grasp of such cultural contexts in their everyday and localized qualities, since it is there that distances and intimacies between and within distinct classes of people become marked and disputed, challenged, asserted, or just neglected, evaded, or forgotten. The concepts of solidary logic and civilizing coalition seem to provide a fruitful starting point to bring such an analysis a step further.[34]

Girls at the Philips Strijp Complex
assembling wireless sets, circa 1930.
Courtesy of SAREK (Regional Archive
of Eindhoven and Vicinity).

Immigrant families in Drents Dorp, circa 1930. Courtesy of Philips Company Archives.

The Drents Dorp project, built in 1929–30. In the background are the apparatus factories. Courtesy of Philips Company Archives.

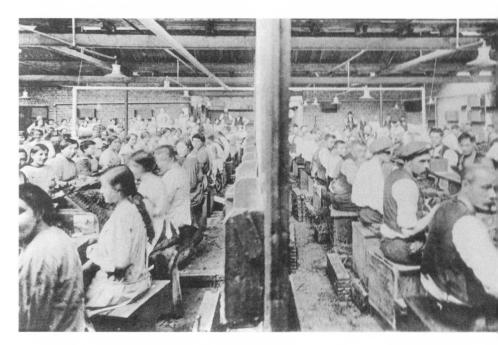

Cigarmaking in Eindhoven, circa 1910: mass production and segregation. Courtesy of SAREK (Regional Archive of Eindhoven and Vicinity).

Philips lamp factory, circa 1910. Courtesy of SAREK (Regional Archive of Eindhoven and Vicinity).

Shoemakers in a cooperative plant, 1910. Courtesy of Toon Ververs (Kaatsheuvel).

PART TWO

The Enigma of Philipsism: Family and

Acquiescence in an Electrical Boomtown,

1850–1950

3   Eindhoven and Its Context

By 1930, the town of Eindhoven, on the southeastern periphery of the Netherlands, had become a national symbol of industrial growth, efficiency, and technological know-how. Or, as the secretary general of the state department of trade and industry at the Hague put it, it was "an oasis in the all too often desert-dry industrial life of the Netherlands." Various expanding firms, for example those in cigarmaking, had contributed to that popular picture. But more than anything else it was the electrical manufacturing complex of the Philips company to which national praise was due.

Philips, indeed, had witnessed an impressive expansion since its start in 1891. In 1929 it employed almost twenty-three thousand workers in its Eindhoven outlays and had become by far the country's single most important earner of sorely needed foreign currency. Especially since the autumn of 1927, when the company had launched itself successfully into the mass production of radio sets, its growth had seemed almost unbelievable to Dutch contemporaries. It enticed some of them to draw historical parallels with the golden age of national maritime power and wealth, suggesting that the economic lead had passed from the seaborne canals, stock market, and merchant capitalists of Amsterdam to the peripheral heathlands, to semiproletarian families, and to industrial capitalism of southeast Brabant. The seemingly insatiable demand for the new electrical products convinced Philips to build a new seven-story industrial complex, erected completely out of concrete, styled in a clear modernist design, which would become one of the very largest manufacturing sites in Europe for decades to come.

This unprecedented industrial growth necessarily engraved its mark upon the Eindhoven landscape, which was quickly transformed into an advanced manufacturing territory. In 1920 the originally small and narrow city had annexed its five satellite villages. This led to an urban polity of some forty-five thousand inhabitants. In the next decade the popula-

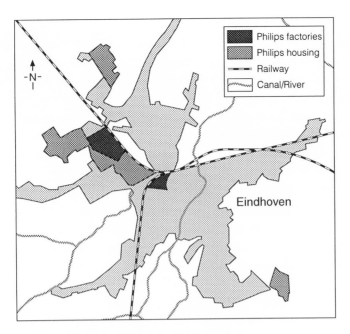

Eindhoven and the Philips industrial complex.

tion had doubled to ninety thousand, with a marked acceleration of growth in the years 1927 to 1930. All over the Eindhoven area construction sites appeared, the majority commissioned and supervised by Philips. Trains, trams, and bus services brought thousands of workers to the city each morning and home again in the evening. The labor market spanned an area of more than sixty kilometers' radius, from Tilburg in the west to Roermond in the east and the Limburg province of Belgium in the south. Government-supported population removal from the crisis-stricken peat districts of the Dutch northeast sent those citizens to Eindhoven as one of their places of salvation.

But in contrast to all the official pride and enthusiasm, the boomtown would quickly learn how vulnerable an industrial community could be that specialized in consumer products for international markets. Starting in late 1929, Philips had cut back its number of Eindhoven workers to some 8,500 by the spring of 1932. Cigarmaking and textiles, the other basic productions of the area, were drawn into crisis and gradually reduced their numbers of employed by a large percentage. Partly due to Dutch conservative monetary policies, this once prospering community would witness one of the highest urban unemployment rates of the country throughout the 1930s. While new factory buildings served only to pile up stock, whole parts of new workers' quarters would stand empty for years.

Unexpected cutbacks, layoffs, and unemployment in the thirties were obviously painful for the people concerned. This certainly was a major drama. But, surprisingly, it in no way triggered concerted collective protest. Although a small group of radicals tried to mobilize the unemployed in the town, the established unions and political parties, however disillusioned, did not feel confident enough to organize popular dissent. Nor did any trace of collective protest appear outside formal organizations. Again, in later times, the city of Eindhoven would be a prime example of Dutch labor quiescence. From the point of view of contemporary social thinking about modern industrial societies, Eindhoven was an anomaly. Both conservative and left-wing thinkers assume the salience of growing anomie, rootlessness, materialism, and popular disobedience to be a feature of modernizing, urban, and industrial societies. However, the nation's prime large-scale industrial area showed little sign of this. The enigma of Philipsism became one of the major historical frustrations of the Dutch left.

Explanations given for working class quiescence in this key area of the Dutch economy, though never seriously elaborated and discussed, take one of three possible routes. The first takes its starting point in the practices of the giant company and refers to its local power structure and its tradition of paternalism and benevolence. The second form of explanation points to the assumed quiescent nature of the young, rural, unskilled, and inexperienced workers typically employed by Philips. Finally, it has become a general and rarely disputed feature of Dutch historiography and much social thought in general that an almost natural deference of workers reigned in "traditional," mostly Catholic areas. This vision, based on the premises of modernization theory, is often thought to be sufficiently illustrated by the unchallenged dominance of conservative Catholicism in local politics and by the popular adherence to deferential Catholic unions instead of "modern" ones. Explanations thus tend to shift between essentialist characterizations of workers' consciousness, on the one hand, to visions "from above" with workers largely left out (which also assumes that in the absence of corporate dominance workers would have become class conscious in the classical sense).

In the virtual absence of sustained historical and comparative questioning, many such explanations all too easily attain a self-referential character. They have attained the value of unquestioned common sense. But despite their superficial matter-of-factness, on closer scrutiny what is most telling about them is not so much their empirical and comparative validity but the rather overwhelming sense of exceptionalism and anomaly that is implied. Here, they appear to say, we encounter a situation that is not provided for by our theories of modernization, capitalist development, and class struggle. Indeed, modernist theories presuppose the growth of utilitarianism, materialism, secular individualism, and awareness of modern conflict in advanced industrial environments, and therefore predict dissent and collective action rather than quiescence in case of popular adversity. In order to explain away the unhappy digression, and indeed to reconfirm their own authority, such theories then start to point to the other anomalous qualities which happen to coexist, such as, in the Eindhoven case, corporate welfarism/paternalism, Catholicism, and "immature" laborers in a technically advanced industry. Subsequently, these anomalous co-presences are then turned into explanations for the noncorrespondence with the a priori assertions of modernist teleologies.

Instead of taking such theories of exceptionalism at face value, then, they are better seen as a mere index of divergences in local trajectories and timings of capitalist development, and of differential ways of local insertion into the world system. It is a bad but widespread habit that successful capitalist configurations that emerge at a later point in time, and in unexpected locations (such as present-day East Asia), are often seen by those theorizing from an earlier topical case as digressions, exceptions, and anomalies, which are either bound to be changed at last into the right and "necessary" direction or hopelessly infused with an alien "traditional" culture and therefore feared, honored, or condemned. The twin idols of teleological evolutionism and cultural essentialism, however, miss the important point of divergent but nevertheless connected capitalist trajectories. Such exceptionalist analyses, moreover, are often found to be imprecise, inadequate, and prone to falsification upon comparison or closer study.

Of the concepts employed by exceptionalist elucidations of the Eindhoven case, dominance, welfarism, and paternalism are, with respect to their empirical validity, the more workable explanatory terms. But in the absence of research on their particular workings "on the ground" and on their specific effects on the visions and motivations of groups of people, they remain inadequate as explanations of quiescent attitudes. Moreover, the dominance displayed by the Philips company over the region, though indeed exceptional when compared to the highly differentiated and nationally dominant Dutch maritime provinces, is in fact encountered in many more sites of twentieth-century capitalist mass production. On closer scrutiny, corporate engagement with regional structures in peripheral places did not so much evolve from a concern with sheer dominance in order to avoid organized protest, as has often been alleged by contemporary labor organizers, but rather from the necessity to modernize the region according to the evolving needs of mass production.[1] And since some such dominated regions, such as the Ruhr, southern Wales, and Lorraine did feature radical popular protest, corporate dominance cannot be taken as a sufficient general explanation for workers' quiescence at Eindhoven. That is, unless it is demonstrated that the structures of Philips dominance were of a peculiarly effective and different character. But then it becomes necessary for their particularity to be highlighted and explained.

Paternalism and welfarism, though easily demonstrated as employers' practices, also generate several difficult-to-handle problems when used as an index or cause of deference. The concept of paternalism has rightly been criticized for not distinguishing between its effects on industrial relations, on the one hand, and on the local public sphere and politics on the other.[2] Moreover, many historical examples can be given where paternalist and welfarist employers were nevertheless fiercely criticized by their workers after crisis-induced layoffs, such as Ford in Detroit and General Motors in Lynn in the thirties, or Siemens in Berlin after the turn of the century.[3] Indeed, languages and practices of paternalism, instead of necessarily instilling contentment, in times of crisis often served to inform the terms of popular critique against the powerful. In this way power holders, both in feudal and capitalist relationships, have often been reminded of their earlier hegemonic claims and paternalist promises. Thus they were accused of violating the terms of the implicit social contract which they themselves had tried to forge and under which the play of popular obeisance would be acted out.[4] Both on theoretical and historical grounds, then, the record of paternalism and welfarism is clearly too uneven and ambiguous for it to be used as a general explanation for quiescence.

This is also true for the Eindhoven case. Unless the particular workings of paternalism at Philips can be demonstrated to have had such a pacifying effect, the simple presence of paternalism cannot be a sufficient causal factor. Moreover, if we want to avoid an outright voluntarism on the part of Philips's management, the particularities of its paternalist package can only be explained by relating it to the particular modes of electrical production and accumulation at Eindhoven.[5]

Deference, and by the same token traditionalism, has recently been subjected to an even more devastating critique. Howard Newby, studying deference among East Anglian agricultural workers, a class known for its quiescence throughout history, could not really establish its existence at all, not even through fieldwork methods. What he found was discontent, disapproval, collective condemnations even, that coexisted with political inactivity. His work suggests that deference is often deduced when in fact merely collective passivity can be found. It strongly warns against taking overt public behavior as a measure of private attitudes.[6] A similar stance can be found in the recent intriguing work of James Scott, who studied everyday forms of peasant resistance in Malaysia through anthropological fieldwork. He even goes so far as to reject fully the idea of hegemony, commonly understood as rule by popular consent. He encountered a whole "underworld" of what he calls "off stage" critique, which did not seem, however, to affect the "on stage" performance of the powerless.[7] Deference, in short, clearly carries too many implications concerning the correspondence of attitudes and actions, private and public behavior, deeds and words. As demonstrated by such researchers as Scott and Newby, in particular when people are studied "from below" in their everyday settings and practices, the distant judgment of deference will often turn out not to be consonant with their practical outlooks.

Exactly the same reservations are true for Catholicism or conservatism as explanatory shorthands for workers' quiescence at Eindhoven. Here again, superficial data on public behavior are taken to correspond unproblematically with private ideas. It is necessary here that the relevance of conservative politico-cultural claims and organizations for the real world in which common people live is demonstrated for each empirical case rather than just assumed a priori. But even then, traditional languages and political practices never unproblematically command the loyalty of subject populations. They always offer something in return, whether it is safety, security, or bread.[8] Thus they also provide a yardstick to measure their own performance with. It has been abundantly demonstrated that such conservative claims can produce downright radical consequences when the promised fruits of obedience do not seem to materialize.

What these considerations suggest is the essential importance for generating any form of collective popular protest of those social institutions, mechanisms, and relationships by which "off stage" and "private" popular angers, indictments, and condemnations can become named, articulated, and acted upon "on stage," in the public and semipublic arena. The question of popular protest, then, depends to a decisive degree on the responsiveness and openness of the formal organizations of associations, trade unions, political parties, and representative institutions, in other words, of the civic realm, for the as yet hardly formalized and theorized, sometimes squarely incoherent and fragmented grievances of groups at the margin.[9] Without linking up with civil mechanisms and interclass relationships that can render dissatisfaction somehow coherent and respectable, collective actions and collective condemnations by the weak can hardly be conceived of.

Although it is true, as has been argued by recent authors such as Gareth Stedman Jones, Joan Scott, and Patrick Joyce, that political and cultural traditions of public life carry a certain historical weight of their own,[10] the above leads to the methodological priority for students of working class formation to assess the particular ways and degrees in which "off stage" angers and grievances become connected and disconnected with the historical narratives circulating "on stage." And these ways and degrees, it is well to emphasize, vary considerably, both locally and nationally. There are specific local, regional, and national patterns of incorporation and marginalization of the weak. Moreover, as is illustrated most forcefully by the work on working class formation of Charles Tilly, Louise Tilly, Michael Hanagan, and Ron Aminzade, this whole process crucially depends on the opportunities for coalitions between social class segments to develop.[11] Building on the work of these authors, I will put the formation and deformation of such coalitions in the center of the analysis of working class formation and working class culture at Eindhoven.

From marxist labor sociology, however, a different and more empirically sustainable explanation has been given for Eindhoven quiescence. In contrast with paternalism, dominance, and deference, this explanation, pointing to the overwhelming presence at Philips of unskilled and inexperienced workers, is rather better established. As the Amsterdam sociologist Ad Teulings has pointed out, Philips thrived to a considerable extent on unskilled, young, and female labor, often from peripheral and agricultural backgrounds.[12] These workers, both in personal outlook and collective capacities, were a far cry from the skilled, urban, and male workers with union experience who by 1900 began to dispute employers' practices in the established industrial regions of continental Europe. Building on the fact that Philips did not grow from the same basis of electrical engineering as had Siemens and AEG in Berlin and General Electric in the United States, but from unskilled work in the new trade of incandescent lighting production for an international consumer market, Teulings sought to explain the characteristics of the Philips factory regime and the absence of collective power by workers. As Harry Braverman has described for monopoly capitalism in general, Teulings found a dependent working class bereft of any autonomous insight into the dynamics of its own work and living conditions, a class that readily let itself be exploited by an almost omniscient technocratic managerial elite.[13]

Though absolutely demystifying in some respects, like Braverman's before him, Teulings's work, on closer scrutiny, only describes what Eindhoven electrical workers were not: that is, not skilled, nor schooled, nor broadly educated, and not tightly organized as were the proverbial male blue-collar workers, who were employed in labor processes that critically depended on their experience and cooperation. In fact, Teulings precisely represented the disillusionment with Philips by the only working class group at Eindhoven that did display such characteristics. His sources on Eindhoven working class culture mainly consisted of social democratic metalworkers' commentaries.

In fact, again like Braverman's, Teulings's work is grounded in a simple, unrealistic, and romantic polarity. On the one hand, there is the skilled class-conscious artisan of the nineteenth century, who could still combine the functions of conception and execution and therefore exert a crucial measure of control over his labor, and on the other hand there looms the deskilled worker of monopoly capitalism who could and would not be more than a confused pawn in the hands of a scientifically supported management.[14] Consequently, Teulings's work is far better at establishing the general lines of development of the Philips corporation within the global electrical arena than in understanding the actual experiences of workers. He completely misses what they themselves might have thought was important to them, what they felt motivated toward, their relevant histories, their hopes, relations, capacities, and incapacities.[15]

In fact, the whole a priori assumption that industrial workers should somehow develop their consciousness and culture around the organization and experience of work has recently come under attack. The American social historian John Bodnar, for example, has not unjustifiably argued that the degradation-of-skill approach that has dominated social history for two decades loses much of its value when used for understanding workers' protest as recent as the interbellum.[16] The degradation-of-skill approach focused on skilled workers' efforts to counter their loss of control over labor processes with the ascent of industrial capitalism.[17] It explained the emergence of workers' solidarity and workers' politics from such defensive efforts. The new semiskilled workers of the mass-producing industries that emerged from 1900 on, however, had histories that differed greatly from those of the unionized skilled artisans of a generation before who had formed the empirical basis and main historical object for the degradation-of-skill approach.

The new industrial workers of the twentieth century, Bodnar convincingly shows, did not primarily bother about specialist skills or dream of collective regulatory power over production processes. In fact they had never had any access to such privileges. What moved them, according to Bodnar, was very much the same as what had moved them in the generations before: the sheer survival and integrity of their families. This is probably just as true for American immigrants as for the majority of Ruhr miners, the steelworkers of Lorraine, and the electrical proletariat of southeast Brabant.

Finally, contrary to what is implied by Braverman's work, Bodnar argues that such new industrial workers were definitely capable of collective protest. But they were only motivated to do so if and when the very livelihoods of their families were acutely threatened. Although this may be too easy an explanation of workers' protest in the light of the recent social-historical and anthropological emphasis on the importance of coalitions and public practices, it is clear that here, rather than in the degradation-of-skill thesis, we have an adequate starting point for analyzing workers' motivations at Eindhoven.

In connection with the poor insights in twentieth-century working class culture emanating from Bravermannian visions, Teulings's work features another vital weakness. Largely based on sources produced by young, skilled, immigrant metalworkers who had just completed their trade schooling in one of the liberal and democratic urban centers of the Dutch north and west and had come to try their luck at the famous Philips plants in the Catholic province, Teulings uncritically reiterates their notable low esteem for the peripheral and unskilled proletariat in electrical mass manufacturing. Indeed, as we shall see, these metalworkers' inability to develop stable and meaningful relations with local workers contributed to a consistently dismissive and undifferentiated opinion about their "lesser" fellow workers. In this context, the prefix *agrarian* tended to attain highly negative connotations. In metalworkers' discourse, to be a Philips worker from "agrarian" or "peasant" background almost became equivalent to having no relevant history and civilization at all. Indeed, this fitted very well with Teulings's Bravermannian inspiration.

But the Philips proletariat did not only, or even mainly, have traditional peasant backgrounds. Though it is true that they were recruited from peripheral regions, they featured social and cultural characteristics that could not simply be reduced to traditional peasant culture. By denying the relevance of their particular histories, left-wing theorists put themselves in a hopeless position for understanding their orientations and practices. And worse, it prevented them from coming to grips with important aspects of the Philips regime itself.

To develop any more penetrating insight into workers quiescence in Eindhoven, we need, first, a much better grasp of the composition, structure, and origins of the Philips proletariat, including the firm's methods for labor recruitment and deployment; and second, a more grounded and comprehensive vision of the patterns of popular alliance formation in the community. But beyond the obvious need for more productive questions and a more adequate empirical base, what is above all necessary to explain the problem of class formation in this key area of Dutch twentieth-century industry (as in any other such setting) is the identification of a whole, historically and spatially defined, dynamic, and interrelated pattern of capitalist accumulation that exerts definite pressures and sets determinate limits on the possible modes of local existence, popular experience, and social action. Toward this end, it is useful to revive the old and fiercely disputed marxist idea of a "structured totality" of class relationships (or David Harvey's more modest variant: the idea of the "structured coherence" of urban settings) and, like scholars such as Eric Wolf and Michael Burawoy, demonstrate its continued usefulness for social research in a nonreductionist and contingent mode of inquiry.[18]

Speaking of such a "structured totality" of class relationships is warranted only if we can show the same coherent pressures, emanating from a specific spatial and temporal pattern of capital accumulation and industrial life, to be operating in such diverse fields as work, coalition formation, social policy, household formation, human reproduction, everyday life, and urban form and culture. In the case of Eindhoven, the close and continuous interweaving of such empirically distinct processes into a more or less coherent and comprehensive path of social change can best be described as "flexible familism." Flexible familism in the southeast Brabant area, as I understand it, was a key property of the regional mode of production, grounded in the long-drawn-out and combined eclipse of peasant and worker-peasant economies, on the one hand, and the rise of labor-intensive export manufacturing in the later nineteenth century on the other. It denotes a class relationship and labor market practice that was based on the increased allocation, within multiple-earner households, of industrial, waged tasks to local daughters. Starting from this basic interdependence between labor-intensive export manufacturing and the structure of working class family economies, the concept of flexible familism seeks to connect such diverse aspects of regional development as the predominant forms of industry, the type of urbanization, the pressures of family and household formation, but also the nature of popular politics and working class culture. Flexible familism, then, describes a comprehensive path of capitalist urbanization and industrialization.

Consequently, I do not treat the Philips company as anything like a separate structure or organization. Rather, in the course of research it became ever more clear to me how fundamentally embedded even this giant corporation was in local life and relationships. Indeed, Philips finally became the most articulate embodiment of such relationships. This insight is expressed in my use of the term *Philipsism*. With Philipsism I denote the totality of managerial social and technical policies that emerged in the late 1920s, as the company, in response to a serious crisis of control, started to incorporate the most basic aspect of flexible familism: the reproduction of multiple-earner families. This insight puts me in a position to see that Philipsism, instead of being an innovative managerial practice, was in fact an attempt to re-create the original characteristics of local labor. A rapid widening of job opportunities in the late twenties shifted the balance of class forces in such a way that customary forms of hegemony and social control over young mass-production workers began to erode, on the shop floor, in families, and in the city. Philipsism, in response, sought to re-create a proletariat of whole families, with multiple earners, many of them daughters, which, supported by a package of social policies, exhibited the same internal disciplinary capacities as local families around 1900. Philipsism thus reproduced exactly those key characteristics of local labor that had given the area its original capitalist impulse. By making the family again the unit of labor recruitment, the corporation sought to reinstall both paternal authority, adolescent obedience, and industrial discipline. The region's key property of flexible familism was at the heart of Philipsism. It was also central to subsequent working class quiescence in the early thirties. Flexible familism, both as a customary practice around 1900 and as an explicit, systematic, though persistently understated management strategy by 1930, fully shaped the reigning patterns of class segmentation and class organization in the locality, as well as its emergent urban form and public culture.

The present approach to an accurate depiction of this complex of forces comes down to combining the old, ambitious, and controversial marxist idea of a "structured totality" of class relationships with a non-reductionist and contingent approach to class and capitalist development, as for example expressed in the notion of the path dependency of local process. This approach invites us to lay bare vital and simultaneous connections between the different composite elements of a total social and spatial development process. It analyzes the determinate interlinkages between the global dynamics of the capitalist world-system, the nature of local production and class relationships, the sorts of local alliances likely to be forged, the forms of family and public life to be fostered, and the consequent structure of everyday power and politics to emerge in industrial localities. In the case of Eindhoven, it alerts us to hitherto barely recognized facts and interrelationships, and helps to inform a vision of local processes that seems at once richer, more comprehensive, more plausible, and more fascinating than existing accounts.

4   The Making of a Flexible Industrial Territory

Traveling through the province of North Brabant in 1818, G. K. van Hogendorp was told more than once that plain citizens, without substantial means, could easily become wealthy businessmen here.[1] Wages in the province rarely attained a level higher than 60 percent of national average, and there was an abundant supply of sons and daughters available for (proto)industrial work. Already in the eighteenth century, textile entrepreneurs in Haarlem and Leiden moved much of their mass production to places such as Tilburg and Helmond. In the case of the Eindhoven area, too, enterprising families with the right resources, entrepreneurial skill, and manufacturing knowledge succeeded in amassing large stocks of capital. Based on the cheap and flexible deployment of local unskilled labor in labor-intensive industries such as textiles, cigar-making, and by the end of the century, light electrical products, their activities created a process of industrialization and urbanization that, accelerating after 1890, would result in the making of the most advanced manufacturing territory of twentieth-century Netherlands.

In important respects the Eindhoven area differed from the Brabant textile towns. Helmond and in particular Tilburg were dominated by a relatively small, locally rooted, and closed elite of Catholic industrial families. In contrast, Eindhoven in the nineteenth century featured an open and dynamic entrepreneurial community. While the majority of manufacturers were locally born and Catholic, the largest enterprises in all local sectors were owned and managed by non-Catholic entrepreneurs with roots outside the community, some of them from foreign countries such as Germany and the United States.[2]

Local industrial labor was rooted in the slow decline of the east Brabant peasant economy. All descriptions of "traditional" agriculture in the region paint the same picture. Mixed farming, first with an emphasis on agriculture and later on livestock, was performed on very small, scattered, and undercapitalized peasant plots. Around 1900 almost 50 percent of peasants worked on less than five hectares. This was deemed just enough to feed a family, provided there were enough family members to work the soil. Somewhat over half the farms were owned by the peasant households that worked them. But small proprietors increasingly suffered from high mortgage payments for buying out other inheriting brothers and sisters (partible inheritance). In the course of the nineteenth century relative autarky gave way to more commercialized and specialized forms of farming, but all sources emphasize that smallholders kept growing potatoes and vegetables and went on breeding small livestock for their own needs, in particular pigs, goats, and chickens.[3]

It is impossible to understand processes of industrialization in the Eindhoven area without understanding their close link with the peasant economy and in particular with the peasant family cycle. Since a new household could only be formed when a farm became available, the frequency of marriage in Brabant, just like other European regions, had been low since early modern times.[4] Age at marriage, accordingly, was often high. Males in the nineteenth century, if marrying, did so at age thirty-two on average. If parents were still active and market conditions adverse, the oldest son would cancel marriage, leaving his second or third brother the chance. Sometimes, no son or daughter married at all. In that case brothers and sisters often stayed together and ran the farm collectively. Since peasant productivity depended fully on the amount of labor inputs, families tended to stick together in order to ensure survival. Without the labor inputs of a sufficient number of family members, Brabant peasant households became impoverished and proletarianized.

This fundamental situation had two important demographic consequences. First, the number of children remained modest, since low marriage frequency and high age at marriage reduced the chances for procreation. Second, households were rarely composed of nuclear families, in that unmarried brothers and sisters remained living with the married sibling. It is a well known fact that almost every Brabant family sent one or more members into monasteries. But more important here is that many of them stayed with the family, to labor in the fields or to earn some extra cash for collective survival.

Rural Brabant households were poor but complex, and so too was their work. While they have always been described as peasants, in fact they hardly limited their labor inputs to agriculture proper. Starting in early modern times, but with a powerful acceleration in the nineteenth century, protoindustrial textile production had spread all over the east Brabant countryside.[5] In the agricultural low season members of peasant families were underemployed and often took up weaving. Most families around the main putting-out centers gradually became primarily dependent on industrial production rather than on agriculture. In the Eindhoven area in 1829, out of a total population of some eleven thousand people, over seventeen hundred protoindustrial workers were employed by local textile entrepreneurs. Around 1860 the greater Eindhoven area hosted more than twenty-five hundred weavers; 85 percent of them worked in their own homes.[6] Though its extent is not exactly known, protoindustrial cigarmaking emerged as another important source of additional household income after 1850. It has been estimated that throughout the nineteenth century about half the working population was engaged first on protoindustrial tasks and later increasingly on industrial jobs, largely in intensive manufacturing such as textiles, cigarmaking, and light bulbs.[7]

As the central place for the regional socioeconomic system, Eindhoven was the paramount engine behind the growth of protoindustrial and industrial activities. When protoindustrial spinning and weaving were gradually concentrated in central workshops after 1850, Eindhoven began to witness the growth of fixed capital outlays: the narrow city became full of factory buildings, warehouses, steam engines. The first conjunctural growth cycle, lasting till about 1880, substantially increased industrial employment as against protoindustrial work in the locality. New entrepreneurs in cigarmaking played a large role in this. Starting in the early 1890s and lasting with some interruptions until the crisis of the 1930s, a second growth cycle put the locality definitely on the list of primary industrial places in the Netherlands.

Protoindustrial and industrial development in the Eindhoven area affected the peasant family cycle in diverse ways. However, local industrialization remained firmly tied to the labor reserves and labor qualities of the slowly declining peasant family economy. Industrialization thus did not lead to an abrupt transformation. On the contrary, by offering increasing numbers of nonagricultural jobs to peasant family members, local industrialization instead subsidized the survival of small peasant holdings. An extensive class of worker-peasants and peasant-workers emerged that did not conform to the neat statistical categories of lower bureaucrats who were ordered to describe whether people earned their living either in the agrarian or in the industrial economy.[8] Industrial cash earnings, in particular by unmarried daughters, enabled peasant families to pay mortgages, rents, and small-scale investments, and added to the self-procured diet that would otherwise have been deficient.

At the same time, however, small-scale agrarian activities and the pooling together of individual incomes within families permitted industrial wage standards to stay far below the level necessary for workers' reproduction. A key role in that respect was played by the daughters of local families. Descriptions of "traditional" relationships in east Brabant peasant families all emphasize the subservient position of females.[9] Daughters were sharply supervised and segregated from the local boys, who were allowed much autonomy. They were expected to serve their parents as long as possible by performing necessary household tasks and bringing in additional cash income. In connection with their subservient function, they were supposed to postpone marriage in order to support the parental household. This would remain true for the whole period up to 1930. Statistics show that the average age at marriage of working class females, though lower in Eindhoven than in the wider region, did not drop below twenty-five years.[10] This was comparatively high for an industrializing city.

Daughters' labor and local industrialization were two sides of the same coin. Their availability in great numbers was the cause of the expansion of local industry and of the pertinence of low wage levels. As we will see, the expansion of cigarmaking in the 1860s beyond the limit imposed by the male labor supply did not lead to proportional wage increases. Rising labor demand would be solved by recruiting ever more cigarmakers' daughters and did not lead to higher male wages. The crisis in local textiles in the 1870s and 1880s would also partly be solved by exchanging daughters for adult males. As a consequence, around 1900 adult male Eindhoven workers still earned no more than 60 percent of the national male average. As we shall see, around half of registered local industrial employment was comprised of jobs for unmarried and adolescent females as well as for children. Their earnings often did not exceed half the male wage. Moreover, they could easily be put on shorter hours or laid off temporarily, since it did not offend their social status.

Thus, within the households of Eindhoven peasants, worker-peasants, peasant-workers, and workers, industrial labor and agricultural labor were combined in many ways, while the gains from both were pooled together for collective survival. Waged and nonwaged labor of all capable members, in particular of adolescent daughters, was customarily required. On the level of the local economy this led to two interrelated processes. First, it ensured the perpetuation of family roots in small-scale agriculture and to some extent in small-scale proprietorship, even when agriculture had lost its primary importance for survival. Secondly, it created an important incentive for labor-intensive industries to concentrate in the community because of uniquely low labor costs and a flexible work force. But (proto)industrialization and (proto)proletarianization did affect people's room for maneuver with respect to courting and household formation. In Brabant, as in the rest of Europe, the average marriage age for wage earners was lower than for peasants or skilled artisans.[11] Proletarianization, or the spread of wage work, eased the constraints of the peasant demographic regime. Since wage work was of increasing importance to the Eindhoven population, one could expect a weakening of "traditional" demographic controls. And indeed, compared with its more agricultural hinterland, in Eindhoven the average age at marriage for females in the later decades of the nineteenth century was lower: twenty-six as against twenty-eight years old.[12] Moreover, it tended to be lowest among unskilled wage workers. Finally, while marriage age of wage workers tended to decline in periods with growing labor demand, it remained comparatively stable at relatively low levels in times of conjunctural downturns.[13] The same was true for marriage frequency. While peasant marriages were relatively rare and tended to fluctuate with market conditions, industrial employment facilitated a remarkable rise in the number of marriages and seemed to liberate them to some extent from the capricious market fluctuations of the agricultural economy.[14]

This weakening of "traditional" peasant demographic constraints did not yet lead to the great population expansion that, diverging from developments in other parts of Europe, would take place in twentieth-century industrial Brabant. But, taken together, these demographic trends did cause a doubling of the Eindhoven population from some 11,000 inhabitants in 1850 to 22,000 in 1900. This population increase was mainly due to internal demographic expansion of the area, although it was also partly produced by short-distance migration.[15] After 1900, immigration, mainly from the wider region but increasingly also from other parts of the Netherlands (and Europe), fostered further urban growth, making the Eindhoven area the nation's quickest urbanizer in the 1910s and twenties. Local population increased from 22,000 inhabitants in 1900 to 48,000 in 1920, and to 95,000 in 1930.

With urban expansion, the "nonagricultural" labor force, as represented in (necessarily flawed) statistics, was growing considerably. Although we cannot count upon reliable primary sources for the distribution of local employment over the primary, secondary, and tertiary sectors during the nineteenth century, the following figures, based on a sample drawn from various registered data on employment by O. Boonstra, gives an idea of the official picture.[16] In 1830 some 30 percent of the Eindhoven working population in his sample was employed in agriculture, either as peasants or as laborers; slightly over 20 percent had skilled jobs in industry; and just over 45 percent performed unskilled industrial tasks. In 1890 these figures were respectively 12, 38, and almost 50 percent.

Two changes were salient: the rise in the percentage of skilled industrial jobs and the decline of agriculture. As to the former, it should be stressed that it is not clear what "skilled" could have meant exactly in this local context. Blacksmiths and metalworkers have certainly and justifiably been registered as skilled. Probably this was also true for the core of established local male cigarmakers. In a national context, however, many of them would not have been considered skilled. As to the decline of agriculture: the 12 percent seems quite a reliable indication of the extent of agricultural work as primary occupation at the end of the century. Other evidence also indicates employment in this sector around 1900 to be some 12 percent.[17]

For the year 1909 there is a relatively reliable nationwide employment census available. Total population for Eindhoven at large in that year was 29,180. Registered working population was 13,244 (45 percent!); 10.4 percent worked in the primary sector, 50.6 percent in the secondary sector, 39.3 percent in services.[18] However, informal work was widespread in the locality, but of course not registered. The category of "services," moreover, is somewhat problematic as it is not clear what exactly was included. But it does indicate that Eindhoven, though emphatically an industrializing town, featured a much more extensive petty bourgeois service class than proverbial hotspots of industrialization such as Oldham in the British Midlands or Bochum in the Ruhr.[19] Indeed, Eindhoven still showed many of the sociostructural characteristics of a "traditional" central place supporting its region with a relatively dense service sector.

This comparative picture of the Eindhoven social structure is confirmed by sample materials recently presented by Boonstra. The local male working class grew above 60 percent of total male jobs only after 1890. It would never attain levels over 75 percent such as reached by thoroughly industrialized towns like Barmen, Bochum, or Oldham. Boonstra's figures also show that local male petty bourgeois jobs, notwithstanding the town's increasing rate of industrialization, maintained their 25 percent share in male occupations. They even rose significantly after 1925, for reasons we will discuss later.

A disconcerting note, however, must be made concerning these apparently clear-cut figures. Percentages based on male occupations are not an accurate description of divisions of labor or class composition in a locality where about 50 percent of manufacturing jobs were performed by (adolescent) children. Male occupations may certainly be used as an index of status distribution in the town, but they do not deliver much insight into both the lived reality and the social dynamics of industrialization in the locality. They completely fail to point to the centrally important complex interdependencies that arose between local accumulation on the one hand and family life on the other, interdependencies that necessarily sprang from a manufacturing base that employed such high numbers of unmarried daughters and children. Any serious student of local culture should somehow come to grips with precisely these unexpected complexities of economic process, as well as with their social, political, and cultural consequences. These are unexpected because they tend to be hidden by superficially innocent and reliable, though seriously anachronistic, statistics based on male occupations and clear-cut sectoral definitions of the labor force.

To conclude, Eindhoven industrialization was based on a large labor supply employed on wages below the level necessary for its own reproduction (for males 60 percent of national average, females and adolescents considerably lower). This low wage level was made possible by the reigning patterns of household formation and family economy in the region. The pooling together of several incomes within the household plus additional earnings from small-scale agriculture and other dealings gave the industrial wage nexus a flexibility that was highly advantageous to employers. Apart from the fact of low wages, it was above all this availability of a large, flexibly employable, local labor reserve that contributed to the locational advantage of the Eindhoven economy.

Indeed, economic history teaches us that all industries in the nineteenth century suffered from recurrent and strong fluctuations in demand, both in certain seasons of the year as well as from year to year. The piling up of stocks was risky and expensive, and not always possible. Consequently, an area that could supply employers with workers whose individual earnings were not considered as the sine qua non for their survival, let alone for the survival of a whole family, was very supportive to them. In the Eindhoven area, most individual earnings, though in particular those of children, were considered as not more than just one type of contribution to an array of sources of income for households. This was a fundamental and characteristic condition for the reproduction of local workers. Rooted in the "traditional" family economy, it made it easy for industrialists to shift part of their seasonal and conjunctural risks to their working families by laying off part of them. In contrast to those places where male breadwinners were gradually becoming a norm, they could do so without devastating proletarian livelihoods or brutally uprooting local labor. Indeed, relying on "traditional" forms of family cohesion and mutual dependency in times of adversity, households would always somehow dispose of some income, both in cash and in kind. For labor-intensive branches of manufacturing, this fundamental quality of the local labor market meant a great social and competitive advantage.

It should be emphasized, however, that flexible labor market practices were fundamental not only to the area's pattern of industrialization. Their meaning went far beyond the formal boundaries of the "economy." They fundamentally shaped relationships within and between families and marked the "field of force" between dependent households and employers. For while flexible treatment held for most unmarried Eindhoven children of working age as well as for mothers working at home, only those adult males were exempt from its rules who brought with them to the factory a good number of obedient children. Labor market flexibility, from the point of view of the employer, favored the recruitment of whole families. For heads of households this meant relative status security during downturns, though some of his children would be laid off, and prosperity in the good times when children were called to the factory again. This little-noted but central fact of local life in the period of industrialization is essential for any understanding of local working class culture. Indeed, family employment was the rule rather than the exception.[20] Though certainly not unique for industrializing Europe, the centrality of flexible family employment for the accumulation of capital as well as the accumulation of households in the Eindhoven area probably turned it into its single most strategic social relationship. Both capitalists and households survived, and sometimes flourished, on what may be called the practice of "flexible familism."

INDUSTRIAL STRUCTURES AND FLEXIBLE LABOR

Thus, the growth of labor-intensive manufacturing in nineteenth-century Eindhoven was triggered by the locational advantage of a low-cost structure and flexible labor-market practices. Let us take a closer look at the structures of Eindhoven industrialization itself.

Textile production (mainly woolens and linen, some mixed cotton) was introduced to the region as a protoindustry already in early modern times. It employed the whole family as a mutually dependent labor unit. Around 1860, as we have seen, this industry employed more than twenty-five hundred local workers. Only 15 percent of them worked in central workshops, on spinning and on diverse auxiliary processes. As weaving was gradually mechanized and centralized after 1880, home weaving slowly declined. The earlier mechanization of spinning had reduced female participation at home because weaving the woolen cloth, which was still done within the household, was considered too heavy for them and remained a male task. The mechanization and centralization of weaving opened up new income opportunities for working class daughters.

The largest Eindhoven textile factories remained relatively small. The factory of J. Elias, for example, employed some two hundred workers in 1914. Several linen factories specialized in the production of high-quality cloth. The factory of C. van Dijk at Stratum, for example, acquired a royal seal of approval for its superb quality. Woolen productions seemed to have catered more to the mass market.[21]

There are no reliable figures on home work in textiles after 1860, but sources agree that it must have been considerable.[22] We do know how many persons were employed in factories. It rose from a mere 120 in 1853 to over 800 in 1871. Then it declined to a low of some 400 in 1895, and grew again to over 1,200 workers in 1913. It would relatively stagnate thereafter and slowly climb to more than 1,600 workers in 1930.[23]

In 1871, adolescent daughters and sons between twelve and sixteen years old occupied 33 percent of factory jobs in textiles. During the years of decline between 1871 and 1890 their share would rise to some 43 percent, facilitating a reduction of the male work force by half. In 1913 it had climbed to 45 percent.[24] Although textile production made less use of unmarried women and children than cigarmaking and lamp manufacturing, the cheap and flexible part of the labor force in the Eindhoven textile industry was in no way insignificant.

Up until 1930 few branches of industry were so little capitalized as cigarmaking. Because machines played a very limited role in the production process of tobacco products, labor costs largely determined final product prices, above all in the lower market segments. In the Netherlands, which had privileged access to fine Java and Sumatra tobaccos, the mass production of tobacco products migrated from the high-wage areas of Amsterdam and Hilversum to the river country first, and then to the low-wage area of southeast Brabant. In the course of the second half of the nineteenth century, Dutch cigarmaking concentrated in and around Eindhoven. There it would be threatened again in the twentieth century by new industrial spaces near, and over, the Belgian border offering even cheaper labor supplies.[25]

In contrast to textiles, cigarmaking at Eindhoven evidently began as a centralized factory production process (or manufacture, strictly speaking, because machines were not important). It started around 1850 and quickly rose to be the largest local industrial employer, remaining so until the First World War. However, while claiming ever more scarce Eindhoven space, it started to put out many preparatory and auxiliary processes such as the cutting of tobacco leaves. Employers thus aimed to limit fix investments. In 1910 a government research team registered 610 home workers, some 18 percent of the local cigarmaking labor force.[26] These protoindustrial workers were either adult men or adolescent males. It is unclear how many children were engaged in auxiliary tasks. In times of decline, home work and small-scale businesses in cigarmaking recurrently increased to become real competitors to centralized production. The key to success of big over small lay in marketing rather than production.

In cigarmaking, daughters' labor on a large scale emerged only in the course of the eighteen sixties. Engaging the daughters of cigarmakers was an employers' response to a shortage of male workers. Women's labor in cigarmaking was not inferior to male work, although it did pay less. As full cigarmakers, both sexes performed the same tasks. Cigarmakers rolled the prepared tobacco leaves in a higher quality coverleaf. It demanded considerable experience to do that quickly yet carefully enough. Children's labor was important from the earliest beginning. Children below sixteen years old performed auxiliary tasks, in particular preparing the "poppen," that is, the less precious insides of the cigar. Children were rewarded by the cigarmaker they worked for, according to their age.

Apart from numerous small-scale manufacturers, Eindhoven hosted the large Mignot and de Block factory, where in 1911 over 750 people worked. A. Mignot was from a family of French Revolution refugees who had settled in the United States. In the late fifties he started a firm at Eindhoven, together with his local companion A. de Block. They would be the first to employ daughters on a large scale, and later females would even form the great majority of their workers. The firm was highly export oriented. In the 1920s, the factory of H. van Abbe, who transferred his production from Amsterdam to Eindhoven, would rise to local preeminence by employing over a thousand workers.[27]

In addition to outworkers, the flexible production in Eindhoven cigarmaking is abundantly documented by the high degree of female and child participation. In 1876, daughters, and sons below sixteen, made up some 55 percent of the total factory labor force in cigarmaking. At that date more than 1,170 workers were employed in the trade. Female labor participation reached a peak of 34 percent of factory occupations in 1895, which in absolute numbers amounted to 643 women workers. Thereafter it would relatively decline because of the demand for female workers at the expanding Philips firm. In cigar factories, the relative decline of the female labor supply after 1895 was countered by engaging an increasing number of boys below sixteen. In 1913, out of a total factory work force of some 2,700 workers, more than 500 boys and 600 daughters were employed. Daughters plus sons below sixteen together made up 46 percent of those employed in cigar factories at that time.[28] In 1930, Eindhoven cigarmaking provided work to slightly under 4,000 workers.

The same cheap and flexible manufacturing facilities that had earlier propelled local textile and cigar production also brought the Philips family to start its incandescent lamp factory in Eindhoven. Frederik Philips was a merchant banker in the old mercantile town of Zaltbommel, in the river country. He knew Eindhoven well since he was connected with the tobacco and cigar trade. His son Gerard Philips, who had been a commercial agent for Algemeine Elektrizäts Gesellschaft (AEG, Berlin) after graduating as an engineer from the Delft technical academy and Glasgow University, proposed to start an incandescent lamp firm. So Frederik bought an old factory in the west Brabant town of Breda. But in the end he decided to sell it again to buy an old textile plant in Eindhoven, because he was convinced of the "good and reliable" quality of local labor.[29] Started in 1891, the Philips company became successful only after 1895. European market conditions were improving by that time, and Frederik's energetic younger son, Anton, had joined the company to take up sales and marketing. In 1899, the firm employed some 450 workers. After 1907, when it launched the production of the successful but much more complicated metal-wire lamp bulb, its number of workers took a great jump. In 1910 employment had increased to 1,750. In 1914 it amounted to 2,370. In 1929, Philips employment reached its pre-1945 height of 23,000 workers. At that moment the company provided some 70 percent of industrial employment in the town.[30]

Apart from the important innovation its products represented, and the cheap and flexible qualities of its home base, what were the conditions for its success? Decisive was the fact that the Netherlands did not yet acknowledge international patent law. Consequently, the Philips company could make use of Edison's invention without being prosecuted by law.[31] Secondly, in a new, highly cartelized but quickly expanding market for electrical products, Philips could outcompete the closely cooperating giants of General Electric, Algemeine Elektrizäts Gesellschaft, and Siemens, by specializing on the one simple mass product provided by the Edison patents. While the established corporations catered to heavy electrical engineering and the use of electricity for public purposes (like urban tram systems, transformers, generators), Philips built a relatively small, commercially oriented organization with low overhead costs that was bent on the most efficient mass production of a relatively simple standard product. Its cheap and flexible home base suited perfectly the company's need for efficiency and flexibility in a fluctuation-prone emerging international market.

Right from the start, Philips specialized in relatively simple production processes that matched the available skills of Eindhoven workers. Glass bowls, for example, were outsourced. Eindhoven workers were exclusively employed on simple but highly specialized tasks that had to do with mounting the filament on to the lightbulb. Leaving exceptions aside, these actions required a training on the job of from one or two days to some months. The socialist engineer Th. van der Waerden, who studied processes of deskilling in industry around 1910, was unequivocal about it: the only skills really needed at Philips were precision, carefulness, reliability, and some literacy.[32] Thus, not only with an eye to costs and flexibility but also for technical and cultural reasons, jobs at Philips were to an unprecedented degree occupied by females. The great care, quietness, obedience, and dexterity required by the highly subdivided and minute tasks on relatively costly and vulnerable materials performed at the Philips plant made young east Brabant females, accustomed to subservient carefulness, ideal workers. In 1910 almost 70 percent of Philips workers were female. In 1914, it rose to 74 percent.[33]

It is clear, then, that the supply of daughters and younger sons of local families was of vital importance to the dynamics of Eindhoven industrialization. Their share of industrial jobs was roughly equal to that of males above age sixteen. Eindhoven industrialization thus was not only based on low wages facilitated by the agrarian activities of wage workers, as has often been noted.[34] More importantly, though surprisingly little incorporated into any systematic understanding of local processes, was the fact that industrialization in the Eindhoven area received much of its impulse from the necessity for young workers to earn cash and the willingness of families to send their children, particularly their daughters, into the factories. Local industrial expansion was inconceivable without the multiple-earning east Brabant household (and vice versa).

The most successful Eindhoven firms were those following this particular logic of local labor market practices to its extreme. Thus all cigar manufacturers were known to prefer daughters over fathers or sons. Daughters, purportedly, were more careful, drank less, and did not pilfer materials.[35] But it was only the American Frenchman A. Mignot, not locally rooted and owner of the largest and most export-oriented cigar factory of the country (85 percent of its production went abroad), who fully used this insight as the basis for his factory organization. Young females occupied over 70 percent of jobs in his plant. Likewise, the Philips brothers, also without local roots, nor historically tied to the local male working class, knew how to exploit the exceptional locational advantages of the east Brabant labor market. Almost all plain tasks at their plant were performed by adolescent females. As we shall see, insofar as males took up tasks in production at Philips, they were generally limited to supervision or skilled work.

Mignot and Philips thus both epitomized the social and spatial relationships of Eindhoven industrialization. Being immigrants to the place, they completely concentrated on its key economic relationship. By deploying unprecedentedly large numbers of cheap, flexible, obedient, and careful local girls, they conquered important international export markets.

SPATIAL DIVISIONS OF FLEXIBLE MANUFACTURING

Notwithstanding the predominantly industrial impression the Eindhoven population makes when looked at from the vantage point of their jobs, in their everyday lives they were closely tied to small-scale agriculture and, to some extent, small-scale proprietorship. In contrast to its firm rate of industrialization, then, Eindhoven urbanization did not reflect the outlook of the proverbially overcrowded industrial city. In 1914, for example, industrial workers formed the majority of the heads of households of Gestel, one of the municipalities of greater Eindhoven. A majority of them, however, still had access to significant pieces of land. There they grew potatoes and vegetables and bred pigs, goats, and chickens.[36] The condition of wage-earning households in other greater Eindhoven municipalities was not much different.

How important access to land was for the survival of local working class households is illustrated by a household budget from Eindhoven published by the labor inspection in 1907/08.[37] It demonstrates that, without the self-procurement of vegetables and potatoes, there was no money whatsoever to spend on meat or dairy produce. The budget was not that of a destitute family but of a family of three able-bodied working persons. The father worked as a cigarmaker, his son too, and the mother enjoyed earnings from tobacco stripping at home. Thus, without access to land, the nutrition even of healthy working class families would have been grossly insufficient, let alone of those households confronted by illness or early deaths. Moreover, this particular budget was recorded in a period in which real wages for the first time since the 1870s were rising again. It has been calculated that real wages between 1900 and 1910 increased by 20 percent.[38] Yet, even under such beneficial conditions local wages evidently remained too low to feed people.

The small proprietary and agricultural ties of local worker households were reflected in a particularly scattered and spread-out pattern of human settlement. This pattern was further reinforced by ecological conditions. Small rivers that used to flood adjacent lands in the spring and autumn crisscrossed the greater Eindhoven area. Human settlements and their interconnecting roads had developed on the higher stretches of land between those currents. From the narrow Eindhoven core, long radial roads reached the municipalities of Gestel, Strijp, Woensel, and Tongelre (the community of Stratum was more centrally located). Along these roads long rows of ribbon development composed of one- or two-story houses had emerged that left wide stretches of agricultural land at the back unsettled, resulting in very low population densities.

Fragmentation of the Eindhoven area was not only the effect of a dispersed pattern of settlement. Although the whole territory indisputably functioned as one single interwoven economic area, it was divided over six independent local political units: apart from the central place of Eindhoven, there were the municipalities of Woensel, Tongelre, Stratum, Gestel, and Strijp. This political division, moreover, overlapped with fundamental social divisions.

In 1890, Eindhoven city proper was almost exclusively inhabited by the regional commercial and industrial bourgeoisie, the latter comprising 77 percent of its heads of households.[39] These undertakings by 1900 had fully occupied the narrow urban territory, and even by 1870 the enterprises had begun to spread out into the low-cost areas of adjacent villages, in particular to invade the spacious community of Woensel.[40]

The satellite communities, in contrast, increasingly hosted the growing population of local poor and working classes. The municipality of Stratum, which neighbored the Eindhoven canal and had direct connections with Rotterdam and Liège, was the most industrialized and cosmopolitan of these satellites. Here 60 percent of heads of households were wage workers in 1890. Woensel was even more proletarianized (64 percent of heads of households in 1890), but was not inhabited by such substantial numbers of notables and entrepreneurs as Stratum was. Woensel, however, was the largest territory of the six municipalities and had the largest and quickest growing population. By 1900 it was the location for an increasing number of new cigar factories. In addition, it was one of the favorite places for working families to settle since it offered the cheapest access to land. Tongelre was the most agricultural community of the six, but even here wage workers comprised 23 percent of heads of households in 1890. Gestel also was less proletarianized and industrial, but already 34 percent of its heads of households in 1890 were wage workers. Strijp was quite petty bourgeois too, although 45 percent of its heads of households had a waged occupation.[41]

It is clear, then, that crucial social inequalities overlapped with local settlement and political divisions. This was most pronounced in the division between the rich Eindhoven core and the poor periphery, though also between the satellites there obtained important social differences.

Because they inhabited different political communities, workers and employers in the Eindhoven area were thoroughly disconnected politically while fully interdependent economically. The origin of political cleavage may seem arbitrary and incidental, no more than a contingent effect of old political boundaries, but it was in fact firmly related to the actual nature of economic ties between the "high" and "low" in the area. Low wage levels necessarily dispelled people from the high-cost core of the urban area. The cheapest access to much-needed land could be obtained on the outskirts of Woensel, Stratum, or Strijp rather than around the Eindhoven core. Thus, while the expansion of flexible manufacturing was largely based on the preexistence of a semirural smallholding population with abundant juvenile labor reserves, it simultaneously reproduced and reinforced its "traditional" dispersed settlement pattern at the moment when the local population began to grow. As the poor were dispelled from the rich through the mechanism of housing markets, and consequently had to settle beyond community borders, a sharpening of sociopolitical and fiscal divisions between the classes necessarily resulted.

The population growth of the satellites relative to the Eindhoven core from, say, 1850 onward was therefore not simply a consequence of a shortage of space in the core but also an inevitable effect of its low-wage manufacturing economy. In 1860, out of a total population of 11,313, the city of Eindhoven proper hosted 28.6 percent with the community of Woensel having an exactly equal share. In 1919, out of a total population of 43,772 persons, however, Eindhoven held a share of not more than 14.7 percent. By then, Woensel had already increased its share to 33.3 percent.[42] The other satellite municipalities also contributed firmly to the growth of the nonurban periphery vis-à-vis the core.

Important social distinctions also obtained between the satellites. While Stratum had been the focal point of expansion in the period before 1900, Woensel received the largest part of the rapidly increasing short-distance migration of proletarian households after 1900. Short-distance migration was the prime engine behind its growth. And, because it resulted in a younger population, it also led to a larger percentage of children relative to the whole population (while marriage fertility remained relatively modest). Thus, Woensel had a more recently proletarianized population than Stratum. Strijp, on the other hand, became the most expansive community after 1910, and received the great majority of long-distance (national and international) working class migrations. Tongelre, finally, which long remained the most agricultural area, was partly turned into a romantic suburb for the wealthy after 1900.[43]

This overlap of social, spatial, and political divisions in the Eindhoven area created a contradictory dynamic. On the one hand, poor families had the privately beneficial opportunity to establish themselves in low-rent, low-price, low-tax spaces. But, on the other hand, the pressures of population expansion thus fell exclusively on the poorest communities. These communities did not possess the resources needed to keep public services in tune with their expansion. As a consequence, local sewer systems, water supply, gas supply, and road systems, let alone housing provisions, were far below the level needed in these satellite communities.[44]

For industrialists who looked for cheaper manufacturing space outside the urban core this situation gradually became a nuisance. Also employers who were concerned with the living conditions of their workers rallied against this. Their engagement, however, was just as contradictory as the situation itself to which they responded. Indeed, they themselves did not subscribe less to the low local wage levels that had produced this particular spatial outcome. Workers were trapped in a similar contradictory situation. While their immediate costs remained low, their immediate environment became shabby, unhealthy, and unpleasant. It even became a source of wage workers' exploitation. As we will see, starting around 1900, a progressive popular alliance emerged that pleaded for political unification as a precondition for the upgrading of infrastructure and services. In 1919 this unification would finally be realized. All municipalities fused into one large political unit.

But the process of political unification as a means of countering underinvestment in the working class reproductive areas of a flexible industrial territory was again highly contradictory. This is best illustrated by the position of the Philips company. Initially, the Philips brothers were the principal supporters of unification, but in the course of the twenties, while their own housing provisions were expanding, they became the principal antagonists of the newly unified polity. They fiercely opposed the ensuing upward pressure on housing and labor costs caused by the political effort to regulate working class reproduction. Thus, instead of being an unfortunate historical circumstance, political and geographical fragmentations really were an integral part of the making of a flexible manufacturing territory.

CONTRADICTORY ALLIANCES AND POLITICAL CONFUSIONS

It is correct that the vocabularies of popular contention do not simply and directly arise from the deficiencies of lived social reality. Authors such as Gareth Stedman Jones and Joan Scott, who criticized the "naturalism" of earlier social-historical studies, in particular E. P. Thompson's influential work *The Making of the English Working Class* (1963), are not mistaken in this respect.[45] On the other hand, their assertion that grievances should first be constituted in a political language before they can be uttered at all, assuming that any human observation by definition depends on the preexisting discriminatory and evaluative tools of human language, misses an important aspect of social change and the dynamics of popular movements. First, there is a universal epistemological objection to this: language should not be treated as sui generis.[46] Language is a practical instrument of human orientation (parole, in Saussure's terms) and not a static, highly systematic determining and signifying structure (like langue in Saussure). Any process of social change implies, generates, and includes changes in practical understandings. Language and meaning must not be set apart from real life.

Moreover, as the work on class formation by authors such as Ron Aminzade, Michael Hanagan, and Marc Steinberg has demonstrated, it is on the level of popular alliance formation that the practical meanings of formal political languages become negotiated, innovated, and established.[47] Canonical texts, therefore, do not deserve a methodological privilege. Political languages can better be approached as vehicles for contention, negotiation, and agreement between sets of human actors. In the short term, they may set certain limits to the politics of meaning. But those limits tend to be highly plastic. They always facilitate the setting of divergent emphases, the introduction of new interpretations, the forging of multiple alliances, and the formation of divergent programs. Their internal coherence may be a case for ideologists or lawyers, but is not, by definition, respected on the battlefields of human practice.

In the analysis of the formation of social and political alliances at the turn of the century in Eindhoven it must be recognized that working class quiescence in the 1930s cannot be understood without looking at the prior constitution of a field of collective political actors, coalitions, and their popular bases. Moreover, the study of political alliance formation between 1890 and 1914 prompts one to focus on the consequences of the contradictory social logic of flexible mass manufacturing as it developed in the Eindhoven area.

Instead of giving rise to a clear-cut political class formation, as both contemporary marxists and liberals assumed would emerge with urban industrialization, the logic of cleavage and alliance in the Eindhoven area produced a highly confusing and contradictory sociopolitical field. As we will see, political working class formation was blurred, crisscrossed, and confused by its close links with political middle class groupings. The two rival bourgeois blocs of liberals and conservative Catholics both succeeded in forging alliances with working class activists. These cross-class alliances gave birth, respectively, to a local social democratic party and to a Catholic labor movement in cigarmaking. Each of these cross-class coalitions enabled its allied workers to emphasize one of their objectives and forced them to repress another. Thus, the Catholic alliance proved much more reliable in combating employers' power at the point of production than the liberal alliance. The liberal alliance, on the other hand, offered decidedly better resources to address deficiencies in the field of human reproduction, in particular in relation to housing and retailing.

Bourgeois political group formation in Eindhoven between 1890 and 1914 turned on two central issues: secondary education and housing.[48] The rival bourgeois class formations that crystallized around these issues were firmly rooted in local society and were based on clearly discernible bourgeois class segments. Both these segments inhabited the central city. In contrast, their allied working class groups originated from the satellite communities, in particular from the municipality of Woensel.

The divide between liberals and conservative Catholics among the Eindhoven citizenry dated from the middle decades of the century. It seems that with the reinstitution of the Catholic clerical hierarchy, banned in the Netherlands since the sixteenth century, local bourgeois society had come under increasing pressure to support the objectives of the emerging Catholic movement. This led to a split in the Concordia society, where the local bourgeoisie used to meet, as liberally inclined families decided to leave and formed the Amicitia society. By the end of the century Amicitia was a focal point of liberal civic life. In contrast to the members of the Concordia society, many of them were relative new-comers to Eindhoven. And although (liberal) Catholics were the largest denomination within its membership, many of them were Protestants or Jews. Among its most prominent members around 1900 were Gerard and Anton Philips, their Belgian nephews, Louis and Eduard Redelé (who owned a soap factory in town), the German E. Brüning (running a large cigar box factory), the French-American R. Mignot (who owned the largest cigar factory in town), and P. Elias (owner of the largest textile factory).

Around the turn of the century, members of the Amicitia society began to organize to win seats in the municipal council in order to realize two broadly supported aims: liberal secondary education (which was not available in the city) and working class housing. They also pleaded for the political unification of the fragmented area by means of annexation. They founded the Eindhoven Vooruit association (Eindhoven in Progress), which published a magazine, and found an ally in the liberal journal the *Peel- en Kempenbode* (later the *Eindhovens dagblad*). In the municipal elections of 1901, they failed to win a majority, but in 1908 they temporarily succeeded. Realization of the program, however, would in the end depend on private financial support for the school and on private and semipublic funding for working class housing.

Catholic conservatism crystallized around the organizations of the clerical Leo Association, the (proto)-party Gemeentebelang (Community Interest), and the daily journal of the Meyerijsche Courant. Already in the first confrontations with the liberal segment, local conservatism did not back away from squarely fundamentalist rhetoric and secretive network tactics. Compared with the liberals, the conservatives recruited their central members from a decidedly less wealthy, less powerful, less nationally and internationally oriented, and more locally rooted citizenry. It contained entrepreneurial families such as De Vlam and Hoppenbrouwers who owned minor cigar factories in town, as well as merchants, shopkeepers, and free professions. They blocked liberal proposals in order to keep both housing and education under their own particularist influence. While education was a serious theme for them, the issue of working class housing did not arouse any sincere interest in their circles. The efforts they made in that respect were transparently ill conceived. And it took them a long time to initiate the smallest of projects.

In these same years, immediately after the turn of the century, key entrepreneurial members of the emerging liberal bloc were actively mobilizing resources to improve the local housing supply. What was the nature of the local housing question? Why was it pressing? Why could it become central to liberal middle class formation at Eindhoven? And what were the strategies of liberal entrepreneurs to improve on it?

As high costs in the Eindhoven core forced workers to settle in the satellites, workers' housing became an object of petty bourgeois village politics. In the community of Woensel, which around 1900 was hosting the greatest part of the new households, only 12 percent of the housing stock was inhabited by owners.[49] Since workers formed more than 60 percent of local households (the percentage figure is from 1890),[50] it is clear that the great majority of them were forced to search for rented accommodation.

The expanding local housing market turned on the relations between two groups: newly formed and newly arriving proletarian households, on the one hand, and the village petty bourgeoisie on the other. In 1900, local retailers owned 80 percent of the total Woensel housing supply.[51] As landlords, they were actively interested in the ongoing process of industrial urbanization, but their interests were nevertheless contradictory to the interests of local industrialists. Retailers and other petty bourgeois families profited heavily from a constant scarcity of working class housing. This scarcity was maintained because they did not dispose of the capital to launch large-scale projects. Large industrialists, however, were faced with an upward trend of housing costs and with a consequent upward pressure on wages. Moreover, it became increasingly hard for them to attract new workers when housing was not available. This became a serious problem, finally, when employers' demand for those skilled workers who were not locally available began to rise. For reasons I will elucidate later, this happened to be the case after 1907.

The consequences of leaving housing to petty bourgeois piecemeal and self-interested investments were clear. While between 1850 and 1900 the average number of inhabitants per house in the Greater Eindhoven area had fallen from 5 to 4.6, the first decade of the twentieth century saw it rise again to 5.1.[52] Housing shortage now became a real problem. For over 60 percent of newly formed households in Woensel in 1913, no independent living space was available.[53] In 1918, 6 percent of the housing stock was occupied by two or more households.[54]

All sources indicate, moreover, that petty bourgeois housing speculation led to a rental housing stock of very low quality and to a detrimental interference of the housing market with the retailing business.[55] In 1900, for example, there reportedly was one baker in Woensel who owned eighty dwellings that were far below normal housing standards.[56] The tenants of these places were forced to buy his low-quality/high-priced products on the threat of expulsion. In Woensel, this was not a problem for tenants only. Retailers, and bakers in particular, provided high renting mortgages to newly arriving propertyless large families on the condition that they buy exclusively at their lenders' stores. In Woensel in 1914 almost 15 percent of the population was subject to "forced shopping."[57] Thus, after 1900 the absence of larger investments in working class housing was in fact reaping the fruits of cheap space and cheap labor from the industrialists on behalf of sections of the local petty bourgeoisie.

A short comparison with the shoemaking district of central Brabant may help to build a more general perspective concerning the problem of the role of petty bourgeoisies in industrial class formation and, in particular, in the formation of "progressive" alliances between workers and large industrialists. This is relevant because in both regions the sociopolitical formation of working classes on the one hand and classes of large industrialists on the other turned, to an important degree, on the problems caused by the self-interested practices of "traditional" classes. Indeed, it is important to emphasize that "modern" industrial political groupings were not yet formed, but were forming themselves in simultaneous and interdependent reaction to their joint problems with petty bourgeois practices.

The central Brabant industrial district featured a comparable problem of "forced shopping" (*gedwongen winkelnering*). Here, however, it originated with a large class of small, declining industrial entrepreneurs who forced their workers to buy from them elementary provisions at high prices in order to compensate for decreasing industrial profits. In contrast, at Eindhoven the problem was not caused by uncompetitive industrial entrepreneurs but by parasitic retailers who turned large-scale industrialization and quick urban expansion to their own profit by exploiting their chances in the housing market. In both cases, there arose a social problem that was inseparably linked to the respective historical conditions and social relations of regional accumulation. In both cases also, this problem became the focal point for alliance formation between large, competitive, and expansive entrepreneurs on the one hand and relatively well-off local workers on the other.

In central Brabant progressive alliances between large entrepreneurs and workers catered to the mobilization and organization of workers in problematic backward sectors of the local economy in order to break the petty bourgeois hold on them. In an industrial district where all entrepreneurs and workers were dependent on the same national sales market they tried to clear up and equalize the terms of their mutual competition on behalf of general prosperity. In Eindhoven, social problems were not caused by "traditional" and "backward" employers but by the "traditional" and "backward" structures of the housing market. Mobilizing workers could offer no solution here as it did in central Brabant. In Eindhoven, expansive, world-market-oriented entrepreneurs either allied to create collective institutions for large-scale housing investments, or did the same single-handedly. However, they were warmly applauded by proletarian clubs for liberating them from the petty bourgeois hold on housing and retailing.

In 1898, Gerard Philips, his nephew Louis Redelé, and other enlightened employers and citizens founded the association Eindhoven Vooruit (Eindhoven in Progress). The association was dedicated to "fostering the interests of trade, industry, popular welfare, health, and leisure." It was broadly supported, as was illustrated by the three hundred citizens present at the opening session. The association immediately appointed a committee of citizens to work out proposals for the improvement of working class housing. During the presentation of its report, enlightened citizens and employers such as Brüning, de Block, and Philips agreed to found a building society and at once provided the capital to do so. But the project they envisioned was not so much a solution to immediate working class problems as a self-confirmation for rich philanthropists.

The plan drawn up consisted of some fifty fancy houses in Woensel that fully corresponded with bourgeois notions of respectable working class living. Inhabitants were supposed to partake in a savings arrangement and to make regular contributions to the organization of philanthropic work by local high-status ladies. As an experiment, a small batch of the houses was realized at once. It turned out, however, that rents were about 75 percent too high for working class budgets in this low-wage area. As a result, the initiators became disillusioned and the remaining set of planned houses was never realized.[58]

In 1901, the new national housing law provided cheap credit facilities for projects by housing associations, provided such projects were approved by local government. This offered the opportunity for large-scale intervention in the Eindhoven housing market. Concerted action, however, would take place only after 1907. A dual strategy emerged from among the largest employers. First, the Philips brothers financed two housing projects in order to house newly recruited immigrant metalworkers, production supervisors, and office clerks. Secondly, an alliance of large employers, among others Philips, Brüning, and Mignot, founded an association in order to claim state loans for working class housing.[59]

In 1907 the Philips firm was preparing the production of metalwire lamps. Its expansion was unprecedented. The Philips brothers lured workers away from other local firms and sent trams to neighboring villages with female labor reserves.[60] What was decisive, however, was the start of the Philips workshop for machine construction. In order to man it, Philips had to attract skilled metalworkers from advanced labor markets outside the region. In 1909 almost two hundred highly skilled fitters, platers, and benchmen were employed in the new shop. For them, and for the expanding staff of office clerks and production supervisors, Philips first bought the failed Eindhoven Vooruit project in Woensel and completed it. Then, in 1909, the Philips brothers decided to build Philipsdorp, a large project in the municipality of Strijp, near the factory. This project originally consisted of two hundred well-designed houses, nicely situated around a spacious sports terrain. During and after the First World War Philipsdorp was substantially enlarged.

In contrast with Philipsdorp, the strategy of associational building was not suited to the preferential allocation of housing to certain groups of workers. This was forbidden by law. Large employers were therefore hesitant to provide the initial capital for a housing association. But finally the community of Eindhoven decided to guarantee part of the initial building costs. In 1914, the Vereniging Volkshuisvesting (Association for

People's Housing), chaired by Anton Philips, realized its first project of fifty-eight houses in Woensel.[61]

In 1915 municipal elections at Eindhoven turned largely on the issue of popular housing and brought a victory for the liberal bloc. Partly because of their considerable financial means, all their 1901 projects were fulfilled or under way. Conservative Catholics, however, had failed in all respects. In response to liberal actions, they too had founded a building association for people's housing, but it was unable to build cheaply enough, failed to mobilize sufficient capital, and was finally denied a state loan. Their wish not to segregate working families in a "workers' colony" in Woensel, because of its purported civilizational disadvantages, left them little room for effective action. From 1915 onward, the dominant liberal faction could proceed with the preparations for the annexation of the satellites, which finally took place in 1919.

How did the formation of political middle class groupings intersect and link up with the emergence of working class political clubs? Like its bourgeoisie, the Eindhoven working class was relatively open and dynamic in comparison with other southern cities.[62] This dynamism was rooted in particular in the working class communities of new industries such as cigarmaking and wood processing. Though little of it has found its way into written documents, it is clear that cigarmakers often displayed independent behavior and were sometimes able to organize independent forms of self-help.

Thus the expansion of work opportunities in the 1870s led to a shift in the balance of class power that seems to have eroded the cultural dominance of entrepreneurial classes. This is suggested by an agreement between all local employers in 1873 not to contract workers dismissed for unruly behavior. It is also indicated by the subsequent popular reactions to this employers' agreement. When it became known, a crowd of angry workers responded with rough music and satirical songs at the houses of employers. As they smashed in the window panes of manufacturer K. van der Putt, the city's mayor obviously feared an all-out rebellion and immediately called for a battalion of the military police. The unit came and did not hesitate to draw swords and intervene violently when the crowd appeared unimpressed. Manufacturers, afterward, felt so relieved that they urged the city to send a reward to the police unit to share among themselves.[63]

More "modern" forms of collective action among cigarmakers emerged in 1888. Probably inspired by contacts with socialist organizers, cigarmakers in Woensel founded the workers' association De Tabaks-plant (the tobacco plant). It aimed at the cooperative purchasing of food and fuel, and offered insurance against illness and unemployment. De Tabaksplant instantaneously became very popular, with a membership of some five hundred. Vehement repression by the Church and employers, however, gave its supporters a hard time. Its membership declined to 217 persons in 1890. In 1892 they decided to become a local department of the somewhat syndicalist Nederlandsche Internationale Sigarenmakers- en Tabaksbewerkersbond (Dutch International Cigarmakers and Tobacco Workers Union). Their activities, however, remained unrecorded. But whatever their actual doings, they did contribute to a relatively open and lively public climate for debate among Woensel cigarmakers. The union succeeded in maintaining a membership of some two hundred workers.[64]

The formation of Catholic workers' associations initially did not at all link up with these internal dynamics of local blue-collar communities. Local clerics were rather hesitant to engage with working families. In Eindhoven, the Catholic trade-based "guilds," uniting under the aus-pices of the local Volksbond (People's Union), founded in 1896, were undoubtedly creations from above that were only meant to act as an ideological bulwark against socialism. Here the left-wing thesis on cleri-cal interventionism as a last defense against socialist intrusion into Catho-lic communities finds unequivocal support. In the Volksbond employers and other citizens could participate as well as industrial workers, but a council of clerical supervisors had the right of veto on each decision. It therefore remained unpopular and inactive for some time. In Septem-ber 1897, however, it faced a breakaway from a group of dissenting workers who condemned its undemocratic and hierarchical operation. These workers now started the independent Christian workers' associa-tion De Eendracht (United).[65]

Responding to both De Eendracht and the socialist cigarmakers, Cath-olic workers' organizations, however, were reshaped, democratized, and rooted in local working class community life. The new populist chaplain of Woensel, L. Poell, a democratic Catholic activist, permitted some genu-ine workers' interests to be represented by Volksbond organizations. Catholic unions now created a real strike fund and an illness and unem-ployment fund, and made contact with Catholic workers' associations in other places. Catholicism gradually succeeded in gaining an impressive membership, in particular among the dynamic community of Woensel cigarmakers. The Catholic guild of St. Franciscus Xaverius, in which the cigarmakers were organized, had grown to 850 male members in 1906. Its female counterpart, the guild of St. Clara, also had a considerable membership of 500 unmarried girls.[66]

As it gradually started to facilitate action from below, the Catholic cigarmakers guild was pushed into an unexpected strike in 1907, leading to a dramatic communitywide lockout.[67] Though this conflict went far beyond the intentions of its leadership, it had momentous consequences. It triggered a membership increase to over 60 percent of local cigarmakers. In time, it caused the virtual clericalization of cigarmaking in the southern Netherlands as employers were gradually pressed to organize under Catholic auspices.[68] Eindhoven became the seat both of the Dutch Catholic Cigarmakers Association and of the Catholic Dutch Cigar Manufacturers. Catholicism now became a strong hegemonic force in cigarmaking communities, penetrating into practices on and off the shop floor. Thus, in response to independent working class initiatives, and due to the will for struggle on the part of Eindhoven workers and employers in 1907, Catholic working class organization in cigarmaking won out definitely over its independent and socialist rivals. We shall see, however, that Catholicism's deliberate attempt to establish itself also in the Philips plant was bound to fail.

In comparison with the Catholic cigarmakers association, independent and socialist working class clubs in Eindhoven remained weak. The socialist cigarmakers at Woensel maintained a membership of some two hundred persons, but they did not play an important role in major class conflict. Among construction workers and woodworkers, socialist and independent clubs existed too, but they remained small and did not attain predominance in their trades. However, in contrast to their failure in shop floor politics, they were relatively successful in offering cooperative alternatives for petty bourgeois retailing. Moreover, independent and socialist candidates succeeded in securing stable popular electoral support, especially among the proletarian community in Woensel. Headed by Henry Rooymans, the workers who split away from the Catholic Volksbond in September 1897 formed the association De Eendracht (United). An isolated club of some seventeen members in the beginning, it was consolidated after becoming the proletarian ally of the bourgeois liberals.[69]

Henry Rooymans was a locally born woodworker at the Brüning cigar box factory. He was not so much a preacher of class struggle as an interconfessional and democratic workers' organizer with an ecumenical religious vision. Evidently his program did not seem antithetical to the liberal employers who formed the Eindhoven Vooruit association in 1898, including his own employer. Rooymans subsequently was chosen as a member of the liberal association's board and of the board of the association's housing society, and was the first worker to inhabit one of the relatively expensive Eindhoven Vooruit houses in Woensel.[70] Whether he was consciously co-opted by the large entrepreneurs for their own ends is not clear. Given the balance of power in the city, it is more probable that progressive employers saw in him a welcome ally for fighting the still dominant conservatives.

By 1900, Rooymans' role as the prime ideologist of non-clerically controlled working class action in Eindhoven had been taken over by the better educated Eduard Redelé. Now the relation between working class action and bourgeois liberalism became even more intimate. Redelé was the co-owner of a soap factory in town, brother of the chairman of Eindhoven Vooruit, and nephew of the Philips brothers. When De Eendracht transformed itself into a local branch of the Sociaal Democratische Arbeiders Party (SDAP) in 1904, Redelé became the chairman. The organization by then had some twenty-five members. It grew to about one hundred members by 1910.

Like Rooymans, Redelé believed emphatically in a synthesis of socialism and religion. He preached a purely "economic socialism" (his words), inspired by Marx's analysis of capital, and supported "this-worldly" workers' interests, though he did not subscribe to any wider materialist philosophy. As for moral and even mythical support, he believed workers were rather in need of a democratic and humanist religion. This stance, however, became gradually untenable. His position, though rooted in local relationships, was increasingly ridiculed and attacked by national SDAP ideologists, while fiercely vindicated by local conservatives. In 1907 religious overtones were completely stripped from the Eindhoven SDAP program. Redelé himself, however, was badly hurt. He completely withdrew from public life, spent some time in sanatoria and psychiatric hospitals, and eventually committed suicide.

While failing to establish themselves in local production, the socialists around De Eendracht did succeed in organizing a cooperative bakery in Woensel and in creating their own meeting place. The co-op aimed at breaking the monopoly of local bakers in retailing and thus to weaken the practices of "forced purchasing" and indebtedness. This was quite a feat, since the establishment of a co-op had been high on the list of all earlier proposals for working class organization at Woensel, including

De Tabaksplant and the Catholic Volksbond. However, the intimate relation with Anton and Gerard Philips had secured De Eendracht the necessary capital.[71]

At the same time, success in elections demonstrated that local workers, though not subscribing in great numbers to explicit socialist or non-Catholic politics, did respect the activities of De Eendracht and the local SDAP. Thus Henry Rooymans won a seat in the first Chamber of Labor for the cigarmaking industry in 1900 by gaining over five hundred votes.[72] While the census remained an obstacle against working class electoral success, socialists in Woensel were nevertheless on the brink of winning a seat in municipal elections from 1906 onward. In 1917, Woensel finally voted three socialists into office. Eindhoven and the other satellites, with the exception of Tongelre, all elected one left-wing candidate.[73]

Eindhoven workers, though not at all corresponding to the proverbial image of obedient pawns of Catholic machinations that a condescending posterity believed them to be, did not succeed well in forming their own political organizations. When collective initiatives emerged, like De Tabaksplant and De Eendracht, they had to retreat in front of united resistance from the clergy and local entrepreneurs. Workers were always forced to find allies outside their own community to sustain their collective efforts. Thus Amsterdam socialists proved helpful for both De Tabaksplant and De Eendracht. Both clubs subsequently became local branches of national left-wing organizations. De Eendracht, moreover, was morally and financially supported by local large-scale entrepreneurs such as the Philips and Redelé brothers. Finally, competition from these non-Catholic clubs as well as pressure from below forced the initially very hierarchical Catholic guilds to open up. After the large-scale cigarmakers conflict, local working class activism was to a large extent channeled into the Catholic framework.

The local political landscape that emerged was highly confusing. Reflecting its social bases, Catholicism was unsuccessful or unimaginative in dealing with the acute problems of housing and retailing. But it turned out to be the workers' only ally capable of supporting serious industrial conflict. Local socialism, on the other hand, was too isolated and too closely tied to some large entrepreneurs to pose a threat to production. But it did succeed in offering relevant alternatives to petty bourgeois politics in the field of reproduction. The electoral support they mobilized demonstrated that many Woensel cigarmakers, although largely organized in the Catholic guild, appreciated their public stance. Thus the sociopolitical allegiances of local workers became divided between two cross-class alliances, producing a highly fragmented and dependent working class public sphere.

CONTENTIONS, CAPACITIES, AND CLEAVAGES: WORKERS' WEAKNESS AND WORKERS' POWER AROUND 1910

Between 1907 and 1912, the Eindhoven area witnessed a series of labor conflicts that expressed the peculiar moods, mentalities, and capacities of local workers. These conflicts facilitate a close view of the "field of force" obtaining between workers, capitalists, and Catholic organizers. Both empowered and constrained by the complex cross-class alliances they themselves had helped to forge, workers for the first time used the "modern" strike weapon to reshape the relations of flexible manufacturing. These conflicts laid down the future terrain of working class loyalties and cleavages, of shop floor relations and urban politics, and of the subsequent chances for popular aspirations to become publicly named and acted upon. They therefore deserve some close attention.

The 1907 Cigarmakers Lockout

As I have shown, Catholic workers' organizations were initially a top-down affair in Eindhoven. Since 1906, however, the guild of Franciscus Xaverius, which brought together male cigarmakers, became more activist.[74] In October 1906 monthly talks were agreed upon by the local cigar employers' association and the Catholic (some five hundred members in 1906) and socialist cigarmakers' unions (some two hundred members), with the purpose of standardizing local wage schemes.

At first glance, it is surprising to learn that this form of collective regulation was initiated at the employers' request. But for them it was one of the ways to control an upward pressure on wages in busy times. Mutual competition for labor had long been their principal weakness. In times of labor shortage, it endangered their profit margins. On the other hand, it offered individual workers a good opportunity to increase their incomes and take a share of employers' profits. Employers were used to making such labor market agreements among each other. But they could easily fail, since there were always one or more entrepreneurs who broke the front in pursuit of immediate self-interest. By adopting this new collective effort to regulate and equalize local wage schemes in collaboration with the labor unions, employers now sought to forestall both unexpected workers' gains as well as the individualist option among their own numbers.

Paradoxically, however, this "containment" strategy placed the cigar-makers' unions in a key position vis-à-vis local wage levels, a position they had as yet never enjoyed. It implied that union leaderships became highly vulnerable to pressure from below. And this in fact was what happened. In early 1907, the Catholic guild was forced to give in to work-ers' grievances concerning piece wages at the Tinchant Frères factory in the municipality of Stratum. Concerted pressure from a group of cigar-makers pushed the guild into supporting exceptional wage demands for this single factory.

After the precedent of workers' success at Tinchant Frères, cigar manu-facturers evidently felt threatened by an impending wave of wage in-creases. They seem to have understood that workers, as an unintended consequence of their own "containment" strategy, could now avail them-selves of collective organization in pushing up wages just as they used to do individually in times of labor shortage. And indeed, in April 1907, a handful of workers again pressed for strikes and wage increases at the minor factories of Aalfs and De Jong and Van der Heyden. Van der Heyden immediately settled the conflict by offering somewhat better wages. But Aalfs and De Jong refused to negotiate. The employers' fear of losing hegemony because of an unfortunate misjudgment was now so great that they at once decided to lock out all 2,800 Eindhoven workers in order to destroy the Catholic organization.

Contrary to superficial interpretations, the conditions of capitalist ac-cumulation in a relatively little-concentrated and even less capitalized trade as cigarmaking around 1900 could well uphold the idea that work-ers were getting a price for their products instead of wages for their labor.[75] Though much is unclear about relations in the trade, a closer examination of the motives behind protest at the Aalfs and De Jong factory suggests that their explication by Catholic union leadership, put-ting their objections down to the legitimate grievance of low wages, was a misinterpretation. Closer analysis suggests that male workers tended to see their world to a significant degree as one of independent producers. This was no simple error of the mind. While their families were stripping tobacco at home, and their sons, brothers, or sisters preparing the "pop-pen" at neighboring work stations in the mill, cigarmakers themselves were rolling the final cigars. From their own point of view, they still worked as a family team on a relatively discrete product.

Entrepreneurs were there to deliver raw materials, make the marketing effort, provide part of the tools, and pay workers a just price for their products. The price that workers received was of course somewhat below the market sale price, but nevertheless had to be closely related thereto. Factory owners, at least so it seems, were believed to have a right to a certain percentage of the product price because they carried the costs of fixed capital outlays, owned the raw materials, and carried the risks of the trade and the responsibility for marketing. But since cigars were also considered the worker's own product, the entrepreneur ought not be allowed to appropriate more than a determined percentage. Conflicts tended to center, therefore, on the respective shares of the final price.

In relation to this, it is important to understand that the cigar trade was relatively transparent. The easy dissemination of information among members of households on the shop floor or in the neighborhood about prices paid to workers by employers and prices paid by customers to retailers guaranteed an openness of market information that was not generally the case in industry. This working class community, therefore, was both tightly knit and surprisingly open to the world. It hosted two rival political persuasions, featured many recent immigrants, was employed in a dynamic industry with transparent market relations, and lived from incomes earned by both sexes, by parents and children, performing jobs at home or in the plant. This greatly enhanced worker awareness of exploitative practices by employers. It sensitized them to popular versions of social critique and made them capable of pushing through monetary demands at the moment that markets gave them a chance.[76]

Induced to conflict by a small group of eight male workers at Aalfs and De Jongh, and confronted with collective employer intransigence in April 1907, a salaried functionary of the Catholic cigarmakers guild first stated that Aalfs and De Jongh had unjustifiably lowered their wages. When it turned out that this was not the case, he switched the issue. He now argued that what cigarmakers really wanted was one single wage contract for all tobacco workers in the Eindhoven region so as to overcome mutual differences in pay. The concrete complaints of workers at Aalfs and De Jongh, however, pointed to a much more prosaic and straightforward issue. Pointedly expressing the cigarmakers' peculiar moral economy, workers at Aalfs and De Jongh were upset about the employer's shrewd way of raising his own share in the price of the product. What exactly had happened?

Even though cigar production was not at the point of being mechanized, cigarmakers faced a myriad of ways in which new production methods and procedures encroached upon their earnings. If such methods did not diminish their earnings outright, they certainly enlarged the employers' profit. At Aalfs and De Jongh, management now succeeded in selling imitation handwork, produced with the help of pre-formed boxes, at the price of real handwork. Thus the owner made a considerable extra profit. Having discovered this, the workers immediately demanded a correspondingly higher "price" for their products (or higher "wage" for their labor), leaving no doubt that this simply was their right.

Their moral argument, however, subsequently became wrapped in a calculative disagreement between the guild's leadership and the employers' association. At first the guild reproduced the workers' argument that they had "made a loss" on this product. Then the guild saw itself forced to accept the employer's assertion that Aalfs and De Jongh in fact paid higher wages for this particular product than all other manufacturers in town. Later, the union's demand for a collective agreement on wages could not be implemented because it would have in fact eroded the wage standard of the workers at Aalfs and De Jongh. The employers, on the other hand, also missed the point by concluding that these particular cigarmakers had no reason whatsoever to complain about their earnings. Both organizations, evidently, treated producers as workers on a wage that was related to their costs of living, whereas workers themselves felt that the prices paid for their produce by entrepreneurs should reflect the final product prices made on the market.

How broadly the contempt of entrepreneurial practices was shared is shown by the impressive solidarity displayed after the guild's membership refused to cancel the strike and the employers proceeded to close all factories and lock out all workers. During the five weeks the lockout lasted, only half of the 2,800 workers were eligible for union assistance. The other half were not organized, or young and female and therefore excluded either from membership or from support. In the beginning employers stopped all local production, probably with an eye on their own mutual solidarity. But after two weeks they consciously tried to break the workers' front by letting unorganized workers in, as well as those who were prepared to distance themselves from the guild. But worker solidarity was strong enough to prevent that from happening. Of course, the unorganized often were simply the younger family members of the organized. The family team thus ensured solidarity among cigarmakers.

But the fact remains that all families incurred substantial reductions in their (low) incomes. And since it was unclear how long the conflict would take, the guild felt vulnerable. As part of its confrontational policy it therefore boasted that all workers, the unorganized included, could temporarily be moved to another cigar-making locality. From the second week on, the guild also claimed that it was about to realize cooperative production in Eindhoven. Clearly, this was an all-out confrontation.[77]

Notwithstanding the high price at stake in the conflict, the union board was insistent and successful in getting local workers to display a highly respectable and even religiously devout behavior. Workers were urged to attend church in their own parishes each morning and not to gather around the public spaces of the city. Public performances were of an exceptionally religious character, even culminating in a kind of collective procession to a semiholy place nearby.[78]

It is a clue to the nature of local relationships and political culture that this strategy of respectable confrontation turned out to be successful. Interestingly, the mayor of Eindhoven had immediately informed the queens' commissar at Den Bosch (provincial governor) that the city had sufficient military police prepared to resist all threats to public order. Municipal authorities in entrepreneurial Eindhoven had always taken a firm stance against crowds, but now that their fears were ridiculed by ostensibly decent workers, other public authorities were drawn into action. The Catholic guild, through the Catholic network, mobilized the support of most of the mayors and secretaries of the satellite municipalities. These mayors made a public statement that they planned to buy tobacco and that they had already rented a large factory building where they would employ all local workers. The Dutch community was asked to place orders and send money in advance for this good cause. Together with the persistence of local worker solidarity, this intervention by municipal authorities was central to the eventual victory of the guild.

It is interesting to take note of a letter in which the mayor of Strijp (one of the satellites) informed the minister of internal affairs on the reasons for this public action.[79] One is struck by the populist and paternalist vein of his arguments. He emphasized the ultimate probability that hunger and need would force these respectable, obedient, poor, and hardworking people to violence; that since it was his task to protect public order, he could not do otherwise than take care of this decent and well-meaning people who were so badly treated by liberal entrepreneurs.

Here we encounter another paradox of the political fragmentation of the Eindhoven area. Though fragmentation prevented the improvement of housing and urban infrastructures in the satellites, it did secure the survival of paternalist political vocabularies. While political functionaries in entrepreneurial Eindhoven stuck to a liberalist and noninterventionist stance, the paternalism of the satellite polities, reinforced by intimate relations with the church, facilitated a powerful alternative local state policy that could clearly be supportive of workers' causes.

Thus the Catholic Volksbond, with its guilds that were never meant to be activist clubs, succeeded in winning the allegiance of the overwhelming majority of local cigarmaking households. It was never noticed that this position of power was the product of pressure from below, nor that the guild had waged its struggle on false grounds, based on a lack of understanding of workers' motivations. Aided by the existing political fragmentation of the area, social Catholicism had shown itself to be capable of waging an all-out class conflict with distrusted and powerful entrepreneurs. By so doing, it not only attained a firm footing among the local population, it now also linked, however contradictory, its own sociopolitical agenda and its paternalist discourse of social intervention with local working class sensibilities. Moreover, it had taken up a position of considerable power in cigarmaking. That position led, within a few years, to the emergence of Catholic employers' organizations and to an increasingly effective corporatist ordering of the tobacco economy. It culminated in one of the earliest and certainly one of the most wide-reaching collective labor contracts in the Dutch south.

Clericalism, Philips, and Catholic Girls: The Lockout of 1910

A Catholic guild in the electrical industry was not created until 1909.[80] The Philips factory differed from other local industries in the way it was embedded in local society. While the percentage of female labor had been high all over the local economy, the Philips shop floor stood out in that it almost exclusively employed girls. In general, the few males employed at Philips in these years performed supervisory or skilled jobs. The Philips factory was therefore hard to enter for any unskilled workers' organization. But what was more important: the Philips unskilled work force was only marginally relevant to local political life because it was largely composed of daughters. In a society where females, let alone young females, were excluded from the political process, each local political actor would first and foremost address the male population.

The conservative bloc nevertheless did have some reasons to organize support on the Philips shop floor. The Philips brothers, financially supporting socialist activities at Woensel and contributing heavily to popular housing efforts, had emerged as their paramount antagonists. This opponent could be weakened considerably if a Catholic guild were to be established among the lampmaking girls. Since cigarmakers had demonstrated the unexpected force of Catholic workers organizations, it was not surprising that local conservatives started to think about threatening the Philips brothers through their backdoor.

The lampmakers' guilds of St. Emerentiana (for daughters) and St. Laurentius (for males), founded in the summer of 1909, featured a structure that deviated significantly from the other guilds. Whereas textile workers and tobacco workers were integrated into national or diocesanal organizations, and were headed by professional labor organizers, the lamp guilds were an exclusively local affair, managed by local politicians. Their newspaper, *De Lamp*, was edited by the staunch conservative J. Vervoort, nicknamed "the Pope of Eindhoven."

In 1910, Philips employed some 1,870 persons on a weekly wage. Almost 1,700 were unmarried (the married were probably not employed on direct production tasks).[81] If we deduct another 200 persons in skilled and supervisory positions, we arrive at an estimated number of 1,500 direct production workers. Almost exclusively they were daughters from families in the region. From this large and relatively homogeneous group, the lamp guilds recruited some 320 girls and 50 males in January 1910.[82] This was not an impressive figure, though it was not totally discouraging either. The clerical leadership decided to try to make a breakthrough. It focused on a relatively recurrent employers' practice as a cause for struggle: working on holy days—a cause that was indeed a flagrant violation of Catholic principles, although no authority had ever made a serious point of it.

Like other employers, Philips would sometimes have people work on Sundays and saints' days in the high season (the winter). Such had also been the case on 6 January 1910, the Catholic day of the Three Kings. Two days later the spokesman for the conservative bloc in the city council demanded that the mayor take action in order to prevent a similar violation of religious sensibilities from happening once more. In subsequent weeks, Catholics attending holy mass were sharply reminded of their Sunday duties. They were ordered not to work, nor let their children work, for people who do so "do not respect the service we owe to God."[83] *De Lamp* appeared with a cover drawing featuring fathers behind musicians on their way to church, wearing their Volksbond insignia, while their daughters were laboring behind machines. The journal foresaw the future rise of a "powerful popular movement" that would demand nothing more than sheer respect for religious convictions.

Already in the autumn of 1909 the Philips brothers had been alarmed by the emergence of the lamp guilds. They knew who were behind them: "personal enemies," as Gerard Philips later said.[84] Moreover, with the recent experience of the Catholic cigarmakers' protest in mind, the Philips brothers could not possibly just ignore them. In October 1909, in a meeting with socialist union leaders, they solicited their support for one or another action against the guilds. But the union leaders deemed it better to stay out of this.[85] Anyhow, it is clear that Gerard Philips in 1909 was already preparing to confront them. "The powerful popular movement" that was prophesied by *De Lamp* did not arise. Instead, it was Gerard Philips who took the initiative. He decided to lock out all members of the guilds unless they gave up their membership. On May 14, in the low season of lamp production, he distributed a pamphlet with that message. Those who refused would be fired. In an oral address he told his workers that he was absolutely in favor of unionism, but that he could not accept the influence of guilds that were led by people totally unrelated to the firm or to labor relations in general.

Faced with an unexpected and total lockout, local conservative protagonists tried once more to place the conflict in the moral perspective of working on Catholic holy days, making an effort to turn it into a principled strike for respect of Catholic traditions. Though they did arouse considerable local response, in the end they were not successful. In a few days the number of those who refused to sign a declaration of nonmembership amounted to 372. Thereafter it gradually rose to 584, 80 percent of whom were female.[86] Principled Catholicism, in short, was supported by 35 percent of the factory workforce at Philips. Philips itself emphasized that everyone had always been free to refuse to work on holy days. He guaranteed this same freedom for the future. Socialist unions, obviously, had a difficult time determining their standpoint. National leadership proposed to become solidary when the number of strikers exceeded one thousand. But the recently recruited unionized metalworkers at Philips were opposed to any form of support for the guilds. They backed Philips's assertion that the clergy should never be conceded any kind of influence in business affairs. In that time, as we shall see, Philips attempted to establish good relationships with the organized metalworkers. He needed their support for the development of his machine construction department.

Without the emergence of wider solidarity, either under the banner of Catholicism or under the heading of class, the guilds were forced to seek a way out of this deadlock situation. The same was true for Philips. He had demonstrated his ability to withstand an upsurge of principled Catholic loyalties among his factory workers. But it threatened to reduce his critically important unskilled workforce by 30 percent. Nor did he know the eventual implications of fostering religious antagonism. A solution was reached when two professional labor organizers from the Catholic labor movement, J. van Rijzewijk and J. van Rijen, took over the leadership of the lamp guilds. Gerard Philips had consistently refused to negotiate with local conservatives. These two professionals, however, did not seem objectionable to him. On 17 June they quickly reached an agreement. Philips recognized Catholic labor organizations, restated the freedom not to work on Catholic holy days, and promised to reemploy all his personnel. Leadership of the guilds would subsequently pass from the local conservative network, since a national Catholic union for incandescent lamp workers was created in February 1911. Later it fused with the Catholic metalworkers union Saint Eloy. The chance to mobilize Philips girls in support for the Eindhoven Catholic bloc had failed.

The conflict created some new realities and institutionalized already existing ones. The workers' households that had their daughters employed at Philips were clearly divided in their allegiance to local Catholicism. Some 35 percent of Philips factory girls were prepared to risk earnings for a public declaration of loyalty to the church, probably with the encouragement of their families. And although this may not have been a decisive percentage to win the struggle, it was surely a notable figure. Hence, principled versions of Catholicism, though far from predominant in the town, could certainly reckon with a solid social base.

But the majority of working girls, again probably on their family's instigation, had chosen either for the advantages of political abstinence or against the group of Catholic conservatives. However, the fact that, in addition to cigarmaking, Philips had also now given birth to Catholic labor institutions had profound consequences for this majority's ability to influence public life in the town. As important as the split within the Catholic working class community was the fact that the social cleavage between unskilled local families and highly skilled immigrant metalworkers had now crystallized into two explicitly antagonist blocs of nationally organized labor. In the end, this would fundamentally weaken both, as it implied the absence of coherent blue-collar politics. Moreover, neither electrical working class segment alone, skilled or unskilled, was strong enough to effectively oppose management policies. Unskilled local labor was easily exchangeable, largely female, and hard to organize. Complex metalwork, on the other hand, could always be outsourced if necessary. Already by 1911, Gerard Philips had shown that a highly unified group of skilled metalworkers, acting in isolation, was highly vulnerable.

Skilled Metalworkers and the Regime
of the Philips Machine Shop

From 1907 Philips was producing the successful but highly complicated metalwire lamp. In order to make sure that the firm kept up with the interconnected monopolists of General Electric, Siemens, and AEG, which were excluding the Dutch manufacturer from their technical knowledge, Gerard Philips started his own machine construction department. Begun with a handful of artisans in 1907, it employed some two hundred gasfitters, turners, and benchmen by 1909 but was gradually cut back to about 125 workers in late 1911.[87]

Since the number of skilled workers and technical employees was rising quickly in these years, an acute housing problem emerged. Such workers were almost exclusively recruited from the advanced, urbanized, and Protestant western part of the country. Their arrival at Eindhoven necessitated that Philips provide its own housing facilities.[88]

The machine shop turned out to confront Gerard Philips with a problem of labor control that he had no experience with. Skilled metalworkers were neither unskilled Brabant daughters nor white-collar employees, and their mode of integration into the factory therefore had to be different. This created a sequence of management problems that were never to be solved. In the course of time, this led to an increasingly strained and conflictual atmosphere between workers and management in the department. Finally, it culminated in the dismissal, on 14 December 1911, of the core group of metalworkers, among them the complete local leadership of the metalworkers union, De Algemene Nederlandse Metaalbewerkers Bond (General Dutch Metalworkers Union). The remaining metalworkers immediately responded with a strike. Supported by national union leadership (ANMB), they proposed to regulate all relevant aspects of their work by collective contract. Philips, however, reacted by firing them all, declaring that he had decided to outsource much of the department's work.

The official Philips historiography has been unduly selective in clarifying the causes of this conflict. It has too hastily accused the metalworkers of an outdated and pointless radicalism, and has consciously played down the extent of mutual solidarity among the group as a whole. Heerding delivers the unjustified suggestion that a small and isolated bunch of troubleseekers had undermined labor-management relations in the department and had alienated themselves from moderate national ANMB leadership.[89]

The immediate cause of the conflict was Philips's order to produce certain metal parts under piecework arrangements. The issue of piecework had had a much longer history in the department, however. Piecework had been ordered repeatedly by management, but had been refused consistently by the metalworkers. As before, Gerard Philips in the autumn of 1911 seemed to accept this. But in a subsequent fit of anger he apparently decided to dismiss the group's core. To understand the conflict, therefore, we need to understand the wider history of piecework in the shop.

Contentions about piecework had been a recurrent feature of the machine shop since 1909. It formed the core of a series of disagreements between workers and management that increasingly troubled their relationships. Initially, these disagreements arose not so much between Gerard Philips and local union leaders, but, as ANMB sources suggest, between Philips and the rank and file.[90] While resistance was organized from below, local union leaders had been sharply divided in the beginning. By more determinedly backing and incorporating their members' rejection of piecework, union leadership gradually succeeded, however, in forging a strong group cohesion. This now cohesive group developed an ever sharper opposition to the overall fashion in which Gerard Philips was managing the department. Thus, already by September 1909, a few months after the first group of metalworkers had arrived, turners went on strike against piecework. Most local ANMB leaders, however, were in favor of accepting it. Due to the intervention of the liberally inclined department's manager, piecework was thwarted for the moment.[91]

A year later, in September 1910, piecework was introduced again, this time for the plateworkers. Union leadership by now appears to have been in control of the issue. After long telephone calls with the national leadership, they decided to try to unify all the department's metalworkers behind a rejection of piecework.[92] In this they succeeded. Considering that they now dared to play their hand on the unanimity of over a hundred workers, it is evident that a strongly unified group had already emerged in the department. Faced with this unanimity, Philips withdrew.

Gerard Philips, however, was probably exasperated with this unexpected workers power in a department that was central to the firm's survival in the worldwide race for new lighting technology. The same day on which he was forced to retreat again on the question of piecework in 1910, he decided to fire thirty-five men and to subcontract some of the work.[93]

In spite of a momentary membership loss, the local union started growing again as new workers were brought in. In late 1910, the union probably organized over 75 percent of the department's workers. But relations became ever more strained. In September 1911, when there purportedly was not so much work to do, Gerard Philips used the occasion to fire some fifty men once again. The union journal, *De Metaalbewerker*, now featured a series of articles and reports on the experiences of its third-largest local branch.[94] They were written by local leaders who exclaimed that Philips company, though initially presenting itself as a progressive employer, had in fact been absolutely "reckless" in the treatment of its personnel.[95] Prefiguring the struggle to come, local leaders, in September 1911, announced that the time for cooperation and consent was now over.

After the layoffs of September 1911, the local union was reduced to a membership of 80. Just a month later, in October 1911, all 125 metalworkers (except three) once again rejected any form of piecework payment. Shortly thereafter, the local union secretary, A. Wiecherink, who was, to judge from his writings, a very moderate and reasonable though certainly moralistic man, refused any overtime work as long as it did not pay better. He was immediately fired. But subsequently all workers (except two) joined his refusal. The fitters even laid down all jobs. Gerard Philips again withdrew and called Wiecherink back. Management was also then forced to accept minor improvements of other arrangements, about which they had always refused to talk. Their firm collective stance immediately brought the union seventeen new members from a group of recently recruited young and little-skilled workers.[96]

Seen as the outcome of an unfolding series of gradually intensifying conflicts about control over the work regime of the Philips machine shop, the events of late 1911 can no longer be treated as the inconsiderate rebellion of a small group of "syndicalist" troubleshooters, as Philips historian A. Heerding would have us believe. Rather, it was the final enactment of a human conflict that had been in the making for over two years. Instead of being ignited by a small and radical union leadership, it had in fact been the rank and file who had forced their irresolute leaders to unite on the relevant issues. This in turn had led to a unique unification of the department's personnel.

Heerding treats the events as if they were nothing more than the enactment of a set of dichotomous principles, one a realistic liberal contractual principle, the other a utopian socialist "all power to the people" variant. Thus he contents himself with justifying Gerard Philips's action in December 1911 by rhetorically stating that the principled Philips was no longer prepared to "bargain" about the rules of the game.[97] Metalworkers, on the other hand, are accused of clinging to an outmoded "syndicalist" refusal of piecework while the ANMB was on the verge of giving up its resistance to it. This is history with the people left out.

Why did the Philips machine shop generate a conflictive development of this kind? And what was the place of piecework within it? The initial hesitations of local union leaders against rejecting piecework reflected an increasing awareness in contemporary left-wing circles that a pertinent refusal would in the end not be sustainable, or necessary. Instead, it was argued by the ANMB leadership that piecework could be allowed on the condition that it was regulated by collective contract.[98] Immediately after the 1909 strike, both local and national ANMB leaders had conferred with Gerard Philips and proposed to arrange for piecework in a collective contract. Philips responded that he was not unwilling to accept, but only on the condition that the majority of metalworkers were organized. Apparently this was not yet the case in 1909.

In September 1910, however, the union was already very strong, probably organizing more than half the metalworkers. When the issue of piecework cropped up again, they rejected it. They were backed by a national leadership that respected the collective opinion of one of its largest and most cohesive local branches. Philips, however, never again made any attempt to negotiate piecework as part of a collective agreement, as had been discussed the year before. Instead, he ruthlessly took revenge by firing thirty-five men the next day. The idea of a collective contract with a piecework arrangement was never taken up again. During the third conflict Philips reacted as brutally as he had in 1910. Reconciliation, of course, became ever more difficult.

Why did Philips not propose a collective contract with piecework arrangements in September 1910? Why not in October 1911? Why not in December 1911? Especially the latter date is puzzling, since the national ANMB leadership had just invited the firm to open negotiations to that end. Why did Gerard Philips prefer to fire all of his unionized workers, more than 75 percent of his metalworkforce, rather than finally negotiate? Philips's actions strongly suggest that he never wanted to share his authority over the workshop floor.[99] Although relations in the machine department grew ever more tense, chances for appeasement abounded. Philips, though, was simply not interested. By recurrently firing workers and bringing young ones in, he tried instead to break their group cohesion.

Gerard Philips has been depicted as a progressive employer who sought to cooperate with skilled workers in creating a "model department." Heerding suggests that he was utterly disillusioned over his relations with the metalworkers, and he explains Philips's abrupt action in December 1911 as embitterment. But for all practical purposes he forgets that Gerard Philips, long before the final confrontation was going on, had recurrently fired whole groups of people.

Gerard Philips's embitterment seems to have been caused by something else. He appears to have been totally offended by the emergence of some workers' power in the machine construction department. He attributed this to the rebelliousness of the workers' spokesmen.[100] To him, therefore, the conflict had become highly personalized. When the fight was on, he immediately threw out all strikers from their (Philips) homes, giving them no chance whatsoever to arrange things. Those who lived with other landlords were virtually hounded by him. Thus he demanded that the priest of the Protestant Young Men's Association evict a striker who happened to lodge in the association's clubhouse. When the priest declined, Philips immediately withdrew his financial support. He even announced that he would probably come and take away the furniture he had lent them the money to buy.[101] It seems as though he wanted a total excommunication of the "radicals." He personally called some of the higher Philips employees to remind them that they should not keep regular contacts with their inferiors. To that end, these employees were pressed to leave the Protestant association.[102]

What Philips's official historiography totally overlooked was how metalworkers themselves were more and more offended by the Philips regime. Their journal abounds with minor complaints about work rules, hierarchy, control. "Each day there was something new, but it was always exactly the same song," A. Wiecherink wrote in his retrospective and highly balanced article on the failed strike. He went out of his way to explain why the painful final collision with management could not be averted. He emphasized how union leadership had in fact often withheld its rank and file from angry and spontaneous action.[103]

These metalworkers had a particular history with Philips, a history that also contributed to their growing bitterness. Philips had explicitly solicited the cooperation of the ANMB in recruiting highly skilled applicants for jobs in the deep south. The ANMB had hoped that a "model relationship" could perhaps be built up in Eindhoven. Gerard Philips initially did his best to confirm that idea. Besides, these metalworkers were employed in an environment in which their immediate superiors boasted identical left-wing political and cultural outlooks. Expectations, in short, were high and could easily be violated.

In spite of the good intentions of everyone, it was basically the advanced form of labor control deployed in a peripheral, mass-producing factory based on the flexible use of unskilled girls' labor that happened to persistently antagonize a group of skilled metalworkers. The strict, Taylorized hierarchy Philips was used to working with did not match their customary expectations.[104] They had felt like "a small bunch of people that was constantly watched over by its opponents."[105] Despite a lot of bitter disagreements in the union press about the strategy behind the failed strike and about the destruction of the third-largest local union branch in one of the country's most advanced factories, all ANMB commentators underwrote that the struggle had in fact been about shop floor power, about the acceptance of a form of collective influence by workers.[106] In retrospect, everyone agreed that a final collision could not have been averted. "Well, it came . . . and we defended ourselves," A. Wiecherink apologized.[107]

Seen in this perspective, the polarity articulated in this struggle, of "piecework" on the one hand, and "collective contract" on the other, merely symbolized more fundamental questions about the Philips work regime. The struggle was in fact about the contradiction between hierarchical, individualizing, Tayloristic, and bureaucratic power, and a more horizontal form of self-regulation. On the surface of the conflict, the themes of "piecework" and "collective contract" appeared to exhaustively demarcate the terrain of contest. But more basically, they were the public symbols by which different "structures of feeling,"[108] interests, and perspectives on work were expressed and communicated.

The dynamics of flexible mass manufacturing of light electrical products at Eindhoven had attained a momentum of their own, irrespective of any good intention. The fall in the power of the socialist metalworkers at Philips implied that Eindhoven industrialization would go without a locally implanted institution to give voice to one of the key human dilemma's inherent in its growth.

The arrival in Eindhoven of a large group of skilled, urban, and left-wing metalworkers had implications for local social democracy too. In 1908, the local SDAP had sixty-two members. In 1910, after their arrival, membership rose to a hundred. And in 1912, after the lost strike, it fell to fifty-five again.[109] Given their cohesion and their age (no family obligations in free time), it was understandable that metalworkers quickly took over local leadership. But as they were becoming ever more critical toward Philips, they antagonized the members of the old party core who still maintained close ties with their old political benefactor and employer.

The conflict centered on the person of Jan Jansen, who was the former secretary of the local party and chief porter of the Philips factory. He became the subject of a long series of letters to the party office in Amsterdam. The new board complained about the atmosphere, "the intense rottenness" of the department, about the sad engagement of many of its members, and above all about the dominance of Jan Jansen, that "highly dangerous figure."[110]

Jansen, indeed, had the confidence of both the Philips brothers. Moreover, his functions and authority at the plant far exceeded those of a porter. He was, for example, responsible for housing and other personnel affairs.[111] Therefore he was well informed and occupied a strategic position in the community. Because Jansen was quite prepared to abuse his powers, local party members were afraid to speak their minds in his presence.[112] Finally, as local correspondent of the socialist daily newspaper *Het Volk*, he also held strategic relationships with nationwide socialist opinion. During the metalworkers' strike, he took the opportunity to sharply condemn their visions and strategies.

The sharp collision of loyalties between the old and new core in Eindhoven socialism is well indicated by a letter from a local party activist to the SDAP board after the departure of the metalworkers. He asked whether it was true, as Jansen had repeatedly asserted, that Philips had subsidized the electoral campaign of Jelle Troelstra, the SDAP's paramount leader.[113]

With the advent of the group of metalworkers, the local SDAP became attentive to domination in the sphere of production. They also sought cooperation with the relatively large group of socialist cigarmakers who had hitherto refrained from an active alliance with the party. When their final strike failed, however, the local SDAP, headed again by, among others, Jan Jansen, returned to its preoccupation with the politics of reproduction. The chance for more assertive left-wing local politics had faded.

CONCLUSION:
THE LANDSCAPE OF FLEXIBLE MANUFACTURING

The ascent of Eindhoven in the world of manufacturing was predicated on low wages, wages well below the level to support an individual. This low wage standard was the result of local labor practices embedded in the structure of local household economies. Gradually declining peasant and protoindustrial households had survived by sending their offspring into industrial wage work, in particular their daughters. This had given rise to the development of a highly labor intensive industrialization, employing large numbers of local girls, based on the relationships of "flexible familism." Industrialists commonly employed several members of a household. In case of adversity, some were dismissed, but others, in particular fathers, were kept. This assured the industrialist of a great measure of labor flexibility, and brought the household a minimal measure of security. During upswings "flexible familism" implied the availability of a large and trained labor reserve for the employer, and meant prosperity for dependent families. Flexible familism was the key relationship of regional development and fundamentally shaped the local patterns of family life and demography. It put pressure on older daughters to postpone marriage and support the parental household as long as possible. Thus regional industrialization did not liberate adolescent individuals for the play and romance modernization theorists would deductively expect, but instead served to reinforce "traditional" parental claims.

This fundamental pattern of working-class reproduction and the related low wage levels also generated the geographic / political pattern of scattered residences and fragmented community formation. As households sought access to land and livestock for securing family survival, they were dispelled from the most densely inhabited areas around the central city of Eindhoven. And indeed, being in need of cheap space, they wished so.

Altogether, "flexible familism" laid down the social foundation for a dynamic landscape of flexible, labor-intensive manufacturing that proved highly competitive and resilient, also in international markets. This local culture of flexible mass production also produced a highly confusing political landscape. While a conservative Catholic section of the Eindhoven bourgeoisie succeeded in aligning themselves with emergent protest among cigarmakers, the liberal section of large entrepreneurs forged a coalition with anticlerical workers that formed the ground for local social democracy. Both were explicit cross-class coalitions. While the latter alliance turned out to support improvements in local infrastructure, such as housing and retailing, and pressed toward political integration of the area, the former alliance proved capable of waging and winning a large-scale conflict in cigarmaking. As Philips girls were partly organized by Catholicism, and metalworkers failed to implant a more production-oriented socialism, the local political arena remained fragmented over two contradictory class alliances. Catholicism, however, would remain dominant, partly because of its strong position in cigar-making, partly also because of the emergence of a highly successful cooperative peasant movement and other petty bourgeois organizations in the wider region from which the town recruited its workers.

5 Cycles and Structures of Electrical

Production, 1910–1930

Arguments that try to explain the quiescence of Eindhoven workers in terms of paternalism, deference, and dominance largely build on the experience of the twenties and early thirties. In those years the Philips company expanded to what contemporaries saw as "Americanist" proportions. In 1930, electrical manufacturing provided some 70 percent of industrial employment in the town, 50 percent of all local jobs. In the course of the twenties, moreover, Philips invested increasing stocks of capital in the supply of "social provisions" such as pensions, illness benefits, workers' housing, social work, leisure opportunities, and a retailing cooperative, as well as in its own police force. In contrast to the early years of the century, Philips now preferred to organize such initiatives on its own account, increasingly bypassing local government or civic coalitions. Its reputation for paternalism, therefore, was firmly established in these years, both in the public image and in the self-understanding of its management. But the period also gave rise to sharp criticism from labor activists and Catholic protagonists who took the firm's social policy to be a conscious effort at domination and control.

"MATURITY" AND "IMMATURITY" IN PHILIPS'S EXPANSION

From 1911 to 1915, employment at Philips remained relatively stable while based on the new metal wire technology developed by General Electric. Production and marketing of this new product in Europe was cartelized among Siemens, AEG, Philips, and several smaller central European manufacturers. After 1915, however, manufacturing at Philips partly shifted to an independently developed "half watt" lamp. This was a cheap and very successful mass product, the result of concerted technical and chemical effort. The east Brabant manufacturer now, for the first time, took advantage over its competitors in Berlin and New York.[1]

The company was very keen on rationalizing production technologies, in particular through intensifying work by applying science. Total employment between 1911 and 1914 therefore tended to decline somewhat. In 1911, it employed some 2,700 people. By 1914, jobs had been cut to 2,350. Due to the "half watt" lamp, jobs then started to rise again to about 2,600 in 1915. Except for three minor conjunctural cuts in 1919, 1921, and 1926, the number of jobs at Eindhoven rose constantly between 1915 and 1930. But in this persistent expansion two clear phases can be discerned, both quantitatively and qualitatively. Up to mid 1927 the company grew at a steady pace. Starting in the autumn of 1927, however, its growth became explosive and beyond precedent in the Netherlands. In the late summer of 1927 it employed some 8,500 people; at the end of that year jobs suddenly increased to 10,000; in October 1929 employment reached a height of 22,800.

Growth in the gradualist phase, up until mid 1927, depended to a considerable extent on the vertical integration of more complex production processes, on the formation of corporate administrative and marketing functions, and on the establishment of an independent research and development capability. Thus, reacting to trade disturbances during the First World War, Philips decided to start its own glass factory at Eindhoven. By 1922, some 800 glassblowers and apprentices, recruited from older glass centers in the Netherlands and abroad, were producing glass bowls in Eindhoven. The machine shop, created in 1909, plus some special technical facilities, expanded rapidly and employed some 2,200 skilled metalworkers at the end of the twenties. In order to keep up with sharp international competition, Philips started its own physical and chemical research laboratories by the mid-tens. Administrative and commercial jobs also grew quickly as the firm developed a more corporate character and acquired several foreign subsidiaries and sales agencies.

In June 1922, overall employment at Philips consisted of over 3,200 jobs in lamp production proper, largely unskilled; 520 skilled jobs in the machine shop; 800 jobs for glassblowers and apprentices in the glass factory; 300 jobs in additional technical services; and over 530 salaried jobs for white-collar employees.[2] Thus, by mid 1922 almost 40 percent of Philips employment consisted of skilled, technical, and service jobs. The first phase of Philips expansion after 1910, then, was mainly realized through the qualitative upgrading of local employment structures and was aimed at the formation of a "mature" corporate industrial complex.

Related to the growth of higher-status job categories, the electrical labor force displayed a marked decrease in the percentage of working daughters and a notable increase in the percentage of fathers. In 1914, about 75 percent of overall Philips employment consisted of (adolescent, unmarried) female jobs, but just ten years later, in 1924, its share was already reduced to slightly over 30 percent. While this substantial relative reduction of young female workers was partly triggered by the expansion of higher-value-added jobs, almost exclusively occupied by men, it was also caused by the exhaustion of the young female labor supply in the region.[3] In 1924, for example, only 50 percent of the work force in the lamp factory was female, although girls were preferred for at least 70 percent of its jobs. The partial shift to skilled and male labor was expressed in the number of married males working at Philips. Of more than 1,870 blue-collar workers in 1910, only 190 had been married. A decade later, in 1920, of 2,860 blue collars, 839 were fathers of families.[4] Thus, in addition to the "maturation" of its job structure, the Philips working class, at first glance, was also gradually assuming the classical image of a "mature" proletariat. Compared to the 1910s, when Philips workers were largely adolescent and female, and only indirectly dependent on industrial wages, a much larger share of its numbers in the early twenties was male and married. They headed families whose survival fully depended on waged work.

By contrast, the phase of explosive growth, starting in the late summer of 1927, featured a renewed and impressive expansion of unskilled jobs. In January 1927 some 7,500 unskilled workers were employed at the Philips plants. This increased to 18,555 in late October 1929.[5] Skilled and white-collar jobs did not remain stagnant in this period, but in contrast to the earlier period, in which higher-status jobs grew quite independently from developments in mass production, their growth now was largely derived from the expansion of unskilled employment, and along the lines set before 1927.

Explosive growth after 1926 was predicated on a new and highly successful mass product, the radio set. In the aftermath of the war, a number of specialized, small-batch productions were started, particularly in the promising field of wireless communications and related products such as loudspeakers and microphones. In this way the company gradually acquired competence in the wireless field. By 1925, it produced all the vital components of radio sets, but they were not yet integrated into one marketable standard product. As demand for components steadily rose, the decision to start the production of complete radio sets was finally taken in 1927. This led to a nationally unprecedented acceleration of job growth in southeast Brabant and resulted in the formation of the largest radio factory in the world.

Thus the first and the second post-1910 growth cycles should be clearly distinguished in terms of their effects on local employment structures, working class composition, and forms and problems of urbanization. In fact, while the first phase of gradual expansion featured a "maturation" of industrial job structures and an immigration of well-paid skilled workers and white-collar people, the explosive employment growth after 1926 was characterized by a complex and contradictory struggle over the nature of the quickly growing unskilled working class. Although this struggle was of course triggered by the sudden and enormous demand for unskilled labor, it was rooted in the exhaustion of the original southeast Brabant reserve of unskilled workers: local working daughters.

Philips's expansion, therefore, required its management to find an answer to a new and difficult question. What were the conditions for the formation of a new unskilled electrical proletariat that could serve as a substitute for local girls, without compromising on the characteristics that had made local girls so profitable: the unusual combination of flexibility, discipline, and obedience? In other words: while building the largest radio factory in the world and supervising, as we shall see, a rapid process of urbanization, Philips's management was exploring a new synthesis of "mature" industrial structures and "immature" industrial workers.

Philipsism, as it emerged in the 1920s as a social and managerial ideology and practice, we can now begin to understand, featured a search for synthesizing two different forms of industrial organization that were at first sight contradictory and mutually exclusive. On the one hand, the dynamics of global competition in electrical products forced the Philips family to build an advanced and innovation-oriented production base, as well as a differentiated corporate hierarchy, with all the dynamizing consequences for the local community it inevitably entailed. But on the other hand, in order to ensure its competitive strength while drastically expanding its production, it sought to renew its historical foundation on a flexibly deployable but nevertheless disciplined unskilled working class.

As we shall see, it was exactly this unique local synthesis of industrial "maturity" and "immaturity," "modernism" and "traditionalism" that forced Philips managers to a growing engagement with urban and family structures. This engagement accounted for a substantial part of its "social policies." This paradoxical dynamic finally induced the company to re-create, under its own auspices, an unskilled working class such as it had found in southeast Brabant at its inception at the end of the nineteenth century.

THE PHILIPSIST PRODUCTION REGIME

In his comparative study of corporate social policies, Sjef Stoop has recently argued that Philips, in 1927, during its leap into radio set production, witnessed a transition from a Tayloristic technology of labor control by task division to a Fordist one based on the integration of separate actions by mechanisms of continuous flow and the assembly line.[6] Now, on closer scrutiny, it is hard to see what exactly this Fordist transition could have meant to Philipsism as a whole. It might well be possible to demonstrate the introduction of Fordist technology in some departments by 1930. But in contrast to, for example, auto making, the electrical industries have always been a highly differentiated and weakly integrated cluster of production processes and organizational arrangements.[7] Philips, without a base in electrical engineering like Siemens and General Electric, and with its orientation to international consumer markets, probably championed this principle of organizational differentiation.[8] Thus, though Fordist techniques were increasingly applied in mass production departments, it hardly makes sense to talk of a whole Fordist technology of production, shaping and unifying social practices and social relationships throughout the Philips plants.[9]

Marxist sociology has argued that a mode of production can analytically be broken down into two sets of relationships. It distinguishes between "relationships in production" on the one hand and "relationships of production" on the other. The first set of relations refers to the everyday forms of the labor process, the actual organization of work, while the latter refers to relations of appropriation, to the social forms through which surplus value is drawn away from the "direct producers" and appropriated by the capitalist.[10] Together, such sets of relationships, Michael Burawoy has suggested, make up specific empirical regimes of production.[11] The Philipsist regime of production was characterized by the combination of two distinct principles of social organization. On the one hand, it left the regimes of everyday production highly differentiated, fragmented, and divided, responsive to the particular demands of technology and labor markets. But on the other, it developed a highly efficient, unifying, and individualizing bureaucratic mechanism in order to register and control the generation and appropriation of surplus value. On the level of Philips's top management it was precisely this particular combination of interrelated characteristics that facilitated the continued product, process, and labor flexibility that Anton Philips, as a salesman, deemed essential for the survival of a young and dynamic industry that remained fully dependent on capricious export markets.[12]

Mass Production and Gendered Discipline

Systems of blue-collar labor control at Philips were strictly divided between, on the one side, the skilled labor in the technical departments and the glass factory, and on the other the unskilled and semiskilled labor in mass production departments. In terms of formal relationships this division became manifest in the fact that the former were quite thoroughly unionized, whereas the latter were absolutely not.[13] However, underpinning this formal contrast was a whole world of everyday relationships, hierarchies, solidarities, expectations, and experiences that made these two fields of industrial production at Philips utterly dissimilar. In the final analysis, this dissimilarity was based on the divisions and differences between what Michael Burawoy has called the "technical relationships in production" of these departments, that is, the relationships as they were determined by the technical properties of labor processes.[14] Crucial for the great social divide in Philipsism were the consequences of divergent technical properties of labor processes for the nature of labor demand and labor control in these departments.

A good way to illustrate this is to start with the rate of young female labor in various departments. This measure roughly indicates the degree and methods of industrial discipline as well as the levels of formal skill required. While the percentage of male labor in Philips as a whole had been rising quickly during the twenties, amounting to more than 75 percent by 1930, the male share in specific departments had remained very uneven. Thus the lamp factory proper had retained a female rate of over 40 percent.[15] And in 1930, some of its mass production departments, as well as some parts of the "apparatus factories" where the radio sets were assembled, depended largely or even exclusively on adolescent female labor.[16]

In these feminized departments a quite harsh and restrictive work regime obtained. It was despotically supervised by male bosses, who, as oral evidence abundantly underscores, often "incredibly got on the nerves" of the working girls. Girls' labor, moreover, was carefully guarded by time and motion studies. The disciplining of their bodies was intensified by a series of rules regulating their movement through space. They were not allowed to move freely through the department, let alone enter other departments. They sat at their work stations, or on "lamp mills," and had to ask permission for alternative movements, such as going to the toilet. Indeed, sanitary stops were strictly regulated, and often became a point of friction between management and workers. The same is true for young workers' behavior at the elevators and stairs. Such sites became outlets for various adolescent reactions against Philipsist regimentation of teenage workers. Though there are no good figures of the participation of girls in the labor unions in Eindhoven, all sources agree that the extent of such was negligible and, so far as it existed, largely confined to the Catholic union, which at the time acted exclusively as an additional moralizer.

To understand Philipsist mass production and female labor, it is centrally important to note that the "despotic" regime under which girls worked was essentially founded on gendered forms of discipline taught in the southeast Brabant family. Girls, though certainly deriving some pleasure from being together with equals, were sent to the factory, explicitly so or by the silent force of custom, by their families at the age of fourteen.[17] Their basic disciplining took place in their households and their home environments, with an eye on their subservient status both in the family economy and in local industry. Moreover, fathers and brothers in such households were very often also employed at the Philips plants.[18] Indeed, in Philips circles the employment of more than one family member was considered the rule rather than the exception. It probably raised workers' dependence on and loyalty to the firm and fostered their collective knowledge and experience of practices at the plants. Remarkably often, fathers executed functions with some measure of authority and status, such as production boss, guard, archivist, or elevator operator.[19] Such male experiences with the day-to-day functioning of local industrial disciplinary structures certainly added to their visions of gendered discipline. Since family incomes and the opportunities, status, and security of fathers substantially depended on the labor of their offspring, in particular of their daughters, socialization practices of families in the region were finely attuned to the demands of industrial discipline, and vice versa.[20] Fathers, and mothers sometimes even more so, tended to be complicit therefore with the industrial despotism under which in particular their daughters had to work. Indeed, their daughters' ability to cope with harsh industrial discipline tended to secure a good part of their local status and means of survival.

It is, then, essential to see that the regime of basic mass production at the electrical plants, and indeed Philips's competitive edge in international markets, was socially preconditioned by, and built upon, aspects of class, gender, and household economy that originated outside the immediate sphere of industrial production and the labor market.[21]

The fundamental importance of gendered forms of labor discipline to the Philips regime of accumulation is underlined by the growth of labor control problems in the later twenties. As we shall see later on, these particular disciplinary problems formed the background for the expansion of social policies and paternalist services by the corporation, including its decision to start building large residential quarters for unskilled labor. In the course of the twenties, many formally unskilled jobs became available at Philips for males. The production of bakelite, for example, like most types of chemical production elsewhere, was an exclusively male process, just like the production of gas. Moreover, there were a thousands of weakly defined actions necessarily to be done by hand, even within the confines of the national champion of mechanization that Philips undoubtedly was. Carrying coal, painting walls, delivering the internal post services, doing archival work, all this kind of weakly supervised work was generally done by men, often of middle age, who had enjoyed little formal education but nevertheless displayed the skills and personalities that made them reliable executors of such tasks, in particular when some of their children were also earning a wage at the plants.

Though the rates of male participation had thus been rising all through the twenties, problems of labor control only seem to have become alarming with the tumultuous start of radio set production in 1927. At that moment, the employment of thousands of unskilled male workers in basic processes of mass production, lured to the factories by a rise in wages, had become inevitable since the regional supply of female labor had long since become exhausted.[22] Initially the firm could hire the very youngest boys, but gradually it was forced to contract also those approaching the age of marriage.[23] Apparently, both the home disciplining of younger working class males and their wider opportunities in an expansive industrial society seem to have made them much less adept than girls to perform those minute tasks, under strict surveillance, that were the essence of electrical mass production.[24]

Seen in this gendered light, the whole interrelated set of labor control questions that by 1929 increasingly demanded the attention of Philips management acquires a wholly different and much more fundamental and interesting character than is on first sight suggested by the dry statistics expressing it. Such evidence as rising illness, absenteeism, deteriorating product quality, falling labor productivity, and, above all, the quickly rising rate of labor turnover, which by 1930 approached 30 percent, then become neat statistical windows onto what happens when basic forms of social discipline, on which regional modes of production and accumulation are built, start to erode.[25]

This whole complex problem of labor control ultimately turned on the possibility of substantially expanding production while maintaining a disciplined regime in the basic departments. The meaning of the years 1927–1930 turned out to have been, as we shall see, that such a disciplined regime of electrical mass production could hardly have been based on market-oriented wage incentives for individual adult male workers. Instead, Philips had to reinvent the family-controlled, gendered styles of obedience produced in the multiple-earner southeast Brabant working family.

In the end, with the building of large-scale workers' quarters such as "Drents Dorp," a solution was found that seemed to liberate Philips from regional labor market constraints. As we will see later, neighborhoods like Drents Dorp provided the company with the necessary supply of girls to secure the functioning of its production regime in the basic departments. Consequently, during the crisis of the early thirties the percentage of female workers at Philips again started to rise.[26] In practice this probably means the refeminization of central processes of electrical mass production.

Reflecting their subordinate status as adolescents in the wider society, regionally recruited "mass" workers, in contrast to nationally recruited skilled workers, were not unionized.[27] First, many would have been too young to be union members, for which you had to be at least eighteen years old. Secondly, a great many were girls and therefore ignored by existing male unions. Moreover, they often came from places and families without traditions of collective labor activism. Finally, most of them probably considered their status as industrial workers temporary.

Philips argued that industrial unions had no popular support among young Brabant unskilled workers and that the firm therefore should not maintain serious communication with their national leaderships. To determine wage levels for the unskilled, Philips assumed the sole right to calculate their minimal costs of living in the area and set their wage standards and secondary conditions accordingly (though, as we shall see later, in the management of some kinds of secondary remunerations some form of labor participation was granted).[28]

As a consequence of the absence of any form of collective bargaining or group self-regulation, mass production department bosses at Philips became, for all practical purposes, the sole executors and controllers of the everyday factory regime. However, from the establishment of the socioeconomic and personnel departments in the early twenties, their power was curtailed somewhat. But during the expansion of radio set production, department bosses again acquired a large degree of autonomy in creating jobs and hiring people.[29] This decentralized and informal form of management lent itself well to quick expansion. But it also led to high wage costs and caused much unrest among workers who felt treated unequally and unjustly. It could even give rise to mutual competition for labor between bosses when production targets could not be realized by the existing number of workers in a department.

By 1930, bureaucratic centralization of budgets, of hiring and firing procedures, of wage stipulations and piece rates, of complaint procedures and free-time allowances, was all aimed at the prevention of arbitrary power wielding from the side of production management.[30] In the absence of any form of collective representation, or self-regulation by group contracts, as was common in much male metal work in older industrializing countries like Great Britain and Germany, bureaucratic control and legitimacy, embodied in the Philips departments of labor and social economy, helped to maintain "mass" workers' cooperation while curbing mutual competition between bosses.

The Insular Male Worlds of Skilled Work

In contrast to mass production departments, the glass factory and the technical departments were largely composed of highly skilled and unionized males (and, in the case of glassmaking, their apprentices).[31] The technical departments employed skilled metalworkers, who often were recruited from outside the region. They had generally enjoyed the best trade schooling obtainable in the country. In collaboration with corporate scientists they were deployed on the construction and maintenance of machines, machine tools, and all kinds of factory installations. Since they had to be recruited on a nationwide labor market, their remuneration was nationally competitive. They enjoyed much freedom of movement, good learning opportunities, and fine career expectations. In fact their whole outlook and experience sharply contrasted with those of local "mass workers."

By 1931, in the midst of the creation of mechanical infrastructures for radio production, more than 2,200 metalworkers were on the Philips payroll.[32] Over 600 of them were members of the Algemene Nederlandse Metaalarbeiders Bond (ANMB; General Dutch Metalworkers Union) affiliated with the Nederlands Verbond van Vakverenigingen (NVV; National Syndicate of Trade Unions), while more than a thousand were organized by the Catholic metalworkers union St. Eloy (which also organized unskilled workers).[33] Though metalworkers often complained of the strict rules and controls at Philips compared with the smaller shops they used to work in along the Dutch coast, they seem to have been satisfied with the earnings, and in particular with the ample opportunities for overtime. For many of them, moreover, Philips seems to have been a good place to become acquainted with the latest techniques and materials. Their training and knowledge could subsequently be put to good use on the labor markets of the north and west.

In contrast to industrial unions, which were kept at bay by Philips, metalworkers' unions had gradually gained a modus vivendi with the corporation after their demise in 1912. By 1930, local and national leaders of the ANMB regularly convened with Philips management in order to negotiate wage questions. The outcomes of such negotiations, however, were never formalized in collective agreements. They were single-handedly translated into company rules which were exclusively applied and controlled by company staff. Though Philips did recognize the legitimacy of labor unions to work for better standards, the company still did not want to accept any form of formal union power on the shop floor in skilled metalworking. In line with that position, Philips refused to sign any sort of collective contract with organized labor. Philips referred to the constant need for flexibility in a technologically young industry that was for 90 percent of its operations dependent on export markets. But notwithstanding this position, working conditions for skilled labor at the firm were generally thought to be among the best nationally.[34]

Again a different regime obtained for glassworkers. All of them were immigrants to Eindhoven. Some were Austrian, Czech, German, or Belgian, but most came from older glass centers in the Netherlands, like Nieuw Buinen, Maastricht, and Leerdam. Glassworkers had always been a group apart in the world of industrial work. Up until the later nineteenth century they had maintained a very large measure of control over their trade. Because they guarded their own knowledge and skills, glass workers' sons often inherited their fathers' positions after an apprenticeship of more than ten years. But in the course of the twentieth century this strong position began to erode as scientists increasingly intruded in the forms of production and application of glass.[35]

Because of their common places of origin and high measure of self-reproduction glassworkers at Philips were quite a cohesive group. Many of them were interrelated by ties of family and friendship and lived close together in the younger part of "Philipsdorp." The glass factory itself was spatially separated from other Philips productions. Despite the fact that glassworkers were divided along the lines of religion and nationality, they all shared in a male culture of independence and sociability centered upon the authority of the more senior and highly skilled artisans.

Although the great majority of glassworkers at Philips seem to have been unionized, national industrial unions did not play a role in determining wages and work conditions in the glass factory. This is explained by the fact that glassmaking was a rare and highly concentrated trade in the Netherlands, of which the three main production centers were spatially isolated and specialized in dissimilar productions. As a result, glassworkers were organized under the general umbrella of the industrial trade unions. But in fact, these national unions of unskilled industrial workers could hardly make a useful contribution to the diverse situations of glassworkers. At the same time, however, the strong position of glassworkers on the shop floor, as well as their social cohesiveness and cultural distinctiveness, made them largely independent of the support of a central leadership.

At the Philips glass factory, their collective power seems to have given rise to what we might call a weak system of shop-stewardism. Representatives from the various unions (Catholic, Protestant, and Socialist) took elected positions in a works council, called the "kern," for negotiation with management. This council was formally instituted in 1918, after a conflict over piece rates.[36] It became the example on which other factory councils at Philips in the twenties and thirties were modeled, but none of them seems to have attained an authority comparable to the original one.[37] Though much is unclear about its record and functioning, the council must have played a large role in negotiating beneficial arrangements for glassworkers. Indeed, encroachments on glassworkers' positions such as the deskilling of manual work, the mechanization of routine glass bowl production, and the abolition of the self-recruitment of apprentices, which all took place in the later twenties and early thirties and had momentous consequences for the daily lives, expectations, and status of glassworkers, did not lead to collective protest. Although lay-offs and strong pressure from above in a time of crisis may well have been decisive in preventing collective action, it can also be seen as an indication of the capacity of the glass factory council to successfully negotiate such restructurings.

The Fragmentation and Unification of Philipsism

Thus the Philips production regime was thoroughly segmented and highly differentiated. The everyday goings on on the shop floor were structured along highly divergent lines of power, discipline, negotiation, and cooperation. As we have seen, at least three different blue-collar work regimes could formally be distinguished: a market despotic regime with increasing bureaucratic regulation in mass manufacturing; a weakly consensual, bureaucratically regulated regime in the technical depart-ments; and finally an increasingly weak version of shop-stewardism at the glass factory. The shapes of these regimes were not just coincidental but corresponded with highly divergent technical properties of labor processes, on the one hand, and greatly different, socially, historically, and geographically separated cultures of work, family, and leisure among blue-collar groups on the other.

However, in the everyday reality of an increasingly diversified and in-tegrated electrical corporation like Philips, there in fact developed many more informal types of work regime. The electrical industries, in contrast with, for example, the automotive industry, textiles, or machine building, featured very fragmented and fluid types of organization and labor con-trol. Dozens of categories of jobs and productions did not fall neatly into one of the regimes described above. In fact their everyday control mecha-nisms varied with the specific historical conditions of work and the labor market characteristics associated with them. Philipsism, then, seen from the point of view of production and the experiences arising from it, appeared not at all as a unified whole, nor could it ever have done so.

The electrical industries in general, and Philips with its orientation on consumer products and capricious international markets in particular, did not resemble the relatively stable and homogeneous processes and regimes of textiles or automobile production. Electrical consumer prod-ucts bridged a whole set of technical, social, and geographical divisions. None of the other key industries of the twentieth century employed so many scientists recruited from advanced research institutes located in core technological regions as did the electrical corporations. But neither did any of them employ so many unskilled young girls as the electrical manufacturers, in particular when, like Philips, they had their roots in mass production for consumer markets.[38] It was this fundamental condition of electrical mass production that provided the groundwork for the differentiation of production processes and segmentation of labor markets and production regimes at Eindhoven.

But over and above this variance, from the later twenties on an increasingly capable "social" bureaucracy was developed that spotted, checked, controlled, and guided the diverse production setups and their workers. The departments of labor and socioeconomic affairs designed, prescribed, and evaluated wage systems, piece rates, and other work-related rights and remunerations. By 1930, this central bureaucratic administration even penetrated so far into the workings of the production departments that central corporate management became capable of spotting the weekly output of each individual laborer and following his or her record of profitability to the company. To researchers from the International Labor Office at Geneva, Anton Philips asserted that each half year, a committee, composed of the directors of both staff departments, assisted by some of their key functionaries and subdepartment chiefs, bent itself over individual profitability rates.[39] Good performance led to higher earnings and to better career chances in the largest internal labor market of the country.

Thus, while day-to-day work regimes at Philips remained highly fragmented over plants, departments, and categories of employees, appearing in a shape well attuned to the accustomed rights and duties of any single working class group, the abstracted threads of their daily efforts, reduced to the key information on individual profitability rates, were increasingly drawn together at the corporate headquarters. It was this peculiar configuration of differentiation/segmentation and centralization/unification, leading to a regime fragmented in its daily workings and relationships but unified in its surveillance of workers as individuals, that permitted Philips, as we shall see, to maintain a crucial measure of flexibility while broadening its corporate capacities and strengthening its global competitiveness.

6   The Culture of Philipsism

Any effort to understand the paternalism of Philips company should start with asking why exactly the firm built such a "kingdom," a "wonderland," outside the factory gates. The main point of my approach is to show that both the cause and peculiarities of its paternalist practices sprang from the dynamic structures and contradictions of Eindhoven's flexible manufacturing as a whole. Without understanding its unfolding logic as a regionally dominant mode of production we cannot hope to understand Philipsist paternalism.

Secondly, we need to question the idea of deference as a natural consequence of paternalism by asking how different categories of workers were actually addressed by the firm's structures, both in production and outside the gates. How did these different categories of workers appropriate the constraints and opportunities inherent to those structures? Only after exploring such questions will it become possible to say anything valid about the effects of paternalism on workers' loyalties and orientations. Indeed, corporate paternalism has never exerted a total embrace, nor has it affected everyone in the same way and to the same degree. Industrial paternalism always operates within a market environment which inevitably serves to constrain its workings and shape its objects. Its structures, moreover, are differentially related to the everyday lives of different working class segments. Accordingly, they differentially affect workers' chances for private or collective empowerment. We need to breathe some actual historical, human life into the paralyzing concept of deference.

These are the guiding questions for the approach that follows. Answers to them will be sought through different openings. Each section studies another aspect of the Philipsist regime in the context of its overall structure and dynamic. Thus, like a hermeneutic circle, I will shed light on the whole by analyzing the development of its constituent parts and will illuminate the parts by approaching them from the vantage point of their insertion in the dynamic whole.

The first section examines the origins of the most salient form of Philips' paternalist provision: large-scale housing for unskilled workers. Contrary to common opinion, I argue that Philips, like most industrialists, did not have a "tradition" of providing housing for the unskilled. The two-thousand-plus houses that were built between 1928 and 1930, claiming more than half the nation's budget for housing loans, was a response to a very particular problem that had no precedent at all in local history: weakening labor discipline among an emergent proletariat of regionally mobile youth. This eventually threatened the work regime of vital mass production departments as well as patriarchic practices in households and the city. Housing investments served to counter precisely this development by re-creating "flexible familism." Large-scale housing facilitated the creation of an immigrant proletariat of large families, with multiple earners, many of them daughters, such as had originally marked the southeast Brabant labor market. As we will see later, the new immigrant proletariat, employed under the conditions of "flexible familism," turned out to be essential for overcoming the 1931 crisis without collective protest. It also enabled Philips to enhance its productivity enormously and secure its position in the highly competitive world markets of the 1930s.

The second section elucidates the forces of Philipsism as they shaped the experiences, lives, and histories of several families from two key Philips neighborhoods, one inhabited by skilled immigrants from northern and western towns and another populated by unskilled, large immigrant families from poor peripheral regions. It also explores the respective neighborhood cultures. This section illustrates the deep cleavage, in terms of experiences, expectations, and everyday life, between skilled and unskilled Philips workers as well as between their neighborhoods. If mutual identification was not easily developed on the shop floor, it was also unlikely to be created from joint experiences in family, leisure, and neighborhood life. This section also touches on the different orientations to work, family, and politics that emerged among families in these neighborhoods. Beneath the surface of formal political and cultural allegiances it explores the wider motivations and experiences of Philips families and points out key ambiguities of living with the electrical corporation.

Not only production, neighborhoods, and families, but also the urban morphology of the city of Eindhoven itself was to an important degree shaped by the social relations of flexible mass production. The third section describes the form of the town, which was generally felt to be ugly and provincial, somehow not corresponding with the idea of a city. It had the unfortunate shape of a spider, a small core with long legs that did not touch each other and stretched far into wild and rural areas, making communication difficult. Its neighborhoods, furthermore, were remarkably idiosyncratic. They did not seem to be part of a quickly expanding city but were socially and culturally insulated and inward-looking. This section points out that the spatial dispersal and cultural fragmentation of the place, as well as its provincial aesthetic, were not caused by "poor popular traditions," as has often been imputed, but by its particular social pattern of industrialization and urbanization epitomized by the Philips upsurge.

No analyst of Philipsism can overlook the extensive range of services and welfare with which the corporation increasingly intervened in local life. In the fourth section I study this redistributional system primarily as a moral program. Beyond its discrete provisions, it amounted to a cultural offensive aimed at promoting, among its working-class population, models of behavior and modes of orientation deemed preferable in the Eindhoven context. Such models served to include those found deserving of Philipsist favors but also to exclude the undeserving. I maintain that throughout the practices, discourses, and rituals of Philips's social system the idea of self-responsible worker citizenship was enacted. Such citizenship claims, however, were generally contradicted by existing social cleavages and sometimes, as in works council elections, intentionally circumscribed by the company so as to exclude those who were most exploited. The spread of its citizenship ideology among local inhabitants, however, was secured by being wedded to the job opportunities of the largest internal labor market in the country. Philips created a local cadre that was, in important respects, culturally unified by repertoires of common sense derived from Philipsist citizenship.

THE ORIGINS AND STRUCTURES OF PHILIPS WORKERS' HOUSING

Philipsism, in its narrower sense as a management strategy, can be understood as an interwoven set of answers to the combined problems of expanding a flexible unskilled working class while at the same time realizing a vertically differentiating and dynamic urban industrial complex. One central societal field on which such problems emerged was housing. What exactly were the problems for which the Philips housing effort was meant to offer solutions? What were the strategies followed by the company? And how did they relate to the company's growth cycles?

In official Philips representations, company housing has always been presented as a single enduring effort, started at the end of the nineteenth century, to alleviate the perennial local shortage of good working class housing in a quickly growing industrial city.[1] Philips, however, up to 1925–27, was almost exclusively interested in providing living space for salaried employees, production bosses, and skilled artisans such as metalworkers and glassblowers, all of whom were recruited from outside the region. Philips, instead of looking to the housing needs of local proletarian families, only provided space for elite workers. Indeed, the firm used its good housing provisions to attract qualified personnel to the underdeveloped south. Only after 1925–1927, with the inception of a new growth cycle based on radio set manufacturing, did the company turn to the large-scale provision of housing for unskilled workers. Instead of a tradition, then, this was a qualitative and quantitative new concern.

The cause of this new concern with housing for unskilled workers was much more complex and fundamental than has been acknowledged. The housing projects of the radio boom years were a key strategy for Philips to counter the unexpected rise of problems with the control over its unskilled labor force. This was a new and extraordinary problem. Had it not occurred, Philips would certainly not have set aside its "traditional" reluctance to immobilize large stocks of capital in housing projects for common laborers. And without a solution, Philips would probably have not succeeded as a world leader in the market for radio sets. This would have had serious consequences for the post-1945 Dutch industrialization program.

Moreover, housing as a method for reestablishing hegemony over unskilled laborers was in itself not sufficient. Rather, large-scale housing programs for workers during the radio boom years was meant to recreate the large semiproletarian family as a basis for Philips labor recruitment. By 1929, quickly rising demand for unskilled labor in radio set manufacturing had at once created a numerous and mobile proletariat of young lodgers and commuters of both sexes. Consequently, patriarchic and sex-segregating practices, which were essential for both industrial shop floor discipline and paternal authority in families, could no longer be upheld. The discourse of "healthy families" and the impressive investments in workers' housing during 1928–30 were a unique and concerted effort on the part of Philips, supported by the central state, to re-create the large, multiple-earner, unskilled families that had served as the social foundation of the southeast Brabant industrial regimes before the dramatic widening of labor market opportunities in the late twenties.

Philipsdorp

"Philipsdorp" (Philips Village) was built as part of the company's effort to integrate more complex production processes. This resulted in the establishment of the machine shop in 1909 and glass and gas production during the First World War. In other words, Philipsdorp was the urban expression of the company's process of vertical integration. What did its origin in this particular phase of the company's growth imply for the form of the neighborhood and for the sort of people being housed there? And how did it come about?

As pointed out earlier, it had been the unwillingness of the conserva-tive Catholic majority in the city council to provide municipal loans for housing projects that had induced the Philips brothers to first support initiatives for associational building projects in Woensel, and then, in 1909, to start its own building program in Strijp. The former project would provide living space for autochthonous workers, the latter for key immigrant personnel of the Philips company.[2]

It says something of the contradictions of Catholic politics in the Eind-hoven area that the community of Strijp had first tried to block Philips's housing plans on its territory, but then could not and would not prevent piece after piece of private lands, community lands, and church lands being sold to the firm. Philips even found its staunchest and most promi-nent Catholic antagonists very willing to sell their properties for a good price.[3] Consequently, the community that had been the most outspoken critic of entrepreneurial politics during the 1907 cigarmakers lockout was now dramatically transformed. After having lost its political inde-pendence to the city of Eindhoven in 1920, and after much of its land was appropriated by the Philips company, the community of Strijp became an extensive industrial landscape. For decades to come it would feature the most advanced manufacturing complex of the country.

Philipsdorp originally consisted of some two hundred well-designed single family houses in a neighborhood that was modeled on the ideas of the garden cities movement. The place was picturesque, with various architectural niceties. All houses featured sloping roofs and large gar-dens. Streets were romantically shaped, with small, orderly green spots and many trees. The community was centered like a half circle around the Philips sports terrain and looked out behind over wild and rural areas. From 1915 on it was gradually extended by some three hundred houses in a northwestern direction. The famous Amsterdam school architect of this extension, K. P. C. de Bazel, who also contributed to the villa park for Philips's top executives on the other side of the town, gave tree names to the streets so as to underline its green aspirations.[4]

After 1927, Philipsdorp began to lose its semirural and romanticist aesthetic and gradually lost its attraction for those who could afford to settle elsewhere. The new high-rise, massive, and modernist factory blocks for radio set manufacturing were located just between the Philipsdorp community and the railways. It now tended to become the sort of appendage to large-scale mass production its original aesthetic had expressly tried to avert. Its attraction was more and more restricted to those categories of higher-skilled blue-collar workers who were responsible for the flow of production processes at the plants.

Nowadays, almost none of the original inhabitants still live in Philipsdorp. While many recent immigrants from southern European countries settle there and mix relatively easily with the local white working class, the community is increasingly overshadowed by the commercial expansion of the Philips sports stadium. Located on the former public sports terrain, the now postmodern and luxurious stadium is host to the Philips sports club, which since the early 1980s has been one of the most wealthy and successful football organizations in the country.

Though Philipsdorp nowadays delivers a fairly proletarian impression, it was designed for highly skilled metalworkers, technicians, technical drawers, and factory supervisors. Here lived that particular heterogeneous population of well paid and technically schooled blue-collar and white-collar workers who together, in a superficially peaceful but increasingly friction-ridden cooperation, managed and innovated the production process in the early years of corporate capitalism. The earlier part of Philipsdorp provided space for the families of supervisors, clerks, works masters, and skilled metalworkers employed in the lamp factory, the machine shop, and the gradually expanding offices and laboratories. Almost without exception they were immigrants from the urban west and north.[5] The later part was largely inhabited by glassblower families recruited from older production sites in Nieuw Buinen (northeast), Leerdam (river country), and Maastricht (south). Reflecting the high incomes of their inhabitants as well as their standards of living, houses in Philipsdorp were charged rents that exceeded those paid for the associational housing projects in Woensel by 30 to 60 percent.[6]

All of the inhabitants being highly skilled and well-paid immigrants, many with an urban background and with Protestant, liberal, or socialist convictions, it was no wonder that the Catholic village of Strijp saw this modernist enclave as "a collective of strangers."[7] The glassblower families, in addition, were a set of highly cohesive groups, exhibiting idiosyncratic cultural forms and customs. Indeed, all of these immigrants posed a challenge to existing Catholic hegemony as they became active in public life or merely displayed their own styles of leisure and sociability. But being a privileged elite, they did not invoke a Catholic cultural embattlement. Rather, their presence reinforced an inward looking and somewhat fundamentalist tendency in local Catholic life that emphatically stressed the values and ties of invented traditions, a tendency that would become much stronger with the urban and labor market expansion of the late 1920s.

Drents Dorp

Drents Dorp, and the other workers' quarters built between 1925 and 1930, were erected for very different reasons, consisted of completely dissimilar households, and developed a neighborhood and working class culture completely distinct from Philipsdorp. Whereas Philipsdorp was built as part of the regional process of vertical integration of more complicated productions that had formerly been organized elsewhere, Drents Dorp was the spatial expression of the mass manufacturing of radio sets. These new, and for Dutch standards at the time, extensive workers' quarters were the urban product of a nationally unprecedented but short wave of industrial and infrastructural investments that also resulted in the impressive factory outlays at Strijp between 1927 and 1930. Drents Dorp, then, in clear distinction with Philipsdorp, came to house the thousands of unskilled laborers required for the expansion of mass production.

Seen from the point of view of the fundamental forces at work, Drents Dorp was the expression of a little-understood transition in the nature of the urban and industrial processes underlying the area's development. For one, it was the first time that Philips itself had invested large quantities of capital in housing for unskilled working families on a grand scale. This decision therefore signaled the emergence of a form of regional commitment that much exceeded, and qualitatively changed, the corporation's earlier engagements with urban structures and provisions. Moreover, by doing so, industrial management in fact decided to incorporate crucial aspects of working class reproduction into its own field of action, aspects that had hitherto been left to "spontaneous" social processes within the southeast Brabant region. And, as will be shown, these aspects were closely related to precisely the social and regional assets on which the firm's ascent in the global world of electrical production had depended: the reproduction of flexible but disciplined unskilled labor. Indeed, Drents Dorp and the other minor projects of these years were Philips's answer to mounting problems of labor control in its vital mass producing departments.

In spite of its centrality for understanding the social patterns of development of both the Philips corporation and the city of Eindhoven, the origins and function of Drents Dorp (and the other neighborhoods that were built between 1925 and 1930) have been little understood. At least three distinct sorts of explanation for the Philips housing effort in the late twenties have traditionally been given. The first one is an example of anachronistic and essentialistic storytelling. It asserts that the Philips family has always tried to provide good houses for its workers and it refers to Philipsdorp and to the Philips brothers' earlier coalition with Eindhoven socialists for the improvement of the local housing supply.[8] Justified as this argument may seem, it does not recognize the crucial innovation in Philips's building policies in the 1920s. It overlooks the fact that only in the later 1920s did Philips begin to envision whole families of unskilled workers as the inhabitants of company houses. It is a voluntarist explanation in terms of benevolence, an explanation more interested in historical legitimation than in analyzing contradictory historical processes.

A more technocratic and seemingly precise explanation has been given under the concept of housing shortage. This explanation was most comprehensively put forward by the urbanist F. Bakker Schut, who headed the Philips building office between 1929 and 1932.[9] On first glance it again seems a totally acceptable story. The electrical industry grew very quickly, the city expanded rapidly, but the community of Eindhoven, for various reasons, did not itself provide for a large-scale building effort. So what else would one expect, except that the large corporation, with peaking labor demand, decided to do it itself. In his dissertation Bakker Schut even concluded that large industries had a responsibility to do just that.[10]

However self-evident this explanation in terms of housing shortage nowadays may seem, on closer inspection it turns out to be a construction by the professional urbanist, a construction that obscures more than it explains. In building his argument for housing shortage, Bakker Schut relied on two basic observations: the rise in the average number of persons per family house (which in Eindhoven increased to 5.72 by 1930), and the quickly increasing number of lodgers in town (doubling between 1927 and 1930 to slightly more than 15 percent of the local population, that is, in absolute numbers over 13,000 people in a population of almost 90,000).[11] These data led him to conclude that the pressure on private living space in Eindhoven by 1930 was quickly increasing. Inevitably, he argued, this implied a deterioration of the conditions for the day-to-day reproduction of labor power in the town. Current literature from Germany and the United States strongly suggested this close relation between spatial overcrowding and insufficient recuperation from work, as did Bakker Schut's own material on the Eindhoven case. He pointed to steadily rising figures for illness at Philips, an increasing rate of absenteeism from work, and, above all, an alarming rise in the rate of labor turnover (20 percent in 1925, 27 percent in 1929).[12] Finally, Bakker Schut mentioned the less solid and less apparently descriptive observation that a "bad spirit" had been rising among Philips workers all through the later twenties.[13]

But was housing shortage a good interpretation and explanation of these correlations? Or did "bad spirits" and other indices relate to a rather different phenomenon, a phenomenon that was not so instantly captured by the conceptual tools of the professional urbanist? For one, the overwhelming majority of the total of some 2,500 houses that Philips built after 1925 were designed for new immigrant families and not at all for the great numbers of young urban lodgers supposedly in need of better housing. Moreover, the average number of persons that would inhabit the houses of Drents Dorp far exceeded the above mentioned 5.72. There it would amount to as many as an average of 10.44.[14]

When such objections are added to the plurality of meanings that can in fact be attributed to data on absenteeism and labor turnover, the slippery concept of "bad spirits" does begin to open up a different configuration of social phenomena. Strictly interpreted, the figures on lodging, for example, can only support the conclusion that the nature of proletarian household forms was changing in a direction away from the closed single family. This alludes to the possibility that the concept of "housing shortage" may have been nothing more than an accepted vehicle of discussing possible options for action to reshape the emerging household forms of local proletarian life. Taking this line of argument further, the contrast between an unskilled proletariat of young urban lodgers and commuters, and a labor force of whole families in single-family company housing may well move center stage in explaining the Philips building projects.

There is a third explanation for the massive Philips housing effort of the late twenties in Bakker Schut's dissertation. The explanation emphasizes the ultimate financial inevitability for the company to provide living space for its workers. Bakker Schut takes pains to show that the large-scale commuter system that Philips initiated in 1927 in order to augment as far as possible its unskilled labor supply quickly led to very high commuting costs. On average, commuting costs amounted to some 10 percent of the weekly wage of about five thousand commuting laborers. But more serious from the standpoint of the company was that the costs for each additional laborer, who tended to live just a bit further away than the one recruited yesterday, exceeded common house rents in Eindhoven by some 25 percent.[15] What would be more rational than to offer a rental place near the factories to this person? And since the literature available to Bakker Schut suggested that the expensive and disruptive phenomena of illness and labor turnover were much more widespread among tired commuters than among workers living comfortably near their workplace, housing provisions would probably lead to a significant reduction of other secondary labor costs.

But following this logic further, one arrives at a major paradox. The great majority of these commuting workers were unmarried young people, mostly from rural households where diverse sources of income were pooled together. More than half of them were female. Thus, the company could have found a very cheap solution for high commuting costs by offering places in lodgers' compounds or hostels. Provided such hostels were large enough, this could also have led to a substantial decrease of lodging among working families in the town, thereby countering the allegedly high and unwelcome measure of overcrowding. In fact, in 1931, such hostels were realized but only for a very minor number of persons, many of them office clerks. Paradoxically, in countering commuting costs for young single workers, Philips exclusively envisioned large-scale housing schemes for whole families. Again, this cannot but add to the suggestion that it was not so much commuting and lodging per se that were the cause of labor cost increases and "bad spirits," but rather the commuting and lodging proletarian adolescents themselves.

There is good reason to suspect, then, that Philips, in working out its housing schemes, was not primarily seeking solutions for the existing working class of purportedly tired commuters and badly housed lodgers. As we will see, other circumstantial evidence strongly adds to the idea that Philips's unprecedented building projects of the later twenties were essentially meant to facilitate the substitution of this young and mobile, regional proletariat of single workers with a newly recruited working class of whole immigrant families. Working class housing, it seems, was a means to definitely reshape proletarian household forms in a way apparently advantageous to the company.

There is a range of disparate and partly contextual clues that supports the apparent centrality of household forms to Philips's social policies in the later twenties. This evidence also points more directly at the causes for the Philips preoccupation with households: a deepening crisis of labor control caused by the expansion of job opportunities since the start of the radio boom. Widening job opportunities led to the weakening of paternalist authority in working class families and the city as young workers started commuting and lodging. They also triggered an erosion of adolescent labor discipline as job mobility suddenly increased and job segregations of gender and age quickly broke down.

Some of this evidence is presented by the Philips urbanist Bakker Schut himself. For all his emphasis on the costs of commuting and the extent of housing shortage, this cannot distract from the fact that, from the standpoint of the industrial capitalist, what was really dysfunctional was above all the increasing rate of labor turnover.[16] Labor turnover, however, is a concept tainted with employers' interests. What from the employers' position appears as turnover may well be mobility and enhanced labor market capacity on the part of workers. Here the opportunities of the one become the additional costs of the other.

Now for electrical manufacturers, labor turnover is even more costly than for other employers. The immensely concentrated, swift, and demanding manual work under piece-work contracts that is the essence of much of electrical mass production can only be competitively performed by experienced workers who have had training of up to three months. Accordingly, in order to offer attractive enough wages for new workers, electrical companies have to add up to 30 percent on the values that they can actually produce.[17] Thus, high job turnover and the consequent large percentage of inexperienced workers cause a drain on profits for electrical producers.

Electrical manufacturing is, moreover, one of the best examples of what labor sociologists have called "short cyclical labor." "Short cyclical labor" is known to be very tiring and boring. It can in fact be coped with only in a very concentrated atmosphere that offers a minimum of distractions and a maximum of quiet. Young girls have everywhere been the best performers of this kind of job.[18] But only on the condition that they are strictly segregated from boys, as play and courting threaten the necessary discipline.[19] Thus, high rates of labor turnover, especially when they necessitate the end of sex segregation, tend to produce a whole set of additional dysfunctional effects on the fragile work regime of electrical mass manufacturing.

But if a mobile working class is dangerously inefficient and costly in electrical production, this means that stable workers who have adapted to its rules and learned to cope with its regime of discipline are highly valued. They will not so easily be laid off, either, when they lack any formal skills or credentials. Electrical manufacturing might well be one of the best examples of what is in effect an important characteristic of twentieth-century corporate industrialization as a whole: offering security to formally unskilled but sober, obedient, precise, careful, and literate workers. It is a phenomenon that has no precedent in history, before nor after.[20]

This essential working class stability, however, is obviously hard to establish with a proletariat of young, unmarried, lodging, and commuting workers, such as was emerging in great numbers in the Eindhoven area from late 1927 onward. The premium on stability, in fact, put a premium on the family, in particular when more members could be employed.[21] In this form of family employment, as had been common to Philips and other Eindhoven manufacturers before 1924, wage dependencies and family dependencies become interrelated, shared, and therefore multiplied and solidified. The larger the number of household members that earn a wage in a specific industry, the higher the collective income, security, and family status will be, and the more likely it becomes that a family will socialize its offspring according to rules that fit with the cultural preconditions of particular regimes of production. Such multistranded overlapping between production and family is not exceptional; on the contrary, it was quite general all over the industrializing world, including Brabant.[22] The problem of labor turnover, then, as it figured in Bakker Schut's dissertation, was not just a naturalistic representation of a technocratic issue. More importantly, it acted as a pregnant metaphor for addressing the discrepancy between the particular household forms of the Eindhoven working class such as it was emerging and the forms it actually ought to have from the point of view of capitalist electrical manufacturing.

Not only was the discipline on the Philips shop floor eroding since late 1927, but urban and parental relations of authority also seem to have been shifting quickly. In any case this is suggested by the combined information of a series of clues from other sources. One of these clues consists of the rate of recorded criminality in the city of Eindhoven. All sorts of minor offenses, like small theft, maltreatment, public drunkenness, and offenses against moral and sexual virtue had been declining in the town since the years immediately following World War One. But from 1927 on they again began to rise, suddenly and steeply. The sum total of all offenses recorded in the city in 1930 was as much as three times higher than in 1926. The figure for recalcitrance against police officers rose by more than a factor of five.[23] This is telling, because this figure is the most direct indication of the moral prestige attributed to representatives of the established order. Their prestige was falling quickly indeed.

The rise in the figures of recorded criminality was accompanied by a wave of moral panic. The vein of this moral panic, however, was already of older standing. It originated in petty bourgeois and clerical efforts to thwart the perceived liberal defiance of traditional hegemonic claims over the local working population emanating from among the "strangers" employed by the Philips corporation. Especially after the inflation, economic expansion, and temporary local working class wealth of the First World War, these conservative Catholic hegemonic concerns had been mainly directed at the public practices of local adolescents. The Eindhoven Catholic journal *Roomsch Leven* (Roman Catholic Life) from 1919 on fiercely condemned and warned against eating sweets, wearing nylons, going to the cinema, visiting pubs, drinking alcohol, working for secular employers (like Philips), dancing, jazz music (nigger music), and modern sports.[24] Most of all, any form of "modern" girls' amusement, sexually appealing female clothing, and sexually mixed public life was held to be absolutely illicit. As in most Catholic actionism of the time, such practices were denounced as a great danger to the specifically female virtues and female personalities that lay at the roots of a dedicated motherhood. Eindhoven boys were called upon not to let themselves be attracted by such immoral and dutiless femininity.

After 1927, with thousands of jobs opening up for young workers, and 15,000 young lodgers in town, the tone of *Roomsch Leven* became shriller, its warnings more ominous and emphatic. Local activists began to undertake a serious effort to expand the Catholic youth movement, especially among girls. But activists had to concede that the souls of very many of them "were already lost," and that, among Eindhoven working girls, priests harvested more contempt than respect. Eindhoven, which in these years was sometimes called "Dutch Brussels," was held to be the place with the most fallen youth in the Netherlands.[25]

This Catholic fundamentalist discourse of threatened femininity in the Eindhoven region has sometimes been treated as representing age-old visions put forward by antimodernist ideologists who wanted women back within the household and kitchen.[26] But while its vocabulary indeed originated in an earlier epoch, it should not be overlooked that the situation to which it reacted was new, real, and exceptional. Fears for fundamental shifts in relationships between generations and sexes were firmly grounded in the reality of the place, and were not simply the product of the uncontrolled sexual fantasies of repressed "traditional" minds. In this region, in which the incomes of households had long since been greatly dependent on the marketing of adolescent children's labor power, the regulation of their sexual encounters had always been central to parental authority.[27] And parental authority, in its turn, had always been central to the collective income, survival, and status of households. The regional public fascination with gender and sexuality, therefore, was closely related to real popular anxieties about liberating shifts in those parental authority relations that were essential to the organization both of household economies and industrial economies in the region. And while such fears might well have been a recurrent aspect of the region's industrialization process, they only culminated in public alarm when the radio boom so dramatically increased the demand for young workers.

That this public alarm was not just created by conservative political organizations is illustrated by its also being highlighted in the two single examples of regional belles lettres that show an explicit interest in social developments in the area. Although never really engaged with the lives of young electrical workers themselves, this regional literature was very much concerned with the moral consequences of Philips's sudden expansion. In *Het donkere licht* (1930, The Dark Light), one of the early novels of the successful author of regional literature Anton Coolen, a girl from a poor and isolated household in the peat area of "De Peel," thirty kilometers southeast of Eindhoven, is sent to the Philips plants. Her father hopes she will help to alleviate the household's permanent financial hardship.[28] The girl, named Maria Magdalena, is quickly drawn into the culture of Eindhoven working girls. She starts buying nylons, pumps, a short skirt, and an attractive hat. Even more tired and bored by long commuting hours and exhaustive labor, she is gradually lured into the evening pleasures of Eindhoven city, just like the more experienced working girls from her area. Taking an apparently meaningless digression into town on her way to the station, she is readily flattered by a fashionable man who appears really interested in her. She has some violent disagreements at home about coming in too late for dinner. Then at once she decides to sleep with this man and becomes pregnant. Procuring an illegal abortion in Amsterdam, she barely gets to "De Peel" the next night. Bleeding dangerously, she is found in the dark by an old neighbor who had been called upon as a godfather at her birth. The old man does not dare to inform the family, and arranges for her transfer to a hospital the next day. Informed by the doctor, her father feels deeply embarrassed over her behavior, and initially does not want to see her anymore. His shame is quickly overcome by the love for his child and they become united again in the hospital under the outspread arms of a crucifix.

Since Anton Coolen worked from a transparent polarity between the "thousand ties" that connected these people with the land and the alien and alienating modernity of the city, symbolized in the "short skirts," "light blouses," and "above all legs, legs, legs, O what a miserable plumage and coquetry,"[29] this novel could easily be dismissed as just another manifestation of the general conservatism and, indeed, anti-Philipsism of the local, autochthonous intelligentsia. But such is not fully the case. It is significant that this novel was written in 1929. In later work, Coolen always showed himself an outright admirer of Philips's social policies.

Despite its moralist vocabulary and suggestive plot, this novel nevertheless precisely describes the situation emerging in Eindhoven between 1927 and 1930. A young and mobile proletariat flocks to the town in their thousands, gradually mixes, and appropriates the streets after work hours. Coolen vividly captures the liveliness of these streets by dawn, the ubiquitous groups of young male workers strolling the town, the urban and ambitious fashions worn by them, and the sounds they make in passing when trying to relate to girls. The book is certainly limited by Coolen's romantic and schematic juxtaposition of modern and traditional, and by its resultant presentation of the ill fate, powerlessness, and, one would almost say, unwilled anomie of a very inexperienced girl from an exceptionally deferent, very poor, and peripheral background. A concentration on urban lodgers, for example, might have been more realistic and convincing, and their affairs would probably not have inspired such a pitiful vocabulary and fateful plot. But in spite of such ethnographic shortcomings, Coolen did portray the particular relations emerging in Eindhoven during the radio boom years, even if his use of allegory often won out over his roots in realism.

Another novel, by the minor local writer and publicist Henri Maas, shows that local popular fears and aversions, when represented in allegory, did tend to be dressed as an obsession with sexual mores. In *Onder der gloeilamp* (1946, Under the Lamp Bulb), a book written in the thirties in Eindhoven, Maas describes the moral and financial failure of a small and traditional stockings entrepreneur in a local society marked by the nouveaux riches, American-style capitalism, and perverted love practices.[30]

Both the book and the author are little known and appreciated. Maas, a failed Catholic teacher, has been accused of fascist and anti-Semitic leanings. The book does give some reason for such accusations, but more basically he seems to have been a proud though sensitive Catholic moralist and romanticist, who developed some pathologies as a consequence of tragic deaths and illness in his own family life. His book is hard reading, since he is often distracted from his story by loose angers and anxieties. In a highly undisciplined way he expands on all sorts of connotations, rumors, anecdotes, and sidetracks. But Maas does maintain that the novel is based on historical facts. People well acquainted with local society of the time may indeed recognize the personalities of employers, industrial managers, and city councilmen. But more interestingly, Maas combines colorful descriptions of town life with the inevitable blowups and exaggerations to which a pathological observer is inclined.

One of the most salient motifs in the book is the perversion of sexual mores. Such perversion not only brings the key figure down; it also seems to have thoroughly invaded the streets, parks, alleys, corridors, cafés, and cinemas in the town. The author everywhere sees and suspects illicit lovemaking. In his mind, young uneducated workers in the Eindhoven evening can everywhere be expected to quickly and secretly enjoy sex. However, he is not too hard on them. To him, it has been the perversion of local political and economic elites that has made this moral decline possible in the first place.

Here again, just as in Anton Coolen, we see a local author developing his own idiosyncratic observations and judgments on the basis of a very real, unexpected, and to established classes clearly alarming urban situation. In combination with the other information, the sheer fact that the only two novels that we have on Eindhoven relationships in these years should concentrate on changes in sexual behavior, urban practices, and paternalist authority seems to firmly underscore the presumption that the crisis of labor at Philips was not at all limited to the electrical workshops, but also extended to urban and paternal relationships as a whole.

This local community, then, in the years of the radio boom, seems to have been taken by a comprehensive social and moral panic. And this panic, I would suggest, in the light of the evidence presented, was produced by a quickly aggravating crisis of control over young workers' labor and leisure. On the one hand, this situation prompted Philips management to come up with a modern "social" program aimed at the re-establishment of "traditional" authority relations over its unskilled labor force. But on the other, it created a heightened public concern with the moral policing of local adolescents. Even in the later fifties, in respectable, locally rooted working class families, young women could be forbidden to work in Philips offices, let alone factories, and were prevented from wearing short skirts or shorts while touring around on their bicycles. To local fantasy, long legs seemed to lure everywhere, always ready to endanger the well-being of Philips as well as the well-being of households.

By now it seems clear that Drents Dorp and the other quarters built in the course of the radio boom were essential for regaining control over young mass production workers. And they were so, precisely because they facilitated the partial substitution of mobile youth with whole immigrant families. It is not fortuitous that the building of these quarters followed the timing of production expansions and the resultant control crisis by some significant six to eighteen months, depending on how you look at it.

Apart from two minor and partly interrupted projects in the second half of 1925, the building of the first substantial part of Drents Dorp was started in the winter of 1927/28 (195 large family houses), several months after large-scale radio manufacturing commenced.[31] Then, starting in August 1928 two scattered settlements were built just outside the Eindhoven area, taking advantage of low ground prices. In this same period a larger project just realized by a construction firm, consisting of 234 one-family houses, was acquired by the company and made available to unemployed families from the Oss region (in northeast Brabant, along the river Meuse; agribusiness, food processing, chemicals). Finally, only in the late spring of 1929, while the first new "apparatus" plants at Strijp were being opened and the number of lodgers and commuters was already peaking, the building of more than 1,700 one-family houses was started: for example in Drents Dorp (570), Woensel (521), and Tivoli (500 houses, partly outside the Eindhoven area).

Thus it is good to emphasize that working class housing on a really large scale was only to be realized when the production expansions had already been well under way for about one and a half years. Building was started at a point in time when already over 20,000 workers were being employed in a factory complex of which the space had just been more than doubled. Both the new workplaces and the city by then exhibited all the forms of juvenile mobility, sociability, and intermingling of the sexes that to managers and authorities ever more clearly began to appear as a crisis of control. Housing for unskilled workers on such a large scale was not a Philips tradition. Neither was it envisioned when Philips's staff first began to talk about providing living space for large families in 1922 or 1923, nor when the proposal came up to build 500 houses for immigrant families in October 1927.[32] It really seems to be the case that the idea of large-scale housing provisions was suggested only by changes in the culture and composition of the electrical working class consequent upon Philips's production expansions.[33]

It is important to note that it was not only the complex of Drents Dorp that served the housing of (large) immigrant families. To a considerable extent so did the other complexes. They too housed many families from Oss, Gelderland, the northeast, Zeeland, and elsewhere, sometimes concentrated as a group, sometimes scattered. Drents Dorp was outstanding because it showed Philips's labor policies in their optimal form. But such designs really were integral to the whole building effort. Other quarters were often inhabited by families in another phase of the family cycle. The majority of them had children too, but they were still too young to be employed. Houses in those quarters were smaller than Drents Dorp houses because family income was much less and rents had therefore necessarily to be lower.[34] Moreover, even if Philips tried to contract as many large families as possible, it was basically the idea of the whole family with its inevitable mutual ties, loyalties, and responsibilities as such that was crucial for its offensive against young mobile labor. The whole massive round of housing investments in the late twenties was really grounded in the loss of hegemony over adolescent workers.

In spite of the centrality of unskilled workers' housing for resolving Philips's problems of labor control, and, of course, for facilitating successful radio set production, the corporation was not at all prepared to use its own capital stocks to that goal. Here again we encounter a fundamental difference with the social dynamics underlying earlier building projects for skilled workers and clerks, which were readily financed by the company. Philips was so reluctant to immobilize capital for "mass" workers that it decided to do so only after the central government agreed to a loan of 80 percent of the costs. This again underscores that, instead of a tradition, this was really a completely new project, realized on greatly different premises and grounded in fundamentally different problems and dynamics. Evidently, also in the midst of a great expansion of mass production, unskilled workers were not to be treated as human capital.

The central government could provide this loan under the stipulations of its "welfare policy." In the 1920s the Dutch state made an effort to diminish unemployment and poverty in regions like the northeastern peat district of Drenthe. It aimed to remove families voluntarily from crisis-striken regions to places with an expanding labor demand. The areas of immigration were the Twente textile region, the Limburg mines in the far south, and Eindhoven. Such immigrant areas received state support for housing provisions and removal costs. It was a very convenient and market-oriented way of combining humanitarian amelioration of supposed hardship without a real regional or industrial engagement by the central state. Simultaneously, it helped to further the expansion of national centers of industrial production and employment by organizing extra supplies of cheap unskilled labor. The Philips housing investments at Eindhoven in the years 1929 and 1930 were the largest projects ever organized on these premises. They claimed over 50 percent of total national housing expenses for these years.[35]

The facilities of this "welfare policy" were very congenial to the labor market aims of the Philips company, as it was not the state that would select the applicants but the future employers themselves. Philips thus could freely realize its highly specific labor demands and could compose a whole new working class after its own appetite. Reflecting the company's labor needs, its selection was based on a combination of household-demographic, sociocultural, and individual capability criteria.[36]

First, the company demanded that the families to be contracted would offer at least three daughters over the age of thirteen, plus some younger children who would enter the factories at a later date. This large number of children was required not only because young and female workers were the human basis of Philips's mass production, but also because Philips felt obliged to pay fathers more than the actual value of their labor. Their jobs, from the viewpoint of the company, were primarily a guarantee for family loyalty and cohesion, as well as a form of parental status support.[37] Subsequently, members of such families had to go through a set of "psychotechnical" tests in a mobile laboratory that would decide on the basis of their exact physical and mental capabilities, the sorts of jobs they could successfully learn to perform. Applicants should not be too intelligent, creative, or ambitious, as that would give them too hard a job with "short cyclical" work in mass producing departments.[38] Finally, the company was expressly not seeking job applicants among the most proletarian groups of the crisis areas. Impoverished peat diggers, for example, were expected to be too mobile and restless to adapt easily to the highly disciplined circumstances of continuous electrical mass production and the urbanization produced by it.[39]

In Drenthe and other northeastern provinces, Philips in this way recruited 554 large families, on average consisting of 10.44 members (including parents). Of all these family members more than six were instantly employed at the factories (one father, 3.16 daughters, 1.88 sons).[40] Families recruited elsewhere often exhibited comparable characteristics. Thus the Dutch state's "welfare policy" and its housing loans made possible the re-creation of an unskilled electrical proletariat such as had successfully been employed by Philips before 1924.[41] Among this new working class of large immigrant families, comparable relationships between generations and sexes developed as had originally reigned among local Philips workers. Collectively dependent on each other for family income, jobs, status, and security, the family would again supervise young workers at home and in their neighborhoods so as to prepare them for the strict regime of electrical mass production. On the shop floor these adolescents would again allow a marked sex segregation, and a strict regimentation and supervision.[42]

SEGMENTED WORKERS, DIVIDED CITY:
PHILIPSISM IN FAMILY BIOGRAPHIES

Human lives in Philipsdorp and Drents Dorp were physically proximate but in terms of the opportunities, histories, and the social experiences of their inhabitants they were widely separated. As I have argued earlier, segmentation of work and workers, and its multiple consequences in the everyday, was probably the inevitable condition of a local society based on export-oriented electrical mass manufacturing. A good way to explore what this fundamental segmentation actually meant beyond the more formal aspects of production regimes and housing structures is to study family histories and biographies. Being a product of the same social forces that also shape the urban and industrial landscapes in which their subjects' lives unfold, family histories and biographies can deliver rich impressions of what such forces meant, presumed, and accomplished on the everyday ground of human existence, in work, family, and leisure.

With this purpose in mind, five such family histories and biographies are explored here, three from Drents Dorp and two from Philipsdorp. However, I will not present them in the manner in which such histories are commonly presented, that is, with the informant as narrator in the first person, answering questions posed by the interviewer, or narrating his or her life story chronologically.[43] Instead, I will paraphrase the informants and will consciously present their stories in a way best suited to illuminate the myriad forms in which the forces of Philipsism became meaningful in their lives. This form of presentation is chosen because it is most economic given its purpose here, which is explicitly not a detailed interest in human lives per se as is often the case in oral history projects. Secondly, even in such "naturalistic" presentations the original materials are thoroughly selected, edited, and retouched by researchers, delivering the incorrect and sometimes indiscreet impression that they really were narrated that way.

Moreover, instead of gathering information on individuals, I primarily searched for insight into families. Like most anthropologists, I did this in various ways, ranging from formal and recorded life interviews to unstructured collective talks and cozy personal chats.[44] Often I also interviewed other family members, sometimes of a different generation, in order to get a more comprehensive, dynamic, and richer picture. Subsequently I had to construct rather dense portraits from disparate materials. These portraits, thus, are to a substantial degree interpretive constructs by the researcher, enabling one to see the intricate interweaving of large-scale and apparently anonymous social forces with the intimate lives of families and individuals in time and space.

I will start with an admittedly flat portrait of A. de Broekert, a central figure in Philipsdorp. It is not a real portrait since it merely mentions some relevant facts of his professional and political life. It only serves to give an impression of the opportunities and social visions of capable technicians and white-collar employees at Philips. This group should not be overlooked in an exploration of Philipsdorp lives because it definitely set the tone in the older parts of the neighborhood.

Then, in order to indicate the distance between a white-collar worker like de Broekert and the skilled blue-collar artisans who also inhabited Philipsdorp, a portrait is presented of the Koopman family, a family of highly skilled glassblowers who lived in a younger part of Philipsdorp.[45] This is a long and dense family portrait, covering a historical period

stretching well into the second half of the nineteenth century. It is pregnant with suggestions as to the multiple and intricate ways in which
skilled blue-collar workers would appropriate the structure of opportunities and constraints of Philipsist accumulation.

The Drents Dorp portraits of the Sipkes, de Bondt, and Van Uden
families that follow all feature the typical backgrounds and experiences
of the large, daughter-rich families from the northeast who passed Philips's "psychotechnical" testing. They are less dense and complicated
than the Koopman portrait, maybe because in spite of their inferior status, their lives, in retrospect, have been more clear-cut and less ambivalent than those of highly skilled artisans at Philips. Nevertheless, they
deliver a close and intimate view of their relevant experiences before and
within Philipsism. Above all, the Drents Dorp portraits collectively underscore the great social divide that lay between their own projects and
capacities and those of the Philipsdorp inhabitants.

(Hi)stories from Philipsdorp

De Broekert

A. de Broekert was born in 1879.[46] He worked at the large shipyards of
De Schelde and Wilton Feynoord at Rotterdam and was contracted by
Philips in 1899 to supervise the maintenance of factory buildings and
technical installations. Although he only enjoyed an intermediate level
technical education (MTS), he made an impressive career at the firm. He
became responsible for safety and sanitary issues in the Philips factories
and neighborhoods, started the Philips fire brigade, and finally, in 1922,
became general manager of Philips's *technische bedrijven* (technical enterprises). In 1929 he assumed the function of director of the newly formed
Philips building office, directing more than a thousand workers who
were then employed on the great housing and factory projects. The corporation's international expansion, starting in the later twenties, gave
him the opportunity to lead the construction of factories and installations all over Europe. Already by 1910 he earned a regular salary of more
than 2,000 guilders a year, which was two or three times as much as the
average skilled blue-collar worker. He became one of the professionals in
whose hands the upsurge of Philips rested.

Around 1910 de Broekert was active in local socialism and in the local
branch of the Algemene Nederlandsche Opzichters en Tekenaars Bond
(General Dutch Union of Supervisors and Drawers). He repeatedly de-

fended local radicals against the more die-hard Philips-minded Eind-hoven socialists like the influential Philips gatekeeper Jansen. In early 1912, however, in the immediate aftermath of the failed metalworkers strike, he was nevertheless one of the initiators of the Philips Association for Higher Personnel, a leisure club undoubtedly inspired by Gerard Philips's unwritten wish to separate skilled workers and supervisors in their leisure time.[47] De Broekert might not have been aware of this inten-tion, but he played a prominent part. In 1915 Philipsdorp voted him into the Strijp council as the representative of Ons Aller Belang (Our Com-mon Interest) party, among other things to curb Catholic plans for a tax-supported church and women's cloister near Philipsdorp. After the 1920 annexation of surrounding municipalities by the city of Eindhoven, he became the paramount local protagonist of the Vrije Democraten (Free Democrats), a left-liberal organization not unsympathetic to socialism though emphatically not underwriting its stronger pleas for workers' power and solidarity.

De Broekert's life course clearly testifies to the great opportunities the ever differentiating and expanding internal labor market at Philips of-fered to the educated and talented people of Philipsdorp. Having en-joyed an intermediate-level technical education, de Broekert became the leader of several academics and hundreds of workers in large projects all over Europe. His close and successful engagement with the Philips ex-pansion, however, led him to part from his earlier collaboration in local socialist clubs with skilled workers and embrace a more elegant, socially enlightened liberalism that fitted better with the circles convening in the Philips Association for Higher Personnel. In fact, similar politico-cultural experiences were common among the more prominent white-collar peo-ple in Philipsdorp. De Broekert's life course may have been outstanding in the neighborhood for how far it got him, but it was not exceptional in the direction it took. Indeed, many of the better educated and more talented inhabitants experienced never expected personal opportunities in the later 1910s and 1920s.

The Koopman Family

Jan Koopman (ca. 1880) had been a specialist artisanal glassblower at the Dutch glassworks in Leerdam. More precisely, he had been one of the artisanal collaborators of Jan Copier, the famous Dutch designer of fine glass products. Jan and his wife Anna had seven children, four of them boys. The three oldest boys were apprenticed to their father. Koopman was a respected though somewhat idiosyncratic inhabitant of the glass-making center of Leerdam, a small town in the old polder landscape between the great rivers. His youngest son Chris (b. 1916) remembers that he used to take a walk through town on Sunday mornings, wearing an impressive black top hat that emphasized his strong tall figure as well as his personal independence. The streets were silent on those Sunday mornings, since everyone, except his father and his older brothers, was attending church. Indeed, Koopman earned more than ordinary workers could ever hope to but refused to share in the bourgeois codes of fine public conduct.

Koopman's enviable position notwithstanding, Philips in 1923 had convinced him to move to Eindhoven by offering a good job not only to himself but also to his glass-blowing sons. No secure jobs had been available for them at Leerdam. As soon as they arrived at their rental house in Philipsdorp, Chris still vividly remembers (1992), that his father took a bottle of brandy from his large cane suitcase, invited his older sons, and quickly emptied it to the bottom. It was a noisy toast on their new collective future. Chris and his mother and sisters could only be spectators. It turned out to have been a good decision to come to Eindhoven. By the late twenties the three older sons were all holding secure and well-paid positions in the expanding glass factory. They had their own families now, and lived in good rental houses in Philipsdorp, close to their parents.

In addition to being some of the best glassblowers in the country, Koopman and his three sons were also renowned billiard players and outspoken socialists. They used to play billiards at a range of cafés near Philipsdorp, which were situated in a plebeian and industrial area between the southernmost part of Woensel and the railways, significantly called *'t eindje* (the dead end). The place had such a bad reputation that the youngest son Chris was absolutely forbidden to go there. The notorious shabbiness of the place, however, did not at all affect the social standing of the proud young glassblowers. They were absolute champions in these surroundings and often brought home money they had won and a wealth of good stories.

Sometimes the Koopman's house was turned into a gathering place for local socialists, some of them colleagues at the glass ovens. They used to talk politics there, tell each other the latest events, drink, and sing socialist songs. The Koopmans also regularly attended local socialist rallies, but none of them ever felt like taking up any formal position in the movement.

Mother Koopman, as remembered by her youngest son, consciously kept distance from this collective male world of glassblower socialists. She was from a wealthy Protestant farmers' family in the river country, and, in contrast to her husband, had remained loyal to her religious affiliation. On Sundays, she and her three daughters always attended church; they were well dressed and left the men alone with their own leisure pursuits. As a housekeeper she was very clean. She woke up at six in the morning to start housework and prepare meals for the workers. She obliged everyone to take a bath twice a week. Evidently, she gave her daughters an outstanding female education, as they were all to become maids with high-standing families in The Hague.

The youngest son Chris, who was seven years old when they moved to Eindhoven, was not intended for glassblowing. He was quite a good student and his father decided that he should learn the necessary skills for a white-collar position. But against his teacher's advice his father would not allow him to go to college. "That is not fitting for him," Jan Koopman often declared. He sent Chris to the Philips Educational Institute, only a hundred yards from the parents' house. Chris took courses in bookkeeping and commercial correspondence and was a dedicated student. In 1930, just before the onset of mass layoffs, he got a job at the institute.

One incident that Chris remembers most vividly took place when he had been chatting with a fine girl from one of the neighboring blocks at the main street of Philipsdorp, just after a course at the Philips institute. She was the daughter of a high-ranking Philips executive. Suddenly he saw his father coming from the direction of the glass factory, much earlier than he was used to. The father approached the two of them with long strides and grasped Chris by the ears. Chris got a powerful kick in the ass and his father growled "go home at once." Chris went off without objections and never talked about the incident again, but now he regrets his silence. He is still not sure what it was that could have made his father so angry. Maybe he was supposed to be studying at home. Maybe he should not have tried to communicate with that girl. But if so, why? He is not sure which explanation is correct. It may well be both. He never talked to the girl again, nor was he ever seen again with another girl from the neighborhood. A year or so later, an older brother took him to the canteen of the football club where he was serving drinks during dance evenings. Chris fell in love there, at first glance, with a quick-witted and beautiful Catholic girl from plebeian Woensel. Later in the thirties he married her.

In the 1930–32 crisis none of the Koopman glassblowers were among the at least fourteen thousand workers who were laid off. Their skills had apparently become indispensable to the firm. Or Philips perhaps did not dare to risk losing them all by firing one. Chris, however, was dismissed. Pleas by Dr. Bonebakker, the director of the Educational Institute, and by his father were without effect. Up until 1937 he worked with traders and shopkeepers in the inner city, performing all kinds of jobs a smart teenage boy was capable of, such as driving lorries and managing minor commercial transactions. His girlfriend too was serving retailers in the inner city and they often saw each other after work, or during lunch, and had a good time together.

Throughout this part of the family portrait, there emerge some suggestive clues as to the experiences, motivations, and sensitivities of a family of self-aware, artisanal glassblowers in the Philips context. The portrait seems to point to a complex relation with the dominant culture of white-collar workers in the corporation and the neighborhood. The ambivalence of this relation was apparently projected onto the youngest son Chris, who was denied access to glassblowing and destined to become a clerk.

Although Chris repeatedly asserted that he had enjoyed a happy youth, it appears that he occupied a rather uneasy position in the family. Being denied access to glassblowing, including the collective male experiences connected with it, he was also effectively barred from the wider male culture in his family. There may have been a good labor market reason for the paternal decision to let him become an office clerk, but in fact it amounted to his virtual exclusion from the male world that dominated his family. Thus, he never learned even to play billiards, nor did he ever enter the cafés that his brothers used to frequent. Never invited to take his part in political happenings, he was excluded from their culture and politics.

Paradoxically, neither was his white-collar career allowed a head start. With the same absence of explanation as when his father had brutally ended his incipient relation with an executive's daughter, he also refused him access to college. There was no financial reason for this. Taking the whole context into account, it does not seem too far-fetched to suggest that Jan Koopman, although silently acknowledging the limits of his trade and background, was not prepared to let his youngest son become completely alienated from it. Probably, the successful and position-conscious artisanal glassblower remained suspicious of the patronizing tone of the dominant white-collar culture at Philips. Accordingly he sent

Chris to the part-time courses of the nearby Educational Institute and kept a close watch over his actions. While Chris was denied access to glassblowing, he was also never given full parental support to enter into the white-collar world either.

It is revealing how Chris's narration and memory become much more detailed, lively, and colorful when he is finally invited to talk about his dealings with inner-city commerce and his friendship with his Catholic girl from Woensel. Evidently, both the inner city and the Woensel girl were distant enough from Philipsdorp for his father, and for Chris himself, to finally breathe again. But the incident with the executive's daughter at Philipsdorp, somehow a condensation of the whole complex of cultural ambiguities, could never be forgotten, nor ever be talked about.

Similar ambiguities were acted out in the family of Koopman's second son Jan (junior).[48] Father Koopman had put high pressure on his glass-blowing sons to become excellent at their trade. Later, his son Jan would often reiterate the story to his own children, how, as an apprentice, he once had failed to perform a task well enough and was suddenly kicked right in his face with his father's wooden shoe. He almost fainted, he said, but didn't think of crying. The story transmitted the idea that his father's harsh teaching methods had been very successful, and had indeed been basic to this household's current wealth.

Jan (jr.) had quickly attained the artistic level of his father and even surpassed him in the course of time. After the Second World War, Jan (jr.) was widely known to be the best artisanal glassblower in the country, if not in Europe. English and American officers, purportedly, were heavily impressed by his craftsmanship. His younger brother Chris still vividly recalls having observed him standing in the top of the glass factory, solemnly moving under the windowed roof, surrounded by a dozen astonished glassblowers, singlehandedly blowing a two-meter glass tube.

While glassblowing at Philips was largely mechanized and deskilled in the thirties, Jan (jr.) became the outstanding artisan working on all kinds of special products like giant lighthouse lamps or complex glass instruments. He became the very richest blue-collar worker in town. In addition to his high regular weekly wage, he earned large amounts of cash for blowing special artistic glassware in his "own time," for the highest Philips executives and others. Jan (jr.) carried his own keys to the glass factory and spent nights and weekends blowing precious objects for whoever could afford them. Finally, he even managed to get a monthly salary and the related advantage of a white-collar pension. At first, management would not allow him this, but then he threatened to move to Maastricht (another glassmaking center), as he often used to recall, and his superiors realized at once that they had no choice but to accept his demands.

Jan junior often took his family out for weekends and short vacations. They went to popular resorts like Scheveningen and Valkenburg, where he arranged the best of hotels. His youngest son Chris (born in 1939, and named after his youngest uncle) recalls (1992) being the first one in Philipsdorp in the fifties to drive a magnificent red Italian scooter.[49] His father used to give him anything he wanted, such as the finest clothes, not only to show him his affection but also, Chris (jr.) believes, to demonstrate his wealth to a by now predominantly blue-collar Philipsdorp.

The atmosphere at home, however, was not good. Chris (jr.), who was a very sensitive boy, openly preferred to be with his Catholic girlfriend's family in Woensel (indeed he also found a girl from a lower status community in Woensel). By so doing, he exposed himself to recurrent parental misgivings about her family's inferior social status. Philipsdorp was not a bad place to live for a teenage boy, but, as Chris says, you never went into the other houses, or, for that matter, invited the other people into your house. In his observations the picture emerges of a privatized local culture riddled with tales of status. Against this culture, and against his parents' failure to escape it, Chris openly demonstrated his love for the more easygoing life among autochthonous Brabant workers. Painful for them as it was, his parents often and impatiently inquired whether they were just not good enough for him.

Chris junior did his best at secondary school, but he was nervous, could hardly concentrate, and finally failed. After a period of not knowing what to do, he reached an existential turning point in which, as he says, he suddenly realized that he wanted to become a glassblower himself, like his older brothers and the other males in his family. He successfully applied to the Philips Industrial School for Boys, and made rapid progress. In 1992 he still wondered about that sudden insightful and almost magical moment in which he chose to fully embrace his family's tradition. He knows that it is hardly believable to an outsider, but from the very moment that he blew his first glass object he felt all through his body that he was finally on the right track. As was the case with most family members, his glassblowing skills gradually attained a high level of excellence. In the early sixties he became a central teacher of glass instrument making at the Philips Industrial School. Later, he was one of the initiators of a glassblowers' professional association in the country.

Finally appearing ready to appropriate his family's tradition, Chris (jr.), in those years, however, turned up less and less at his parents' house in Philipsdorp. The atmosphere was not pleasant. There were constant frictions. Among other things, their habit of spending several hours each Sunday on that long and silent walk to Grandfather's grave annoyed him greatly. One late night, Grandfather had returned from playing billiards at the Philips leisure locale, just opposite Philipsdorp. He had probably drunk too much. Crossing the main street, he was hit by a car, lay there bleeding on the street for several hours, was finally found and carried home, but died some time afterward. Grandfather, subsequently, never left his son's mind. On family occasions Jan Koopman junior used to offend his wife by endlessly singing socialist songs like those he had sung with Koopman senior and his brothers in their early Philips years. He went on and on, evading contact with anyone. This obsessive habit finally alienated him irrevocably from his youngest son Chris junior. When Jan Koopman (jr.) again started humming such songs at his wife's funeral, Chris (jr.) felt like leaving him alone forever.

A complex and compressed family (hi)story like this Koopman portrait gives a wealth of indications as to how skilled working people, entering into the new and specific practices, places, and relationships of Philipsist accumulation succeeded or didn't succeed in connecting the new with the old; their private lives, families, and capabilities with those of others; their own histories with that of Philips corporation. I do not want to try to explain at length the structures of the Koopman story, but it is clear that for the Philipsdorp people the possibilities of forging relatively solid and coherent ties among each other were, in a multitude of ways, crisscrossed by their possible ties, opportunities, and responsibilities with and within the patterns of the Philipsist expansion.

Both de Broekert and the Koopmans were peculiarly successful. But each paid their particular price for career and prosperity. The Koopmans uneasily struggled with their trade and their family cohesion, with their pride and their independence in the context of a dominant, self-assured, and prospering white-collar corporate culture. For themselves and each other they certainly created less happiness than they longed for. Theirs is a victorious but nevertheless tragic family story. Of course, it is highly idiosyncratic in its particular composition. But the Koopmans' inability to find a really comfortable place in the Philips world was certainly exemplary of the many ambivalences skilled blue-collar families experienced. Such ambivalences could spring from diverse sources, such as unequal cultural competition at work and in the neighborhood, the insecurity and loneliness of career, or the perennial threat of deskilling on the Philips shop floor. But in each case, Philipsism as a mode of accumulation clearly did give something to people as well as appropriating something from them.

The two histories presented here, then, deliver some sense of the backgrounds and careers of the people of Philipsdorp. Although many inhabitants were certainly less successful than de Broekert or the Koopmans, the place nevertheless was pregnant with aspiration. Generally well placed to take a chance when the opportunities arose, many people from Philipsdorp, either through their hands, their heads, or their character, though mostly by combining the three, came to embody the popular advancement in which the Philips corporation increasingly and not unjustifiably took pride.

(Hi)stories from Drents Dorp

(Hi)stories of Drents Dorp families were different. They did not possess the skills that could propel them forward in the large corporation. Lacking marketable skills, they were explicitly recruited for their large, daughter-rich families and the undemanding, highly adaptive, and quiet personalities they had brought. Though living in adjacent, and at first glance quite identical neighborhoods, these worlds of Philips labor were far apart.

The Sipkes Family

In February 1928, the Sipkes family had migrated to Eindhoven. Seven of the thirteen children were girls. They came from Onstwedde, a small dispersed village in the empty northeastern marshes, where, during the season, they had been employed as a team of landless laborers. All family members above ten years old had been hired for the potato harvest on one of the large Groningen farms. In winter, their situation had been precarious as they had rarely had an income. Later in the twenties this improved somewhat because father Sipkes found a winter job in a nearby fertilizer factory, carrying sacks from and to the ships. He also used to make some money by hiring out his horse on calm days to the captains of sailing vessels. But with the rise of motor power in the course of the twenties this source of income dried up.

Mother too had earned some cash by serving as a maid at the nearby

Protestant school. In that task she was assisted by Elsien, her third oldest daughter. As a little girl Elsien had to wake up each morning before the others and take care of the coal stoves in the two classrooms, and during the day she was often called for various housekeeping tasks. Later she failed at school because she had hardly been able to follow lessons.

In spite of their unrelenting, multiple, and strenuous collective efforts, both members of the family whom I interviewed (1991), Elsien (b. 1915) and Jan (b. 1917), passionately described how, before their Eindhoven years, they had been living in dire poverty. After the Philips recruiting team had offered them the opportunity to move to Eindhoven, their conditions changed for the better, as both interviewees independently agreed. Father Sipkes, his oldest son, and the two oldest daughters were able to start work immediately. The son (just like Jan at a later date) went to the glass factory to become a glassblower's apprentice and learn the new mechanized production processes. The father and the two girls were placed in the "apparatenfabriek," where they mounted radio lamps. One child after the other, following their fourteenth birthday, entered the Philips factories, except for the two youngest. The youngest boy enjoyed extensive trade schooling at the Philips industrial school and became a glass instrument maker. The youngest daughter made a lifelong career as a waitress at the Philips headquarters, and never married. Thus, in the early thirties, although its members were now employed on individual industrial tasks, the household still functioned as a wage-earning collective. But in contrast to comparable households in the northeast, this family could now earn a considerable and steady income of more than seventy guilders a week. This was far above the earnings unskilled laborers could ever make in most other places in the Netherlands at the time.[50]

The memories of their arrival in Eindhoven seem to be shaped by their consciousness, in retrospect, of how right their decision to move to the south had in fact been. Their memories emphasize the great cultural distance between the electrical town and the northeastern countryside. Jan is still amused when he tells his story. Sitting in the train and approaching Eindhoven, he had looked out from the window and seen football teams playing. He had never seen anything like this before and he was excited. He called the others and commented that a magnificent public festival was going on. Up until today, this anecdote is often reiterated in the family. Elsien remembers the delight of seeing for the first time large red tomatoes, and of their putting on the electric lamp above their beds with just one simple action. Indeed, it was the first time they had enjoyed the pleasure of sleeping in a bed that was exclusively made for that purpose.

The ugliness of life in the northeast could not have been better inscribed in memory than through the story Elsien and Jan both told about their departure from Onstwedde. Just one day before the departure was planned, the village baker had discovered that the Sipkes boy who had been his servant had shared out bread to several poor families for free. Before they were allowed to depart, the whole family was now forced to labor one long day in the baker's fields. Through this story, also frequently narrated, Onstwedde was condensed to the inescapability of unremitting and unrewarding labor. In collective memory, it was Philips that had helped them to escape both the place and the poverty.

But in spite of this positive memory, Elsien does not make an attempt to deny that their daily work in the *apparatenfabriek* had been "absolutely without hope," worse even than the harsh and long labor on the northern soil. Like so many other young girls, she had wept many times. "The coats," as the Philips supervisors were commonly called, had "driven her mad." And that was also true for her sisters. Even nowadays, she can still physically sense the fear she had experienced as a girl.

The mother kept the household running and tried to keep up the sometimes sad spirits of the young. The father was now much more exhausted by his work than he had ever been before, and tended to withdraw from the liveliness of his large family.[51] With thirteen children the small house was terribly overpopulated. The older children were all introducing friends and lovers from the neighborhood, and all these friends and lovers very much liked the family's open and busy atmosphere. The large living room downstairs was often crowded by groups of young workers playing cards, telling stories, preparing for a ball game, or whatever. During weekends the number of eaters sometimes exceeded twenty. Assisted by her daughters, mother Sipkes saw no problem. To her this was nothing compared to her tasks in Onstwedde.

But though one never ran the risk of feeling alone, Elsien emphasized that the absence of any secure form of privacy could also be very oppressive. Indeed, it could make one feel very lonely. Sometimes she would cry and run away from home. She would hang around for some hours in the neighborhood until she finally calmed down. Really, there was nowhere else to go. The oppressive shortage of private space and time was aggravated still further by the mother's habit of helping migrants from the north and taking them in as lodgers. One of those lodgers even ran a milkman's business, which claimed a lot of scarce space in the home and the garden. Elsien, after so many years, could still feel the shame she had had for the "perennial mess" at home. Although emphatically underlining her mother's clean and civilized habits, she confided that as a girl she had always refused to accept this overcrowding as normal. She had made constant efforts at seclusion from goings-on in the family. And she had frequently demonstrated her disapproval by an ostensible silence.

In the north the family had felt in tune with the growing wave of agricultural socialism in the region. Never real activists, they had been silent but convinced supporters of any sort of emancipatory thinking. In Eindhoven, too, everyone in the family voted for social democracy. Some of the older girls also participated in local socialist leisure life, such as the socialist musical association and the theater club. But they were not really drawn into practical politics. Only once or twice they had walked in the march on the first of May. None of the boys got into this. In Eindhoven all of them became fervent football players. Like so many other boys in the Philips neighborhoods, they spent all their free time with sports. Some of the girls also played handball.

The crisis of the early thirties meant the dismissal of two of the then five electrical workers in the family. Two girls were fired, one was kept; the father and the oldest son were also able to hold their jobs. Elsien was among the dismissed, exchanging the drudging work at the plants for the busy tasks of housekeeping. She believes she and her sister were called back to work after some three months.

The de Bondts Family

The de Bondts were a family of six, with four daughters between thirteen and seventeen years old at the time of arrival in Eindhoven. They had migrated from Nieuw Buinen (Drenthe) to Eindhoven in the autumn of 1927. Father and mother had run a grocery store there, but the worsening crisis in peat digging and local agriculture after the First World War had made it harder and harder to survive. In Nieuw Buinen they had been respected members of the local citizenry, closely and actively engaged with the Dutch Reformed Church. In Eindhoven their religious conviction was actively sustained, and the family, as before, kept away from other forms of public life.

The three oldest daughters were offered jobs in the assembly departments of the *apparatenfabriek*. Though Ellen (b. 1913), the third daughter and one of the two daughters I interviewed, no longer had any precise memories of work at the plants, she was still easily overwhelmed by the feeling of how oppressive the work had been. The pace was just as high as neighborhood girls had warned them of, and supervision by "the coats" had made them very nervous indeed. Their youth in Drents Dorp had been happy, but the girls did not so often mix with the numerous groups of teenagers out on the street, as they spent their free hours in the Protestant Youth Association or indoors.

The father, not being skilled in an industrial occupation, became the operator of a large factory elevator, bringing crowds of young laborers to and from their departments. He had a uniform and a cap, and, as his two surviving daughters underlined (1992) with a smile, he had been visibly proud of wearing it. All, including the mother, had been silently impressed when he returned from work wearing his dark uniform over his tall upright figure. Sometimes he used to tell stories about workers he had debunked for not behaving orderly in "his" elevator. He himself had always been a very punctual person and he expected all other people, above all his own family, to be the same.

As far as his daughters know, their father had never been a member of a labor organization or of a political party, nor had he ever shown interest in such worldly things. Of basic importance to him and their mother had been the Reformed Church. Religious education was a central part of the daily life of the household. Before each meal, which was always enjoyed together, the father used to read prayers. Everyone listened with deference until the father, sitting at the head of the table, had finished reading and praying and had invited them to take the food.

The youngest daughter Petra (b. 1916), who was initially too young to be employed, often read the Bible, both alone and with her father. She was very careful and concentrated and liked learning. After the Philips primary school she was unexpectedly offered a place at the Philips department for social work. This was really extraordinary since the women working there had all enjoyed a professional education at the Amsterdam school for social work, and came from middle-class urban backgrounds. Her family's respectability and religious devotion as well as her own seriousness had probably so impressed the responsible people at the Philips social and educational services that they decided to keep her away from the factories and offer her the opportunity for a different career.

During the thirties crisis, Petra was the only earner in the family not to be dismissed. The three other girls were all laid off temporarily. Ellen cannot remember well how long the period of her unemployment had been, but she can very well recall how delightful it had been not to go to the plants early each morning. Father de Bondt too was fired. But how he had felt about that, or how their mother had dealt with her sorrows, had been absolutely beyond the sorts of knowledge permitted to the women I interviewed. Their parents do not seem to have talked about it either. Everyone suffered in silence, my interviewees supposed. Both daughters are sure, however, that their father had been painfully offended by his dismissal. They tend to think that all of them returned to work within a few weeks.

Though of course very diverse, both these family histories point to key features of the social experiences that shaped the working class culture of Drents Dorp. For one, both families did not at all resemble the then current stereotypes of the mobile seasonal workers and rude peat diggers from the northeast that were produced by the national "welfare" policy effort. Indeed, the migration campaign as organized by Philips corporation was simply not directed at the most poverty-stricken northeastern population groups. Philips expressly tried to recruit respectable families. They had to show a longing for a stable life and steady earnings, and had to exhibit the social discipline and hygienic habits deemed necessary for a "healthy" working life in mass-producing industry.[52]

The de Bondt family very much coincided with the Philips picture of the ideal working class family. They had no proletarian experience at all, no industrial and no wage work history. Instead, their history was marked by a difficult struggle for maintaining independence, expressed in everyday life as a religiously sanctioned exercise in respectability and a sober, disciplined lifestyle. The father took the same stature of the solid, responsible, hierarchic though benevolent authority that within Philips official imagery was increasingly attributed to the Philips family itself. Moreover, they had led the inner-directed, privatized lives that were thought to be most "healthy" for electrical workers.[53]

Although much more open to the world and without religious convictions, the Sipkes too had a collective experience of passionately trying to keep up respectable habits. Unsteady earnings served as the grand explanation for the family to move to Eindhoven. Moreover, the Sipkes parents also had evident and symbolically important roots in small-scale ownership and independence. Grandparents from both sides had been smallholding and house-owning peasant workers. Father Sipkes himself still cultivated this background by retaining his horse, which, though enabling some income sometimes, certainly became an expensive affair later in the twenties. Indeed, the earliest memory of his father that son Jan was still able to evoke was on horseback, wearing a large broadsided black hat. Such memories are not fortuitous. As students of popular memory insist, it is not without significance that one remembers this thing and forgets another. Amnesia is very selective. Indeed, a reminiscence such as this is intimately connected with the deep historical symbolism of family orientations. And finally, although the Sipkes knew none of the paternalist hierarchy that ordered female lives at the de Bondts' house, it appears that the Sipkes women themselves, in a much more egalitarian way, formed the backbone of their family's everyday work and morality. Among the Sipkes girls there was probably more open condemnation of work regimes at Philips, and perhaps more crying too. But they all went to the plants, day after day. And none of them gave up the responsibility vis-à-vis the family. All remained attached to the collective cause.

Is there a better illustration of respective family capabilities imaginable than the fact that the Philips company chose the youngest de Bondt daughter for its prestigious and austere social work department, while employing the youngest Sipkes daughter as a favorite waitress for top management? Such clues reveal important characteristics of family structures and the personalities they fostered. With these two families, then, we seem to approach the extremes on a scale of internal family relationships that could function as a collective resource in Philipsism. The one represented the more hierarchical and closed form, the other the more open and egalitarian. But however different, both were conducive to sustained labor and the maintenance of crucial family ties. And as a result and reward, both could foster a fragile collective welfare amidst various setbacks. How well the Philips personnel department used to operate is finally illustrated by the destinies of the fathers of these two families. Sipkes was put to work in a mass production department, which was not quite common for adult males, while de Bondt got a completely unskilled though nevertheless authoritative position as an elevator operator. Both jobs fitted very well with their work experiences and with their capacities and positions within their families.

The Van Uden Family

In 1928, the Van Uden family was recruited by Philips. Coming from Emmercompascuüm in the Drenthe peat district, they brought eleven children with them, five of whom were daughters, four of working age.

The father got a job at the Philite factory (bakelite) while the four girls were employed on the mounting of radio bulbs in the *apparatenfabriek*. The family had run a small farm in the peat district and had supplemented its cash income with peat digging and related activities. The father had been a respected protagonist of the Catholic Farmers' Association, which entailed repeated travel to The Hague for political meetings. He had also taken up the function of alderman in the community of Emmercompascuüm. Indeed, he was held in high local esteem. He supported a dynamic social Catholicism that responded to the problems of small farmers and rallied against the rise of agricultural socialism in adjacent regions. The family was not quite trapped in poverty. On the contrary, as family members still emphasize, they could well uphold a decent living in Drenthe. The reason for moving to Eindhoven originated in anxiety about the children's future. Employment opportunities in the northeast were ultimately scarce and meager, and were not likely to recover in the foreseeable future.

Like all the Philips girls, the Van Uden daughters quickly united in their aversion of the Philips regime, but they understood very well that their father had an even harder job adapting to life in industry. The story is still told with compassion how painful it was for him to have to sit it out until his pension. All recognize how just it was that in 1935, after some seven years in Drents Dorp, he bought himself a small peasant holding just over the border in the rural community of Veldhoven. But aside from work, there was another feature of life at Eindhoven that made it hard for Van Uden to feel at home. His former public engagement as a Catholic protagonist and popular organizer seemed to lose all its significance. Though having emigrated to the Catholic south, and therefore apparently staging a homecoming, his cultural experience of public activism seemed to be entirely out of place here. After two years of trying to shape Catholic popular activism in Drents Dorp, he retreated from any kind of wider public involvements and started to think of a way back to rural life.

His partisanship was picked up subsequently by some of his children and sons-in-law, who all seem to have loved him dearly. But in their case too, efforts at public engagement were rather unsuccessful. The greatest effect was on their reputation in the neighborhood. In the stories told by the youngest son of the oldest daughter, Karel van Kampen (b. 1943), it becomes clear that by taking ideological causes seriously some of the Van Uden children set themselves painfully apart from the wider community and harvested more contempt than respect. Some of the grandchildren, like their grandfather, were negatively stereotyped in the neighborhood and had an unduly hard time. The only grandchild to successfully translate the family's public energies and undeniable expressive capacities into practice found himself preaching the Philips cause of competitiveness in the postwar Philips Workers Council.

The radio boom neighborhoods have always been thought of as marked by religion and status. They were an outright denial of the close connection assumed by left-wing orthodoxy between industrial capitalist concentration and the rise of class consciousness. On closer scrutiny, however, status and religion also tend to lose their primacy. It seems that the only political and religious organizations that were successful in arousing sustained popular support were exclusively those that catered to the industrial workers' new leisure needs, in particular those providing "modern" leisure for young workers and children. Whether Catholic, Protestant, or Socialist, all organizations tended to become focused on play instead of on work or politics. A good deal of the Drents Dorp stories relate the local centrality of sports and leisure and the gangs and clubs and everyday pleasures that formed around them. The Sipkes girls were connected with the socialist movement not so much to support left-wing public actions but to play theater or music. Protestantism, in itself already emphasizing the separation between public and private life, appeared to the de Bondt girls primarily as a specific approach to leisure time. The most successful popular organizations were not at all based on ideology or religion, because most outdoor activities like football were organized by specialized leisure clubs based in the neighborhood. Boys, therefore, tended to have even less contact with religion and ideology than girls. Of the parents themselves only a few actively participated in public life. But here again, those who became active, whether in religious, ideological, or secular form, often happened to do so in youth and leisure clubs. This is understandable since the great number of children put high claims on parents' time and responsibilities. As far as their own leisure was concerned, mothers had very little, while fathers often withdrew into hobbies at home or in gardening on the small allotments provided by the company.[54]

The failure of an orientation on wider public issues to develop in the radio boom quarters is well illustrated by the story of the Van Uden family. Though Catholicism and its organizations were prominently present in the city of Eindhoven, and were not absent in Drents Dorp either, a true popular organizer and activist like Van Uden set himself painfully apart from the blue-collar community. In a neighborhood that became focused on the leisure needs of its omnipresent youth, Van Uden had too much sense of purpose, too much urgency.

But more fundamental than leisure, it was the family itself which attained a practical and emotional centrality in the radio boom quarters that may have been unique to modern industrial society. While the blue-collar community at Drents Dorp became segmented along lines of religion and ideology like the Dutch polity at large, precisely those aspects of religion and ideology became salient that tied in most intimately with the everyday practices, solidarities, and hierarchies of electrical workers' families. Thus, instead of producing secularization and class consciousness, this locality gave rise to a process of working class formation in which tradition and the family became paramount and tended to mutually reinforce each other. And since the large family was the very foundation of the Eindhoven process of industrial urbanization, it was the family rather than tradition that was basic to this dialectic, and not the other way around.

The practical centrality of the family was partly derived from the large family's inevitable orientation on youth and socialization practices. Partly also from the wide range of collective leisure opportunities and relationships that arose among brothers and sisters. But more importantly, it was due to the fundamental collective experience, reflecting the fundamental power structures shaping their lives. As a tight family collective with intense mutual interdependencies, they were able to gain some elementary welfare and in the end maybe some material security and a future for the next generation.

This experience was a vital collective resource. Many seem to have understood that no individual family member could easily have realized this security and welfare alone, and that as a collectivity they would probably not have realized it somewhere else. Indeed, how else can we explain that Drents Dorp families did not easily disintegrate in spite of the intense pressures on individual members (with the possible exception of boys, who seem to have lived with milder constraints).

Of course there is an alternative account that seeks an explanation for strong local family cohesion in terms of sheer power and exploitation.[55] It would abstract from actual forms of life and straightforwardly deduce from the relevant politico-economic dynamics that children were simply sent to the factories by their parents in order to provide them a comfortable life. It would say that parents collaborated with the corporate capitalist in the exploitation of their adolescent children. It could even conclude that class consciousness was absent because the income and positions of adult males were amply subsidized by the work of their daughters; hence the parental and male concern with status. Status was the stick with which to beat the subordinate class of young females. Subsequently, it could maintain that, given the repression of children by parents, leisure was their only domain of self-expression. It could even see the organization of leisure as an attempt to contain its dangerous load and find confirmation in the fact that less exploited boys were enjoying less regulated leisure.

Although such an argument may seem crude, it does hold a significant measure of truth. Its weakness springs from the fact that it deduces human reality from structural relationships without any sense of the ability of human people to invest their lives and their relationships with meaning, thereby trying to reconciliate, if only for a moment, the contradictions between and within them. Drents Dorp families were not simply the capitalist class struggle writ small. They were a primary human arena in which hope and exploitation, interests and intimacy, emotions and calculations formed an intricate and complex web. To understand this web better, it may be instructive to take a comparative look at a somewhat earlier Philips project that, in contrast to the later workers' quarters, failed to give a solid base to families as wage-earning collectives.

In 1927–28 Philips first seemed more interested in providing immigrant families with small farmsteads instead of working class neighborhoods.[56] The firm hoped to attract large peasant families that could send their daughters to the plants while the parents remained on the farm. Philips erected a small complex of this type in the neighboring village of Son, but intended to build some more extensive ones. However, this turned out not to be a viable strategy. First, it was hard to find peasant families willing to establish themselves in this way. But more importantly, these families tended to disintegrate quickly as older adolescent sons and daughters refused their assigned role and left the family as soon as they were old enough to support themselves. Parents, subsequently, were left in an insecure position.[57]

Compared with the cohesive family structures of Drents Dorp, the failure of this small Philips neighborhood at Son suggests that fathers played a key role in forging solid ties within families.[58] Fathers, it seems, had to share in the industrial experience. If not, older children did not so readily accept their own exploitation and often opted for the most likely way out: depart for a better future. Even if working fathers in the electrical industry were generally not so regimented and controlled as their children, they did suffer much from the Philipsist regime, as shown by the examples of the Van Uden and Sipkes families. The suffering and fatigue of fathers on the one hand, and the constant household efforts of mothers in adverse conditions on the other, could inspire a strong compassion with and commitment to the family's plight on the part of children. It could create great loyalty and give them a strong feeling for family solidarity.

People brought up in Drents Dorp use many symbols to compare the life of their parents in Eindhoven with their earlier situation, and some such symbols imply deficiencies in the electrical town. Jan Sipkes's memory of his father on horseback in a large hat was not only referential for a real historic situation, it also connoted the loss of freedom and human worth that had later beset his father when he spent his days on the production line and lost his position in the family. The Van Uden family, like so many other Philips families, had a drawing on the wall of the small farmers' house in which their grandparents used to live. This was no cheap popular romanticism but a realistic way to remind each other of what had been lost. In many subtle ways, then, Drents Dorp families register the pains that were suffered. And such perceived pains cannot but translate into a commitment to the emotions, motivations, and sufferings of the parents, and vice versa.

Parents therefore did not easily become the targets of criticism. Elsien Sipkes's objection against Drents Dorp life centered on overcrowding and the absence of privacy, and not on the factory work that caused her to cry, nor on her parents who sent her to the factory. Not only the Van Uden children but even the grandchildren were still emotionally committed to their grandfather's suffering as it was handed over from one generation to the next. Nobody compared the parents' suffering directly with the extent of the children's labor efforts, thereby implying that these were unequal things. Thus, the labors of parents (in the original Latin sense of heavy duty) rather than the labors of children tended to shape ideas of justice in Drents Dorp family culture.

This analysis does not negate the fundamental fact that Philips paid the fathers of Drents Dorp a wage higher than the market value of their own labor, only because they brought in enough exploitable daughters to balance the account. There is no denying children's exploitation here. The approach starts rather from the other empirical fact that the whole web of exploitation, interdependency, and intimacy that arose from the triangular connection between the Philips company, immigrant parents, and the children of Drents Dorp evidently contained more encouragements for perceiving the justness of family solidarity than for justifying the escape of the older children. Drents Dorp family solidarity was inspired by hope. And all Drents Dorp life histories in one way or another testify to this fundamentally hopeful family culture. In Philipsdorp, family status was vested in the secure high incomes and career chances of the well-skilled and well-educated individual adult men. In Drents Dorp it was not status but rather a strong collective hope and belief in a good ending of the collective endeavor, derived from some elementary welfare as a tight family team, and from the anticipated future chances of the children.

There obtained, then, a fundamental difference in family circumstances, orientations, and neighborhood cultures between Philipsdorp and Drents Dorp. This difference was a combined effect of, on the one hand, fundamentally divergent life histories, demographic conditions, and start positions, and on the other the sharp differentiation and segmentation of Philipsist production. Philipsdorp people were highly skilled and privatized and their families were closed, except to other branches of the family. The streets were quiet. Drents Dorp people were recruited for their demographic and family characteristics, not for their skills. Their neighborhood featured a vital street culture rooted in the omnipresent youth. Many of its households were relatively open to their neighbors and their neighbors' children.

Both communities, then, have been called privatized. But it is immediately clear that this general concept attains a totally different meaning in each case. While, for example, courting in Philipsdorp was circumscribed by an intricate set of parental considerations of status and respectability, in Drents Dorp it tended to be the largely autonomous domain of the industrial youth. Even the segregation along ideological and religious lines did not hold in the next generation as many youngsters married over the demarcation lines that had seemed of such paramount relevance to their parents. Moreover, many of them seem to have married within the neighborhood, something which appears to have been rather rare in Philipsdorp. Privatization then in Drents Dorp was generally limited to the inability and unwillingness of parents to uphold wider public and political commitments beyond the boundaries of family life or immediate neighborhood affairs. While the dominant culture at Philipsdorp emphasized the individual capacities of persons well situated within Philipsist practice, Drents Dorp was permeated by hope, pain, and trust based on the collective efforts of large and cohesive unskilled families.

In the end, the enduring strength of the Drents Dorp family was translated in the surprising habit of many children to stay near to the parents' place after marriage. Even nowadays it is remarkable how frequently the second and sometimes even the third generation of families that had originally inhabited the workers' quarter still cluster in the immediate environment of the old neighborhood. While social and geographical mobility already began to change the relationships and social composition of Philipsdorp in the twenties, post-1950 social mobility did not easily break the ties and orientations created by an earlier regime of accumulation within the families of Drents Dorp. Not even in the case of those people, like Elsien Sipkes, who intensely longed for more privacy and less family entanglements.

The strong Drents Dorp family acted as a collective resource for its members, but not less so for the Philips corporation. It provided the company with a large, loyal, and well-adapted future labor reserve.[59] The corporation made use of that reserve in a very thoughtful way, a way that supported the expectations of the immigrant families. In the course of the thirties and forties many Drents Dorp boys were taught vital industrial skills, either through learning by doing or through formal (Philips) education. As the company started ever more complex production processes at its Eindhoven plants after 1930, and gradually removed mass production to peripheral regions, the recently skilled male workers from the radio boom neighborhoods became the lieutenants of the Philips production apparatus in the city. And when the Eindhoven girls married them, they could afford to do what they had long dreamt of: leave industrial work. The gradual realization of male breadwinner wages in a more skilled industry now permitted the formation of small families that offered more privacy. The large stock of relatively spacious houses originally designed for large families, plus a range of new Philips housing initiatives, provided them with cheap and relatively comfortable living.

By exploring family histories I have tried to show what Philipsism meant and presupposed for the family histories that shaped the neighborhood cultures of Philipsdorp and Drents Dorp. There was a great cultural gap, a cultural dualization even, between the inhabitants of the two adjacent neighborhoods. Their family structures, skills, capacities, and outlooks were sharply contrasted. Indeed, this contrast was a virtual precondition for their being employed by the electrical company. If, as we have seen, the fragmented and segmented shop floor did not give rise to forms of solidarity and collective action, neither could a collective identity easily be assembled from the highly distinct family and neighborhood cultures of the skilled and unskilled. Furthermore, the ambivalent experiences of highly skilled artisans at Philips somehow seemed to paralyze their politics and collective capacities. In that Drents Dorp was not primarily marked by status and religion, as is so often assumed, but rather by the centrality of the family, both as practice and ideal, the absence of group efforts in the face of the workers' situations is not out of character.

THE SPINELESS SPIDER OR THE URBAN FORM
OF FLEXIBLE MANUFACTURING

Since the expansion of the Philips corporation after the First World War there has existed a marked contrast between the outward appearance of the factories and that of the community. When J. Beyen, later Dutch foreign minister, arrived at Eindhoven in 1925 to start work as Anton Philips's secretary, he was impressed by the contrast between the enormous factory layouts and the humbleness, poor form, the ugliness even, of the community.[60] Likewise, the city's historian Van Oorschot wrote that with the building of the Philips Tower in 1922 the factories acquired a definitely more urban outlook than the city itself.[61]

By 1930 that contrast had become even more pronounced. Visitors entering the city of Eindhoven from the north by train were impressed by the gigantic seven-story-high concrete factory blocks of the Philips "Strijp" complex (named after the old municipality) to their right-hand side. First one came along by the bakelite factory, by then the largest in the world, putting out the shells of radio sets. Next there were the two "apparatus factories" where the radio sets were assembled, also the world's largest plant of the sort. Then came the glass factories, behind which the Philips Educational Institute impressively towered. There followed a short picturesque intermezzo: the Philips sports terrain, surrounded by the smartly styled housing complex of Philipsdorp. Finally, there were the layouts of the lamp factory with the somewhat robust and authoritarian Philips Tower on top, rising like a big tooth from the building's casco shape. A walk along the seven-story-high factories took more than three quarters of an hour.

Eindhoven and its municipalities showed a striking aesthetic contrast to the factories. All through the century the city had experienced quick growth. Especially after 1920, when the center annexed the satellite villages and employment at Philips accelerated, the locality featured the fastest urbanization process of the Dutch twentieth century. Nevertheless, the town had kept its poor and provincial appearance. It did not even form a spatial unity.

Coming out of the railway station, still impressed by the concentrated industrial landscapes just passed, visitors were struck by a paradoxical experience. To the north of the station were large stretches of rural and wild lands bordering on the river De Dommel. Somewhat to the left of this were the beginnings of the older municipality of Woensel, including some of its commercial sites and working class residential neighborhoods built by housing associations after the turn of the century. Woensel seemed a world unto itself, disconnected from the urban goings on. This was true in a real physical sense. A busy network of railways which could only be crossed at a single point and only during certain times of the day virtually cut the community off from the main urban area. But it was also true in another sense. The community of Woensel consisted of small one- and two-story houses and imperceptibly merged into the rural lands to the north and east. Indeed, it hardly distinguished itself from the rural surroundings since it lay scattered over several smaller clusters, each apparently with its own social identity. Most of these clusters featured large gardens and stretches of land used for small cattle breeding and vegetable gardening, marked by rough-built sheds for any and all purposes. On the surface, Woensel did not seem related to the impressive electrical manufacturing complex, except for some modern quarters near the railways to the west, disconnected from the rest of the community and partly built by Philips.

Standing before the railway station and looking southwest, visitors faced the town center. It was still evident that Eindhoven had once been a small though fairly rich entrepreneurial market town (in Max Weber's sense of a *Verlegerstadt*). Shops seemed to cater primarily to the better situated. The market square, with a grand old lime tree on one of the southern corners, still paid tribute to the traditional Brabantine inner city designs. But a large chain store of the Dutch-German Vroom and Dreesmann enterprise, with an iron and glass art deco entrance on one of the main urban crossings, was definitely a sign of the locality's modernity. Except for that store, however, there were few modern buildings to be found. The fancy small council house was a nineteenth-century neo-gothic design, already outdated before it was built. And further south rose the contours of two large churches, the church of St. Catherina with its tall twin towers, built in the 1850s, and the church of the Augustinian order of monks, with its impressive statue of Christ overlooking the adjacent schools and cloister complex from the top of its tower. Modern public amenities were scarce. There was the "Chicago" cinema, near the Vroom and Dreesmann store, owned by an Amsterdam family specializing in commercial entertainment. A musical and theatrical program was offered in the old nineteenth-century wooden locale Appollo's Lust, on the eastern filled-in urban canal, run by the liberal Amicitia society. And finally, on the opposite part of town, there was Roomsch Leven, the Catholic associational place, which offered a determined Catholic program of theater and music that competed with the liberals. Workers did not inhabit the city proper, though on its western border, near the tramways to the Campina villages, some small and shabby workers' quarters were still located.

Walking south through the main street of the old town one entered the former village of Stratum. This was probably the most differentiated community of the Eindhoven area. Situated near the nineteenth-century canal (1854) that connected Eindhoven with the global ports of Amsterdam and Rotterdam and with the heavy industrial district of Liège, this community was industrialized long before the turn of the century. It featured diverse textile, cigar, and woodworking enterprises. Part of the entrepreneurial classes lived in the community itself, as did many shopkeepers and several innkeepers and barbers. Catholics, Protestants, and Jews intermingled, and there seems to have been a quiet but steady in- and outmigration. By 1930, a new villa park was being planned in the heath lands west of the Stratum church, providing new and respectable residential spaces for Philips executives. And further away, to the south, in the vicinity of a somewhat older bourgeois garden community, some working class quarters for unskilled families had just been completed, including the one inhabited by the immigrant families from Oss. Two miles further south, well beyond a forested terrain, on the territory of the village of Waalre, one of the smaller, low-rent Philips quarters was erected. Two miles from the village core to the southeast, behind a stretch of wild land, the Philips colony of Tivoli was in 1930 on the point of being finished.

East of the center, north of the canal, the romantically styled *villapark* was located. "Huize de Laak," Anton Philips's residence, had been the first house to be built in this low swampy area on the former territory of the now annexed village of Tongelre. Other entrepreneurs had followed suit and had had new villas and country houses built in the park, often moving from one of the more classical residences in the town center. Moreover, many of the key engineers, managers, and executives of Philips corporation lived there, following the cultural lead of their boss out of town and into romantic suburban and segregated living. This area, then, with its lime-tree-lined streets and its English garden architecture, was a romantic bourgeois and upper professional refuge from the vagaries of economic life. Like Woensel, but infinitely richer, it was almost an island unto itself. It too was physically barred from the life of other Eindhoven communities by the insurmountable railways in the north, the canal in the south, and the Dommel river in the southwest.

To the west and southwest of the center lay the former villages of Strijp and Gestel. Gestel was still a largely petty bourgeois community in 1930. It was separated from Stratum by the Dommel river and the surrounding wetlands (no bridges), and from Strijp by the wetlands of the small Gender creek. Strijp hosted the greater part of the recent Philips immigrants. The railways barred it from Woensel, the factories from the center.

Although all of the Eindhoven area had long been subjected to identical economic forces, its social space was nevertheless highly fragmented, to such an extent that, except via the old town, it was hardly possible to move between the constituent communities. Eindhoven, urban planners realized, had the form of a spider, the old town being the body and the former villages forming the legs. Between the legs lay broad stretches of wild and rural land, often crisscrossed by small currents that used to flood the neighboring areas in spring and autumn. A dense network of railways and a canal finally served to reinforce these spatial barriers. In addition, real divisions of labor were projected onto space as insular territories were shaped by specific population segments and acquired specific functions.

In a country where urban form was evaluated according to the standards of the world-famous, elegantly concentrated, and collectively managed towns of early modern, bourgeois, mercantile Holland, the Eindhoven spider was an absolute failure.[62] Urban planners blamed the town's particular history, the environmental ecology, the dominant type of one-family houses that created low densities but abused space, and the "traditional" system of radial roads with ribbon building. They asserted that the effect was not only ugliness and a circulation problem in the center, but also the absence of mutual ties between the constituent parts.[63] After 1945, politicians also sensed that it hindered the emergence of what was considered essential for a real contemporary city, a dynamic, trend-setting, modern urban culture, concentrated on a city center. Urban planners after the 1920 annexation immediately started to conceive of a large and representative circular road connecting the former villages with each other. And after the bombardments of World War II, the town's politicians prepared themselves to dynamize the appearance of the center, to give the place a "modern heart," as they would say, so as to match the dynamism of its economy.[64]

But however adequate such technical reasoning from the viewpoint of urban planners may have seemed, their explanations for urban failure were at best partial. But isolating space they failed to conceive of the crucial interdependencies between space and the social dynamics of the territory. These interdependencies in the Eindhoven area around 1930 were still based on the key social relationships of flexible manufacturing, as is illustrated by a conflict that arose between the Philips Building Office and the urban planning department of the community of Eindhoven around 1928, a conflict that may serve as a clue to the sociospatial dynamics of the area.

In 1928 Philips sought to realize a series of housing projects just over the Eindhoven town boundary with adjacent villages like Son, Waalre, Geldrop, and Veldhoven (which was never realized).[65] The Son and Waalre projects were small, but the Geldrop and Veldhoven projects were major undertakings of over five hundred one-family houses. The Philips Building Office had two good reasons to start projects outside the urban area. The first reason was the difference in land prices, which in many cases exceeded a factor of five.[66] The other reason was a conflict with the urban development department of the municipality of Eindhoven. This conflict turned on a set of requirements to which the Philips Building Office had to adhere before the city of Eindhoven would approve of the projects (which was again necessary for getting central government housing loans, which had to pass city government). These requirements concerned the measurements of streets, sidewalks, and public space in general. Philips would not concede to these prescriptions because it would result in higher building costs per unit and therefore in higher rents per house. And since wages paid to the unskilled were a function of local costs of living, the company's labor costs would subsequently have to rise too.[67] To Philips, a corporation that depended on the world competitive production of labor-intensive mass products, this seemed irrational. In the end, the conflict was resolved by the central government, which responded to pressure from Anton Philips, threatening to direct his investments in radio set making to Belgium and Germany. On behalf of "welfare policy" the minister of labor bypassed the city of Eindhoven and made the housing loan directly available to a new building association (Thuis Best) installed by Philips.[68]

Two aspects of this conflict are relevant for the question of spatial fragmentation and urban concentration. For one, electrical mass manufacturing, as we have seen earlier, based as it was on the large-scale deployment of formally unskilled female and adolescent labor, by itself caused a centrifugal tendency in urban development as it sought to exploit the cheapest possible space for workers' housing. Such locations were by definition not situated near the urban core. Further, even a minimum of collectively imposed costs, in this case on behalf of public space, would have led to an increase of local wage standards. While it had precisely been the low costs and flexible quality of local pools of unskilled labor that had given the region its momentum, such a politically enforced and permanent cost increase tended to slow down the motor behind it. Even a large and well-capitalized employer such as Philips felt induced to circumvent such measures.

From this episode we can derive the more generally valid insight that an urban region that accumulates on the basis of flexible mass manufacturing does not tend to a concentration of workers, nor to the high collective investments in public space or public provisions that are the logical consequence of such concentration. The pressure put on its capitalists by international competition to maintain low and flexible labor costs simply does not facilitate the formation of local alliances to support such policies in the first place.

In the Eindhoven case, as we have seen, this very same spatial dynamic of flexible mass manufacturing had functioned all during the nineteenth century. It had led to high population increases in surrounding proletarian villages, where land rents had been low enough to make cheap and simple housing possible with large gardens for food provision. It had also served to reinforce the regional tendency of housing to be located along radial roads. Ribbon building was not simply an effect of bad regional tastes or "backward traditions"; it was caused by the absence of large investors like local communities, capitalists, or associations that could have provided the capital and organizational capabilities needed for additional infrastructure. For example, 80 percent of the housing stock of the community of Woensel by 1900 had been under the control of local petty bourgeois citizens like bakers and construction contractors for whom housing investments had been a normal method of securing family capital.[69] Of course they had only the capacity to build small batches of houses along existing roads. Larger projects, with higher costs for infrastructure, could not have been realized on this social and organizational basis. Thus, by 1930, if the Eindhoven population was divided over several disconnected clusters, it was not a function of ecology, as suggested by the urbanist Beekman,[70] but of its particular path of capitalist accumulation. Technically speaking, it would have been easy to bring working families close to the center and to build roads and bridges to enlarge the habitable territory near the core. But who would have paid for it? And who would have supported the necessary taxation?

It is interesting to see that Eindhoven entrepreneurs in the nineteenth century were well able to form a coalition to collectively generate the large amounts of money needed to build a thirty-kilometer canal. But housing investments for the ever larger number of ordinary working families who increasingly began to overcrowd the surrounding villages never became a general interest to them. In flexible mass manufacturing areas, unskilled workers, by definition, were not conceived of as part of private or collective capital. As a consequence their housing, and the communities they lived in, either remained their own "traditional" business or the "traditional" business of petty capitalists.[71] Such areas, therefore, consistently tended to spatial deconcentration and fragmentation.

The high spatial fragmentation and deconcentration of the Eindhoven urban area were a consequence, or rather an inseparable part, of a regional process of accumulation that was anchored in the social dynamics of flexible mass manufacturing. Paradoxically, then, precisely by keeping the accumulation of capital and the reproduction of working families apart, by on the one hand concentrating and enlarging the scale of productive capital and on the other hand creating "villages," the development of social space and the development of industrial production were conjoined. They were two sides of the same coin.

With the large-scale housing projects for unskilled families after 1927, the organization of space and housing for the first time became incorporated in the circuits of capital.[72] This was an important transition. But it was only a very partial transition. In spite of the enormous increase of capital outlay between 1925 and 1930, in factories, laboratories, skilled people, and urban infrastructures, the rules of regional accumulation did not yet change. Notwithstanding the large technological and organizational gap between radio receivers and cigars, regional development was still fundamentally based on flexible mass manufacturing. Indeed, as we have seen, Philips housing investments precisely served to reinvent its basic original relations. The implications were inescapable. The Philips

Building Office was now building in a rational and functionalist manner workers "colonies" that were in spatial respects almost the equivalent of the "traditional villages." While the round of investments in productive apparatuses in the late twenties led to an unprecedented concentration of "modern" production in the vicinity of the center, the large-scale housing efforts again fostered the fragmentation and deconcentration of local space. The Philips company not only reproduced under its own auspices the "traditional" family structures of the region, it also re-created the "traditional" distances of some three kilometers between communities and the center.[73] Philips also encouraged the "traditional" use of garden allotments as cheap providers of both food and "healthy leisure." Indeed, the company tried to create a large-scale project with hundreds of separate houses on large gardens of up to five hundred square meters.[74] Although this particular project failed, the "modern" creation of "province" and "tradition" in the context of a highly capitalized regional process based on flexible mass manufacturing could not be halted.

THE PHILIPS GOSPEL OF SELF-RESPONSIBLE WORKER CITIZENSHIP

In the fragmented polity, segmented society, and divided urban space of the city of Eindhoven, a flourishing, lively, and engaging public sphere could hardly be expected. While the urban landscapes emerging around the key complexes of twentieth-century corporate industry never offered good instances of democratic and popular public life—indeed, how could they ever have done so, considering the great differences in resources between the giant corporation that determined these localities' destinies and their dependent populations?—the Dutch electrical town was probably one of its worst examples.

One important cause lay in the segmented, indeed dualized, nature of local relations. The social, cultural, and spatial distance between corporate elites and subelites, on the one hand, and the "mass" of workers on the other was simply greater in an electrical manufacturing town like Eindhoven than in a mining town like Bochum, or in an automobile city like Coventry. We only need to consider how a well-educated and well-paid electrical engineer with an urban background in the thirties probably related to an unskilled, sixteen-year-old proletarian girl, to understand that high and low in local society could hardly dance the tango together. In less scientifically oriented and more male based industrial centers, social relations were necessarily less asymmetrical. Add to this the inevitable complicity of parents with reigning disciplinary regimes in electrical manufacturing and local life, and we arrive at the rather bleak condition of local citizenship that probably materialized in the Eindhoven of the early thirties.

But the dualized and segmented nature of local society per se was not the whole story. Public life in the town was also, and increasingly, affected by the Philips redistributional system. Philips' social policy, as we have seen, was essentially meant to reshape local proletarian life and household forms, reacting against a local working class culture that started to escape Philipsist hegemony in the later twenties. The company developed a comprehensive set of social policies, the most basic of which were the large-scale housing provisions, in order to regain a measure of social control and moral leadership. Philipsist social practice was shaped by what I call the "gospel of self-responsible worker citizenship," and its moral messages were a powerful force in local public life. It invaded the narrow public sphere of the Eindhoven community, not so much by persuading everyone of its inherent correctness, but by offering the ascendant Philips cadres a coherent and unified cultural outlook.

In the later twenties and early thirties, the Philips redistributional system was gradually extended over the whole social terrain, from leisure services, via social work, health care, housing, and educational facilities, to more work-place related programs.[75] The threads of this wide-branching social apparatus came together in the staff of the socioeconomic department at Philips headquarters. Intentionally or not, the company thus erected what political scientists have called a unitary structure of power in the town.[76] Practiced by this unitary structure of social power and wedded to the job opportunities of the largest and most differentiated internal labor market in the country, the Philips gospel of self-responsible worker citizenship became an influential cultural force in the community.

What were the contents of this cultural force? How did it operate? And what were its effects on the outlook of working class communities? Of course it is not possible to give an exact estimate of its influence over local people. As a cultural force it tended to be described as either omnipotent or nonexistent.[77] This is an unfruitful and unrealistic polarity. As a start it makes sense to point out, however, that the absence of any other general, nonparticularist, organized and institutionally supported cultural frame in local public life did guarantee the eminence of the Philips gospel. In the course of the twenties and thirties everyone in town was, whether they liked it or not, confronted by its messages, sanctions, and encouragements. Whatever its exact power of persuasion, each worker had to develop an attitude toward it. This single fact obliges any author on Eindhoven and Philipsism to study its workings and contents, even though the cultural program may not yet have been extensive enough to shape workers' reactions to mass layoffs in 1930–32.

Historians and sociologists have tended to concentrate on the specific rules and provisions of redistributional systems, and so did those studying Philips's social policy.[78] But beyond specific regulations, provisions, and entitlements there are two largely neglected aspects of redistributional systems that are of eminent comparative and anthropological interest. For one: each system of social redistribution invokes certain key images of the ideal human recipient of its expenses and efforts. Redistribution needs moral legitimation vis-à-vis its contributors and the wider outside world. Moreover, it puts moral claims on the recipients of its services.[79] As Michael Katz has again illustrated, redistributive systems always distinguish between those who deserve care and those who do not. This is important, because it means that the formation of new systems of social redistribution also always implies the formation of new moral and cultural codes. As Corrigan and Sayer have argued, in the longer term, social policy regimes sometimes constitute outright cultural revolutions.[80]

Systems of social redistribution are so culturally formative precisely because their managers and protagonists generally undertake action in order to shape their recipients in the light of their own moral motivations. In the case of modern forms of company welfare, which are by definition little susceptible to struggles between contradictory social interests, their everyday functioning may be very coherent and very consonant with their wilder cultural claims.[81] Such a system, then, boasts clear messages on desirable behavior, everyday proprieties, and the sorts of conduct deemed at the limit or out of order. These cultural and civilizational programs have however been neglected by historians and sociologists not only because they deployed one-sided theories, but also because these moral programs cannot be found on the naïve empirical level of single and distinct provisions. They are, rather, established both on the level of the totality of rules and images, on the one hand, and in their everyday practice on the other.

But what then were the central cultural rules and images of Philips's social policy? Even when it has steadily been described as utterly varied and unsystematic,[82] one of the oldest texts on the subject, the report on labor relations at Philips from the International Labor Office at Geneva (1932), left no doubt about Philips's civilizing tenets. Approvingly, it concluded that the employer clearly "sought to develop among his workers a good taste for order and hygiene, for initiatives based on administrative experience, a good feeling for private and collective discipline, and a habit for fine recreations and social advancement."[83]

Philipsism, through its social policies and in accordance with its individualizing form of labor control and its dynamic and differentiating character, boasted a very Dutch, Protestant, and individualist civic moralism. It stressed the virtues of self-help and self-improvement and pressed for sobriety, rational leisure, and self-control.[84] It emphatically believed in the collective welfare that would inevitably arise in a society based on the rules of individual duties, talents, efforts, and responsibilities, and saw this expressed in devoted labor, "healthy families," respect for education and knowledge, and civic actionism to improve the quality of life and labor. In the division of labor, differential rewards were legitimized and naturalized by referring to the interest of all in putting "the right man in the right place." Among the Philips cadres, the ideology of meritocratic rule and reward was enacted in their stress on capability and responsibility, in their minor rituals of respectful greeting and deferential addressing, the great weight they put on quiet and rational argument. Downward, to the shop floor, meritocracy was ritualized and legitimized by such practices as psychotechnical research on individual capabilities and constant evaluation of performance. Paradoxically, then, the dominant corporate class in the town made a consistent and large-scale effort to authorize and promote the self-responsible worker citizen.

The gospel of self-responsible worker citizenship in Philips's social policy was first enacted in the basic guideline that it was not up to the corporation to take the lead in the launching and management of social policy initiatives, and that it should rather be the responsibility of "its" citizens to air their needs themselves.[85] Authority over sponsored initiatives was generally delegated to foundations which were formally (semi-)independent of the corporation. In those bodies workers often also had a formal voice. Pensions and illness benefits, for example, were controlled by committees in which elected worker delegates held half the seats. In the whole series of leisure organizations subsidized by Philips, workers were quasi-autonomous. They managed their own daily affairs while being generously funded, and ultimately evaluated and approved, by the "Philips-de Jongh Leisure Fund."[86]

One permanent edifice for the fruits of self-responsible worker citizenship was erected with the establishment of the Philips Vereniging voor Onderwijs en Volksontwikkeling (Philips Association for Popular Education). This association organized primary schools in the Philips neighborhoods; a school for incandescent lamp manufacturing, to train thirteen-year-old girls for a factory job to which they were only formally admitted at age fourteen; and a famous industrial school in glass, metal-working, and electrical engineering for local boys. Apart from these regular schools, it offered a whole array of voluntary evening courses, from working class cuisine and sewing work (to satisfy parents and local moralists with the idea that their daughters were not only exploited but also educated to good motherhood, if they wanted to be) to bookkeeping, accounting, typing, stenography, commercial correspondence, foreign languages, and technical drawing. Those voluntary evening courses attracted a substantial public.[87]

By itself already a stimulus for "popular advancement" because suggesting the possibility of career by self-help, the association further reinforced its civilizing message by offering its teaching in such a way as to make the pupil himself appear responsible for his or her skills and knowledge. Courses were never offered freely. The director of the association, Dr. E. Bonebakker, a famous educator, had discovered that if students were obliged to pay a small fee this would foster the impression that they had themselves chosen this particular subject and should therefore be held responsible for its successful completion. For primary schooling Bonebakker preferred the system propagandized by Maria Montessori, since of all schooling systems he believed this would contribute most to the Philipsist ideal of self-responsible worker citizens.[88]

In apparent contradiction to its despotic regime of production, Philips even wished to stress worker citizenship on the shop floor. Top management decided that the works council as developed from below in the glass factory should also be introduced in other departments in order to inform on and negotiate recurrent problems of production and factory life. In order to help induce more trust in the anonymous functioning of piece wage systems, committees of workers were formed to check the fair application of the rules that governed their work and income.[89]

But despite efforts to suggest the contrary, the rules, rituals, and routines of the Philips social apparatus did not operate in a social vacuum composed of unconstrained and individual *citoyens* who could freely sign up to a contract that suited them best. Social policies were closely wedded to the dynamics of an industrial complex that had to combine the expansion of flexible mass manufacturing with the formation of a differentiated and mature corporate base. Necessarily, the gospel of worker citizenship and the practices of the social department somehow had to deal with the social divides between the different class segments employed by the company. In effect, these basic divisions became projected onto its citizenship practice and discourse. Unskilled families, juvenile workers, and female workers got a particularist treatment within Philipsist worker citizenship practice.

In accordance with its idea of healthy family life as a civic prerequisite for both individual well-being and profitable mass production, Philips kept a close watch on goings on within unskilled families. Philips has been complimented with its much larger staff of social workers employed at the socioeconomic department than was provided by the city of Eindhoven itself. However, this was but the expression of the centrality of family policy in the effort of Philips managers to regain control over unskilled labor. The extraordinary high pressures on the large families of unskilled Philips workers, the sheer number of family members living together, the large number of earners within families, the intricate relationship between parental love, status, and children's exploitation, their nonindustrial backgrounds and problems of adaptation, all made the family's stability both highly fragile and at the same time highly central to production management. Each threat to the stability of any single family unit at once threatened the productivity and loyalty of several workers. In particular in girls departments, a lack of concentration by some girls could easily lead to a weakening of overall discipline. Philips feared that unmanaged stress in one family could disturb wider relationships in the overcrowded neighborhoods. In addition to the relatively large number of trained social workers employed by the company (Philips employed seven of them, while the community of Eindhoven employed only one), there was a small army of almost thirty female "house supervisors" who had the right to enter workers' private space, inspect the performance of households, and give unsolicited advice. In a sense they were the scouts of the social department, registering weak spots in the industrial bulwark of the family.[90]

In combination with the information from the Philips medical office (paid by the Philips illness benefit fund) and the Philips police force (paid by Philips but carrying public authority as volunteers in the municipal police force), the social department developed quite an intimate knowledge of working class families.[91] They knew who deserved favorable treatment, who needed what kind of special attentions, and who would never learn the rules of the Philipsist game. The Philips emergency fund, which, significantly, was exclusively administered by top executives, closely followed the advice of these agencies in deciding who was favored with what kind of means in case of adverse family fortunes.[92]

Though it is of course impossible to assess the specific influence of such institutions on working class families in Eindhoven, oral evidence clearly indicates that their presence has been felt as ubiquitous, demanding, and in many respects uncognizant of workers' own capacities for decency and respectability. In particular the "house supervisors" were confronted with much distrust, and are nowadays openly repudiated in the neighborhoods.[93] The names of prominent female employees of the Philips social work department are still memorized wth an ambiguous mixture of anger and deference, both among men and women.

A good illustration of the more enforcing sides of the Philips gospel is offered by the workings of the illness benefit fund. Arguing in 1930 that the fund was the workers' own resource, the board, of which half the seats were held by manual workers, decided to organize a grassroots network in the neighborhoods to check whether people were not unjustifiably home and faking illness. The city was divided over seven districts, and in each of them a commission composed of eight men and eight women, recruited from the eight main corporate subdivisions, started tracing fraud. While by 1930 individual conduct and productivity at work were ever better spotted, supervised, and rationalized, an "irresponsible" withdrawal in illness was not allowed.[94]

While working class families were closely watched and regulated, their daughter-workers were heavily discriminated against in Philipsist citizenship discourse. Although, or because of, being the very social basis of electrical production, they were exclusively addressed as unaspiring mass producers and future mothers. Schooling for girls meant either training them before their fourteenth birthday for mass-production jobs or teaching working girls to be good working class mothers after marriage. In contrast, men and boys were eligible for special training programs to become part of a pool of local cadres. While male workers saved for their pensions, girls were sponsored to save for a dowry.[95]

Citizenship on the shop floor, as expressed in the Philips works councils, was not as liberal as might seem on first sight. Notwithstanding the large number and centrality of young workers (more than 8,000 under age eighteen in October 1930, which is more than half the total number of blue-collar workers at the time),[96] all of them were excluded from works council practice. Participation in works council elections was open only to male wage workers over twenty-one and to women over eighteen. Those who were most exploited, that is, the adolescents, thus were not allowed a voice. In addition, one had to have been employed at Philips for a continuous period of more than two years. Through this single rule, again about half the Philips personnel was excluded. Together these limitations served to establish a highly restricted census for shop floor citizenship. In effect, it was exclusively granted to those workers who had long been adapted to the Philips regime and, more significantly, to those older male workers who drew the greatest advantages from a system basically held up by the labor of their adolescent children.[97]

In addition to their restricted constituency, the field of operation of Philips works councils was also strictly circumscribed. The corporation was willing to promote and authorize work councils only as long as the basic conditions of production were kept from open discussion and awareness. Worker delegates were therefore not permitted to talk about pay levels or about wage practice at Philips. Management maintained that these issues were subject to general and national rules which were decided elsewhere, such as in negotiations with national union leadership. Instead of general rules, works councils should debate the local and particular problems that arose from the application of general rules to everyday production.[98] Council meetings were always led by higher managers, who used to stop discussion at the moment that delegates went beyond the council's official mandate. In spite of some superficial similarities, therefore, Philips worker citizenship did not at all resemble British shop stewardism or the majority of German *Betriebsräte*.

As a consequence of restricted constituency and limited authority, worker delegates to Philips works councils were often deemed sloppy by union organizers. Indeed, they were more concerned with indecent toilet graffiti or illicit women's clothing than with advancing collective workers' causes as perceived by union leadership.[99] At the same time, labor leaders completely seemed to misunderstand the crucial relevance of questions of women's clothing and feminine respectability in the Eindhoven context. Such issues did not simply originate from misplaced moralist obsessions but were a key aspect of power and production regimes in this locality. The fact that works councils often pleaded for more segregation of sexes and for stricter policing of female morality reflects their particular base in constituencies of older male workers who drew most of the fruits of adolescent and female exploitation. Instead of being sloppy, then, worker delegates seem to have known very well what their interests were.

However, there is no denying that union complaints about the quality of delegates were justified. On behalf of the Philips version of worker citizenship, everyday factory reality as represented in public discourse was emptied from any and all discussion that might have given rise to wider theoretical and political insights. For Philipsist common sense the single relevant distinctions for life in Eindhoven almost came down to those of correct and incorrect individual conduct. Eindhoven was miles beyond social and historical theory, let alone class theory.

The Philipsist practice of worker citizenship, then, was highly circumscribed. Like the regime of industrial production on which it was based, Philips citizenship discriminated very strictly between the sexes, between skilled and educated families on the one hand and unskilled families on the other, and between older and younger workers. And since alternative discourses failed to establish themselves in the public domain, role models and images of class, gender, and age, anchored in work and reinforced through corporate social practice, attained a coherence rarely found in older and more differentiated urban regions where politics and private accumulation were more securely separated.[100]

The Philips gospel favored those who were, because of their sex, cultural background, capabilities, starting positions, patience, age, or endurance capable of taking their chance in the expanding internal labor market. The single fact that the rules of the gospel were wedded to the dynamics of the largest and most differentiated internal labor market in the country may have given them a material meaning well beyond their intrinsic power of persuasion in a segmented, low-wage industrial economy. The noting of one's cultural performance of the Philips creed quickly became an important vehicle by which careers could be made. Let us take a last look at the internal workings of Philips production and hierarchy in order to establish this.

One of the key changes taking place in the organization of production from 1929 on was the centralization of hiring and firing procedures. Many of the production bosses up till then had functioned as subcontractors who were ordered to produce a certain quantity of goods while retaining a substantial freedom as to how they managed their daily affairs.[101] For this system to work, it had been essential for bosses to retain the right to hire and fire. This provided them with the necessary power to enforce discipline. In 1929, however, central management, confronted with the need to cut costs and increase efficiency, proceeded to take centralized control over hiring and firing procedures. At the same time, it put back in the hands of production management the whole expanding repertoire of the social system. Production bosses became the everyday representatives of Philips social benevolence. They acquired a substantial measure of discretionary power to decide who would be eligible for better living space or for strategic courses that would further one's career.[102] And if the boss himself was successful, he could again decide which of his collaborators would follow him on his way up. Assisted by the data on people's capabilities from psychotechnical research, the figures on daily productivity, and the information on home life gathered by the socioeconomic department, it was he who would select the people that the organization would put its trust in. The department boss, then, instead of being a petty tyrant driving his labor force forward, became the most proximate judge over one's cultural resources. By 1930 he may have lost his personal power in production to the distant bureaucracy of the labor department, but he gained strategic status as a gatekeeper in culturally selecting the recruits for the expanding Philips cadres and in the distribution of other forms of corporate favor.

Thus, as long as internal labor markets at Philips were the best guarantee for family survival and individual advancement in the region, the Philips gospel of self-responsible worker citizenship, however illusory compared to the real power-chances of local dependent people, would retain a very material meaning in one's life and in the urban culture of Eindhoven. It did so, not so much by persuading everyone of its rightness, but by guarding the cultural boundaries of an expanding cadre of convinced clerks, salesmen, social workers, production bosses, and professionals that was, despite its internal divisions, remarkably unified in social outlook.

In the absence of a class or a coalition that could have defied the hegemony of the Philips in-crowd, it was the Philips common sense, its rules of correct behavior and decency, of obedience and competence, its paternalist ideology, and family values, that defined the public ways and debates in the town. While local proletarian adolescents often develop a loud and coarse voice in order to claim public freedom, reasoned public antagonizing is still not done in Eindhoven. It does not belong to the cultural repertoire of "order, decency, and correctness"[103] that local adults have learned to respect, whatever their actual dissatisfaction and angers. And, significantly, when they do express their disagreements, they tend to do so in that same coarse voice of the "street kids."

7 The Fruits of Flexible Familism

The crisis came, in 1929. But it did not break the expansion drive of the bureaucratic leaders of the now unsurveyable industrial giant. Although the deplorable condition of tens of thousands is indeed caused by the general crisis of world capitalism, it is certain that this disaster has been much worsened by reckless, incompetent, and frivolous management.—*Philips of de Neergang van het Nederlandse Kapitalisme*, communist brochure, Amsterdam 1931, p. 7; trans. DK

In the period of depression, Philips management tried as much as possible to maintain the continuity of employment of its army of workers.—*Les Usines Philips*, ILO, Geneva 1932, p. 34; trans. DK

As long as possible, Dr. Philips would avoid laying off his personnel. He preferred a different solution . . . that seemed more socially acceptable to him than cutting jobs: reducing hours.—P. J. Bouman, *Anton Philips: De mens, de ondernemer*, Nijmegen 1956, p. 183; trans. DK

PHILIPSISM IN CRISIS, 1929–1932

In November 1929 the Philips corporation started a long process of job reduction. Total employment at the Eindhoven plants was cut from a height of almost 23,000 to some 9,500 in the spring of 1932.[1] Following a unique expansion, this decline was unexpected and dramatic. And though it may not have caused severe open conflict, it did generate significant disagreement, as illustrated by the above quotations, as to the performance of the management. Was Philips indeed reckless? Or did the company live up to its proclaimed loyalty toward its personnel?

An analysis of the structure of Philips's problems and strategies and the ways in which they have been experienced and explained by the organizations of different working class segments will demonstrate that the corporation's reaction might well have been both: reckless *and* loyal. This suggests that the fate of different segments may have been dissimilar. A closer study of the timing and structure of job cuts and their effect on the composition of the work force shows that this indeed has been the case. Regionally recruited young workers, skilled immigrant metalworkers, and large immigrant families were affected in different ways and at different moments in time.

Moreover, evidence demonstrates that the first year of job reduction, from November 1929 to the early days of January 1931, was not at all related to the consequences of global crisis. This period, instead, witnessed the completion of Philips efforts to reshape the household forms of unskilled labor and regain hegemony over local adolescent "mass workers." Almost totally neglected by contemporary sources and earlier studies, thousands of regionally recruited young workers were probably replaced by a smaller number of highly disciplined adolescents from large immigrant families. The new structures of Philipsism that came out of this struggle for control over unskilled labor, that is, the newly created proletariat of imported large families, plus the package of social policies directed toward it, inherently provided for the possibility of a substantial temporary reduction of jobs without either generating collective protest or threatening its future labor reserve. Flexible familism, as I have named the whole configuration of Philipsist labor practices, also enabled the company to overcome the contradiction of highly labor intensive, export-oriented manufacturing, based in a hard-currency country, in times of dramatically falling world market prices.

Philips, Workers, and World Crisis

The Philips crisis was complex. It was composed of several distinct phases and processes of restructuring. What was the nature and timing of these processes? And how were different blue-collar groups affected? Given the segmentation of manual workers at Philips, we should also ask how workers' organizations perceived and explained their members' grievances. This question is important because answering it can lead to an assessment of the relative power of groups to conceive of and act upon their interests in case of collective adversity. It also points to the chances for wider solidarities to develop.

One form in which the crisis manifested itself to electrical workers was rationalization. Together with the related intensification of work, the popular experience of this particular process at Philips could be interpreted as an instance of the "crisis of labor." The theory of the crisis of labor was originally coined by left-wing theorists abroad. In the Philips case, it was partly echoed in the communist and labor union press, and reproduced later, without much argument, by the Amsterdam sociologist Teulings (1976). This theory maintained that the crisis of the early thirties was not simply the effect of falling world demand but more basically caused by capitalist rationalization.[2] By applying science to production, for example through Fordism and Taylorism, productivity increases outran the slow rise of world demand, caused growing unemployment, and subsequently destroyed their own preconditions. This argument bears at least a partial truth. But it does apply much more directly, and with more force and clarity, to countries industrializing on the basis of home demand and internal forms of accumulation, like the United States and Germany. Philips, however, was entirely bound to growth through export. Apart, then, from its independent, not-crisis-induced efforts at rationalization, Philips's job cuts were really caused by the effects of capitalist crisis on international trade, as will be shown below.

But the experience of rationalization and labor intensification of course was real. In line with the literature on skilled workers and proletarianization, it was the skilled immigrant metalworkers of the technical departments in particular who gave voice to this concern as early as late 1929.[3] However, the theme of rationalization was quickly overshadowed, first by selective dismissals of metalworker activists, then by the steady reduction throughout 1931 of the technical departments from around 2,200 jobs to a mere 770 in early 1932.[4]

Left-wing concerns with the Philips company increasingly focused on the growing repression of local union activities by the Philips police forces. These armed forces were permitted to operate outside the factory gates since the time that the city's mayor, ruling as an autocrat in the moral panic of 1929, had given them the status of voluntary municipal police.[5] Led by inspector Dijs, who under Nazi occupation would become commander of the municipal police, they started to harass union activists by the summer of 1930.[6] Moreover, it seems that Philips in that same year, before starting the reduction of its technical departments, selectively dismissed radical union members.[7] Communist questions in parliament on the repression in Eindhoven were not responded to by the minister of interior affairs, who referred to national interest and public safety.[8] Thus, the experience of activist metalworkers and the Dutch left with Philips in the early thirties was above all shaped by state-backed repression.

The more locally entrenched, though never popular or strong Catholic metalworkers union St. Eloy voiced a concern that differed fundamentally from the left. This highlights the lack of communication and identification between the key blue-collar groups at Eindhoven. Moreover, in contrast with the position of the left, St. Eloy's version of the electrical workers' grievances was never picked up by politicians, nor elaborated or discussed in social or historical studies. St. Eloy's intellectual isolation and political weakness, indeed, was lamentable. Only slowly and hesitantly did the union discover its central grievance.

The first theme that St. Eloy in the late twenties concentrated on was the uncommonly large gap between wages at Philips for the skilled and the unskilled.[9] For the former group Philips was forced to compete on the national labor market and had to pay competitive wages. But wages for the latter were only slightly above the regional average, calculated according to the minimal survival costs for an adult individual living in Eindhoven. Gradually, wholly new fears and grievances were developing among local male workers organized in St. Eloy. With Philips completing its housing projects, and an increasing number of immigrant families knocking at the town's door, their low wages were ever more perceived as reflecting the company's strategy to employ whole families instead of the young and single, in effect to pay family wages.[10] They began to suspect that if you were not part of a family with multiple earners, Philips just would not allow you to earn a decent living. In contrast with all other contemporary interpretations of Eindhoven, this local and little-noted theory seems to have truly identified the key processes affecting unskilled workers in Eindhoven.

Early in 1930, St. Eloy finally felt forced to draw uncomfortable conclusions. It complained that Philips was now not just creating "family wages" but outrightly replacing commuting workers and young lodgers with members of large immigrant families.[11] However, reflecting its powerlessness and its clerically induced fear of public antagonism, the Catholic union tried to sound as casual and resigned as possible when it finally addressed this potentially explosive issue openly in April. Though existing studies and documents make no mention at all of this process of proletarian replacement, it is likely that it was in fact taking place, and that the casualness of St. Eloy's attitude was misleading.

Thus, the wider public attention to repression, rationalization, and job reduction tended to mask the ongoing and simultaneous transition in the nature of the Philips blue-collar labor force. Little sympathy was aroused by its young victims; indeed it went largely unnoticed, by the organized and skilled metalworkers and by the Catholic activists alike.[12] A central part of the appearance of crisis at Philips, then, was not at all related to the world depression. The loss for later Dutch social science and political culture of never having captured this feature of the Philips crisis may be clear: the lately often-discussed emphasis on obedient labor and sober working class family life in the context of a concerted export-led industrialization program in the postwar Netherlands found its chief experimental model here.[13]

To the Philips management the world crisis manifested itself both as a fall in demand caused by diminishing buying power and as an intensification of global price competition. Internally the organization was confronted with problems of location, efficiency, and labor control.[14] Yet, before the management was faced with the need to deal with the direct effects of the global crisis, it was dealing with and completing two distinct and internal processes that affected employment at Eindhoven. The first of these processes was the centralizing and recapturing of control over the production and sales organization, which during the stormy buildup of the radio factory had largely come into the hands of department bosses.[15] This in itself already led to personnel cuts as it prepared the way for a further rationalization of production. Secondly, while immigrant families were being housed in the new quarters, management was transforming its base of local unskilled labor.[16] Philips, consequently, fired thousands of workers during 1930. Only following these internally determined restructurings, probably starting in late December 1930 or early January 1931, did the company begin to respond to the global crisis proper.

Though the crisis of world capitalism following the 1929 crash of New York's stock exchange has become known as a demand crisis, the Philips company hardly faced any fall in nominal demand for its products. Rather, it was the decline of real purchasing power in nations leaving the gold standard that triggered the enormous intensification of global competition in the markets for electrical consumer products. Buyers remained willing to spend part of their reduced monetary means on lamps and radios, but they now searched for the best offer. At the same time, some companies were willing to accept temporary losses in order to enlarge their shares of the market. Thus, cheap Japanese bulbs temporarily made inroads in the established markets of European manufacturers. In addition, the still quickly growing market for radio sets remained an outright battleground where stable market partitions among firms could not yet emerge. As a result of these market structures, average prices for lamps between 1931 and 1937 dropped by 46 percent, for radios by as much as 53 percent.

Philips was utterly vulnerable to this process since it was based in a small mercantile nation without a substantial home market. Moreover, the Netherlands, in accordance with its commercial orientation, only grudgingly left the gold standard, and not before 1936.[17] Philips's reaction was twofold. First, it decentralized the production of its main mature product, incandescent lamps, to a whole range of countries. The company preferred relatively inefficient and small-scale "local for local" production, paid for in local currency, over large-scale export from an expensive hard currency country. Consequently, in 1933, when Philips had adapted to the new terms of trade, Dutch jobs in lamp making had been cut to some 33 percent of its strength in 1929.[18]

In contrast, the production of radio sets was largely retained in the new Eindhoven complex. In the fast-growing market for these sets the company developed an aggressive marketing strategy, based on concentrated mass production and thorough rationalization and mechanization of labor processes. Whereas Philips in 1930 sold almost 310,000 radios, this figure had more than doubled by 1935. The majority of these products were assembled in Eindhoven. In 1933, with its labor force reduced to a third of the 1929 figure, Eindhoven production had nevertheless increased by more than 10 percent.[19] This implies a rise of labor productivity of over 300 percent in less than four years! Thus Philips jobs in Eindhoven were affected by the twin processes of rationalization in radio making and decentralization of lamp production. Together, these processes caused a steep decline in local jobs and a steady increase of Philips workers abroad.

The Anatomy of Philips Job Cuts

How was the long-drawn-out process of job reduction structured? Who was fired, at which moment, and who was not? Two paternalist policy lines have been highlighted in the company's self-representation at the time and reproduced in recent historiography: First, the attempt in January 1931 to forestall personnel cuts by reducing labor time to forty-two and forty hours; and second, the intention to preserve the jobs of fathers over those of teenagers and the unmarried.[20] A glance at existing evidence, however, shows that cuts and measures have been significantly more complicated than is suggested by such official voices.[21]

Let us start with the timing of the process: All figures make clear that total employment at Philips Eindhoven had reached its peak of 22,800 in October 1929. Of those workers 18,555 earned weekly wages in production departments. From November 1929 on, the number of jobs suddenly started a decline. In February 1931, when Philips first introduced the compulsory reduction of hours, the company had already cut some 5,500 jobs. Notwithstanding this substantial reduction, it had been only in the middle of November 1930 that Philips's top managers, in one of their regular meetings, for the first time referred to an emergency situation demanding emergency measures.[22] This dismissal of over 5,000 workers in the period before the reduction of labor time in February 1931 was never presented as part of any crisis measure.

On closer scrutiny, 1930 was the decisive year of the transformation of Philips's base of production workers. While up until the spring of 1930 immigrant families were arriving in large numbers, in November 1929 Philips started to fire the young, regionally recruited proletariat that had become the source of problems with labor control. Instead of world crisis, then, 1930 witnessed the attack on undisciplined labor.

Although there are no specified figures available, it is possible to make a plausible estimation of the dismissals. All sources agree that the first cuts concerned commuters.[23] How many jobs could be reduced in this way? In March 1929 Philips employed almost 5,000 commuters, all of whom received monetary compensation for their expenses. Somewhat less than half of them were women. If we assume that all of those receiving more than one guilder commuting expenses per week were fired, we arrive at 4,200 dismissals.[24] It may well be all 5,000 commuting workers were laid off, as suggested by most sources. Thus, starting in November 1929 with the most expensive commuters, that is, the women and girls from the Belgian Campina and Dutch Limburg, commuting workers were fired one group after another.

It is pertinent to recall that Philips's disciplinary complaints were not limited to the single category of commuters. More generally, they were aimed at all those workers whose behavior was not shaped and disciplined by family relationships and concomitant household economic responsibilities. In this light it is highly significant that between January 1930 and January 1931 the percentage of Eindhoven inhabitants "not living in families," that is, lodgers, declined by more than a third, which amounts to some 5,000 people.[25] Considering the fact that between 1 January 1930 and 1 January 1931 only 1,400 new nuclear families were registered at City Hall,[26] we can infer that at the very minimum some 3,000 young lodgers were dismissed by Philips and subsequently left town.[27]

Thus we arrive at a realistic number of possible layoffs from November 1929 to February 1931 of somewhere between 7,000 and 8,000 workers. The difference with the actual reduction of jobs of 5,500 is probably explained by the approximately 2,050 workers from immigrant families who arrived in the course of 1929–30. Altogether, Philips recruited 554 large northeastern families with an average of 8.44 children, of whom five plus the father were employed by the company. The majority of them, 342 families, were housed in quarters that were only completed in the autumn of 1929 or later. It is beyond doubt that 161 of them arrived after January 1930.[28] These figures, then, suggest that new immigrant workers were introduced to the production lines at the very moment that the mobile regional youth were being fired. Combined with the little-noted complaint of the Catholic metalworkers union, this suggestion almost acquires the status of evidence.

The 7,000 or 8,000 layoffs of 1929–30, in short, had nothing at all to do with the consequences of global crisis. Nor were they simply the outcome of mechanization or rationalization *tout court*. Rather, they were the necessary outcome of a shrewd and innovative labor policy that replaced one unskilled working class group with another. The new immigrant, large-family proletariat, just as expected, developed a much more disciplined and stable attitude toward the wage relationship than the young mobile proletariat that had been emerging before 1930. Without them, a tripling of labor productivity would not easily have been realized.

Beginning in January 1931, however, it was no longer a difficult internal transition that the Philips management was coping with but an unprecedented global crisis. Philips official historiography has pointed out that top executives as late as November 1930 did not anticipate the acuteness and painfulness of the measures they would implement only three months later.[29] This claim seems wholly justified. Metalworkers, for example, were told in October 1930 that employment in the technical departments would be reduced by some 30 percent. It would turn out to be well over 60 percent.[30] In a meeting of the "rationalization committee" in the first days of January 1931, Piet Staal, general manager of the lamp factory, was still objecting to further cuts in production departments. He emphatically stated that production jobs had already been reduced substantially in the year before. In his view, it was now the staff department's turn to cut down. But only two weeks later, in a meeting with commercial planners, Staal had to face the message of quickly falling sales and prices and agree to a sharp reduction of output which led to thousands of layoffs.[31]

Top management at Philips, in fact, was so predisposed to dynamic growth and so unprepared for crisis that the realities of 1931 brought about a complete shift in power. Anton Philips and his older production managers, such as Piet Staal, gave in to a much younger generation of qualified professionals headed by his son-in-law Frans Otten. This same young top cadre had already supervised the infrastructural investments at Eindhoven and implemented the centralization of corporate control, the rationalization of production, and the transformation of the company's blue-collar base in the years before. They already controlled the organization in a very real sense, without as yet replacing the older class of production managers. In a coalition with the commercial departments they were willing and capable of pushing through fundamental restructuring in the face of serious setbacks.[32]

From February 1931 to May 1932 the totality of jobs at Philips in Eindhoven declined from around 17,000 to 9,500; waged jobs in production departments were reduced from 13,050 to about 8,500, that is, by 4,500 workers.[33] Again, we have no clear specifications on who exactly was fired. Nevertheless, it can be demonstrated that Philips management went as far as it could go without fundamentally endangering the premises of its organization or generating open conflict. Further cuts in mass production in 1931, I argue, were wholly predicated on the great employment flexibility that was inherent in the characteristics of the new unskilled working class created only a good year before.

In February 1931 Philips announced a compulsory reduction of the work week to forty-two hours. Only a month later it was further limited to forty hours (with payment for forty-two). The company declared that in this way it was trying to save the jobs of some 2,000 workers, especially fathers.[34] At the same moment, however, the corporation, within a few months, dismissed over 3,000 workers, reducing its waged jobs to around 10,500 in the early summer.[35] From July 1931 another wave of dismissals brought the number down again, to about 9,000 in October / November, after which another round of reductions began. How did the company achieve this second extensive set of reductions of 5,000 production workers in 1931–32? In the absence of exact data the following hypothesis seems plausible.

As we have seen, already long before January 1931 the Philips technical departments were planning a reduction of some 30 percent. Evidently, the completion of the new radio factories by itself led to a considerable labor redundancy in skilled metalwork. Also, now that a large part of lamp production was being moved abroad and an investment pause in new means of production was announced,[36] many more skilled metalworkers could be dismissed. In the course of 1931 and early 1932 Philips fired a 1,300 of them, which left the department with not more than 770 workers (the number 1,300 assumes that a good 100 had already been fired selectively in 1930).[37] The majority of the dismissed were young, did not have families or other roots in the community, and had recently arrived from the west and north. The company now paid their return journey, thus helping the number of unemployed Eindhoven citizens not to peak and to prevent local meetings of unemployed socialist metalworkers.[38] In addition, Philips probably fired some 200 foreign glassworkers, whose return journey was also covered by the company. Together these dismissals amounted to 1,500.

Finally, the most painful part of the operation came into view: cutting back the number of mass-production workers. This was painful because it hit precisely those newly established families that were recently recruited to replace local adolescents. By reducing their numbers only months after their arrival, Philips took the great risk of endangering the quality and quantity of its future unskilled labor supply. No company can easily survive two devastating rounds of dismissals in two years.

Both in the process of restructuring the unskilled working class and reducing its jobs, the Philips managers had quickly learned how flexibly this new proletariat could be deployed. The drastic cuts that were realized in 1931–32 do not appear to have been fully necessitated by the firm's profits or cashflow position.[39] But Philips managers thought these measures could and should be taken because they were a very powerful way to instantly propel productivity by facilitating sharper selection.

Management, armed with an intimate knowledge of its new unskilled working class, appears to have reasoned like this: The 554 large families in Drents Dorp average six workers per family: one father, 3.16 daughters, and 1.88 sons. If, temporarily, four earners per family are dismissed, each family will still be left with two earners. If one was the father and the other a daughter, a crucial measure of loyalty and connectedness with the firm will be upheld (though on shorter hours) while a limited but disciplined and therefore profitable mass production can somehow be sustained (and stocks be reduced). In this way it is possible to cut an additional 2,200 mass-production jobs without fundamentally endangering the labor reserve that might be needed in the near future. Added to the layoffs in glass- and metalwork, this will amount to a reduction of 3,700 direct jobs between February 1931 and May 1932. If we recall that other quarters, too, housed substantial numbers of similar large families, which could also survive a temporary reduction in their ratio of earners per unit, it becomes visible how management arrived at 4,500 layoffs in 1931–32. Indeed, it is arguable that other large families would collectively have suffered some 800 layoffs, making up exactly for the sum total.[40]

This analysis is nothing but a hypothesis. It is, however, based on all the scattered information available and accounts for all relevant processes and relationships. The real process may have been slightly different, but the conjecture seems thoroughly realistic and plausible. Its understanding of the respective roles of local unskilled adolescents and immigrant large families, moreover, is clearly supported by the picture emerging from the other sections of this study and is not refuted by any counter evidence.

Overviewing the whole record, it is clear that different working class segments were treated differently and were affected at different moments in time. Commuters and lodgers were treated mercilessly in the course of the rationalizations and speedups. From late 1929 to early 1931, almost all regionally recruited lodgers and commuters were replaced with labor from large immigrant families. Subsequently, after the completion of the radio factories and the decentralization of lamp production, two thirds of supraregionally recruited metalworkers, largely again bachelor lodgers, were laid off. Lodgers and commuters, in short, were treated as nothing more than an easily substitutable turnover pool.

Family labor, in contrast, occupied a central place in the corporation's strategies and was treated cautiously. For unskilled labor this was particularly true if several members of such "Philips" families were employed simultaneously, and were efficient and disciplined producers. To them, Philips may not have been sentimental, but it did take some measure of self-interested caution. While two thirds of Drents Dorp workers were probably dismissed, the company made a point of equally distributing the pain over those families displaying the right "Philipsist" characteristics. It turned out that the large number of workers per family, combined with the intimate information the company permanently processed about them, facilitated a surprising degree of flexibility in their deployment. Large families initially do not seem to have been recruited with an eye to this potential, as they were exclusively selected on their possible contribution to future growth. But during the crisis period Philips management discovered the flexibility potentials inherent to its earlier labor policies. In his dissertation Philips's urbanist Bakker Schut noted that "a secondary, not to be underestimated advantage of such a [large family] policy was its contribution to the formation of a labor reserve." He goes on, very cool and with scientific distance, revealing small pieces of Philips's practices: "If, in case of a sudden reduction of operations, cuts are equally spread over such families, the subsistence of the great majority of them will not be endangered, despite the fall in their incomes."[41]

In order to understand the subtle workings of the Philips regime as a whole, it should moreover be pointed out that the preservation of the new working class of immigrant large families was made possible by two other sources of control. For one, as a large landlord Philips was in a position to secure worker ties with the company and the community by reducing the costs of living. House rents during the crisis were adjusted in such a way that large families with reduced collective incomes could enjoy uniquely low housing costs.[42] Thus the urban investments, instead of limiting the company's space of maneuver, turned out to be another mechanism for flexibility.

Secondly, the proclaimed respect for fathers' jobs needs to be reconsidered. The single fact that one of the fathers of the immigrant families of which I collected biographic materials was dismissed points to the possibility that a more fundamental calculation might have been made. It is not without significance that this was the father of the de Bondt family. His high moral responsibility and religious dedication, plus the honorable job that his youngest daughter had just acquired in the Philips social work department (she was not dismissed), made him more vulnerable to dismissal than others. Evidently, the Philips personnel department saw enough reasons for this family to stay and be able to endure their misfortune.

It may, then, have been not so much the proclaimed respect for fathers per se that informed the job cuts; rather, the company seems to have carefully weighed the balance of power, status, and interest within families before it determined how dismissals could best be distributed over family members. In this way the company could prevent destroying the family's capacity to collectively endure adversity, while it was able to save the maximum on wage costs. In general, this policy meant retaining the father. But the de Bondt case demonstrates that it could as well turn out differently. Depending on the composition of and relationships within families, the goal of trying to maintain a minimal measure of loyalty could lead to different outcomes in different families. Such evaluations, then, were very intricate and could only be made on the basis of extensive information on families and individuals such as provided by the firm's social agencies that penetrated the life of workers outside the factory gates. Here, as was the case with the Philips housing stock, flexibility was enhanced rather than limited by corporate social policy.

Philips, thanks to its urban service bureaucracy and its large unskilled families, did not only generate a remarkable measure of flexibility. Together, these features of Philipsism also enabled an unprecedented speedup of productivity. After having transformed its base of unskilled labor, Philips thus created a major paradox: achieving world-competitive prices in a notoriously labor-intensive industry operating from a hard-currency country.

Drents Dorp thus first helped Philips to regain control over young production workers and subsequently enabled it to survive the developments of the thirties. Given the centrality of electrical manufacturing in postwar Dutch industrialization, we might almost say that Drents Dorp helped secure a good part of post-war Dutch prosperity.

CLASS STRUCTURES AND REGIONAL PATHS OF ACCUMULATION: EXPLAINING FORDIST AND PHILIPSIST REGIMES

Macro-historical comparisons are a method well suited for defining the diacritical features of historical social structures that bear a certain elective affinity. To conclude this exploration of the city of Eindhoven and the Philipsist mode of production, it might therefore be worthwhile to compare their patterns of development, key relationships, and social arrangements with their influential mirror image in the United States, Detroit's Fordism.[43]

In contrast to the usual abstract ways of theorizing about Fordism and accumulation regimes, it is the purpose of this local/regional comparison of Fordism and Philipsism to situate their emergence and structure in the specific social conditions and relationships of their home regions. Such a comparison shows that their particular managerial innovations were not simply a product of enlightened managerial minds. Rather, both Fordism and Philipsism expanded upon, reproduced, and deepened the particular key social mechanisms of growth in their respective regions. Regional class structures fundamentally determined the methods available to these corporate capitalists for countering problems of weak labor discipline among unskilled workers in periods of expansion. These methods, subsequently, had great consequences for the emergence and issues of class protest during the crisis of the 1930s, and they contributed much to the formation of national production regimes under postwar welfare state arrangements in the respective countries.

Monetary Moralism and Flexible Familism

While Philipsism became famous for its social policies and housing provisions, Fordism made history with two wholly different innovations: the five-dollar workday and, related to it, "sociological investigations."[44] Fordism has also become credited with the invention of modern mass production. But in that respect it was not unique, although of course very advanced.[45] Assembly line production, as developed by the Ford company, was a powerful symbol of mass production in automobile making, but it was not the only form of mass production emerging in those years. Philips, for example, also pioneered mass production methods. But it did so in a different locality and a different branch where processes of production did not generally allow for forms of process organization, such as the assembly line, that were developed in carmaking. In electrical consumer products, such as the core of Philipsist manufacturing, mass production was primarily embodied in the utterly subdivided and Taylorized work stations of large numbers of yellow-skirted girls. The assembly line served by (teams of) blue-collar males, as developed in carmaking, has never been the single paradigm of twentieth-century mass-producing industry. In fact, the case could be made that, by isolating mass production as its defining feature, the current debate on Fordism and post-Fordism has lost a critical measure of historical, comparative, and analytical value.[46]

Grounded in these two divergent forms of labor process in modern mass production—the assembly line "manned" mostly by males, on the one hand, and the rows of work stations served by girls on the other—there arose a whole array of significant asymmetries in what regulation theorists would call "the modes of regulation" of Detroit's and Eindhoven's industrial complexes. Labor relations, corporate policies, family structures, and urban forms that developed in conjunction with the characteristic local forms of production and accumulation were not identical among these cases. A good way to start an exploration of these different structures is to study the social origins and consequences of Ford's five-dollar day.

Between 1913 and 1916, Ford, by then a company employing some 10,000 workers, proceeded to centralize hiring and firing procedures and to standardize wage schemes. In the process it created an employment department and a sociological department. Just as at Philips fifteen years later, this development had been triggered by mounting labor control problems as manifested in rising rates of labor turnover (amounting to more than 300 percent). This weakening of workers' discipline was caused by a similar process to that of the Philips' case: a rapidly increasing demand for unskilled labor shifted the balance of power to the workers' side of the wage relation. Like Philips, the Ford company also started in those years to provide medical, recreational, and educational facilities. But, unlike Philips, it did not provide housing. Instead, it launched a profit-sharing program known as the five-dollar day and created continuous sociological investigation of workers' private lives and situations.

The five-dollar day, established in 1914, was, in Stephen Meyer's words, "a unique profit sharing plan with a powerful monetary incentive to mold and to shape Ford workers in order to nurture more disciplined work habits for mechanized factory work."[47] Breadwinners and unmarried persons over age twenty-two, who conformed to Ford's standards of productivity, were eligible to receive back part of the company's profits in the form of a permanent premium on wages. That premium was considerable; it could even amount to a doubling of the worker's income. Those who did not yet quite deserve a share in the plan had their short-fall premiums clearly mentioned on their wage slip. They were entitled to a part of the sum if they attained the necessary productivity level within six months. The earlier they got there, the larger the sum they received. By 1916, about 50 percent of Ford workers shared in the plan.

Related to this profit-sharing scheme, Ford also installed in 1914 a "sociological department." With the Ford medical department as its antecedent, this new department investigated the private causes for workers' weakening shop floor discipline. It also monitored whether workers receiving profit shares were maintaining thrift, steadiness, and sobriety in their home life. Sociological department employees not only collected shop floor information on productivity, income, illness, and absenteeism but also data on nationality, religion, bank savings, property, amusements, place of residence, number of dependents, domestic troubles, etc. In order to do so, they visited workers' houses and interviewed family members. In the course of 1914–16 eligibility for the five-dollar day was made dependent upon the sociological department's approval of the worker's lifestyle. Thus the department could urge a family to move to a better neighborhood, or even help to reconcile family quarrels using the profit premium as sanction. All of private life was perceived to be of relevance to shop floor performance. Meyer concludes that "the principal objective of the Ford welfare program was to remake social and cultural values for men to fit the regimen of the mechanized plant."[48]

Comparison thus again shows that Philips's concern with working class culture was not unique: not in its causes, nor in its objectives. Rather, it seems to have been part of a broad movement among early-twentieth-century corporate capitalists to counter crises of labor discipline by developing a rooted and steady work force that could be employed on calculable profits. However, in the comparison with Fordism, two interesting and interrelated features of Philipsism stand out. Where Philips tried to counter its labor control problems first and foremost through housing investments and social policies underpinning its labor policy of "flexible familism," Ford launched the "monetary moralism" of the five-dollar day and associated sociological investigation. In order to achieve the same goal of expanding, stabilizing, and disciplining local unskilled labor forces, Philipsism and Fordism implemented highly divergent strategies.

Beyond their connections with ideology, these dissimilarities of strategy were principally caused by their being embedded in, and reacting to, different regional paths of accumulation. These different paths were among others reflected in different labor processes and product specializations, different compositions of the work force, and different markets for labor and final products. Both corporate capitalists, in developing new local solutions for weakening labor discipline, expanded on the respective key mechanisms of growth and accumulations in their home regions.

Patterns of Regional Accumulation

The importance of region, that is, its population, its internal markets, its insertion in the world economy, its class structures, cannot be emphasized enough.[49] The Philips family of bankers, financiers, and merchants started its incandescent lamp firm in Brabant only because of the availability of "good and loyal," cheap and flexible young female workers. It was the abundance of juvenile surplus labor that gave the region its industrial impetus. Southeast Brabant industrialization hinged centrally on the juvenile and female labor surplus of the impoverishing regional agricultural economy, as well as on the input of children from proto-industrial, semi-industrial, fully industrial, and poor petty bourgeois households. The region's development was based, one could say, on an "immature" and dominated surplus work force, dependent on additional family incomes. Like so many other regional development processes, it did not mirror the standard adult, individual, "sovereign," male workers of neoclassical economic theory, who "freely" responded to well-developed market incentives. It was based on dominated young workers, whose comparatively small earnings were only one contribution to complex and multiple-earner household economies.

Regional industrialization thus did not originate in strong markets for labor or final products. While its workers were not lured by high wages but sent by their parents, its final products were largely exported. Urbanization consequently remained weak compared to its industrial dynamism. As we have seen, large multiple-earner households necessarily allocated themselves to low-rent/low-price areas with sufficient space for additional productive activities. Strong housing markets, therefore, could not develop. Up until 1928 urbanization was to a significant extent caused by the immigration of educated white-collar and skilled blue-collar workers, recruited from more advanced urban regions. As far as internal processes of population concentration within the region were concerned, the growth of semiproletarian villages (part of which were annexed to the city of Eindhoven in 1920) had been more significant than urbanization of the core itself. By 1925, this regional dynamic based on "immature labor" and "immature markets" had resulted in a scattered urban settlement of some sixty thousand inhabitants.

By contrast, in 1920 Detroit and its immediate environment were already populated by over a million persons.[50] Together with other centers in the Midwest, the region featured a dynamic industrialization process based on local demand for, above all, metalwares. Grounded in mature markets for innovative products and male labor, the region was the quickest urbanizer in the United States in those years, and became the destiny of a large portion of the migrants to the New World. After 1900, of all metalwork trades, carmaking grew fastest. This led to the development in Detroit not only of the Ford corporation but also of Chrysler and General Motors and a whole lot of smaller carmaking and engine making firms, all with their clusters of hundreds of suppliers. As a consequence of the greatly differentiated, advanced regional production structure, and its well-established markets, the region generally featured high wages. Its internal dynamism was also reflected in its giving birth to its own corporate capitalist classes. Unlike Anton and Gerard Philips, Henry Ford and hundreds of less well known entrepreneurs were firmly rooted in the area.[51] Indeed, Ford had been a skilled metalworker himself. In contrast to southeast Brabant, then, this process was based on, and reinforced, the full development of market forces for many factors of production and reproduction.

In this highly differentiated and monetized regional context, labor discipline of adult male workers at Ford could only be controlled by purely monetary incentives. Both the booming and competitive labor market as well as the fully developed capitalist supply of urban housing made any alternative strategy impractical. It becomes clear, then, that by offering additional monetary rewards to workers displaying the correct cultural traits, Ford in fact turned to the key mechanism of Detroit's regional process, that is, market forces and monetary incentives. Other social mechanisms, let alone outright social pressure, could not have worked here, and indeed were not necessary. In addition to the classical assertion by Antonio Gramsci that in the Midwest cultural hegemony was created in the sphere of production itself, it seems necessary to emphasize that it could also be "bought" in the marketplace.

Ford's sociological investigations reflected this liberal nature of the locality. No employer could physically get a hold over parts of the city or the private lives of its employees. In order to find out more about his workers' families, and accordingly sharpen the discriminatory function of the profit-sharing plan, Ford had no other means than to visit them privately for an interview. This practice was understandably controversial, and often judged to be a violation of liberal American principles. But given the cultural objectives of the Ford social department, and given the liberal and differentiated nature of the region, the company had no choice.

In combatting deteriorating labor discipline, Philips, just like Ford, turned to the key mechanism of accumulation in the region. In southeast Brabant this key mechanism did not consist of a fully developed labor market featuring strong monetary incentives. On the contrary. It had precisely been the gradual emergence of a mature regional labor market that had caused the weakening of local labor discipline. Instead of a dependence on markets, regional accumulation here had crucially depended on the absence of "mature" markets for labor, indeed on their active prevention. Industrialization had been based on nonmarket wages for "immature," juvenile, and female workers from semiproletarian, multiple-earner families. The incomes for these families were primarily realized by their adolescent children, particularly their daughters.

But this form of "immature" labor supply, as we have seen, had no longer been available in sufficient numbers since 1924. The expansion of radio production after 1926, with its consequently booming labor demand, had necessitated a rise in wages in order to attract increasingly older adolescents and young male adults to the factories. Eindhoven for the first time witnessed the emergence of a growing class of young mobile workers, many of them lodgers and commuters, who gradually began to escape parental supervision and family bonds. The incipient "mature" labor market had instant liberating effects on local working class youths. But as it called into question a whole range of "extraeconomic" patriarchal practices that had been central to the reproduction of local, obedient, juvenile, and sex-segregated labor, the disciplinary foundations of local production began to erode.

It is not surprising, therefore, that the core of Philipsist strategy in 1928–31 consisted of managerial attempts to prevent the development of "mature" labor markets and re-create an identical working class of multiple-earner families as had characterized southeast Brabant industry earlier. While Ford developed its monetary moralism, Philips created its flexible familism, based on the importation of large multiple-earner families, large-scale investments in workers housing, and supportive social policy.

In a famous discussion with Immanuel Wallerstein and several prominent agrarian historians, Robert Brenner demonstrated that late medieval landlords were not free to choose the most suitable ways to exploit their peasants but were fully constrained by the historical power relationships between classes that had emerged in their regions.[52] It was not their self-interested managerial choices that determined the different regional outcomes of the late medieval crisis, but their space for maneuver within the class structures of their region. He referred to the marxist position on capitalist transition taken up by Maurice Dobb against Adam Smith, and suggested that Wallerstein, in spite of his supposedly marxist approach, had restated the point of view of classical liberalism.

In comparing different outcomes of twentieth-century corporate capitalist struggle with problems of labor discipline, a similar point seems to come to the fore. Indeed, while both Fordism and Philipsism emerged as systematic and innovative managerial efforts to counter identical problems of labor discipline, regional comparison shows that the divergent strategies developed did not come out of the blue. Instead of being invented by unorthodox managerial minds, divergent outcomes were primarily caused by, and were a reflection of, systematic differences in the social class structures of regional development. Different key mechanisms of regional accumulation, grounded in different structures of production and appropriation, had shaped divergent patterns of industrial development, industrial relations, and industrial regimes in those regions. Consequently, regionally dominant configurations of class largely determined the sorts of strategy open to corporate capitalists in countering problems of expansion and labor discipline.

The Philips corporation in 1927–31 and the Ford company in 1913–16 took important steps in their own development and the development of their regional base. In those years they both became celebrated models for organized capitalist development, at a later stage powerfully influencing visions of societal reconstruction by new national political alliances. But however much these new capitalist practices spoke to the contemporary social imagination, they in fact merely re-created, expanded, and deepened exactly those social mechanisms from which the industrialization of their respective home regions had originated: dynamic market relations, high wages and monetary incentives in the case of Detroit; multiple-earner, daughter-exploiting families, on "family wages," in the Eindhoven case.

The historical consequences of these different outcomes deserve note. David Brody has argued that if the crisis of the thirties had not hit the industrial localities that had formed around expansive "welfarist" employers such as Ford, General Motors, and General Electric in the United States, mass union formation, class conflict, and the New Deal might never have emerged.[53] However, the crisis did come and threw a large percentage of the U.S. labor force out of work. These were male breadwinners who had become accustomed to good and steady wages and high consumption levels during more than a decade. Their dismissal often left their households suddenly without any substantial source of income. Many of them lived in newly built mortgaged houses, and were threatened with expulsion. Their communities were being uprooted in a very real sense.

In the Eindhoven case, however, crisis did not result in the destitution of the majority of unskilled families. As we have seen, even though Philips laid off more than half its production workers, the large multiple-earner families in company housing were well equipped to survive the crisis. When half their working members were fired and the other half were kept on contract, they could still keep life going. The Philips company, moreover, was in a position to strategically lower its house rents, thus helping families survive and keeping its labor reserve intact. All in all, crisis here did not so much result in sudden destitution and uprooting as in collectively shared but "decent" poverty.

Turning Brody's counterfactual hypothesis on its head, then, it might well be argued that without the multiple-earner and daughter-exploiting large family, without flexible familism, the early-thirties crisis in Eindhoven would probably have resulted in much more widespread and concerted protest than was the case. Indeed, such sharp labor segmentation would not have occurred, and forms of solidarity between different working groups would certainly have been nurtured. It is even possible to refine Brody's thesis: If U.S. regions such as Michigan had developed a comparable form of multiple-earner proletariat, supported by corporate housing provisions and other social policies, class conflict and mass mobilization in the thirties might well have been averted.

But, as we have seen, such reasoning is futile. Industrialists had not much choice in the key social mechanisms of their growth and survival. Southeast Brabant at that stage could never have developed a large car industry or an electrical industry for professional equipment and large-scale custom-made installations such as General Electric or Siemens, nor would lamp manufacturing in Detroit have been as competitive as that of Philips. Region, products, class relationships, and class cultures really form one dynamic whole.

8 A Dumb Girl and an Epileptic *Bricoleur:*

Clues on Culture and Class in Popular Memory

and Narration

Work and family, demography and production, the accumulation of capital and the accumulation of households were inextricably intertwined in the industrializing region of southeast Brabant. Large families had a significance far beyond their conventionally imputed relation with Catholic prescriptions. As cash earners and guarantees of parental status, teenage children, and daughters in particular, were vital to the survival of households. Not Catholicism, not paternalism, let alone deference, could really be the primary characteristic of local popular culture. It was precisely this specific articulation of (semiproletarian) family survival and industrial accumulation which formed the social and cultural core of a dynamic regional process that lasted from about 1850 to, say, 1950.

Instead of class, this region gave rise to wholly different forms of struggle, which were centered on different issues and waged by different contenders. As exploitation was mediated through the family and was generally sex specific, it was generation and gender rather than class that would form the crux of social conflict and contention. Whereas in some other industrializing places the discourse of class drew public attention to the unjustified subordination and inequality of supposedly freeborn and sovereign (male) citizens, exploitation through gender and generation in the Eindhoven area hit marginalized categories of people that did not commonly have access to those social and cultural resources that were needed to collectively name, explain, and decry their plight. Their experience, consequently, was decentered, fragmented, and privatized. Moreover, it was generally overlaid and confused with the ambiguities of love and loyalty that parenthood and family always somehow seem to foster.

But how can we get at these displaced struggles? Of course, one could point to the year 1928–29, when mobile regional youth succeeded in appropriating parts of urban and industrial space for their courting, pleasure making, and short-lived collective refusal to live highly regimented lives. But, regrettably, we know little about it, as it left traces only in the discourse and practice of policing institutions and morally panicking authors. The postwar period also witnessed several such moments. But I would like to probe a bit deeper.

It would be worthwhile to get an idea of how the regional forms of exploitation were in fact embedded in the daily routines of social life. How were they connected with parental love and loyalty toward the family? How were such ambivalent experiences handled in cultural ways, in words, orientations, loyalties, and actions outside those little-documented and short historical moments (and isolated spaces) of apparent liberation?

Without believing in clear-cut and representative answers, I think we can learn a great deal from a closer exploration of aspects of memory, life history, and popular narration. There, we can still find multitudes of disparate traces of everyday exploitation, struggle, resistance, accommodation and appropriation, and the ways they are worked up in memory. When placed in the context of the key mechanisms of social life in the region, this can offer significant clues to important questions which we cannot hope to answer in more straightforward ways.

Below I present at length two encounters with Eindhoven inhabitants, one male, one female, both now between fifty-five and seventy years old. Their narrations about their youth and family are far from representative. Indeed, they are highly idiosyncratic, and are not meant to be otherwise. It is my contention, however, that the forms, structures, and issues of memory and narration expressed in these stories are certainly not unique. They are exemplary for the way the region's key dynamic could be translated into human agency, experience, culture, memory, and narration among common people. That is, the configuration of social relationships as represented in these stories does recur regularly in numerous versions of comparable stories that express the multifarious experience of youth, work, and family in the locality. These narrations sensitize us to the range of experiences of key relationships in the region, and to their possible consequences for the thought and action of the women and men concerned. In short, the following presentations should not be misunderstood as ill-conceived efforts at representative life history analysis. They are essays aiming for a deeper cultural understanding.

It should be emphasized that these presentations do not concern encounters with immigrant people from the Philips neighborhoods, but autochthonous local people. The latter not only had different and less paternalistic relationships with Philips; they also embodied regional relationships in a much more organic way. Moreover, boys from immigrant families generally had a much closer relation with Philips than the sons of regionally rooted families. Accordingly, they were socialized differently.

MARIA VAN DE VELDE

It was my second encounter with the family Van de Velde (July 1992). The first time, half a year earlier, I had interviewed the man of the family, Hennie; now I wanted to talk with Maria, his wife. They live in a neat Eindhoven middle class suburb, built in the mid-1970s on the northern outskirts of Woensel. Their house is comfortably furnished with thick, brown-leather chairs. They have a lot of time nowadays. Their three daughters have left the household to live on their own, and Hennie, who had been a gifted toolmaker and technical manager at Philips, has been given early retirement because of corporate restructuring.

They appear to enjoy my unannounced visit. It had been a good interview the first time, and they seemed to like talking about their lives and history with an informed outsider like me. They cordially invited me in. Hennie called for his wife to come and see who had entered. Still standing in the corridor, I told Maria that I would like to interview her on the memories of her youth. Last time I had questioned her on her experiences as a young girl at Philips but, I told her, we had not yet addressed her relationships with her family. I said I was particularly interested in how much of her income she had to give up to her parents and how such things were generally arranged and talked about in her family. She had shown herself to be an open informant with a very detailed memory, so I did not expect problems. I had decided to reveal the point of my visit right at the outset, so as to optimally focus our talk.

Consequently, I was ill prepared when she showed serious doubts. She paled slightly and wanted to move to the kitchen in order to prevent Hennie and me from trying to persuade her. But Hennie, in his relaxed and friendly manner, threw an arm around her and argued that there was no reason not to start with the interview when she could always stop it when she wanted to. I emphatically agreed with this. She probably trusted me just enough to give me the chance.

When we were seated in the sitting room (Hennie was preparing tea) she explained, somewhat embarrassed, that she had been ill some years ago and that her youth and her family had played a large part in that. She had been overstressed, could not sleep, was very anxious, and often had painful reminiscences of her adolescent years. It was hard for her to talk about it now, she said, because she did not want to denounce her own family. Whatever happened, she said, these people were still her family. And there had also been many moments of great pleasure.

But in spite of her initial hesitation and fears for the integrity of her family, it took less than a minute for her to start narrating without wanting to stop. She quickly got irritated when Hennie appeared intending to interrupt her. She only needed some initial questions and all the rest of her story came by itself. Everything she told me fully satisfied my incipient hypotheses on the complexity of father-daughter relations in the region. I was prepared to pose a whole lot of specific questions which I deemed necessary to reach clarification on the possible frictions in those relationships. But Maria needed no prompting. During short pauses she exclaimed: "It's hardly believable nowadays, but this was how it was"; "What's the use of all this today? My children keep saying shut up mother, the past is the past and today is today"; "It's my own history, but it is worthless."

I started the interview by asking how much she had earned as a girl of fifteen in the early fifties (born in 1936), and how much she was expected to hand over to her parents. She still knew it exactly: She had made about twenty-three guilders a week, had given it all to her parents, and had received two guilders and fifty cents pocket money. She had been one of eleven daughters; six were older than her, and everyone above age twelve was expected to somehow contribute to the household income. As a young girl, for example, she used to go along the streets selling sweets prepared by her mother.

First they had lived in the isolated Philips settlement adjacent to the village of Aalst. In 1951 they had moved to Drents Dorp, where a larger house for the thirteen-member family was available. Father worked in a stockroom of the Philips bulb factory. "He used to work always, always. He never came late to his job at Philips, not even a minute, not in thirty years. And we too had to work always, even when we were ill."

Hennie interrupts and says that everyone had to hand over all their money to their parents but that he himself had been lucky. "I got twenty-five guilders pocket money a week." Maria becomes angry with the suggestion that Hennie had had a better time: "Okay, but you too were working like a dog. Even all your earnings from overtime were given to your parents." "Yes," Hennie says, "but I was making fifty guilders a week by then as a toolmaker, because of overtime of course, but also because I used to be 30 percent above the norm. But, in fact, I was simply lucky to be the youngest at home. The others had had less privilege. And my parents, father being a building contractor, were much better off than yours."

Maria determinedly brings the subject back to her own youth. How hard she used to work! At age sixteen she was employed at the BATA shoemaking plant in the village of Best. She got up at 5:30 in the morning; set the table for everyone; took a bus at 6:30; started work at 7:30; worked well above the norm and arrived home again at 5:30 P.M. Then she tidied up the house, which was often a mess, and started peeling potatoes for dinner. She cleaned up the dishes afterward and went to bed totally exhausted. "But I have always been really dumb," she says. "They used to say I was just dumb. 'Bleu,' they said. I was obedient and I was my mother's dearest child. She was always lying in bed with her sicknesses, but she made pretty clothes for me. My oldest sister had left the household by that time. She could not stand it anymore. My father was often drunk and aggressive. Nellie, my second oldest sister, was in fact running the household. The other four older sisters had boyfriends and were withdrawing from their responsibilities. I had to do everything.

"When I left school at age twelve, Nellie sent me as a maid to a small farmer's family in the nearby countryside. My parents turned out not to know about it. The money was paid directly to my sister; I never saw any of it. I was treated badly there, especially by the farmer's wife. I wasn't even allowed to sit at the table. She had five children, but madam just stayed in bed and I had to arrange everything. I was not permitted to go home during weekends. I very often wept. And because they gave me no time off to visit my family during Christmas I ran away. But I didn't know where I was, so I got lost. I was picked up by the police and brought home. Only then did my parents realize that I had been gone for some time. That's how it used to be in those days. You simply needed to get rid of a child. But I can tell you, such things are not easily forgotten. . . . And then my father . . . well . . . you were not supposed to say so . . . but he was always drinking.

"Not that he took anything from his wage from Philips. No, he never did that. But he was serving at the café of a sister of his. So he had money for himself. And then . . . he was always watching on Sundays to see whether we were in time for church. One time we didn't show up and he got very angry. 'But you yourself are always drinking on Sundays in that pub there on the corner,' I said. But I wasn't supposed to say that, and he beat me. He also used to beat my mother when he was drunk."

"Yeah, he was a sharp guy," Hennie intervened. It was silent for a moment. Maria suddenly shifted the emphasis, "But at a certain moment, he was sitting in his chair, softly stammering some words. Everyone must have thought he was drunk. Mother had called him twice for dinner. But he didn't come. She wanted to keep up appearances for the children and didn't get angry. It turned out he had had a stroke! And later in the evening he was hit once again. Some weeks later he died. He had just retired, three months before. He had never been ill. But at that age, you wouldn't believe it, he still had the nerve to hang upside down with his toes behind a high bar. And there he was, dangling for minutes! Looking around, grinning at the amazement all around." Maria springs up: "But as little kids we also used to climb to the very top of a tree, catch frogs, roast them, and eat their legs, or catch birds and cook them. We were also full of tricks!

"However, in his relationship with authorities father used to be very obedient too. When I was sixteen years old I was working at the bulb factory. To make more money the Belgians had tipped me to put small pieces of cardboard in the box. And so I did. But somehow someone must have talked. And the Belgians had probably pointed at me as the initiator of the deceit. After a few weeks of good earnings a calculator came checking my speed. 'You don't work so swiftly uh . . . it does not quite match with the units you score.' I had to confess it all. But I didn't dare to betray the Belgians. They would have beaten me up at the gate! Then the department boss ordered my father to come. Father got very angry with me and I feared he would kick me. But still I did not tell the two of them about the Belgians. At home, however, I started to weep. Mother knew how honest I was. She often left small coins around in the house to check whether anybody would take them. But I never did, and she knew it well. It was decided that I should tell everything to the highest boss of the department. But still I did not dare. In the end I told everything. I said that whole row behind me was doing it, and the other one too, and she also and she. Some were fired, others were fined, and I was moved to another department. I could even have started as a maid with Frits Philips. But I did not dare to . . . or maybe my mother wanted to keep me home, so there was someone around—she was always ill. . . . I don't know anymore."

Someone calls at the door. It is an ex-Philips scientist who needs Hennie for some private business. Maria and I are alone now. She starts to repeat much of what she has told. But in a low voice this time, as if we were collaborators in some obscure affair. Then she turns to new stories.

"After Philips I went to work at BATA because the wages were better there. As a girl of sixteen I used to walk to all the factories, alone, looking for a better job. I walked hours doing so, because I never got any money for the bus." I wondered why she did so since she had to give it all up. "They needed the money," she answered, "everyone had to work." "When I was eighteen years old my mother made me a beautiful and narrowly fitting tweed suit. We very often went out. Each Sunday, but also on Saturdays. You couldn't afford nylons, so you went with your bare legs in high heels. There was no money to take a bus. We walked all the way to the dancings of Stratum or Gestel. That could be more than an hour. Sometimes your legs were like ice.

"But in general it was no fun. It was work, work, and work again. Maybe it is true that I have always been dumb, like they used to say. I met Hennie at a dance. But I knew him already from stories. He could drink! He told my brothers-in-law that he would make me pregnant so I could leave home.

"Some ten years ago I got ill. Overstressed. Was afraid of everything. Shivered all the time. I went to a psychiatrist in the hospital. I thought they'd say I was crazy. But they didn't. Apparently the past came back. I wouldn't have my husband with me in the psychiatrist's room, but he came of his own accord. He knew that everything would come out, that I would tell the whole story, of the past and so. . . . It is no good to keep it all for yourself . . . all those memories . . . it should come out one time. But still, I don't easily tell it. . . . I've often been afraid of my father. When he was drunk you'd better look out for him. Because . . . he tried the kids too. . . . And incidentally, my friend—she's living in the next street, they also had twelve children—she's had a really disgusting youth. She was forced to go to bed with her father! Otherwise he would beat her up. And still she's one of the two normal sisters. The rest are wrecks. And she had to do it often enough! Your own daughters! But you do not have a mother anymore then, do you? As a mother you ought to drag him before court. Nowadays they'll do that. My father too, when I saw him drunk, I kept away from him. Not when he was sober . . . no, no, not then.

"At the time I met Hennie we often used to go to dances. Many girls behaved like sluts, hanging on the bar and flirting. Me too, sometimes. When you went to the toilets and came along the bar I was flirting, too. But I was always afraid of what would happen. I don't know . . . I was of a special sort. I quickly got 'bleu.' Also when I had a fiancé. I had one before Hennie. But he never touched me, because I didn't dare to. Nowadays, when they know each other only for two days they just go to bed. . . . Is that true? Nowadays? . . . Well, in any case there will certainly be many who. . . . But that was totally different then. Although . . . it is true that also then there were many who. . . . We were simply not informed! We looked for babies under the cabbages in the gardens because we were told so! Is it not true then that I have been so awfully dumb? An awfully dumb person!"

Maria's history cannot be generalized. Some of her experiences are certainly far from representative for other girls in the region at that time. But apart from the numerous fascinating events in Maria's story, which do suggest the sorts of social pressure under which girls grew up, it is the deeper structure that is the most significant. Maria's story brings out surprisingly clearly a rather characteristic experience of social relationships. That is why I present her story.

To begin with, she does not want to narrate it to outsiders because she feels both embarrassed and guilty toward her family. But when she does start relating it, there are few areas she does not freely touch upon. And the most confidential parts and thoughts were only told when her husband had gone and we were left alone. In addition, she does not easily allow her husband to criticize her father, in spite of her own serious dismay about him. Obviously, it was hard for her to draw definitive conclusions about his personality. Hostility and respect, both in her story and her life, seem to have been intricately connected.

It seems impossible for Maria to be unequivocal about her father. In her story, he certainly appears as a potential aggressor. Indirectly, through the association she makes with her friend's experience, she even alludes to him as being capable of rape and incest. But when Hennie underlined the ferocity of his character, Maria immediately turned to the pity she had felt about his sudden death. This in turn brought her at once to admiring his idiosyncrasies as a person, his tricks and the pride they gave him—and his family as well, it seems, in spite of all their misgivings. More importantly even, in the same breath she suggests that it was really from him that she had learned much of her own special, courageous, and smart ways of joy and play as a child. These were precious experiences to her, experiences that still somehow appeared central to her own personality.

Ambivalences abound. In her recollections, her father's behavior and trustworthiness is strictly divided between being drunk and being sober. She would never have felt threatened while he was sober, she says. That is also the case with his income. She maintains that his regular earnings from Philips were exclusively destined for regular family expenses. She suggests that it was his irregular work that enabled his irregularities as a person. Father, in short, seems to be credited with at least the sincere effort to be a good father, and maybe he could even have been so in fact, except for some unfortunate traits in his personality, "about which you were not allowed to talk." But notwithstanding the taboo on words, in retrospect it was these dark and irregular sides that happened to take possession of his daughter's mind decades later.

We do not learn much about her mother. Maria appears to have loved her most of all and was allegedly most loved by her. But Maria, evidently, did not agree completely with her "illnesses." Somehow Maria suggests that her mother was not as engaged with the household as she should have been as a mother. Indeed, her mother, like her friend's mother, was also absent when it came to giving her child the feeling of protection against abuse. Their apparent mutual love, accordingly, never seemed to crystallize into a dependable relationship.

Indeed, despite the efforts of her father and mother to relate with her, and her own ostensible efforts to respect and love them, in the final analysis they both just "wanted to get rid of a child." That was the single and overarching unequivocal observation Maria made. In retrospect, this was the key experience of her youth, which she indeed could not forget and which would bring her down thirty years later.

Maria's story illustrates with many empirical examples how young working class girls were exploited in the Eindhoven area. It also shows how loyalty to the family even made them intensify their own exploitation. They worked very hard and searched out, on their own initiative, the best-paying employers. Compared with their perennial efforts, their actual rewards, in terms of love, care, esteem, money, and freedoms, were grossly limited. In the summarizing statement of Maria's: "My history is worthless."

Was Maria dumb? And is she perhaps not a good example for a general phenomenon because of her father's exceptionally bad habits and her family structure? Maria was not dumb, I think, but courageous. Her play as a child was courageous; her running away from the farmer's household was courageous; her lonely walks as a sixteen-year-old girl seeking out possible industrial employers were courageous; her going out as a teenager was courageous; and the attempt at analysis and seeing the relationships of her youth was courageous. What made her afraid of the encounter with flirting boys at dances was not her lack of courage but her lack of trust in intimacy.

Immediately following on the story of her friend who was raped by her father, just as she expected her own father to try if he got his chance, Maria turned to her courting and flirting experiences. She had not only been afraid of her father, but also of other boys if they approached her too closely and too purposefully. Even her fiancé was not allowed to touch her. This sequential clustering of such heterogeneous subjects is remarkable. To Maria, however, her father and the boys were wholly similar subjects. She feared that in the end both would abuse her longing for intimacy, either by physically threatening her or simply by giving too little in return. She feared what she was in fact already suffering, "worthless" relationships: exploitation, in a word.

Maria was not representative in that her subjection was more multiple and her relationships with her parents more asymmetrical than was probably the case with most other working class girls. It paralyzed her more thoroughly than most others. It left her with a "useless" history and made her think she was dumb. She tended to hate herself rather than her aggressors, even while she had a crystal-clear perception of the oppressive relationships that determined her range of action and experience. But in terms of the fundamental mechanism at work, Maria was not at all exceptional. The tight interweaving of love and exploitation, of loyalty and abuse somehow seemed to operate in the relationships of each adolescent girl with her family. In the case of some, the balance certainly was more asymmetrical than in the case of others. Marginal families also tended to have more asymmetrical relationships than more "respectable" ones, even though courting and leisure may have been less parentally regulated. But very many female adolescents coped with a similar configuration of ambiguities. The whole of regional culture was imbued with similar forms of oppression.

Whether they were heavily exploited or not, adolescent girls tended to be highly restricted in their space for thought and action. They were supervised, dominated, and segregated. They were subjected to the arbitrary will of parents and authorities. Their pleasure was highly circumscribed, their courting hindered. Marriage often seemed the only way out, but not easily realized. In Hennie's words, "I'll just make her pregnant so she can leave home." But in general, that could only have been a solution in the mind, as the shame would have been unbearable. While industrialization elsewhere tended to liberate youth, the specific pattern of southeast Brabant industrialization served to intensify or in any case maintain "traditional" controls.

That was the case not only with unskilled working class families. In the early fifties, Anna Vermeulen, twenty years old and a teacher at a primary school, decided to leave home. She wanted to move to a cloister, as she could no longer reconcile the dozens of futile and arbitrary restrictions at home with the public status conferred by her job. But she was simply not allowed to. Her father indignantly told her that the family was finally beginning to see some money from her (she gave up almost all her salary, which almost matched her father's income as a lower civil clerk) and that he did not intend to let that go. This was a family of good reputation. Also in more "respectable" working class circles such explicit instrumental reasoning about children was not considered immoral. Note further that a cloister appeared to Anna as the most practical way out. And finally consider that Anna would later think that she had loved her father dearly and that she had had a satisfying and intimate relation with him. If it had not been for the memory of her husband and her sister, whom I also interviewed, and who remembered this episode, amnesia would have spared Anna a painful and confusing part of her personal history.

In a fine analysis of traditional southeast Brabant peasant family structures around 1900, Dr. P. A. Barentsen, who had been working in the southern part of the area in the beginning of the century, has described two features of familial relationships that still seemed largely in place by the middle of the century.[1] The first of these features was that adolescent girls were heavily curtailed in their liberties. They were made into obedient and undemanding persons. They were strictly segregated from men, and female bodies were completely covered so as not to invite sexual desires. Dr. Barentsen explained this as stemming primarily from parents' fear of losing income because of early marriage. Adolescents had to earn first for the young children and then for the parents themselves. He described children as a vital asset in a peasant economy in which the well-being of households largely depended on the command over the labor of adolescent children and other dependents.

The second feature he described was the "materialistic" way in which emotions were expressed. He gave two examples: At the death of a young boy people tried to console parents by saying, "It's a pity, he would have been a good earner very quickly"; or at the death of a grown up man, "It's a harmful corpse," referring to the loss of labor power.[2] Barentsen did not fall in the wide-open trap of attributing to them a lack of romantic sensibilities, as modernization theorists have tended to do.[3]

Such words were spoken by people who, he maintained, demonstrably loved the casualties, and who in general dealt very sympathetically with other people. Rather, he interpreted it as reflecting the inescapable structure of traditional households in a mostly uncommercialized peasant economy.

Both customs, it seems, were still in place in the thoroughly industrialized context of Eindhoven up to the 1950s. Of course urban industrialization had transformed them. Working class girls were certainly allowed more pleasures than peasant daughters around the turn of the century. Their clothing was much more sexually attractive, sometimes even straightforwardly so. And they could mix with males not only at fairs or carnivals once or twice a year but each weekend. The fundamental condition of their availability for household incomes, however, had not changed much. Similarly, as the example of Anna Vermeulen showed, the explanations given by more articulate parents for their curtailment could be very materialistic indeed.

In the cases of both Maria Van de Velde and Anna Vermeulen there was not simply a lack of love on the part of their fathers. As girls, both had learned precious things from them, things they would rather not have missed in their lives. Maria had learned much from the play and humor of her father. Anna had great respect for her father's carefulness and sensitivity, and certainly was his preferred child. However, leaving excesses aside, these fathers (and mothers, and whole families) went on to dominate and exploit their daughters in the numerous ways suggested by regional "customs" and "traditional" practices. But these customs were now functionally operating within the "modern" framework of local industrial class structures. Indeed, they were at the heart of these "modern" structures. That will have weakened some forms of domination, while it will have intensified others. Moreover, since girls were now drawing on incipient subcultures of their own and led lives spatially and socially differentiated from their parents, the points of possible friction and discontent on both sides had multiplied.

In industrializing southeast Brabant the mechanisms of class and exploitation were mediated through the family and were principally directed at adolescent girls. Consequently, I would suggest, father-daughter relations in particular became the vehicle of appropriation and social friction. But such conflict tended to be individualized and decentered. Moreover, since it was intricately connected with love and identification, it was very hard for children to perceive and address it. Generally it needed the distance of time to understand, or forget, its complex mechanisms. The death of parents could therefore be squarely liberating to grown-up children, as one informant told me.

In this context, longings for liberation on the part of working daughters did not primarily tie up with politics. They tended to focus on marriage as the sole event that could really transform their world. And since marriage was so central, the single large-scale force or process that would help them out was housing and suburbanization. Here we encounter a paradox. The corporation that had partially been built on their exploitation as younger females also acted as their largest benefactor by offering, more than any other single situation, the private space precisely needed for escape.

There is another relevant aspect to time, gender, liberation, and exploitation in southeast Brabant. As the local economy in the postwar period quickly built up a high skill base and the region became one of the more prosperous places in the Netherlands at large, the "worthless histories" Maria Van de Velde complained of lost all the orienting power they might have retained. Females, in particular, had been brought up with a high emphasis on the virtues of abstention, sacrifice, and loyalty. The hedonism that seemed to become the norm in mass consumption, from the early sixties on, confronted them with their repressed youth that had not offered them much occasion to experiment with pleasure—indeed had made it suspect. That was the case everywhere, of course, but in east Brabant, especially for females, the transition was much more abrupt and unexpected, and was felt more intensely than in other industrial regions.

PIET KUIPER

The second encounter I want to present shifts the emphasis to the more enjoyable aspects of east Brabant configurations of culture, class, and household. And though I should not wish to suggest that male working class socialization was by definition more pleasant than that of females, it should not surprise us that this part of the story builds on male experiences. Neither is it strange that the Philips corporation figures much less centrally in this encounter. Before the war, Philips did not primarily employ local males, nor did young males automatically turn to Philips after primary school as they would do in the postwar period.

After discussing his youth and his family's experiences during the crisis of the thirties, Piet Kuiper's narration seems to move away from the Eindhoven relationships proper. I had learned to try to keep male informants from endlessly talking about the local events of war. They all had a wealth of stories about it, which seemed to me to diverge from my interests. But Piet Kuiper strongly insisted on doing so. In the course of his stories, however, I began to realize that the war actually functioned as a historical magnifying glass for highlighting central aspects of local male culture.

When you explain to local people that you want to interview them on their life history in order to get more intimate knowledge of how local life was organized, more often than not people will respond by saying, "Oh, that's interesting, but then you'd better talk with my brother X. I've worked all my life at Philips, what do I know? My brother is different, he's seen more of it." Some families have celebrated storytellers in their midst. Sometimes they have truly led more adventurous lives. And though it has been on the wane in the postwar period, storytelling is generally much appreciated among autochthonous people in the region. Good story-tellers represent a source of wisdom that is peculiarly, though ambigu-ously, valued. When I met Gerard Kuiper, he immediately referred me to his older brother Piet (born in 1923, second oldest son in a family of eight). Gerard arranged a meeting at his house for the middle of July (1992). The weather was hot, and we sat together in the garden. Piet was a lovely man, and he felt supported by my interest and my questions. Three hours later, Piet was to conclude our talk and invite me for a next visit by saying: "Joy is the most important thing in life. And what I for instance enjoy much is your ability to laugh about my stories, because I like them too." Piet immediately wanted to talk about his adventures as a twenty-year-old boy during the war. But I pressed him to start with his family and his years as a child. Although his stories are interesting in their own right, and well narrated, not all of them will be reproduced here. I limit the presentation to the first part of our first conversation, which I will repre-sent chronologically and in his own (transcribed) words.

"My father came from Vlijmen, thirty kilometers north of Eindhoven, near the river Meuse. He was a basketmaker, weaving cane and branches into baskets and selling them to shopkeepers. My grandfather was a small-scale peasant. But he was also a day laborer and did a thousand other things he could earn money from, like growing flowers and ma-sonry work. Grandfather from mother's side was also a small-scale peas-ant and a *bricoleur*.

"My parents came to Eindhoven, I think, in 1927, to work in the build-ing sector. They needed a lot of people there. My father simply said he was a foreman, and they took him. We lived in an old and miserable workers' house in Gestel, near the railway to the Campina villages. The house was so old and rotten that the authorities decided to pull it down; that was even before the war, so you can imagine how miserable it really was. After some two years my father got a job as a foreman with a road building contractor who had some large orders in the region. Now my parents had to start living in a caravan, and except for my oldest sister all children were lodged with other family members.

"I went to my grandparents from mother's side. My grandfather was an epileptic. He used to fall down somewhere and would lie there trembling for a minute or two. It was no problem, except that when he stood up he no longer knew where he was or what he was doing. I was four years old and I became his steady companion. I even slept in his bed. When he'd suffered an attack and came back to himself again, I would tell him the point of his being there. We didn't leave each other alone for a minute. Grandad was very fond of me. For entertaining the village people, he'd taught me to read, write, and calculate. As a four-year-old boy I often had to show to others what I was able to do.

"On Sundays grandad always went to church, and afterwards to the pub. He lit a cigar when we left home and put it on a stone near the church porch before entering mass. When he left, he took it up again. Many males did so. I was fascinated by that neat line of used, wet, and still somewhat burning cigars near that grand porch. I asked him for a cigar too. He said: 'You're not yet old enough. But on your fifth birthday you'll get one.' On my anniversary he gave me a large box of fifty cigars, to smoke a year long on Sundays while walking together to our Sunday obligations, the church and the pub.

"After two years I came back to my parents. They rented a small workers' house with a large garden in Woensel, near the Dommel river. After a while, however, there was no more work in road building and my father became unemployed. But we were a fine household, and everyone was convinced that something had to be done. My father had several small-scale businesses. The garden was turned into a stockyard for building materials and other stuff which he collected and sold. He raised a pig every year, plus some forty rabbits. We also had chickens. Everyone had to work and we wanted to do so. My sister started at Philips in the mid-thirties. Me and my brother, when we had time off from school, we helped father with his dealings and cut grass each day near the river for the small livestock. Mother was the only one not working, but she cooked and did that very well. Being unemployed, my father was forced to labor on public works, in particular on opening up new agricultural land. Very heavy work. During school holidays he took me with him. Working with two was much better. By 1935 my father got his job in road building again.

"I went to high school, to the very bourgeois St. Joris college. I don't know why. It is true, it was exceptional. Nobody else did. I could learn well. But my older brother was no less good and he went to the Philips trade school. Perhaps my granddad's teaching made a difference. And my mother too, she constantly insisted on the importance of learning. And father actually not less so. So it was really in the family. My mother had an uncle who had been in love with a girl from another village. His face was covered with scars from knife cuts received during fights with rival local boys and their gangs. But in spite of his wild look he managed to become the vice mayor of the village of Houten, with eighteen scars on his face!

"It was really in the family. My mother's father was a Belgian orphan. Nobody knew how he had come here. He owned nothing except his house, which was actually too small for any human being to live in, though it had a large garden. He'd never really been to school. But he was not crazy! He could read and write and knew how to make money from a thousand things. Just enough to stay alive in good shape. And then there was uncle Simon. He had bought himself the most fancy cottage of the municipality. It came right out of a fairy tale. He'd bought it for almost nothing 'cause it was in poor shape. He lived there up till his death. That cottage made him rich! The house was gradually encircled by new neighborhoods and was protected by the community as a monument. They gave him a lot of money to restore it. It's now in a condition it never had, complete with sheepfold and chicken barn. And there he was, living as a rich man in a fairy tale in the middle of a modern and wealthy suburb!

"But whatever . . . there, suddenly, came the war. The weather was good, we slept with open windows. We were awakened at four in the morning by heavy noise in the air. The sky was dark with airplanes. I climbed on top of the house. Adriaansens, our neighbor from Zeeland, said: 'What could that be?' I said, 'Don't you see that man, it's war, it's the Germans!' That's how the war began.

"The war was a catastrophe to many people, but . . . especially to people who did not have the opportunity to arrange extra food and things. But we still had many relatives in the countryside, our grandfathers and some uncles. The first three years were no problem for us. Each week we killed a rabbit, twice a year we clandestinely slaughtered a pig. We had eggs, we had everything.

"But take our uncle Sjef. He was a cop in Eindhoven and lived near us. They had eight children but he could do nothing. He would have lost his job. He had no chance to do anything illegal. Whereas my father . . . .

"The Germans wanted that airport here renovated. The building contractor my father had worked for had been a Nazi long before the war, so he got the order. My mother didn't like it, but father said 'What the hell, we need money.' Well, I can tell you, that airport cost the Germans twenty times more than would normally have been the case. A lorry with bricks, for instance, would come through the gate. It was registered. The driver drank some coffee, left, still loaded, through a provisional gate on the other side of the terrain, returned, and let his load be registered again. A guy bringing grass sods, to cover the bunkers, was known to have driven around with the same load for four weeks. With that old truck of his, you know! Another round, and another round again! That was his way of sabotage and survival.

"My father too, he was a foreman, he just took what he wanted. He simply told a driver: 'Take these bricks or whatever and throw them in my backyard.' The stuff was stored all over our place, up in the garden of that old bachelor aunt, on that terrain behind the cigar factory.

"In any case . . . the war, the war . . . to me, it was not all that beneficial. I was interned for one and a half years in the camps of Ommen and Wolfenbüttel, because of the 'Arbeitseinsatz.' All boys aged nineteen and twenty had to go. I worked at Philips then, so I had an 'Ausweis.' But the department where I worked, the Röntgen, had to stop because there were no supplies anymore. I was moved to the transformer department. But that one declined too. Finally we worked twenty-four hours, then eighteen, and then it was over.

"I went into hiding with relatives of mine in Vlijmen (near the river Meuse). They had a horticultural business. They couldn't find personnel, so they had some seven people hiding. We slept together above the cows. However, I wanted to see the soccer match between Philips and Ajax (Amsterdam) in Eindhoven. My mother said to me, 'Don't do it, it's a risk.' But I wouldn't miss it. And she was right. At the end of the match, the stadium was surrounded by police. Seventy boys without 'Ausweis' were arrested, me included. We were put on a lorry and brought to 'Arbeitseinsatz Lager Erica' in Ommen. Jan van Hout, the cyclist, was among them. But except him I knew none of them.

"In the camps you were thrown back on yourself and you didn't relate to anybody. It didn't really touch you when someone was suffering. Franske Klein from Eindhoven was working with me at the Göringwerke. We had to perform very heavy tasks, preparing the ground for a large new factory complex by hand. We all grew weaker and weaker. Everyone was at his limit, and we were starving. Suddenly Franske fell to the ground and did not get up when ordered so. He was kicked to death by the guards while we were watching. But it didn't really touch me. I've often thought what's wrong with me. . . .

"At the Göringwerke we were working with heavy dump carts. One hit my foot and I fell. The SS thought I was play acting and they kicked me downhill. I was really injured but I'd say nothing. In the barracks I went to the 'Sanitäter' and showed him the scar. He was a Dutchman, Aad de Vrij, a good guy. I said, I simply can't do this work with a foot like this. He agreed, and decided to keep me in the nursing barrack. That was my luck.

"In November 1942 the Swiss Red Cross came. They found me and sent me back to the Sophia Hospital in Zwolle (NL), together with Aad de Vrij, the 'Sanitäter.' The department I was allocated to was managed by nurse Bremer, who was a Nazi. But she liked some of us, including me, and I owe her a lot of gratitude. With Christmas, she arranged a visit from my parents, and they would often return. They regularly brought me cigarettes and stuff. I left the hospital only at the end of February 1943. When I arrived, my weight was eighty pounds. When I left it was eighty kilos. They really fattened me up there. I'm still very grateful for that.

"Then the Germans came from the concentration camp in Ommen in order to pick me up and force me to labor again: 'Tomorrow on transport.' But I chatted with them and gave them cigarettes. They'd tell me: 'Be patient, we'll take care of you.' Goddamn, they brought me straight to the nursing department! And who was there? Aad de Vrij, the 'Sanitäter.' He kept me in bed for another week and a half. But then I was sent to the woods to cut lumber. After some days I thought, I can't manage this. I was still too weak. I talked with Aad de Vrij, who suggested to me to faint. I did so. I fell down between the lumber, was kicked a couple of times, but didn't stand up. So I was brought to the nursing barracks again. The doctor there saw me and cried, 'Ill? Carry off!' I was terrified, but kept up the appearance of being unconscious. They brought me to the first floor, to a large room with thirty beds. It turned out there had been some German officers in the room below and this doctor didn't want them to see me, so he'd sent me up immediately.

"I was allowed to stay in that department. I had to serve as a cook for the staff and patients. Moreover, I wrote petitions to bid for mercy for all the fellows there. Many in fact were allowed to leave. Except myself. In May 1943 a nurse came to me and said, 'There are some people for you down at the counter.' 'That's not possible,' I said, 'my parents were here only yesterday.' At once I was terrified and began to shiver . . . I went down very slowly . . . two SS'ers were standing there, waiting for some-one . . . I couldn't move . . . didn't know what to do . . . At last they noticed me . . . '1094?' they called. I nodded uncertainly. 'You have mercy, you may leave.' "

Piet's narration, by ordering experience and representing relations in a determinate way, again harbors a whole series of relevant insights into regional culture. While Maria highlights an important strain of young female working class experience, Piet opens up key themes in the world of young males. The insights concern first the nature of family relation-ships, and, secondly, the particular outlooks and capacities they ideally fostered in the males brought up by them.

The story shows, as could of course be expected, that southeast Bra-bant families did not necessarily become tension-ridden sites of exploita-tion. Families could also become vital organs for self-defense, as the Kuiper family seems to illustrate. At the same time it shows that they could not easily become so as a single household unit. For the family to work as a collective resource it seemed necessary in the first place for the links between the constitutive nuclear household units to be well main-tained. For this to happen, of course, it was inevitable that the family had to be firmly rooted in the wider region. If the whole of the family func-tioned as a network, making multiple sorts of resources available to its members, it became a strategic asset for survival and security. This is a well-known fact among students of developing countries, but it was no different in industrializing Brabant.[4] Piet and his parents, for instance, called upon family for food, lodging, hiding, and other sorts of help, and in general such help seems to have been forthcoming. But the family experience in a wider sense also concerned the sorts of skills developed within family networks. Piet's story suggests that even his own genius was an integral part of that family experience, however poor in material terms the lives of its members may have been.

Two other conditions seem to have been essential for shaping the family network as a collective resource: property (however small, or at least access to some land) and boys. Small property (or access to some land) put households, and boys in particular, in a position to develop diverse forms of informal business and security. Even cultivating flowers could be a welcome source of cash, as Piet Kuiper's grandad teaches us.

In addition, the range of skills learned in relation to small proprietary activities, such as building and dealing, widened both the opportunities for the whole familial network and the flexibility of the individual male member in the labor market. Piet's father could simply boast that he was a foreman in the building industry because he knew how to deal with materials and how to deal with people. Such a position subsequently gave him access to construction materials and knowledge of the relevant markets. And this again ensured his family's survival during crisis and war.

In a highly sex-segregated society, moreover, boys were the ones developing the technical and entrepreneurial skills necessary for flexible behavior in informal labor markets. And as such they also contributed to the opportunities and capacities within the familial network. Girls, on the other hand, were treated as an internal resource to households. They were trained for hierarchy and had to be available for parental purposes until marriage, and this included their formal industrial cash earnings. This is again illustrated by Piet's only sister, who also happened to be the oldest child. When her parents had to reside in a caravan, she was kept in the household to help her mother while the boys were lodged with the family. During the crisis, she was the first child responsible for cash earnings. She was immediately sent to Philips when she was old enough, whereas the two boys were permitted a costly education (costly because the parents had to abstain from an important source of cash). Thus, while it is generally agreed that in east Brabant families the mothers were sovereign within the household, it was the network of males within (and beyond) the family that secured wider opportunities in an informal labor market.

A later part of Piet's story may be relevant here. When the allies had occupied Eindhoven, the airport was intensively used for, among other things, distributing food. Piet's father was working there again, just like Piet himself. Piet had found an opportunity to steal a large quantity of potatoes destined for the army. He sold them for three hundred guilders to a retailer in Drents Dorp. An incredible amount of money. "Then I went to my parents and gave them a hundred guilders. And to uncle Jan, whom I also gave a hundred. The rest I kept for myself." In a well-functioning family network, boys not only were the ones creating the links with informal markets and opportunities, but also appear to have been conscious about their network function within the family. Moreover, their informal gains were apparently conceived of as their own, in contrast to girls' earnings.

As a consequence of their particular position in the family and in the regional economy, adult males had developed a highly flexible and independent outlook on life. They were well equipped to take a chance when it occurred, both because of their broad and largely informal skills and capacities and because of the way they had learned to deal with people. In this respect, stories about the war, such as narrated by Piet Kuiper, were not simply referential. They were models of society "writ small," as it was perceived "from below" by local males. At the same time they were also "models for society," containing prescriptions for dealing with people, in particular for dealing with the powerful and the structures built by them.

In his war story, Piet begins by emphasizing that people who were dependent on higher authorities for their survival had a very hard time. This is an opening statement pregnant with local meaning. It puts him in a position to immediately turn to the strategic capacities of his father, both regarding his rural family and regarding his opportunities as a foreman in the airport works. The informal and indeed illegal survival method his father had learned during the crisis (and before) were of great use in his advantageous dealings with German commissioners. As we have just learned, Piet did the same in relation with the Allies some years later. He expressly highlights the shrewdness of a small dealer who comes back again and again with the same load "in his old truck." This was not felt to be illegitimate. And not only so because it happened to be in relation with the Germans, as is shown by Piet's own action against Allied food supplies in 1944. Moral and physical independence from authorities, and calculation in your dealings with them, are presented as self-evident rules of local survival.

The story of his own experiences in the "Arbeitseinsatz" is also instructive in this respect. Dragging your feet is presented as the natural way of survival in these circumstances. But it adds another feature. And that is the relevance of seeking good personal relationships with strategic people such as the "Sanitäter," the Nazi nurse, and even some SS'ers. In fact, in his stories, the luck you need in finding the right people comes out as a wholly natural fact of life. You hope for it, and you do your best to influence the conditions, but luck you will need. And luck has a name too. The names of nurse Bremer and Sanitäter de Vrij will never be forgotten by Piet. Social structures exist of course, but Piet's stories emphasize that it is in a personalized form that you normally encounter them. And this creates room for luck, as well as for influencing your fate. Boys like Piet, with their particular local cultural backgrounds, were well equipped to deal with such situations.

The vital importance and ultimate unexpectedness of luck is woven, in an almost classical way, into the end of Piet's concentration camp story. He feels terrified by the two SS men waiting for him at the counter. The next step confirms his fear, as the SS'ers start to address him by way of his administrative number. It suggests that there will only be structure this time, and no luck or mutual identification. The tension builds up. But then, paradoxically and suddenly, there is mercy and freedom. Without luck you clearly won't survive, the story says. And though you may try to influence it, it is its ultimate unpredictability that is crucial.

There is, at least to my mind, a last relevant narrative structure in Piet's stories. This structure seems to signify that while luck may be capricious, and official powers not trustworthy, in the final analysis there is no reason not to trust your own capacities, your practical knowledge, and your preferences in dealing with the circumstances at hand. This structure is for example found in the story of his uncle, who had dived deep into the less respectable traits of local village life. The experience was inscribed on his face by eighteen frightening scars. But in the end he became a vice mayor of an utterly respectable community nevertheless. It also occurs in the story of another uncle, who lived by very modest means and had bought himself that small "fairy-tale house." In the end, this "fairy-tale" uncle would not withstand the forces of modernity. He was spatially fully incorporated by modern suburban society. But, and this is significant, it did not happen without making him rich and without endowing him with the romanticized and official status of a monument while he had simply held to his own. Indeed, the story not only referred to the house but connoted the man and his idiosyncrasies as well: both had become monuments. This meaning of the story was clear, if not to the world, then at least to Piet and his brother. Both were laughing cordially during the story.

Fragments structured in this particular way, moreover, were narrated for putting Piet's own genius in historical perspective. Both his talents and his favorite narrative structures were brought in relation to the idiosyncrasies of his grandfather. It didn't matter if you were just plain common people, or even if you were an orphaned, poor, epileptic, small-scale, jack-of-all-trades, annexed peasant like his grandfather, you could lead a very worthwhile life nevertheless. You would, for a moment, put down the wet butt of your cigar in front of the church porch, but simply go on smoking when you came out. This is the fundamental but covert message of those stories. It is, in the end, the same meaningful sequence as found in the story of the small turf dealer with his "old truck" cheating the German army in a grotesque way. Piet's narration, by emphasizing the alienness of large institutions and powers, the necessity and unpredictability of personal luck, and finally the genius of little people, is an outright homage to regional, male, popular wisdom.

For the period around the turn of the twentieth century, P. A. Barentsen, the aforementioned doctor in the region, wrote that southeast Brabant rural boys were generally spoiled during their socialization at home.[5] They were very unmanageable. Mothers used to send them out onto the streets and the fields where they could do less harm. There they were socialized by peers and people from the neighborhood. In contrast with outdoor socialization in cities, Barentsen evaluated this custom positively. People watched and disciplined each others' children permanently, as did older children with younger ones. Consequently, as boys grew up they rapidly acquired a measure of independence and competence and were soon allowed to join adult males in their activities.

Barentsen was located in one of the most peripheral districts of the region. That may explain why he interpreted local family culture largely in terms of the dynamics of an agricultural economy. However, this is probably too neat a classification. Historians and social scientists have now begun to rediscover the composite nature of the economic activities of east Brabant households.[6] These households strived to develop multiple scores of income and security. Agricultural activities certainly were a part of this, as was sometimes domestic service and industrial employment for girls. But, in addition, there was a whole field of more or less informal, flexible, and heterogeneous activities, from protoindustry to petty trading, from seasonal work to construction, from simple artisanal work with wood or metals to transport, a field that lay between industry and agriculture proper. This was what, in the absence of a generic concept, might be termed the "popular or folk economy." It was a domain not captured by existing statistics, not directly regulated by authorities, and largely occupied by adolescent boys and young adult males.

Male adolescents were the ideal performers of such "popular economic" tasks. Their practical outdoor training with diverse jobs and different people made them well prepared for the inherent difficulties and possibilities. Such activities fed into the network of male family members, and the network in its turn disseminated the necessary skills and information. Moreover, adolescent males could maintain their independence while learning essential male skills and acquiring some income. If adult males in southeast Brabant were generally little inclined to take over small parental holdings and form families, the reason for this was certainly related to their earlier experience of flexible work in the "popular economy." This was the domain of the proverbial independent *bricoleur*. The triple theme of male popular wisdom articulated in Piet's stories sprang precisely from this experience.

As agricultural holdings were steadily decreasing in size and fragmenting to the point of losing their primary relevance for household incomes, both formal industrial labor and popular economy gained in importance. War and crisis in the first half of the century, moreover, resulted in recurring temporary revaluations of informal sources of income. Thus, though formal industrial labor would triumph in the end, its ascent was significantly interrupted by downturn periods that breathed life again into the male popular wisdom of popular economy.

There is no simple antithesis, moreover, between urban industrialization and popular economy. Except for a short interlude in the early thirties, the regional economy also created many opportunities outside basic manufacturing proper. In retailing, services, transport, construction, and some nonmanufacturing industrial jobs much of the skill base of the folk economy could be applied. Piet Kuiper's father abandoned his basket making business for a much better rewarded job in construction. Many others saw similar chances to trade in their "traditional" low-income activities for better-paying formal employment in the later twenties and later thirties. Some of the fathers of my informants also succeeded in exchanging tiring industrial work for less formal jobs in the "popular" sector, such as building. In such jobs they were not necessarily exposed to the harsh discipline of despotic manufacturing regimes, which local males, like males anywhere, often found degrading.[7]

Instead of class consciousness, then, male adolescent experience was generally expressed in the popular triple themes we encountered in Piet's stories. The untrustworthiness and alienness of large institutions and formal powers, the importance of personalized luck in one's life, and the "folk" pride in the autonomy of the little man were the guiding themes in the worldview of adolescent and younger adult local males. Such a view was embedded in, and instrumental for the practical relationships of popular economy with which these people had to deal. Also when seeking formalized jobs, young local adult males tried to find and often succeeded in finding those opportunities that recognized the specifically flexible capacities nurtured by this experience.

It is, therefore, not complete nonsense to state that industrializing east Brabant, instead of giving rise to class consciousness among its younger working class males, nurtured many good storytellers. Attractive stories, in one way or another, always make use of precisely the themes shaping Piet Kuiper's narration. In their comic versions, they come down to the idea of a Charlie Chaplin as folk hero, bringing the large wheels of modernity to a standstill not by concerted resistance but by moral innocence. Moreover, up until, say, 1950, such ideals were not merely stories from far away. They were still deeply anchored in "down to the ground" Brabant male working class experience. That is why local people often refer you to good storytellers in their families. Good storytellers, by allegorically expressing these cultural themes, simply tell you more about shared local truths than can be rendered by any flat factual account.

We need a last word on representativeness. Like Maria Van de Velde, Piet Kuiper was of course not representative. I have used his story to explore key mechanisms and key images shaping the experience of east Brabant younger working class males up to 1950. There is no doubt that the experiences and outlooks that come out of his stories were widely shared by young local males, also those growing up in slighty different contexts. But that does not deny the obvious fact that the actual coloring and content of individual experiences and outlooks can vary greatly. Different local, occupational, and family contexts certainly caused significant differences in personal outlook and individual action. The Kuiper family, as Piet immediately acknowledged, was a "fine household." To some extent they really embodied the more flexible, cooperative, and creative aspects of Brabant male popular culture. Other households of course were more constrained and will have put great pressures on their individual members. It also seems that households which were more firmly enmeshed in manufacturing proper encountered ever greater obstacles in living up to the "populist" ideals articulated in Piet's stories. But the fact remains that males from such households often told similar stories and embraced comparable values, even when other cultural repertoires, derived from Catholicism, socialism, or, increasingly, the imagery of the "organization man,"[8] competed for primacy in certain contexts.

Epilogue: Pathways to Labor-Intensive

Manufacturing

If Edward Thompson was right to believe that "history knows no regular verbs," it becomes the paradoxical task of any historical social science to find regularity in the constitution of historical irregularity.[1] In that case, we should really take to heart Antonio Gramsci's singularly important methodological discovery vis-à-vis the Marxist tradition, which is, as Ira Katznelson has recently made clear, that "the different dimensions in any specific society do not move in sealed, logically determined orbits . . . but interconnect in a single historical rhythm."[2] With that in mind, I have proposed my relational materialist rethinking of the problematic of class and class formation in social history, anthropology, and urban sociology. My analysis of industrial class formation in North Brabant, a classic instance of anomaly and irregularity, where extensive industrialization coincided with a seemingly immovable workers' deference and acquiescence, takes its empirical, methodological, and epistemological course exactly to recapture this central Gramscian insight. It explored ways to show, in two specific temporal and spatial cases, how superficially distinct empirical fields actually interacted to grow into one, whole, singular rhythm of industrialization and class formation, a rhythm spanning the conventional bipolarities of structure and action, micro and macro, social organization and social being.

Class analysis, as I see it, ought not be the positivist/reductionist study of a "sealed" economic base and its supposed reflections in a thing called superstructure. Neither should it be replaced, as postmodernists/poststructuralists will have it, by a new cultural history of political vocabularies, canonical texts, cultural traditions, status systems, or consumption preferences. The choice between positivist economic reductionism and postmaterialist literary culturalism is a hopeless one.

When I maintain that, in North Brabant, gender, generation, and fam-

ily have regularly become one prime locus for exploitation and contention, I obviously refuse to adhere to economic reductionist dogma. I also
do so when I study the influence of organized religion on working class
culture and protest, and vice versa. However, this does not imply that I
am succumbing to the culturalist camp in any meaningful way. Rather , it
is to try to account for how dimensions of economy, family, civic life,
space, and urbanism can all become entwined in the making of a particular regional path of capitalist industrialization and development, based
on class-oriented networks of power which lay down the regionally specific character of trajectories of class formation, popular politics, and
everyday life.

In a recent review of studies of class in Britain, sociologist Mike Savage has advocated that class analysis should take an interpretive turn.[3]
However, this is not necessarily a good advice. For, unless we see that
interpretation as a method cannot be limited to what is commonly referred to as cultural meanings and shared values, we will find ourselves
in the same blind alley where the debate between the reductionists and
the culturalists is played out. In order to decode meanings, values, signi-
fications, they must always be dynamically related to the wider practical,
historical, material, and experiential context in which they are actually
used by people (by some more than by others), and where they become
meaningful to them in the first place (and in diverse ways to diverse
agents).

What is, after all, so eminently cultural, in the idealistic sense of the
term, about family practices or clerical activism? What is so cultural
about a southeast Brabant working class mother giving her daughter a
nice tweed suit to wear to the Eindhoven dance halls? Or about groupings of young shoemakers in industrial villages urging others to abstain
from drinking? Such happenings cannot be reasonably interpreted without placing them in the determinate patterns of social practices and relationships from which they arise and which give them their meaning.
Such relationships, moreover, are shaped by, and express, crucial inequalities and asymmetries of social power. They are also inextricably
embedded in more comprehensive, temporally and spatially situated trajectories of social change. Power, inequality, and patterned social change
thus become part of any meaning, both actual, desirable, and possible.

Instead of expressing meaning and value straightaway, human practice should rather be seen, as theorists such as Pierre Bourdieu and Raymond Williams have been propounding, as a complex and simultaneous
combination of externalized necessities and internalized virtues—as ar-

ticulations of both the ways in which people have learned to work and survive and the wider dreams and projects they have learned to envision. Human practice is just not situated in dream-time. It is always part of a real and specific history, which sets definite limits and exerts typical pressures on the everyday politics and resources of groups of people.

But in a different, wider, "relational" and "materialist" sense, an interpretive method does indeed become a prerequisite for grasping the mutually constitutive interweaving of nominally distinct empirical fields that make up a society's singularity. This is a plea against empiricism. It proposes that *data* should be turned into *relata*, and that, after a phase of breaking an object down into its constituent elements, it can only be successfully understood when the parts are again inserted into a wider whole. If there is something to be learned from anthropology, I believe it is this rather than cultural hermeneutics.[4]

In addition, and following authors such as Eric Wolf, it has been my particular contention throughout this book, first, that such social totality should be defined by its key relational dynamics; second, that these key relations can fruitfully be described by a broad and nonreductionist notion of class; and, third, that this puts methodological priority on linkages of (and in) time and space, rather than on the search for fixed structural determinations. The fates and historical trajectories of groups and territories are never simply open. They are crucially shaped by the networks that link local history with global process, and vice versa. Their chances, resources, and directions of development are "path-dependent." This path-dependency structures, constrains, motivates, and empowers their relevant (collective) actors. Most importantly for class analysis, such historical and spatial relationships shape the basic social patterns of local production and reproduction, and structure the whole fields of force in which local actors come to perceive their needs and interests and develop their resources to act. Such materialist studies need not discard local culture, local meanings, and the "actor's point of view." Rather, they help to direct our attention precisely to how human meaning arises from, and feeds back into, the key social interdependencies, conflicts, and historical experiences that motivate actors and structure the immediate context of any signification.

What I have argued and tried to demonstrate is that class-oriented research should adopt this expanded form of "structurist" or "relational" interpretivism, along with its narrativist methodology for analysis and exposition. Such class-oriented research should seek to establish the particular character of a whole, socially structured, spatially and temporally defined totality of capitalist relationships and development, trace its key mechanisms and divisions, and explore the capacities and incapacities of its constituent classes to shape their destiny, create meaningful relationships, and envision possible worlds. Such a methodological turn will decisively change the terms of the debate about class and class formation in the modern world, and will help to give it a new substance as well as relevance.

There is a crucial question about contingency in my argument for broad, relational notions of production and class. In synchronic, positivist methodologies, contingency is often held to be the absolute absence of determination. It can then be read as the "randomness" or "arbitrariness" of a social phenomenon. Instead of being determined by an economic base, gendered conceptions of pleasure and duty, for example, may be seen as at any one moment in time being wholly contingent vis-à-vis such a base.

But in my relational and expanded approach to class formation in history, the idea of contingency does not necessarily imply the absence of any relation. Instead of "arbitrariness," contingency here merely implies that there cannot be a logically (pre)determined, deducible, internal relationship between capital accumulation and other social processes and phenomena. It thus leaves the possibility open that in certain spatially and temporally defined trajectories there might very well be a close and systematic relation between, for instance, such diverse processes as class formation, household formation, and the formation of gender ideologies. Instead of gender at any one moment in time being deducible to a supposed independent economic base, we need to establish their systematic co-variance, or better, their interweaving and mutual constitution in a longer course of time and in a given area. Distinct spheres, then, may well be logically contingent in a model but nevertheless be systematically interconnected in history. It is this specific, and therefore contingent, interweaving within a whole, spatially and temporally defined sequence that produces Thompson's "irregular verbs," that is, the particularist outcomes within a more general process such as capitalist industrialization and class formation.

However, time and space, in particular in the modern capitalist era, are still more substantial than this. Instead of being just the medium for exposing particularism, they even help to produce it. This is so because time and space, as Abbott and Aminzade have argued, are not fixed entities. Rather, they are relationally defined: "place" because of its relation to space and other places; "time" in its relation with what has happened before and with abstract, linear time. When these relations differ, the properties of the time-space configuration under study differ too. Moreover, as world-system theorists and critical geographers have taught us, capitalism by definition features, produces, and reproduces temporal and spatial unevenness. Sometimes this even seems its very essence. Divergences in local trajectories of capitalist and precapitalist development, as well as different timings and ways of insertion in wider networks of capitalist exchange, thus by themselves produce particularist outcomes. This is why I have argued for the substitution of the synchronic and nonspatial structure-action polarity, which also underlies positivist and reductionist class analysis, with the dialectic between local and global histories.

The specific set of interacting, temporal, spatial, and internal relationships that produced a particular path of capitalist industrialization and class formation in North Brabant remained in place from the late eighteenth century until the later 1950s. What were the basic properties of these relationships, and, next, how did they work out respectively in the shoemaking district of central Brabant and in the electrical boomtown of Eindhoven?

The industrialization of North Brabant was to some extent the effect of Dutch merchant capital, originating in the early modern "golden age" of the United Provinces, defending its profitability under the less congenial circumstances of modern-age competition with the territorial states of England, France, and Germany. Largely unspecialized and little commercialized peasant regions, such as North Brabant and Twente, allowed for cheap, not guild-regulated, protoindustrial production. To a large degree, this external origin of industrial capital was still true for the early twentieth century, when cigar and lamp bulb production in the Eindhoven area were the main targets of such flows of investments.

North Brabant industrialization after its protoindustrial period, moreover, was a "reflective" second-phase industrialization, oriented on product markets and technologies that were pioneered and occupied by others more advanced. As is always the case when industrial starter regions face the competition from those more advanced, this had repercussions for the characteristic capital / labor mix deployed here: lower investments in fixed capital outlays and infrastructure combined with a higher input of labor, facilitated by lower wages and the incorporation of less protected categories of workers, often daughters. Hence the region's specialization on low-value-added, highly labor intensive products, often in overcrowded markets such as cigarmaking and shoemaking. In such branches, its locational properties could well be turned into competitive advantage.

Since the Netherlands were an early-modern political creation, resembling a small, trade-oriented Italian city-state rather than a modern, territorial, industrial nation-state, home demand was small. As a consequence, the product markets of large-scale manufacturers, such as in North Brabant, were often foreign. This annihilated their chances to influence trade market conditions and caused important pressures on the social arrangements of their local production sites. Apart from low wages, flexibility was therefore a basic requirement for industrial success.

Even in their own country, regional industrial interests did not attain the measure of market regulation common to large-scale producers elsewhere. Being peripheral to the Dutch polity, they were generally barred from political influence. Where industries catered to consumer demand from the urban parts of Holland, such as in shoemaking, they were always exposed to fierce competition from advanced foreign producers, who regularly dumped their overstocks on the unprotected Dutch market. The Dutch state, supported by trade-oriented financial and commercial interests, retained its traditional free-trade and hard-currency commitment.

This was not only a question of older merchant-capitalist elites, oriented on colonial trade, controlling the polity. It was more fundamentally an effect of national dependency and international economic power balances. Even such a basic economic fact as the gradual rise of home demand between 1850 and 1930 was largely predicated on the industrialization and (renewed) urbanization of the great ports of Rotterdam and Amsterdam, responding to the needs of the rapidly expanding German economy. Dutch industrialization and economic growth thus were dependent on processes taking place elsewhere. On its own, the country would not have generated a sustained impulse for large-scale investments in industry.

Finally, the (liberal) Dutch central state not only wished to abstain from macroeconomic regulation; it also left socioeconomic arrangements and infrastructure largely in the hands of local and regional actors. This was also true on fields where state arrangements were conducive to interventionism, such as housing after the law of 1901. While the government *enquête* of 1889 on labor conditions and relationships gradually produced some central state intervention on behalf of children's and females' labor (conditions and workdays) and on safety control, central regulation seriously took off only after 1945.

How did the combined effect of Dutch capital seeking cheap and flexible labor reserves, central state absenteeism in the economy, and industrial backwardness and dependence vis-à-vis the relevant foreign economic actors materialize in North Brabant? How did such external pressures interact with the particular internal socioeconomic processes within the respective districts studied? When one compares the morphology of the province in 1800 with that in 1900, one is immediately struck by the emergence of extensive conglomerations of industrial settlements, sometimes, as in the case of Tilburg and Eindhoven, merging into more or less consolidated cities. Such spaces had not existed in 1800. Within a few decades their populations had surpassed the number of inhabitants of the older urban centers of Den Bosch and Breda. In the twentieth century, North Brabant urbanization would produce the most populous urban region of the country outside the metropolitan core area. These new concentrations of people were the spatial expression of the accumulation, multiplication, or concentration of manufacturing capital and the related expansion of industrial labor forces. Here, factories emerged near to rural workers' residences and vice versa. And increased income opportunities triggered population growth while the older urban centers remained stagnant. The movement of population in nineteenth-century Brabant thus betrayed the origin of regional industrialization and urbanization in protoindustrial, worker-peasant economies outside the older urban areas. This regional process closely reflected the characteristic pressures of a labor-intensive and flexible industrialization under the temporal and spatial conditions set out above.

In this context, class formation could not resemble the emergence of apparently clear-cut, relatively segregated, more or less internally unified and externally bounded groupings, such as witnessed in the industrial heartlands of Germany or England or the proletarian neighborhoods of Amsterdam or Vienna. Josef Ehmer, for example, has shown how the Viennese proletariat had remained fully separate from other classes for several generations and, as a consequence, developed rather autonomous political practices when they attained the power to do so.[5] Vienna may be an extreme case, but Brabant certainly tends to the opposite extreme. Class formation here, as we have seen, was a very muted and dependent process, where the boundaries between classes often became blurred in politics or production; or were crisscrossed, displaced, and subsumed by family ties; or were relativized by occupational multiplicity; and sometimes even were made irrelevant by their very permeability. In the (liberal) sociopolitical arena, working class formation remained captured within cross-class political alliances, either Catholic or social democratic, and would not easily develop into an independent voice. While this may have been a much more general phenomenon than hitherto acknowledged by class-oriented analysts, again, the degree to which it seems to have been the case here was certainly rare. And the effects of this were even magnified, or in any case consolidated, by the absence of any political breakdown or caesura such as was experienced in most other places of northwestern Europe in relation with war.

Let us consider, in summarizing fashion, the two regional trajectories of industrial class formation studied in this book: central Brabant shoemakers and Eindhoven electrical workers. I am a bit reluctant to bring down these complex cases to their bare bones, as I have repeatedly argued against reification and the isolation of variables, and instead advocated a thick description of their simultaneous working "on the ground." I think our theory-making should enable us to do just that. Nevertheless, when we bear in mind that we are dealing with complex, dynamic, mutually constitutive relations within whole pathways of social change, and not with simple facts or factors, the framework can serve heuristic and comparative purposes. I will consciously abstain from discussing cultural aspects, working class culture, everyday life, and biographies. But I am sure that without studying culture in depth I would not have been able to spell out any such framework.

If the general pressures of North Brabant industrialization were evidently strong enough to produce an overall outcome where class-oriented protest was marginal, my two regions got there along thoroughly different historical routes. Why did social Catholicism play the contradictory role it played in the shoemaking village cluster of central Brabant, and why did Eindhoven become the theater for the emergence and subsequent large-scale managerial re-creation of flexible familism with its associated daughters' exploitation and workers' dependence? We must identify respectively (1) the spatial and temporal properties of these diverse trajectories; (2) the origins and composition of their typical labor/capital mixes; (3) the obstacles for regional development, welfare, and well-being that were inherent to (1) and (2); and (4) the opportunities for class organizations and class alliances to be created and be successful in alleviating such barriers. Finally, in order to prevent teleology, we should ask which possible choices, at which "key forks in the road," at which "junctions," could have triggered alternative directions, and why they were not realized.

Shoemaking villages and the Philips / Eindhoven industrial complex represent two poles within the spectrum of North Brabant's regional development. The polarity concerns the degree of capital concentration, spatial linkages, and time: that is, the scale of investments, the degree and mode in which external capital and long-distance trade was involved, as well as the moment in which a fully wage-dependent working population had emerged. These "factors" were closely interrelated. They produced contrasting paths of intensive and extensive accumulation in Eindhoven and central Brabant.

The central internal fact of the Eindhoven area was its slow and long drawn-out emergence of wage dependency of households all through the nineteenth century. Here worker-peasant families, "folk-economies," and occupational multiplicity held out longest. As a result, it became a favored locale for the deployment of external capital, searching for cheap and flexible labor inputs from members of semiproletarian families maintaining access to multiple sources of income. Wages, accordingly, could be held below the level necessary for the reproduction of an individual adult. The great entrepreneurs in this region were oriented to international trade networks, and originally had weak roots in the community. These characteristics combined to produce what I have called flexible familism: the large-scale deployment of local daughters in labor-intensive manufacturing branches, who became increasingly socialized and disciplined (and dominated) for that task, and whose wages counted as additional family income. This intersection of households and capital accumulation gradually grew into the area's key dynamic. While its entrepreneurs were initially reluctant to create fixed capital outlays, regional industry, on this basis, became so successful that it would eventually respond to competitive pressures by producing a concentrated large-scale factory landscape (with, as we have seen, a highly scattered residential pattern, which was also inherent to flexible familist relationships).

The shoemaking region, however, located near the urban markets of Holland, with a soil too barren for small-scale agricultural activities, seems already in the eighteenth century to have been home to a relatively large, very poor, and indeed highly disrespected, mobile, petty-industrial population. These protoproletarian groups specialized in the simple production and marketing of low-grade consumer products, such as baskets, matches, and cheap shoes. In the course of the nineteenth century, an internal and fluctuating entrepreneurial class gradually succeeded in entering the intermediate quality segment of ready-made leather shoes. These shoes were produced by combining central workshops for (female) stitching with a protoindustrial organization for (male) lasting. Internal entrepreneurship, low capital requirements, and easy entry into the trade, augmented by the low wages, long hours, and hard work of young and old of both sexes, led to the virtually complete concentration of Dutch shoemaking in this single region by 1900. It produced a decentralized, nonurban manufacturing landscape, consisting of a cluster of villages that contained thousands of households. These households were connected among each other by numerous networks of production, exchange, family, and friendship. Some of these networks, those with access to credit and river transportation, mainly located in Waalwijk, transformed themselves into centralized production sites in the decade after 1900. New technologies now started to favor large, mechanized, steam-driven factories over protoindustry. But only some years after this first movement toward concentration, a new phase of decentralization took place, as cheap gas motors and accessible leasing facilities even for the most advanced Good Year Welt technologies allowed numerous central Brabant entrepreneurs, as well as aspiring workers, access to factory formation.

Note that external sources of capital were not absent in this path of industrialization. Rather, in contrast to Eindhoven, it was the agents providing the capital who were themselves not part of the community. Capital was made available in the form of credit, either through lending or leasing. Central Brabant was served by absentee capitalists, who shifted the risks of investment to local populations, employers as well as workers. In particular the leasing facilities offered by the American monopolist United Shoe Machinery Company in Boston kept the barriers to entry into the trade low, while simultaneously allowing for the appropriation of the fruits of intensified competition, hard work, and insecurity on the part of shoemaking populations.

These are the particular paths to labor-intensive manufacturing: The Eindhoven area featured a concentrated, large-scale manufacturing industry based on a nexus of flexible familism and aimed at distant markets. The accumulated capital, though originating from outside the area, was after 1900 increasingly invested in large-scale, internally owned, fixed-capital outlays including the accordant industrial hierarchies. This route was increasingly capital intensive and led in the end to a highly concentrated factory landscape.

Central Brabant, in contrast, experienced a highly decentralized (proto)industrialization in the lowly capitalized shoe trade. Based on internal entrepreneurialism, it became increasingly dependent on external capitalists in the course of twentieth-century mechanization. Instead of concentrating labor and capital in a few large units, such as in Eindhoven, units here were multiplied time and again. Moreover, external dependency on monopolist providers of capital goods reinforced this older trend. Within each subsequent technological / organizational paradigm, there occurred the same cycle of concentration and deconcentration. The region featured a decentralized and capital-extensive route. The capital deployed in the region typically helped to increase external dependency and to siphon off local profits, not to foster local accumulation.

Note that the extensive / intensive divide also carried implications for spatial processes and processes within the household. While both paths to labor-intensive manufacturing tended to draw firmly on daughters' labor, the intensive regime of the Eindhoven area strongly increased its importance. It also tended to deepen parental and managerial domination over local daughters, as well as to create more solid liaisons between parents and industrial managers, even leading to a closely knit, implicit alliance. It also produced much stronger demographic dynamics and a more concentrated residential pattern relative to the capital-extensive path, though its continued basis in flexible familism led again to new rounds of urban sprawl and satellite development around its industrial core rather than to a consolidated city.

What were the typical development obstacles produced by these respective regional paths? And which actors (private or collective) emerged, which alliances were forged, to counter such obstacles? Inherent to the route of extensive accumulation taken by central Brabant was the constant tendency of more advanced producers to be undercut by backward neighbors, as well as their associated inability to dictate, or even negotiate, the terms of trade in shoemaking. This was facilitated by the characteristic protoindustrial relationships and truck systems of regional industry, which allowed backward entrepreneurs to stay in the market by passing the costs of increased competition on to dependent households. This blocked the further development of the regional economy, led to widespread popular indebtedness, rising costs of living, downward pressure on wages, and upward pressure on work time: a downward regional development spiral.

In the particular conjuncture of 1900–1910, the simultaneous processes of emergent factory formation, on the one hand, and the rise within the Catholic Church of a socially activist stratum of lower level clergy on the other, underlay the creation of a broad coalition to counter this downward trend. It was a coalition centered on Catholic labor unions, which were in their turn based on a core of elite factory artisans employed and supported by advanced entrepreneurs. This alliance aimed to put a floor under local labor conditions by way of collective action and social policy, and campaigned against the popular culture associated with stagnation. After the failure of earlier attempts at market regulation, the collective enforcement of social policy was the only way left for large industrialists to force backward entrepreneurs out of the market. Instead of squeezing their workers and underselling actually viable competitors, they now had to invest in production or go out of business.

How should we understand the role of Catholic social action in this process? The solidary practices of factory artisans in European industrialization have recently enjoyed much scholarly attention, but Catholicism and religion have been neglected. While the motivations and positions of factory artisans were the same here as elsewhere, that is, in general defensive, social Catholicism could play a crucial facilitating role in the making of labor unions and collective action. It could do so in particular where potential class actors were too weak, and too internally divided and heterogeneous, to translate latent but structural logics of solidarity into manifest action. Social Catholicism could help to break the deadlock between actors: either between employers, leading to a corporatist ordering of sales markets; or between employers and workers, leading to solidary corporatism and social intervention (or both). It could do the latter in three ways: by rendering working class activists some legitimacy and protection; by providing them with an articulate language that did not seem particularly self-interested because it emphasized universal (even supernatural) morality and the general good; and by modifying and channeling their actions in nonclass and cross-class ways.

To see social Catholicism in this way (or other religions, or nonclass and cross-class ideologies and organizations for that matter), is taking it out of the exceptionalist frame in which it has usually been treated. Indeed, its rise among shoemakers was inseparably linked with the regional conditions and typical development obstacles inherent to the extensive path to labor-intensive manufacturing taken by central Brabant. Social Catholicism was the vehicle for making an unexpected coalition of advanced employers, elite factory artisans, and dependent homeworking households. The two former groups were essential in bringing in enough social power and prestige to promote an organization that could run up against the immediate interests of a large, established citizenry of small-scale entrepreneurs. As my studies revealed, dependent home workers on their own would never have achieved this. But neither would they have joined in such large numbers without the support and protection of the local church. Moreover, given the historical presence and prestige of the clergy in local politics, its attitude toward local action would always be central to any outcome. When it condemned incipient collective action, it soon failed. But where the internal clerical struggle was decided in favor of social-interventionist *petits vicaires*, it meant a strong and immediate, though not easily manipulable, support for local organizers. Especially in a case such as central Brabant, where organizers, being members of a small working class elite, were relatively isolated, and their potential rank and file was too weak to act concertedly in public, support from the church caused a rapid shift of local power balances on their behalf.

The contradictory role of social Catholicism became apparent when, after about 1908, the interests of the class segments that had originally built the shoemakers' unions started to diverge, even to antagonize, and could no longer be mediated and focused by solidarist-corporatist ideology. The alliance had been relatively successful in combating the "super-exploiting" practices of backward entrepreneurs up to that date, but the large-scale and potentially violent conflict that suddenly broke out in the country's largest shoe factory in Waalwijk in 1910 signified its collapse. New technologies and leasing facilities allowed advanced employers a new competitive strategy. Collective action and social policy now gave way to full-scale mechanization, productivity drives, and intensified marketing on their part. Moreover, the new conditions led to the degradation of precisely the core group of activist factory artisans. Clerical supervision of their public institutions, however, deprived them of adequate and autonomous collective insight into the new antagonistic conditions. When they finally came out in strike, it was, significantly, only on their daughters' and sisters' instigation, whose dismay with the increasingly harsh discipline employers demanded from them helped ignite popular protest in 1910. Their fathers, however, were unprepared and hopelessly confused. Their spontaneous action devolved into a potentially violent popular rebellion that caused the authorities to declare martial law, while shoemakers were rapidly abandoned by Catholic public opinion. In the aftermath of defeat and embarrassment, many of them chose to take part in the next round of small business creation. Their Catholic unions quickly lost cultural focus, social power, and mobilizing force.

While the extensive path of the shoemaking cluster caused an endemic, production-based spiral of downward regional development, the highly capitalized, flexible familist route to labor-intensive manufacturing as taken by the Eindhoven area inherently led to recurrent crises of urban underinvestment and working class reproduction. Consequently, the Eindhoven analogy to sociopolitical regulation of labor markets by cross-class and Catholic shoemakers unions should precisely consist of a large-scale alliance on behalf of innovations in urban and family policy. The key to solving local problems lay in gaining control over the dysfunctions and contradictions of flexible familism.

The Eindhoven path combined large-scale investments in production facilities with permanent and structural underinvestment in working class reproduction. My approach has emphasized the centrality of the practice of flexible familism for urban industrial development in the Eindhoven region. The clue to local accumulation, industrial structures, urban form, class formation, and working class culture in the Eindhoven area lay in the specific ways the local tradition of multi-earner households was picked up by external capitalists producing for international consumer markets.

A long drawn-out process of proletarianization forced worker-peasant families in the course of the nineteenth century to increasingly seek industrial incomes. An emerging labor-intensive industry in textiles, cigarmaking, and later lamp bulb manufacturing catered in particular to the cheap, large, and flexible supply of local daughters. Up to 1910, local industry paid male wages far below the national average and exhibited percentages of formal female labor force participation between 50 and 80 percent. Around 1900, these were often daughters of local families, employed in mass-production departments, whose fathers (and brothers, and other family members) worked in slightly higher status jobs or on less tiring tasks in the same plant. Parental status and the job opportunities for fathers in local industry thus became increasingly linked to the number and discipline of the daughters that fathers could bring in. Though local wages were far below the level necessary for individual reproduction, let alone male breadwinnership, collective family income, in this way, could sometimes be relatively high.

Flexible familism enabled industrialists to create not only a very flexible but also a uniquely disciplined production regime. In slack periods a large number of young female workers could temporarily be laid off, while a large labor reserve would always be available for the next up-swing. Flexible familism offered some security during downturns in the business cycle for the higher-status dependent households, as at least one earner would probably hold his job. Upswings would then again bring rising prosperity since more children would start earning a wage.

Not unimportantly, this labor practice also ensured a high degree of discipline among its underpaid workers. In the household economies of southeast Brabant, daughters in particular were socialized for obedience and availability for household needs. Since the discipline of their daughters became a vital asset for their status and survival, parents started to control their dispositions and attitudes toward highly regimented industrial work in a way that underrated wages would never have done. Thus the classical problem of flexible and underpaid labor forces, a persistent lack of dedication to work, could be solved in a nonmarket way by making parents responsible. A flexible industrial base could be built up that specialized in small, fragile, carefully manufactured consumer products for capricious international markets, as demonstrated by the lamp bulb. Thus the accumulation of capital and the accumulation of households intimately interacted to produce a highly flexible, low-cost, and highly disciplined, labor-intensive, and export-oriented manufacturing territory.

But the flexible familist, low-wage base of local industry caused an endemic underdevelopment of housing markets and housing provision. For one, it put a premium on local families sticking together, and prevented a decline of the female age at marriage to the "really modern standard" of Amsterdam or Rotterdam, thus causing a constant tendency toward overcrowding. Population growth and family formation remained substantially dependent on immigration. But given the low wages, acceptable housing provision by large-scale investors emerged only after 1905. Local housing supply, especially for unskilled families, therefore became increasingly insufficient. And, being an ideal source for petty bourgeois profit-making, it became qualitatively ever more deplorable. Low wage levels, moreover, did not allow for the creation of a tax base for infrastructural investments such as roads, sewerage, and water supply, particularly not in the low-value/low-rent areas of the urban periphery where working class households tended to concentrate. Thus overcrowding in low-grade, one-family housing became the Eindhoven complement to the overcrowding of sales markets in shoemaking. And the sprawl of underdeveloped proletarian settlements around an impressive industrial core was the Eindhoven equivalent to centrifugal business formation in the shoemaking village cluster.

The endemic issue of urban underinvestment posed itself in three historical/sociospatial forms. The first affected local, established, unskilled working families, who were hit by such problems as rising house rents, forced and expensive shopping with retailer-landlords, and overcrowding in sad conditions. This particular form also threatened to reap the fruits of flexible familist industrialization from the industrialists, as high rent payments to small landlords caused an upward pressure on wages. The second form was the absence of housing for immigrant specialist workers. And third, and in the long run most fundamental, the overarching tendency to a general exhaustion of the local unskilled labor supply as the accumulation and concentration of industrial capital structurally outmatched the urban concentration of population. Flexible familism and underurbanization were two sides of the same coin.

Local alliances of classes were only made to alleviate version one of this urban underinvestment problem. Dissident local workers after 1900 were encouraged by large capitalists such as the Philips brothers to develop social democratic politics. Liberal entrepreneurs thus hoped to gain wider electoral support for a progressive program proposing the annexation of the underfunded satellite communities as well as the start of a serious social housing effort (made possible by the national housing law of 1901, but dependent on local policy). The large role played by capitalists in this left-liberal coalition, and in particular by the Philips brothers, allowed activists access to the necessary funds to finance their local initiatives. But in the long run it prevented them from developing an independent voice and turning to the conditions of work. As we have seen, it created a strained and quarrelsome atmosphere among the community of the left when younger immigrants started to question labor relationships at Philips. The division of the local left was endemic and paralyzing, and fostered its eventual demise after 1911. At the same time the cultural gap dividing highly skilled, bachelor, immigrant, left-wing metalworkers from local working families was growing wider.

Since it was essential to any further steps on the capital-intensive path, the second form taken by the urban underinvestment problem was addressed quickly and singlehandedly by large employers themselves. As fixed capital assets grew, an increasing number of specialist workers, usually immigrants from the advanced west and north, were necessary to serve, devise, construct, and maintain the increasingly complex installations, especially at the Philips firm. Accordingly, as we have seen, rounds of new factory development after 1900 were steadily accompanied by new rounds of housing investment by employers for this single purpose. For one, without offering good housing opportunities, they would not attract and commit the necessary skilled specialists. Moreover, the wage standards of these skilled workers were high enough to allow for nonsubsidized, market-oriented rents for good housing. This again contributed to the segmentation between working class groups in the locality, as new neighborhoods were spatially segregated from older ones and generally catered to the housing needs of specific income categories with specific skills.

The overarching problem three, finally, could not be solved on the local level. Indeed, it presupposed precisely the large-scale urban investments that a regional economy based on the low-wage relationships of flexible familism did not permit. Neither Philips nor the urban community nor working class parents were able to step over their immediate interests. Philips was not prepared to immobilize its capital to create affordable housing for the unskilled, and would rather locate new production facilities in peripheral regions with a labor reserve or near small cities with an abundant supply of worker-daughters. The city also remained unwilling since it feared the responsibility to support large numbers of unemployed during downturns and only provided housing for established inhabitants. Parents, evidently, were more interested in keeping their children's earning power for themselves than in helping them to create independent households, since local elections after 1910 never again featured housing provision as a major issue.

Though already evident before 1910, the structural and endemic undersupply of local unskilled labor would be solved only by 1930. By this date, as we have seen, the ensuing problems had culminated in a deep crisis of flexible familist arrangements. This crisis was eroding the very forms of hegemony that were basic to profitable mass manufacturing in the region. The concentrated electrical complex of the Eindhoven area, however, had by then attained national weight. Its structural obstacle to further growth could now be attacked by a powerful alliance between the Philips corporation and the central state. As I have shown, this supralocal alliance with the Dutch state allowed the giant firm to liberate itself from its local constraints, which now also included its local workers. The description and systematic interpretation of disparate data and phenomena that were hitherto merely looked at in empiricist isolation demonstrate the origin and logic of Philipsist social policy and explains the popular acquiescence during several shocking downturns in the early thirties.

Together, these phenomena amounted to a serious crisis of hegemonic practices based on flexible familism. Since the local female labor supply was practically exhausted by 1924, the rapid rise of job opportunities during the radio-boom years after 1927 called forth a young and mobile regional proletariat of lodgers and commuters that gradually started to escape parental and managerial controls. Morally panicking local authorities, rising criminality rates, rising rates of illness, absenteeism, labor turnover, managerial discourses on "healthy families," stable labor, and housing shortages—all signaled the end of flexible familism as a dominant labor relationship. Indeed, how could it have been prolonged in a locality where the number of lodgers tripled in three years, while thousands of young commuters entered the city each day, and the percentage of young females in mass production started to decline rapidly?

In an earlier period Ford of Detroit had countered a similar weakening of labor discipline among the unskilled in times of rapid expansion by encouraging moral rectitude through discriminatory wage increases. I have called this strategy monetary moralism, and, building on Robert Brenner, I have suggested it is rooted in the historical power relationships between classes in the midwestern American region. Philips, likewise, in conceiving its package of social policies, rediscovered key aspects of class relationships in its home region. Accordingly, it reinvented a managerial form of flexible familism as its "natural" way out of labor crisis. While high wages were the central remedy for Ford in the liberal society and "mature" markets of the midwest, Philips, in the "immature" and basically juvenile labor market of southeast Brabant, which was dominated by labor-intensive and despotic manufacturing regimes, started large-scale housing programs to re-create "obligatory" daughters' labor from large immigrant families. Other Philipsist policies largely responded to the consequences of this single strategy.

The Philipsist re-creation of flexible familism had momentous and systematically interrelated consequences for the community and the corporation. It is likely that it implied the silent layoff of possibly seven thousand young regional workers even before the advent of world crisis. Starting in late 1929, "undisciplined" lodgers, commuters, and young adult males were substituted with a smaller number of disciplined girls from immigrant families. The moral panic among local authorities faded as mobile youth returned to their homesteads or otherwise left town.

The re-creation of flexible familism, apart from reinforcing existing segmentations between skilled and unskilled workers and neighborhoods, also facilitated a massive temporary reduction in the active labor force in the electrical industry during the crisis of 1931–32. This was not unlike the ways in which local industrialists had probably managed cyclical downturns around 1900. When half the earners in each unskilled family were temporarily dismissed, the others still brought home some necessary income. Philips, along this line, limited its number of mass-production workers to the absolute minimum. Without seriously threatening the stability of its new immigrant proletariat, it could thus bring down existing stocks while stepping up productivity by way of renewed selection and norm-setting. The managerial appropriation and reintroduction of flexible familism thus forestalled uprooting and protest among the unskilled in the early thirties. It also enabled Philips to realize a dramatic productivity increase of 300 percent, which was an absolute precondition for survival in world markets for labor-intensive products given its location in the last hard-currency country in Europe.

But while the new round of investments in radio set making were accompanied by a large-scale, state-sponsored, urbanization based on government social housing expenses, the contradiction between flexible familism and urbanization in fact did not disappear. Rather, it was postponed and displaced. The next (post–World-War-II) expansionary phase necessitated the sprawling of branch plants for mature production processes in search for new, cheap, "immature," and flexible labor forces, first in the Dutch periphery, then in Europe, and since the seventies in particular in Southeast Asia. Instead of creating sprawling and underdeveloped proletarian settlements around a concentrated, capitalized core, such as was the case in Eindhoven after 1900, capital now decentralized itself to find and re-create underdevelopment elsewhere.

Which alternative paths, at which "key forks" in the road, could have been taken by these respective regions? My approach suggests that the key moments in a "branching process" can analytically be broken down into three possible sets of events. The first set contains all those actions in which the organizational power derived from the integration in wider spatial networks of exchange is used to change internal class relationships and the development obstacles inherent to them. The second concerns all those actions in which internal class power, or the power of local class alliances, is deployed to shift and restructure the pattern of external linkages and the inherent problems of development they pose. The third set, finally, concerns efforts to change both (1) and (2) by political or civic means, that is, the means mobilized through access to the instruments of the national state or the organizations of civil society.

The key dilemma in the pathway of Eindhoven was this: In order to acquire a more secure oligopolist status in the international and highly competitive market for light consumer goods, Philips had to expand and intensify the local arrangements of flexible familism (that is, it had to make use of strategy number two mentioned above). But flexible familism, at the same time, made the next step to the luxuries of capital goods production for a national market more unlikely than it already was, given Philips's small home market and trade-oriented political environment. It did so, as we have seen, because flexible familism precisely brought with it a fundamental division between skilled and unskilled workers in Eindhoven. It thus blocked the opportunities for strong and focused labor politics in this national, though peripheral, industrial heartland. As a consequence, it closed the road to political influence through popular action.

Certainly, the Dutch state after 1848 was much more oriented to colonial and international trade than to internal economic growth. Nevertheless, in the course of the twentieth century it could well have started to promote an internal capital goods industry, for example in naval technologies such as radar, or in civic technologies such as power suppliers, electrical motors, and electrical transport. After all, the Netherlands was still a highly urbanized society and a naval power. Though I am not acquainted with specialist research in this field, there seems only one good reason for not having done so, and that is the internal logic of national power balances.

A vigorous local politics and class struggle in Eindhoven, in alliance with left-wing initiatives elsewhere, could well have made a difference here. After the introduction of universal suffrage in 1917, there is no reason why it would have been impossible for a strong labor movement in Eindhoven to press in this direction, in particular when acting in alliance with industrial interests. From this counter-factual vantage point, the fall of local labor politics in 1911 signified the closure of an alternative path based on skilled and specialist labor. This pathway could have led to a different alliance with the central government than the one actually realized in the late 1920s. Instead of an export-oriented, conservative alliance between the corporation and the state, aimed at the re-creation of flexible familism through large-scale, state-sponsored housing projects, it might have promoted a nationally oriented alliance of labor, industrial interests, and the state, supporting industrial specialization and internal growth. Eindhoven would then have looked different, and would have allowed different relationships and experiences than those encountered in this study.

However, as we have seen, there was a strong internal logic to the isolation and fall of socialist metalworkers in 1911. Flexible familist production by itself implied a deep division of local workers, as well as a production regime uncongenial to regulation by collective consent. As is mostly the case, I suspect, the actual path taken had much the better chances already from the very start of electrical production in Eindhoven.

Turning to the shoemaking district, it is hard to perceive possible alternative pathways. Here the key moment also lies around 1910. Two hypothetical alternatives to mass production, artisan degradation, and the decline of Catholic labor in these years can be detected. But, in contrast to Eindhoven, they were hardly conditioned by local relations and therefore not quite affectable by local actors.

First, a more democratic, transparent, and laborist Catholicism, as for example flourishing in the German *Ruhrgebiet*, would probably have enabled factory artisans to respond more effectively to the new employers' strategy. However, the absence of competition with socialist groups *in situ*, and the general conservative position of Catholicism within the Dutch political system (in contrast to Catholicism in Germany) precluded such an outcome of Catholic class formation.

The second possible opening to an alternative path was decided over in the United States and was therefore beyond the reach of any central Brabant actor. The rise to high monopolist status of the Bostonian capital goods industry could have been mitigated through antimonopoly judicial action. In these years, law suits against the United Shoe Machinery Company indeed took place, but did not lead to fundamental changes in the position or the leasing strategies of the monopolist. Central Brabant, like other shoemaking regions, was even more subsumed by processes of accumulation taking place elsewhere. Its potentials for prosperity were time and again exported.

The North Brabant area of large-scale, labor-intensive manufacturing, with its prevailing workers' acquiescence, has always been a classic instance of exceptionalism and anomaly for modernist class theory. Accordingly, it has been explained either in culturalist terms, ranging from Catholicism to lightheartedness, connoting the absence of popular enlightenment, or by top-down notions of capitalist (and clerical) control, suggesting the irrelevance of workers' agency and commitments. By rethinking class analysis, I have done the nonobvious and nonfashionable. The version of historicized and spatialized class analysis adopted here leads to the identification, description, and historical explanation of two particular local pathways within a general regional process of capitalist industrialization, including the attendant patterns of class formation, cleavage, and alliance. To the extent that, in the case of Philips/Eindhoven, the idea of dominance must be retained, we are now at least in a position to specify why this could be so.

The bare bones of these pathways have been presented in summary form in this epilogue. But they should not be seen as the final product of this work. They have been deployed throughout my analysis of industrialization, popular experience, class power, and everyday politics. They are heuristic starting points, a way to get at the real dynamics of real places and real people. They're nothing less, and nothing more.

Class analysis, I firmly believe, must come back to the ground. It must help us to come to grips with the great historical variety of singular but interconnected rhythms of class formation/deformation and experience. Instead of promoting reductionism of any kind, it must encourage us to comprehend complexity. Class theory should point at the specific interconnections between Marx's "modes of production" and his "modes of life," between work, family, and community, between capital accumulation, hegemony, and the everyday politics of mutually connected groups of people. As both Edward Thompson and Antonio Gramsci knew, such interconnections are always singular. But singularity in this regard is not homologous to irregularity. Its causes are largely systematic: they are situated in divergences of timing, position, prior properties, and subsequent trajectories of (people and) places within wider, evolving networks of capitalist accumulation and exchange. Starting from this premise, and aiming at the complexity sought here, will help a bit, I hope, to rid class-oriented social analysts from the obsession not to become obsolete in the face of current culturalist and postmaterialist charms. Let us combat the "intellectual deforestation" of those trends.

Notes

INTRODUCTION

1. Mike Savage, "Class Analysis and Its Futures," *The Sociological Review* 42, no. 3 (1994): 531–48.

2. Nicholas Dirks, Geoff Eley, and Sherry Ortner, Introduction, *Culture/Power/ History: A Reader in Contemporary Social Theory*, ed. Dirks, Eley, and Ortner (Princeton: Princeton University Press, 1994), 3–47, elaborate a program based on the same concepts while consciously avoiding serious engagement with class.

3. See Charles Tilly, *Big Structures, Large Processes, Huge Comparisons* (New York: Russell Sage, 1984a); Eric Wolf, *Europe and the People without History* (Berkeley: University of California Press, 1982).

4. Edward P. Thompson, particularly the following works: *The Making of the English Working Class* (New York: Vintage, 1963); *The Poverty of Theory and Other Essays* (London: Merlin, 1978); *Whigs and Hunters* (New York: Pantheon Books, 1976); "The Moral Economy of the English Crowd in the Eighteenth Century," *Past and Present* 50 (1971): 76–136; "Patrician Society, Plebeian Culture," *Journal of Social History* 7 (1974): 382–405; "Eighteenth-century English Society: Class Struggle without Class?" *Social History* 3, no. 2 (1978): 133–65. On Thompson, see the recent collection by Harvey J. Kaye and Keith McClelland, eds., *E. P. Thompson: Critical Perspectives* (Cambridge: Polity Press, 1990). Eric Wolf, in particular the following works: *Peasant Wars of the Twentieth Century* (New York: Harper and Row, 1969); *Europe and the People without History* (Berkeley: University of California Press, 1982); "Facing Power: Old Insights, New Questions," *American Anthropologist* 92 (1990): 586–96. On Wolf see J. Abbink and H. Vermeulen, eds., *History and Culture: Essays on the Work of Eric R. Wolf* (Amsterdam: Het Spinhuis, 1992); Jane Schneider and Rayna Rapp, eds., *Articulating Hidden Histories: Exploring the Influence of Eric R. Wolf* (Berkeley: University of California Press, 1995); and Don Kalb, Herman Tak, and Hans Marks, eds., "Historical Anthropology: The Unwaged Debate," *FOCAAL*, no. 26/27.

5. For example: Erik Olin Wright, *Classes* (London: Verso, 1985); Gordon Marshall et al., *Social Class in Modern Britain* (London: Hutchinson, 1988); G. Cohen, *Karl Marx's Theory of History: A Defence* (Oxford: Oxford University Press, 1978); Jon Elster, *Making Sense of Marx* (Cambridge: Cambridge University Press, 1985), and *Nuts and Bolts for the Social Sciences* (Cambridge: Cambridge University Press, 1989).

6. The term "relational marxism" is coined by Christopher Lloyd in *The Structures of History* (Oxford: Basil Blackwell, 1993).

7. E. P. Thompson, particularly 1978b, *Poverty of Theory*; Raymond Williams, (in particular) *Marxism and Literature* (Oxford: Oxford University Press, 1977); Derek Sayer, *The Violence of Abstraction* (Oxford: Basil Blackwell, 1987); Jorge Larrain, *A Reconstruction of Historical Materialism* (London: Allen and Unwin, 1986); Richard Miller, *Analyzing Marx: Morality, Power, and History* (Princeton: Princeton University Press, 1984); Arthur Stinchcombe, *Economic Sociology* (New York: Academic Press, 1983); Maurice Godelier, *The Mental and the Material* (London: Verso, 1986); Wolf 1982; David Harvey, *The Urbanization of Capital: Studies in the History and Theory of Capitalist Urbanization* (Baltimore: Johns Hopkins University Press, 1985), and *Consciousness and the Urban Experience: Studies in the History and Theory of Capitalist Urbanization* (Baltimore: Johns Hopkins University Press, 1985).

8. Neil Smelser, *Social Change in the Industrial Revolution* (Chicago: Chicago University Press, 1959); Patrick Joyce, *Work, Society, and Politics: The Culture of the Factory in Later Victorian England* (New Brunswick: Rutgers University Press, 1980), and *Visions of the People* (Cambridge: Cambridge University Press, 1991); Raphael Samuel, "Workshop of the World: Steam Power and Hand Technology in Mid-Victorian Britain," *History Workshop* 3 (1977): 7–72; Michael Burawoy, *The Politics of Production* (London: Verso, 1985); David Levine, *Reproducing Families: The Political Economy of English Population History* (Cambridge: Cambridge University Press, 1987); Michael Anderson, *Family Structure in Nineteenth-Century Lancashire* (Cambridge: Cambridge University Press, 1971); Joan Scott and Louise Tilly, "Women's Work and the Family in Nineteenth-Century Europe," *Comparative Studies in Society and History* 17, no. 1 (1975): 36–64.

9. In addition to the works by Thompson and Williams cited earlier, see Rodney Hilton, *Bond Men Made Free* (London: Methuen, 1973).

10. Sayer 1987.

11. Sayer 1987, 77.

12. Sayer 1987, 77.

13. The term is E. P. Thompson's; see Thompson 1978a, 133–65.

14. Tilly 1984a; Tilly, *As Sociology Meets History* (New York: Academic Press, 1981).

15. Peter Worsley, "A Landmark in Anthropology," *American Ethnologist* 11, no. 1 (1984): 174.

16. For the concept of path dependency in historical sociology see the seminal article by Ron Aminzade, "Historical Sociology and Time," *Sociological Methods and Research* 20, no. 4 (1992): 456–80.

17. Lloyd 1993, 62–65. Antony Giddens, in particular his *The Constitution of Society* (Cambridge: Polity Press, 1984); Pierre Bourdieu, *Outline of a Theory of Practice* (Cambridge: Cambridge University Press, 1977), and *Distinction: A Social Critique of the Judgement of Taste* (London: Routledge, 1984).

18. Andrew Abbott, "From Causes to Events: Notes on Narrative Positivism," *Sociological Methods and Research* 20, no. 4 (1992): 428–55; Aminzade 1992.

19. See, among others, Douglas Holmes, *Cultural Disenchantments: Worker Peasantries in Northeast Italy* (Princeton: Princeton University Press, 1989); Louise

Lamphere, *From Working Daughters to Working Mothers: Immigrant Women in a New England Industrial Community* (Ithaca: Cornell University Press, 1987); June Nash, *We Eat the Mines and the Mines Eat Us* (New York: Columbia University Press, 1979), and *From Tank Town to High Tech: The Clash of Community and Industrial Cycles* (Albany: State University of New York Press, 1989); Katherine Newman, *Falling from Grace: The Experience of Downward Mobility in the American Middle Class* (New York: Vintage Books, 1988), and *Declining Fortunes: The Withering of the American Dream* (New York: Basic Books, 1993); William Roseberry, *Anthropologies and Histories: Essays in Culture, History, and Political Economy* (New Brunswick: Rutgers University Press, 1989); Gerald Sider, *Culture and Class in Anthropology and History: A Newfoundland Illustration* (Cambridge: Cambridge University Press, 1986); Gavin Smith, *Livelihood and Resistance* (Berkeley: University of California Press, 1989); Michael Taussig, *The Devil and Commodity Fetishism in South America* (Chapel Hill: University of North Carolina Press, 1980); Wolf 1982.

20. See, among others, Manuell Castells, *The City and the Grassroots* (Berkeley: University of California Press, 1983), and *The Informational City: Information Technology, Economic Restructuring, and the Urban-Regional Process* (Oxford: Basil Blackwell, 1989); Susan Fainstein, Ian Gordon, and Michael Harloe, eds., *Divided Cities: New York and London in the Contemporary World* (Oxford: Basil Blackwell, 1992); Harvey 1989; John Logan and Harvey Molotch, *Urban Fortunes: The Political Economy of Place* (Berkeley: University of California Press, 1987); Doreen Massey, *Spatial Divisions of Labour* (London: Macmillan, 1984); Allan Pred, *Making Histories and Constructing Human Geographies: The Local Transformation of Practice, Power Relations, and Consciousness* (Boulder: Westview Press, 1990); John Scott and Allan Storper, *Production, Work, Territory: The Geographical Anatomy of Industrial Capitalism* (Boston: Allen and Unwin, 1986); Michael Peter Smith and Joe Feagin, eds., *The Capitalist City: Global Restructuring and Community Politics* (Oxford: Basil Blackwell, 1987); Allan Storper and Richard Walker, *The Capitalist Imperative: Territory, Technology, and Industrial Growth* (Oxford: Basil Blackwell, 1989); Sharon Zukin, *Landscapes of Power: From Detroit to Disney World* (Berkeley: University of California Press, 1991). For a recent sympathetic and seminal critique, see Ira Katznelson, *Marxism and the City* (Oxford: Clarendon Press, 1992).

21. For example: Ron Aminzade, *Class, Politics, and Early Industrial Capitalism: A Study of Mid–Nineteenth-Century Toulouse, France* (Albany: State University of New York Press, 1981), and *Ballots and Barricades: Class Formation and Republican Politics in France, 1830–1871* (Princeton: Princeton University Press, 1993); John Foster, *Class Struggle and the Industrial Revolution: Early Industrial Capitalism in Three English Towns* (London: Methuen, 1974); John Gaventa, *Power and Powerlessness: Quiescence and Rebellion in an Appalachian Valley* (Urbana: University of Illinois Press, 1980); Michael Hanagan, *The Logic of Solidarity: Artisans and Industrial Workers in Three French Towns, 1871–1914* (Urbana: University of Illinois Press, 1981), and *Nascent Proletarians: Class Formation in Post-Revolutionary France* (Oxford: Basil Blackwell, 1989); Joyce 1980, 1991; Erhard Lucas, *Arbeiterradikalismus: Zwei Formen von Radikalismus in der deutschen Arbeiterbewegung* (Frankfurt: Verlag Roter Stern, 1976); Alf Lüdtke, *Eigen-Sinn: Fabrikalltag, Arbeitererfahrungen und Politik vom Kaiserreich bis in den Faschismus* (Hamburg: Ergebnisse Verlag, 1993);

John Merriman, ed., *Consciousness and Class Experience in Nineteenth-Century Europe* (New York: Holmes and Meier, 1979); Barrington Moore Jr., *Injustice: The Social Bases of Obedience and Revolt* (New York: M. E. Sharpe, 1978); Jacques Ranciere, *The Nights of Labor: The Worker's Dream in Nineteenth-Century France* (Philadelphia: Temple University Press, 1989); William Reddy, *The Rise of Market Culture: The Textile Trade and French Society, 1750–1900* (Cambridge: Cambridge University Press, 1984); Donald Reid, *The Miners of Decazeville: A Genealogy of Deindustrialization* (Cambridge: Cambridge University Press, 1985); E. P. Thompson 1963; Charles Tilly, *The Contentious French* (Cambridge, Mass.: Harvard University Press, 1986); Louise Tilly and Joan Scott, *Women, Work, and Family* (New York: Basic Books, 1978).

22. The formulation is Raymond Williams's (1977).

23. The concept of "key relationships" comes from Wolf 1982.

24. Craig Calhoun, *The Question of Class Struggle* (Chicago: University of Chicago Press, 1982).

25. See Charles Tilly, "Demographic Origins of the European Proletariat," in David Levine, ed., *Proletarianization and Family History* (New York: Academic Press, 1984b), 1–87.

26. Samuel 1977.

27. Joyce 1980; Burawoy 1985.

28. Joyce 1980; Burawoy 1985.

29. Lüdtke 1993.

30. Charles Sabel and Jonathan Zeitlin, "Historical Alternatives to Mass Production: Politics, Markets, and Technology in Nineteenth-Century Industrialization," *Past and Present* 108 (1985): 133–74.

31. Stephen Wood ed., *The Degradation of Work? Skill, Deskilling, and the Labor Process* (London: Heinemann, 1982).

32. Dick Geary's *European Labour Protest, 1848–1939* (London: Methuen, 1981) is still a good comparative survey. See the more recent and more far-reaching Ira Katznelson and Ari Zolberg, eds., *Working Class Formation* (Princeton: Princeton University Press, 1986).

33. Among others, exemplified by: Joyce 1980; Lüdtke 1993; Reddy 1984; William Reddy, *Money and Liberty in Modern Europe: A Critique of Historical Understanding* (Cambridge: Cambridge University Press, 1987); Joan Scott, *Gender and the Politics of History* (New York: Basic Books, 1988); William Sewell, *Work and Revolution in France: The Language of Labor from the Old Regime to 1848* (Cambridge: Cambridge University Press, 1980). To the extent that they embrace a (heavily) language-centered alternative, see the (heavy-handed) critiques by, among others, Brian Palmer, *Descent into Discourse: The Reification of Language and the Writing of Social History* (Philadelphia: Temple University Press, 1990); Ellen Meiksins Wood, *The Retreat from Class* (London: Verso, 1986); John Foster, "The Declassing of Language," *New Left Review* 150 (1985). See for comments on the wider shift to cultural analysis: Harvey J. Kaye, *The Powers of the Past* (Minneapolis: University of Minnesota Press, 1991), which defends the social-historical approach based on a broad concept of class, and Lynn Hunt, ed., *The New Cultural History* (Berkeley: University of California Press, 1989), for a positive acclaim. See also Don Kalb,

"Frameworks of Culture and Class in Historical Research," *Theory and Society* 22 (1993): 513–37. My subsequent critique is not universally valid for all "anthropologizing" authors.

34. As exemplified by Ira Katznelson and Aristide Zolberg 1986.

35. Patrick Joyce, *Visions of the People*, 15, for example. I must concede that his work is very careful in its treatment of questions of culture and class. Nevertheless, I think, it is unsatisfactory.

36. Reddy 1984 and 1987.

37. See, for example, Sider 1986; Wolf 1982.

38. Ira Katznelson, "Working Class Formation: Constructing Cases and Comparisons," in Katznelson and Zolberg, *Working Class Formation: Nineteenth-Century Patterns in Western Europe and the United States* (Princeton: Princeton University Press, 1986), 3–45.

39. Julian Steward et al., *The People of Puerto Rico* (Urbana: University of Illinois Press, 1956).

40. I think in particular of Aminzade 1981 and 1993; Foster 1973; Hanagan 1981 and 1989.

41. Where, to my mind, the work of authors like Alf Lüdtke (1993), James Scott (1985), and Gerald Sider (1986) points the way.

42. In this respect, Christopher Lloyd, in his comprehensive discussion of "structurist" approaches in historical social science, fails to highlight the central methodological importance of scale reduction for authors such as Clifford Geertz and Le Roy Ladurie, whom he presents as examples of persuasive social analysis. Reduction of scale and expansion of scope are intimately connected. See Lloyd 1993, in particular pp. 89–130.

43. Burawoy 1985; Michael Burawoy, "Marxism without Micro-Foundations," *Socialist Review* 19, no. 2 (1989): 53–86; Geoff Eley, "Labor History, Social History, Alltagsgeschichte: Experience, culture, and the politics of the everyday," *Journal of Modern History* 61 (1989): 297–343; Lüdtke 1993; Alf Lüdtke, ed., *Alltagsgeschichte* (Frankfurt: Campus Verlag, 1989); James Scott 1985. Of course the work of Italian microhistorians such as Carlo Ginzburg and Giovanni Levi should be included here; see the discussion in Giovanni Levi, "On Microhistory," in Peter Burke, ed., *New Perspectives on Historical Writing* (University Park: Pennsylvania State University Press, 1991).

44. Exemplified by some of the work of Clifford Geertz, in particular *The Interpretation of Cultures* (New York: Basic Books, 1973).

45. See for example Dirks et al. 1994; Roger Keesing, "Theories of culture," *Annual Review of Anthropology* 3 (1974): 73–97, and "Theories of Culture Revisited," paper presented at annual meeting of American Anthropological Association, Washington, D.C., 1989; Levi 1991; Sider 1986; E. Valentine-Daniel, *Is There a Counterpoint to Culture?* (Amsterdam: Center for Asian Studies, 1991).

46. Robert Lowie, *The History of Ethnological Theory* (New York: Reinhart, 1937); Robert Redfield, *Tepoztlan, a Mexican Village: A Study of Folk Life* (Chicago: University of Chicago Press, 1930); Wolf 1982.

47. Antonio Gramsci, *Selections from The Prison Notebooks*, ed. and trans. Q. Hoare and G. Smith (New York: International Publishers, 1971); see Geoff Eley,

"Nations, Publics, and Political Cultures: Placing Habermas in the Nineteenth Century," in Dirks et al. 1994, 297–336; and in particular the reading of Gramsci by Raymond Williams 1997.

48. See Alf Lüdtke, in particular his recent collection *Eigensinn: Fabrikalltag, Arbeitererfahrungen und Politik vom Kaiserreich bis in den Faschismus* (Hamburg: Ergebnisse Verlag, 1993), which contains many of the relevant earlier articles. Other authors have used notions similar to "everyday politics." See, for example, James Scott, *Weapons of the Weak: Everyday Forms of Peasant Resistance* (New Haven: Yale University Press, 1985), and *Domination and the Arts of Resistance: Hidden Transcripts* (New Haven: Yale University Press, 1990); Eley 1989, 297–343, and 1994, 297–336. What matters here is the relevance of a prosaic approach to power, politics, interest, and identity. In fact, one could say that the idea is a realization of the more radical tendencies in anthropology and social history, while referring to the critical tradition in European philosophy by authors such as Ernst Bloch, Henri Lefebvre, and Antonio Gramsci.

49. Michael Burawoy's idea of state politics as the "politics of politics" is useful in this regard; see *The Politics of Production*.

50. Pierre Bourdieu, *Outline of a Theory of Practice* (Cambridge: Cambridge University Press, 1977), and *Distinction: A Social Critique of the Judgement of Taste* (London: Routledge, 1984).

51. For example, the different judgments by F. A. M. Messing in *Het ontstaan van Groot Eindhoven, 1890–1920* (Tilburg: Stichting Zuidelijk Historisch Contact, 1980); and van Puijenbroek, *Beginnen in Eindhoven* (Eindhoven: Van Pierre, 1985).

52. K. Mandemakers and J. van Meeuwen, *Industrial Modernization* (Rotterdam: Erasmus University, 1983); Marinus Huijbrechts, "Het verloren paradijs verlaten," in Gerrit Kruis, ed., *De oplossing van Brabant* (Tilburg: Provinciaal Opbouworgaan, 1987); Cornelis Verhoeven, "Afscheid van Brabant?," in Verhoeven, *Als een dief in de nacht* (Baarn: Ambo, 1980).

53. Recent books are much more dynamic and interdisciplinary than earlier studies. See van den Brink et al., eds., *Werk, kerk, en bed in Brabant: Demografische ontwikkelingen in Oostelijk Noord-Brabant, 1700–1920* ('s Hertogenbosch: Stichting Brabantse Regionale Geschiedschrijving, 1989); Peter Meurkens, *Bevolking, Economie, en Cultuur van het Oude Kempenland* (Bergeyk: Eicha, 1984); and J. van Oudheusden and G. Trienekens, *Een pront wijf, een mager paard en een zoon op het seminarie: Aanzetten tot een integrale geschiedenis van oostelijk Noord-Brabant* ('s Hertogenbosch: Stichting Brabantse Regionale Geschiedschrijving, 1993). The theoretical acumen of the former two books, however, is lost by the latter.

54. I. J. Brugmans, *De arbeidende klasse in Nederland in de 19e eeuw, 1813–1870* (1925; Utrecht: Het Spectrum, 1975); J. A. de Jonge, *De industrialisatie in Nederland tussen 1850 en 1914* (Nijmegen: Sun, 1969); Roland Holst, *Kapitaal en arbeid in Nederland* (1902; Nijmegen: Sun, 1971).

55. For general literature on Catholic bloc-formation and "pillarization" in the Netherlands: J. C. Blom, *Verzuiling in Nederland, 1850–1925* (Amsterdam: Historisch Seminarium, 1981); J. Ramakers and H. Righart, "Het katholicisme," in P. Luykx and N. Bootsma, eds., *De laatste tijd: Geschiedschrijving over Nederland in de 20e eeuw* (Utrecht: Het Spectrum, 1987); Hans Righart, *De katholieke zuil in Europa:*

Het ontstaan van verzuiling onder katholieken in Oostenrijk, Zwitserland, Belgie en Nederland (Meppel, Boom, 1986); Siep Stuurman, *Verzuiling, kapitalisme en patriarchaat: Aspecten van de ontwikkeling van de moderne staat in Nederland* (Nijmegen: Sun, 1983). An English-language overview of Catholic bloc-formation is H. Bakvis, *Catholic Power in the Netherlands* (Montreal and Kingston: 1981). For the classic treatment of Dutch "pacification" politics: Arend Lijphart, *The Politics of Accommodation* (Berkeley: University of California Press,1968). An overview of modern Dutch political history in English: Ken Gladdish, *Governing from the Centre: Politics and Policy-Making in the Netherlands* (London / The Hague: Hurst / SDU, 1991).

56. The discussions were published in *Sociologische Gids* 4 (1957) and *Socialisme en Democratie* 14 (1957).

57. Ger Harmsen et al., *Mensenwerk: Industriële vakbonden op weg naar eenheid* (Baarn: Ambo, 1980); Jos Perry, *Roomsche kinine tegen roode koorts: Arbeidersbeweging en katholieke kerk in Maastricht, 1880–1920* (Amsterdam: SUA, 1983); Bob Reinalda, *Bedienden georganiseerd* (Nijmegen: Sun, 1981). For further studies of Catholic union formation at the national level see J. Roes, ed., *Katholieke arbeidersbeweging: Studies over KAB en NKV in de economische en politieke ontwikkeling van Nederland na 1945* (Baarn: Ambo, 1985).

58. C. Kuiper, *Uit het Rijk van de Arbeid: Onstaan, groei en werk van de katholieke arbeidersbeweging in Nederland*, 3 vols. (Utrecht, 1953).

59. J. van Meeuwen, *Zoo rood als de roodste socialisten* (Amsterdam: SUA, 1981); Don Kalb, "Moral Production, Class Capacities, and Communal Commotion: An Illustration from Central Brabant Shoemaking, c. 1900–1920," *Social History* 16 (1991): 279–99 (an adapted version is reprinted here as chapter 1).

60. For the demographic transition in the Netherlands see, for example, E. Hofstee, "De groei van de Nederlandse bevolking. Drift en koers," in A. den Hollander, ed., *Drift en koers: Een halve eeuw sociale verandering in Nederland* (Assen: van Gorcum, 1962), and *Korte demografische geschiedenis van Nederland van 1800 tot heden* (Haarlem: Fibula van Dishoeck, 1981). O. Boonstra and A. van der Woude, "Demographic Transition in the Netherlands: A Statistical Analysis of Regional Differences in the Level and Development of the Birth Rate and of Fertility, 1850–1890," *A.A.G.-bijdragen* 24 (1984): 1–57.

61. D. J. Noordam, "De demografische ontwikkeling in West-Europa van omstreeks 1750 tot 1985," in H. Diederiks et al., *Van agrarische samenleving naar verzorgingsstaat* (Groningen: Wolters-Noordhof, 1987), 238.

62. A classical text is van F. van Heek, *Het geboorteniveau der Nederlandse roomskatholieken: Een demografische-sociologische studie van een geëmancipeerde minderheidsgroep* (Leiden, 1954), but it is often reiterated, for example by Noordam 1987.

63. See O. Boonstra, *De waardij van eene vroege opleiding* (Wageningen: AAG Bijdragen, 1993); van den Brink et al. 1989; Noordam 1987. For the general literature on the demographic transition see, for example, John Hajnal, "European Marriage Patterns in Perspective," in D. Glass, ed., *Population in History* (London, 1965), 101–43; Charles Tilly, "Demographic Origins of the European Proletariat," in David Levine, ed., *Proletarianization and Family History* (Orlando: Academic Press, 1984b), and *Reproducing Families: The Political Economy of English Population History* (Cambridge: Cambridge University Press, 1987); David Levine, *Family*

Formation in an Age of Nascent Capitalism (Cambridge: Cambridge University Press, 1977); Hans Medick, "The Proto-industrial Family Economy," *Social History* 3 (1976): 291–315.

64. Meurkens, 1984; Peter Meurkens, "Kinderrijk en katholiek: De stijging van de huwelijksvruchtbaarheid in het Kempenland, 1840–1920," in G. van den Brink et al. 1989.

65. Kriedte et al., *Industrialisierung vor der Industrialisierung: Gewerbliche Waren-produktion auf dem Land in der Formationsperiode des Kapitalismus* (Göttingen: van den Hoeck und Ruprecht, 1977); Levine 1977 and 1987; Medick 1976; Noordam 1987.

66. For still useful overviews see H. van Velthoven, *Noord-Brabant op weg naar groei en welvaart* (Nijmegen, 1963); L. G. J. Verberne, *Noord-Brabant in de negen-tiende eeuw tot omstreeks 1870: De sociaal-economische structuur* (Nijmegen, 1947).

67. See the discussion between Messing (1980) and van Puyenbroek (1985). Van Drenth has pointed most consistently at the high degree of feminization of Bra-bant manufacturing: Annemieke van Drenth, *De zorg om het Philipsmeisje: Fabrieks-meisjes in de elektrotechnische industrie in Eindhoven, 1900–1960* (Zutphen: Walburg Pers, 1991).

68. Mandemakers 1985; De Jonge 1968.

69. Van Drenth 1991. See for Eindhoven in particular A. Bogaart, *Industriële kinder- en vrouwenarbeid tussen 1850 en 1914* (M.A. thesis, Catholic University of Nijmegen, 1980).

70. Marjolein Moree, "Vrouwen en arbeidsmarktbeleid 1950–1985," in Kees Schuyt et al., *De verdeelde samenleving: Een inleiding in de ontwikkeling van de Neder-landse verzorgingsstaat* (Leiden: Stenfert Kroese, 1986), 73–96.

71. Rudolf Braun, *Industrialisierung und Volksleben* (1960; Göttingen: Vanden-hoeck und Ruprecht, 1979); Kriedte et al. 1977; Franklin Mendels, "Agriculture and Peasant Industry in Eighteenth-Century Flanders," in Kriedte et al., *Industri-alization before Industrialization* (Cambridge: Cambridge University Press, 1981).

72. For the concept and relevance of the peasant-worker phenomenon see Douglas R. Holmes and Jean Quataert, "An Approach to Modern Labor: Worker Peasantries in Historic Saxony and the Friuli Region over Three Centuries," *Com-parative Studies in Society and History* 28 (1986): 191–216; Douglas Holmes, *Cultural Disenchantments: Worker Peasantries in Northeast Italy* (Princeton: Princeton Uni-versity Press, 1989).

73. This is of course not limited to North Brabant. It is my contention, however, that the practice may have been more central for regional development and sur-vival here than elsewhere.

1 COMMUNAL COMMOTION

This chapter is an adapted version of my article "Moral Production, Class Capaci-ties, and Communal Commotion: An Illustration from Central Brabant Shoemak-ing (ca. 1900–1920)" in *Social History* 16 (1991): 279–99.

1. *Gemeenteverslag* (Waalwijk, 1900), and most subsequent years.

2. Shoemaking was a central economic activity in almost all central Brabant communities. Dutch shoemaking had been largely concentrated here during the course of the nineteenth century; see Kees Mandemakers, "De ontwikkeling van de factor arbeid binnen de Nederlandse schoennijverheid, 1860–1910," *Jaarboek voor de Geschiedenis van Bedrijf en Techniek* 2 (1985): 104–26. Communities in which more than 40 percent of the male working population were shoemakers include Baardwijk, Besoyen, Drunen, Kaatsheuvel, Loon op Zand, Sprang en Waalwijk.

3. *Onderzoekingen naar de toestanden in de Nederlandsche huisindustrie* (The Hague: Directie van de Arbeid, 1911), 2:339–71. The *Onderzoekingen* reports on government-sponsored research on industrialization and homeworking in the Dutch countryside, a practice which was quite widespread around the turn of the century, especially in shoemaking and cigarmaking, and was associated with the truck system. See also the report on the truck system: *Gedwongen Winkelnering* (The Hague: Directie van de Arbeid, 1909).

4. The story is based on information from the local daily paper *Echo van het Zuiden* (28 August 1910, 1 September 1910, 4 September 1910, 29 September 1910); the Catholic labor journal, *De Katholieke lederbewerker* (27 August 1910 to 12 November 1910); see also A. Kleyngeld, *Een staking in historisch perspektief* (M.A. thesis, Catholic University of Brabant, Tilburg, 1976); J. van Meeuwen, *Zoo Rood als de Roodste socialisten* (Amsterdam: SUA, 1981); Don Kalb, "De Anatomie van Katholiek Schoenmakersprotest: Proletarisering, Arbeiderskultuur, en Katholieke hegemonie in Midden-Brabant, 1880–1918" (M.A. thesis, University of Nijmegen, 1988).

5. As oral evidence indicates, the practice of family employment seems to have become increasingly widespread. By 1910 a shortage of young female labor began to develop, increasing the employment opportunities of fathers who brought their daughters.

6. Except for the highly unusual diamond trade in Amsterdam, which was also the strongest base of socialism in the Netherlands by that time, no collective agreement yet existed. There was, however, growing argument in favor of the recognition of labor unions. See especially J. Windmuller and C. de Galan, *Labor Relations in the Netherlands* (Ithaca: Cornell University Press, 1969).

7. See K. Mandemakers and J. van Meeuwen, *Industrial Modernization and Social Developments in the Center of the Dutch Shoe Industry: Central Noord-Brabant, 1890–1930* (Rotterdam: Erasmus University Press, 1983); Van Meeuwen 1981.

8. *Echo van het Zuiden*, 1 September 1910.

9. *Echo van het Zuiden*, 4 September 1910; *De Katholieke Lederbewerker*, 3 September 1910.

10. *De Katholieke Lederbewerker*, 3 September 1910.

11. *Echo*, 1 September 1910.

12. Both Van Schijndel and Van Dortmond had been promoters of union formation in central Brabant shoemaking, and both had been central in the public life of local class solidarity. See Kalb 1988, 63–81.

13. Kalb 1988.

14. *Echo van het Zuiden*, 28 August 1910.

15. *Echo van het Zuiden*, 2 March 1911.

16. *De Katholieke Lederbewerker* (from 24 September 1910 onwards); Van Meeuwen 1981, 80–87.

17. Van Meeuwen 1981, 80–87.

18. See particularly Hans Daalder, "On Building Consociational Nations: The Cases of the Netherlands and Switzerland," *International Social Science Journal* 23 (1971): 355–70; Arend Lijphart, *Verzuiling, pacificatie en kentering in de Nederlandse politiek* (Amsterdam: de Bussy, 1968); Hans Righart, *De katholieke zuil in Europa: Het ontstaan van verzuiling van katholieken in Oostenrijk, Zwitserland, Belgie en Nederland* (Meppel: Boom, 1986); Siep Stuurman, *Verzuiling, Kapitalisme en Patriarchaat: aspecten van de ontwikkeling van de moderne staat in Nederland* (Nijmegen: Sun, 1983).

19. The long-time authoritative history of the Catholic labor movement (Katholieke Arbeiders Beweging) by one of its leading functionaries, C. J. Kuiper, *Uit het Rijk van de Arbeid: Ontstaan, groei en werk van de katholieke arbeidersbeweging in Nederland*, 3 vols. (Utrecht, 1953), held that Catholic workers who were attracted initially to secular unions did not accept the class struggle as a leading principle and thus decided autonomously to establish Catholic unions. The later standard history of industrial unionism in the Netherlands is by the left-wing historians Ger Harmsen, Jos Perry, and Floor van Gelder, *Mensenwerk: Industriële vakbonden op weg naar eenheid* (Baarn: Ambo, 1980); see also Jos Perry's history of socialism in the southern town of Maastricht, *Roomsche kinine tegen roode koorts: Arbeidersbeweging en katholieke kerk in Maastricht, 1880–1920* (Amsterdam: SUA, 1983). These studies emphasized that the initiative was taken by clerics, not by workers, and that the whole enterprise was designed as a new form of social control.

20. See Perry 1983.

21. Van Meeuwen, *Zoo Rood als de Roodste Socialisten* (Amsterdam: SUA, 1981); K. Mandemakers and J. van Meeuwen, *Industrial Modernization and Social Developments in the Centre of the Dutch Shoe Industry: Central Noord-Brabant, 1890–1930* (Rotterdam: Erasmus University Press, 1983).

22. Mandemakers and van Meeuwen 1983, 30, 32.

23. For a more detailed analysis, see Kalb 1988.

24. Richard Johnson, in an important text, maintains that "ideologies always work upon a ground; that ground is culture." See his "Three Problematics: Elements of a Theory of Working-class Culture," in J. Clarke, C. Critcher, and R. Johnson, eds., *Working-Class Culture* (London: Hutchinson, 1979), 234. My formulation, however, points to the problem of how to interpret and analyze the development of particular historical connections between elaborate and formalized ideologies, produced by the apparatuses of dominating classes, and practical knowledge as produced by particular working classes. Whereas historians have mainly been concerned to reintroduce in their work culture and daily life (see in particular Alf Lüdtke, ed., *Alltagsgeschichte* [Frankfurt: Campus, 1989]), anthropologists have rather been engaged with the problem of historicizing culture and relating it to power contexts (see, for example, the interview with Eric Wolf in *Current Anthropology* 28, no. 1 (1987). The increasing influence of Gramsci and Raymond Williams in both currents of cultural studies promises to bring them more in contact with each other; see among others Herman Rebell, "Cultural Hegemony and Class

Experience: A Critical Reading of Recent Ethnological-historical Approaches" parts 1 and 2, *American Ethnologist* 16, no. 1 (1989): 117–36, and idem., no. 2: 350–65; William Roseberry, *Anthropologies and Histories* (New Brunswick: Rutgers University Press, 1989); Gerald Sider, *Culture and Class in Anthropology and History* (Cambridge: Cambridge University Press, 1986); Roger Keesing, "Theories of culture revisited" (paper presented at annual meeting of American Anthropological Association, Washington, D.C., 1989). Geoff Eley's review article "Labour History, Social History, *Alltagsgeschichte*: Experience, Culture, and the Politics of the Culture of Everyday—A New Direction for German Social History?" *Journal of Modern History* 61 (1989): 297–343, describes comparable developments in German social history.

25. K. Mandemakers, "De ontwikkeling van de faktor arbeid binnen de Nederlandse schoennijverheid, 1860–1910," *Jaarboek voor de geschiedenis van Bedrijf en Techniek*, jrg. 2 (1985): 104–26.

26. Ruralization of shoemaking in continental Europe was a rather general phenomenon in the late nineteenth century. The "political shoemakers" of the great cities around the middle of the centry, so sympathetically described by Eric Hobsbawm and Joan Scott (see Hobsbawm and Scott, "Political Shoemakers" in Hobsbawm's *Workers* [New York: Pantheon, 1984]), in my view did not primarily disappear from the political scene as the result of machinofacture but rather because of the ruralization of the industry, which left urban shoemakers either as retailers or as an impoverished and dependent urban subproletariat. On shoemaking see among others Friedrich Behr, *Die Wirkung der fortschreitenden Technik auf die Schuhindustrie* (Leipzig, 1909); W. A. A. Brekelmans, *Huiden, Looistoffen, Lederen schoennijverheid: Een algemeen informatieve beschrijving* (Doetinchem: Misset, 1938); Alan Dawley, *Class and Community: The Industrial Revolution in Lynn* (Cambridge, Mass.: Harvard University Press, 1976); John Foster, *Class Struggle and the Industrial Revolution: Early Industrial Capitalism in Three English Towns* (London: Methuen, 1974); Mandemakers and van Meeuwen 1983; W. Nolens, "Van klopsteen tot zwikmachine: Een beschouwing over de industriële revolutie in de Noord-Brabantse schoenindustrie" (unpublished manuscript, Tilburg, 1965); Carl Rehe, *Die deutsche Schuhgrossindustrie* (Jena, 1908); Wilhelm Schröder, *Arbeitergeschichte und Arbeiterbewegung: Industriearbeit und Organisationsverhalten im 19. und frühen 20. Jahrhundert* (Frankfurt: Campus, 1976); and the numerous references by Hobsbawm and Scott 1984.

27. For an elaborate and more detailed treatment of the development of Catholic shoemakers' unions in central Brabant, see van Meeuwen 1981 and Kalb 1988. This particular logic of solidarity, in which the support of workers by advanced employers was crucial, is comparable with the logics experienced by Amsterdam diamond workers (see T. van Tijn, "De algemene Nederlandsche Diamantbewerkersbond: Een succes en zijn verklaring," in P. Geurts and F. Messing, eds., *Economische ontwikkeling en sociale emancipatie*, part 2 [The Hague, 93–109]), and ironworkers in Solingen and Remscheid (see E. Lucas, *Arbeiterradikalismus* [Frankfurt: Verlag Roter Stern, 1976]).

28. For more details, see *Onderzoekingen*, and Kalb 1988.

29. Kalb 1988 and van Meeuwen 1981.

30. The most important contributor to Catholic and Continental Christian historical theories of politico-economic development and the social question was the German Jesuit Heinrich Pesch. The clearest articulation of his vision is to be found in his *Liberalismus, Sozialismus und Christliche Gesellschaftsordnung* (Freiburg, 1896). In the Netherlands his theories were promoted by, among others, P. J. M. Aalberse, a theoretician and Catholic social organizer who, after the First World War, became the first minister of social affairs in a coalition between the Protestant and Catholic parties.

31. For a more detailed account of shoemakers' culture and Catholic ideology as found in the Catholic shoemakers' press see Kalb 1988.

32. *De Katholieke Lederbewerker*, 27 September 1910; see Kalb 1988.

33. *Echo van het Zuiden*, 4 June 1903. See van Meeuwen 1981; Kalb 1988.

34. For more details see Kalb 1988; Schröder 1976 gives a fine account of relationships and technology in shoemaking in Germany. T. van der Waerden, *Geschooldheid en techniek* (Technical University, Delft, 1911), contains some detailed inquiries into the development of Dutch shoemaking around the turn of the century.

35. Van der Waerden 1911, 193.

36. This is also noted for German shoemaking by Schröder 1976, 172–81. Oral history in the Dutch shoemaking district, which was part of this research project, delivers an overwhelming sense of the restrictiveness of work regimes in those years.

37. This was insistently stressed by interviewed shoemakers. It was, however, nowhere explicitly mentioned in written sources; it could only be calculated from the estimated income of shoemakers in tax lists.

38. This was also concluded in 1910 by the chairman of the Catholic shoemakers' union, C. Roestenberg, in his interview with Th. van der Waerden. See van der Waerden 1911, 193.

39. For more details see Kalb 1988. The word *hidden* is not meant to imply explicit subversive activities. It only refers to common complaints and angers not being picked up by people having access to ideologically articulating practices like the Catholic union.

40. Kalb 1988.

41. There is by now a fairly voluminous literature stressing the importance of "factory artisans" in the emergence of organized class protest. See Michael Hanagan and others in an issue of *Theory and Society* devoted to solidarity logics, 17 (1988): 309–27.

42. Göran Therborn makes much of the presence or absence of workers' collectivity; see his "Why Some Classes Are More Successful Than Others," *New Left Review* 138 (1983): 37–55. Much can be learned of factory regimes from Michael Burawoy's *The Politics of Production* (London: Verso, 1986).

43. For a more detailed and elaborate discussion of the dialectic of shoemakers' culture and Catholic ideology see Kalb 1988. It should be mentioned that rising prices and new, small gas motors made small businesses more profitable again in the 1910s.

44. *De Katholieke Lederbewerker*, 3 September 1910.

45. Hobsbawm and Scott, 1984.

46. See, for example, M. L. Blim, *Made in Italy: Small-Scale Industrialization and Its Consequences* (New York: Praeger, 1990).

47. This has been most strongly stated by Charles Tilly. See, for example, the review of his work by Lynn Hunt in Theda Skocpol, ed., *Vision and Method in Historical Sociology* (Cambridge: Cambridge University Press, 1984); see also Dick Geary, *European Labour Protest, 1848–1939* (London: Methuen, 1981). The stress on rationality also prevails in the moral economy literature, from E. P. Thompson to James Scott; see the criticism by Timothy Mitchell, "Everyday Metaphors of Power," *Theory and Society* 19, no. 5 (1990).

48. See Mitchell 1990.

49. See, for example, the *Theory and Society* issue on solidarity logics, and the foreword by Michael Hanagan, vol. 17 (1988). See also the remarks on this point by Geoff Eley 1989, and his "Edward Thompson, Social History, and Political Culture: The Making of a Working-class Public, 1780–1850," in Harvey Kaye and Keith McClelland, eds., *E. P. Thompson: Critical Perspectives* (Cambridge: Polity Press, 1990).

50. German historians like Karl Heinz Roth and Erhard Lucas seem to have been more sensitive to this fact than some of their English counterparts. See Karl Heinz Roth, *Die andere Arbeiterbewegung* (Munich, 1974); Erhard Lucas, *Arbeiterradikalismus* (Frankfurt: Verlag Roter Stern, 1976).

51. See also John Clarke, "Capital and Culture: The Post-war Working Class Revisited," in John Clarke, Chas Critcher, and Richard Johnson, eds., *Working Class Culture: Studies in History and Theory* (London: Hutchison, 1979).

52. See also Rick Fantasia's criticism of conventional approaches to class consciousness in sociology, in his *Cultures of Solidarity: Consciousness, Action, and Contemporary American Workers* (Berkeley: University of California Press, 1988).

53. This assumption is a welcome and charming aspect of William Reddy's *Money and Liberty in Modern Europe* (Cambridge: Cambridge University Press, 1987). See also Sherry Ortner's remarks on the concept of strategy in "Theory in Anthropology since the Sixties," *Comparative Studies in Society and History* 26, no. 1 (1984): 151–52. Alf Lüdtke's concept of Eigensinn, and his effort to go beyond simple dichotomies of domination and resistance is helpful here; see his "Practising Eigensinn: Workers beyond Domination and Resistance," *Focaal* 19 (1992): 16–36.

54. Patrick Joyce, ed., *The Historical Meanings of Work* (Cambridge: Cambridge University Press, 1987), is remarkable for its attention to such languages. See also Joyce, "Labour, Capital, and Compromise: A Response to Richard Price" and "Languages of Reciprocity and Conflict," *Social History* 9, no. 1 (1984) and no. 2 (1984). Eley 1990 approaches the same question primarily from the organizational point of view. Marc Steinberg's contribution to the discussion on class and language following Gareth Stedmans Jones's "Languages of Class" is profitable reading for his attention to the distinction between the political dynamics of languages and the practical construction of collective experiences. See his "The Role of

Discourse in the Making of Working-class Consciousness in the Early Nineteenth Century," paper presented at the ASA meeting, San Francisco, 1989.

2 SOLIDARY LOGIC OR CIVILIZING PROCESS?

This chapter is a slightly adapted version of my article "On Class, the Logic of Solidarity, and the Civilizing Process: Workers, Priests, and Alcohol in Dutch Shoemaking Communities, 1900–1920," published in *Social Science History* 18, no. 1 (1994): 127–52.

1. The central author of figurational sociology is the German-born sociologist Norbert Elias. His key works are: *Über den Prozess der Zivilisation*, 2 vols. (Frankfurt: Suhrkamp, 1939); *Die höfische Gesellschaft* (Frankfurt: Suhrkamp, 1969); *Was ist Soziologie?* (Munich: Juventa Verlag, 1970). Due mainly to Johan Goudsblom and the "Amsterdam school" of historical sociology, his work has had a broad influence in the Netherlands. See Johan Goudsblom, *Sociology in the Balance* (Oxford: Oxford University Press, 1977); Ali de Regt, *Arbeidersgezinnen en beschavingsarbeid: Ontwikkelingen in Nederland 1870–1940* (Meppel: Boom, 1984); Abram de Swaan, *In Care of the State: Health Care, Education, and Welfare in Europe and the USA during the Modern Era* (London: Polity Press, 1991); Cas Wouters, *Over Minnen en Sterven* (Amsterdam: Van Gennep, 1991). Recently, figurational sociology has attracted wide attention among the new sociologists of culture as organized around the journal *Theory, Culture, and Society*; see the special issue vol. 4, no. 3 (1987). For evaluations in English, see, for example, Richard Killminster, "Evaluating Elias," *Theory, Culture, and Society* 8, no. 2 (1991): 165–77; and Dick Pels, "Elias and the Politics of Theory," ibid., 177–83.

2. See, for example, Ali de Regt 1984, on civilizing offensives aimed at the Amsterdam working class. Working households are studied not so much in the particular context of the Amsterdam economy as an illustration of bourgeois cultural intervention trends on a national level. Compare the much more localized social historical approach by Ben Sanders and Gertjan de Groot, "Without Hope of Improvement: Casual Laborers and Bourgeois Reformers in Amsterdam 1850–1920," in L. Heerma van Voss and F. van Holthoon, eds., *Working Class and Popular Culture* (Amsterdam: International Institute for Social History, 1988).

3. See for further recent debate Ira Katznelson, *Marxism and the City* (Oxford: Oxford University Press, 1992); Patrick Joyce, *Visions of the People* (Cambridge: Cambridge University Press, 1991). Also, Don Kalb, "Frameworks of Culture and Class in Historical Research," *Theory and Society* 22 (1993): 513–37.

4. See among others Brüggemeier 1984; Eley 1989, 297–343. Joyce 1991 is very instructive for the moralizing tone of union life in nineteenth-century England. See also Peter Bailey, *Leisure and Class in Victorian England: Rational Recreation and the Contest for Control, 1830–1885* (London: Routledge, 1978). On British socialism and its attitudes toward popular culture, see Chris Waters, *British Socialists and the Politics of Popular Culture, 1884–1914* (Manchester: Manchester University Press, 1990).

5. For the Netherlands, where social Catholicism has been more conservative than in Germany or Belgium, see G. J. M. Wentholt, *Een arbeidersbeweging en haar priesters, het einde van een relatie* (Nijmegen: KDC, 1984).

6. Elias, *Wat is Sociologie* (Utrecht: Het Spectrum, 1971), 155–62.

7. Elias, however, is aware of the differentiating effects of class on the *Selbstzwang* capacities of people (cf. Elias, *Über den Prozess der Zivilisation* [Frankfurt: Suhrkamp, 1939], 2:319). But he reduces them to a corollary of differences in work habits and professions, and, more importantly, does not conceive of them in terms of a systematic process.

8. Michael Hanagan, "Solidary Logics: Introduction," *Theory and Society* 17 (1988): 309–27; and Charles Tilly, "Solidary Logics: Conclusion," ibid., 17 (1988): 451–88. See Hanagan's very interesting study of solidary logics in nineteenth-century Stephanois communities: *The Logic of Solidarity* (Urbana: University of Illinois Press, 1981).

9. In the Netherlands the work of Ali de Regt (1984) has contributed to grounding Elias's notion of civilizing process to historical agency by bourgeois and social democratic reformers. Her concept of "civilizational work" creates a link between Elias and Michel Foucault and Jacques Donzelot in France; cf. especially J. Donzelot, *La Police des Familles* (Paris: Gallimard, 1977). The idea of a "civilizing coalition," in contradistinction, looks explicitly to alliances and cleavages as structured by the forms of social production, and is thus less tainted with notions of social control "from above." On the contrary, it consciously seeks to establish the motivations of "common people" who support civilizing campaigns.

10. The most important communities are Waalwijk, Kaatsheuvel, Loon op Zand, Drunen, Oisterwijk, Dongen, Besoyen, Baardwijk, Sprang.

11. Source material was derived from the biweekly journal *De Leerbewerker* (1908–9), *De Katholieke Lederbewerker* (1909–13), and the monthly magazines *De Schoen en Lederbewerker* (1913–18) and *De Lederbewerker* (1918); the regional newspaper *Echo van het Zuiden* (1900–1911); the *Vakblad voor de Schoenmakerij* (1900–1905); the municipal reports for the communities of Loon op Zand, Oisterwijk, and Waalwijk (*de Gemeenteverslagen*), (1870–1920); and the reports of the chambers of commerce (*Verslagen van de kamer van koophandel en fabrieken te Waalwijk*, 1876–1920). Oral interviews formed an important part of the research process and turned out to be indispensable for sorting out the relevant information from documentary sources.

12. See the large-scale researches on behalf of the department of labor, Directie van de Arbeid, *Gedwongen winkelnering* (The Hague, 1909); *Onderzoekingen naar de toestanden in de Nederlandsche huisindustrie* (The Hague, 1911).

13. Directie van de Arbeid 1911, 2:258–371.

14. For details see Kalb 1988, 59–88.

15. Kalb 1988, 81–96.

16. Gerard Brom, *De nieuwe kruistocht: Drankweergeschiedenis van Rooms Nederland, 1895–1907* (Helmond, 1909), 19.

17. W. Donker, *Gedenkboek voor de schoen- en lederindustrie* (Waalwijk, n.d.); Kalb 1988, 59–63.

18. See for developments in shoemaking in general, Friedrich Behr, *Die Wirkung der fortschreitenden Technik auf die Schuhindustrie* (Leipzig, 1909); W. A. A. Brekelmans, *Huiden, Looistoffen, Leder- en schoennijverheid* (Doetinchem: Misset, 1938); W. H. Schröder, *Arbeitergeschichte und Arbeiterbewegung* (Frankfurt: Campus Verlag, 1976). Further the numerous references by Hobsbawm and Scott, "Political Shoemakers," in Hobsbawm, *Workers* (New York: Pantheon, 1984).

19. Details in Kalb 1988, 44–55.

20. See van Meeuwen, *Zoo rood als de roodste socialisten* (Amsterdam: SUA, 1981), 60; Kalb 1988, 53–54; Verslag inspecteur van de arbeid (1908); Police notebook 1900, in Municipal Archive, Loon op Zand.

21. Details in Kalb 1988, 81–96.

22. Kalb 1988, 81–98.

23. *Leerbewerker*, 7 November 1908.

24. *Leerbewerker*, 16 January 1909.

25. More details in Kalb 1988, 106–29.

26. Van Delft, "De schoenindustrie als hoofdmiddel van bestaan." M.A. thesis, Economische Hogeschool Tilburg, 1949).

27. Kalb 1988, 112–29.

28. *De Lederbewerker*, 9 January 1920.

29. Kalb 1988, 131.

30. Kalb 1988, 138–43.

31. *De Schoen- en Lederbewerker*, 26 February 1915; Kalb 1988, 138–43.

32. *De Lederbewerker*, 4 October 1918.

33. *De Lederbewerker*, 5 September 1919, 9 January 1920.

34. The argument for everyday life approaches is consistently put forward in Alf Lüdtke's work, *Alltagsgeschichte: Zur Rekonstruktion historischer Erfahrungen und Lebensweisen* (Frankfurt: Campus Verlag, 1989); and *Eigensinn: Fabrikalltag, Arbeitererfahrungen und Politik vom Kaiserreich bis in den Faschismus* (Hamburg: Ergebnisse Verlag, 1993); see also the review article by Eley (1989). A remarkable contribution from anthropological circles is Sider, *Culture and Class in Anthropology and History* (Cambridge: Cambridge University Press, 1986). See also the discussion in Kalb, "Frameworks of Culture and Class in Historical Research," *Theory and Society* 22 (1993): 513–37. It seems necessary, however, to protect everyday life approaches from antiquarianism and theoretical emptiness. The starting point in solidary logics as demonstrated in this study can fruitfully be expanded by a closer articulation with marxist geography. This should lead to an understanding of localities as particular historical-spatial ensembles of relations of production and reproduction. See among others Alan Warde, "Industrial Restructuring, Local Politics and the Reproduction of Labour Power: Some Theoretical Considerations," *Society and Space* 6 (1988): 75–95; Sharon Zukin, *Landscapes of Power: From Detroit to Disney World* (Berkeley: University of California Press, 1992); and Edward Soja, *Postmodern Geographies: The Reassertion of Space in Critical Social Theory* (London: Verso, 1989). Also Ron Aminzade's insistence on studying local politico-cultural alliances in industrializing communities in the light of the locality's specific insertion in the wider world system is a salutary alternative for the bipolarity of class reductionist approaches to working class life on the one hand and

discourse-centered studies on the other; see his "Class Analysis, Politics, and French Labor History," in Lenard Berlanstein, ed., *Rethinking Labor History* (Urbana: University of Illinois Press, 1993b).

3 EINDHOVEN AND ITS CONTEXT

1. See the recent dissertation by Sjef Stoop, *De sociale fabriek: Sociale politiek bij Philips Eindhoven, Bayer Leverkusen en Hoogovens Ijmuiden* (Leiden: Stenfert Kroese, 1992).

2. Alan Warde, "Conditions of Dependence: Working Class Quiescence in Lancaster in the Twentieth Century," *Lancaster Regionalism Group, Working paper 30* (Lancaster: University of Lancaster, 1989), 27–28; H. Newby, *The Deferential Worker* (Harmondsworth: Penguin, 1979).

3. Ronald Edsforth, *Class Conflict and Cultural Consensus: The Making of a Mass Consumer Society in Flint, Michigan* (New Brunswick: Rutgers University Press, 1987); Ilse Costas, "Arbeitskämpfe in der Berliner Elektroindustrie 1905 und 1906," in Klaus Tenfelde and Heinrich Volkmann, eds., *Streik: Zur Geschichte des Arbeitskampfes in Deutschland während der Industrialisierung* (Munich: Beck, 1981), 91–107.

4. Barrington Moore Jr., *Injustice: The Social Bases of Obedience and Revolt* (New York: Sharp, 1978); Dick Geary, *European Labour Protest, 1848–1939* (London: Methuen, 1981); Victoria Bonnel, *Roots of Rebellion: Workers' Politics and Organizations in St. Petersburg and Moscow, 1900–1914* (Berkeley: University of California Press, 1983).

5. This is done by Stoop (1992), but his comparison with Bayer and Hoogovens does not allow him to come closer to workers' culture. Moreover, he reproduces the contemporary emphasis on the function of territorial modernization, whereas my account shows that family forms were central to Philipsist paternalism. Stoop should however be credited with a pretheoretical awareness of this. See Stoop, "Fordism in the Netherlands? The Case of Philips: A Critical Test of the Concept of Fordism" (unpublished paper, University of Nijmegen, n.d.).

6. Newby 1979.

7. James Scott, *Weapons of the Weak: Everyday Forms of Peasant Resistance* (New Haven: Yale University Press, 1985), and *Domination and the Arts of Resistance: Hidden Transcripts* (New Haven: Yale University Press, 1990).

8. Moore 1979.

9. Ron Aminzade's new study, *Ballots and Barricades: Class Formation and Republican Politics in France, 1830–1871* (Princeton: Princeton University Press, 1993), is a very cogent study of the differential degree of responsiveness for workers' grievances of republican coalitions in three French industrial cities. William Reddy is also very sensitive to the nonincorporated elements of working class life; see *The Rise of Market Culture: The Textile Trade and French Society, 1750–1900* (Cambridge: Cambridge University Press, 1984).

10. Gareth Stedman Jones, *Languages of Class: Studies in English Working Class History, 1832–1982* (Cambridge: Cambridge University Press, 1983); Joan Scott,

Gender and the Politics of History (New York: Basic Books, 1988); Patrick Joyce, *Visions of the People: Industrial England and the Question of Class, 1840–1914* (Cambridge: Cambridge University Press, 1991).

11. Ron Aminzade, *Class, Politics, and Early Industrial Capitalism* (Albany: State University of New York Press, 1981), and *Ballots and Barricades* (1993); Michael Hanagan, *The Logic of Solidarity: Artisans and Industrial Workers in Three French Towns, 1871–1914* (Urbana: University of Illinois Press, 1980), and *Nascent Proletarians: Class Formation in Post-Revolutionary France* (Oxford: Basil Blackwell, 1989); Charles Tilly, "Solidary Logics: Conclusion," in *Theory and Society* 17 (1988): 451–58; Louise Tilly, *Politics and Class in Milan, 1881–1901* (Oxford: Oxford University Press, 1992). See also the seminal text by Göran Therborn, "Why Some Classes Are More Successful Than Others," in *New Left Review* 138 (1983): 37–55.

12. Ad Teulings, *Philips: Geschiedenis en praktijk van een wereldconcern* (Amsterdam: Van Gennep, 1976).

13. Harry Braverman, *Labor and Monopoly Capital: The Degradation of Work in the Twentieth Century* (New York: Monthly Review Press, 1974).

14. See the criticisms in, for example, Stephen Wood, ed., *The Degradation of Work? Skill, Deskilling, and the Labour Process* (London: Heinemann, 1982).

15. Compare the critique on Braverman by Michael Burawoy, *The Politics of Production: Factory Regimes under Capitalism and Socialism* (London: Verso, 1985), 21–85; and Anthony Giddens, "Power, the Dialectic of Control, and Class Structuration," in A. Giddens and G. Mackenzie, eds., *Social Class and the Division of Labour* (Cambridge: Cambridge University Press, 1982), 29–45.

16. John Bodnar, *Workers' World: Kinship, Community, and Protest in an Industrial Society, 1900–1940* (Baltimore: Johns Hopkins University Press, 1986).

17. See for example David Montgomery, *Workers' Control in America: Studies in the History of Work, Technology, and Labor Struggles* (Cambridge: Cambridge University Press, 1979). Also for the nineteenth century, there is by now a fairly universal doubt about the epistemological priority of the proletarianization process for studies of workers' culture and politics; see the interesting collection of articles in Lenard R. Berlanstein, ed., *Rethinking Labor History: Essays on Discourse and Class Analysis* (Urbana: University of Illinois Press, 1993).

18. Eric Wolf, *Europe and the People without History* (Berkeley: University of California Press, 1982); David Harvey, *Consciousness and the Urban Experience* (Baltimore: Johns Hopkins University Press, 1985), and *The Urbanization of Capital* (Baltimore: Johns Hopkins University Press, 1985); Michael Burawoy, *The Politics of Production* (London: Verso, 1985). Like these authors, I embrace a concept of totality as a socially structured whole (and therefore diversified, stratified, layered, differentiated, indeed dynamic, antagonistic, dialectic). This is fundamentally different from the expressive totality found in Marxist authors like Georg Lukács and Harry Braverman; see Burawoy 1985, chap. 1. See also the discussion in Ira Katznelson, *Marxism and the City* (Oxford: Clarendon Press Oxford, 1992), 79–84. The concept of an expressive totality is often derived from the rightly discredited marxist finalist philosophy of history. Gerald Sider, *Culture and Class in Anthropology and History: A Newfoundland Illustration* (Cambridge: Cambridge University Press, 1986), is a good illustration of the silent application of a cultur-

ally sensitive, structurist concept of totality. See Martin Jay, *Marxism and Totality* (Berkeley: University of California Press, 1984), for a spirited attack on the idea.

4 THE MAKING OF A FLEXIBLE INDUSTRIAL TERRITORY

1. Jan van Oorschot, *Eindhoven, een samenleving in verandering* (Eindhoven: gemeente Eindhoven, 1982), 147.

2. Main studies of the area are: F. A. M. Messing, *Het ontstaan van Groot Eindhoven, 1890–1920* (Tilburg: Stichting Zuidelijk Historisch Contact, 1980); and van Oorschot 1982. F. J. M. van Puijenbroek stressed the dynamism and openness of local society in *Beginnen in Eindhoven* (Eindhoven: van Pierre, 1985). In his general overview of regional industrial history H. F. J. M. van den Eerenbeemt also pointed at the exceptional structure of the Eindhoven area; see *Ontwikkelingslijnen en scharnierpunten in het Brabants industrieel bedrijf, 1777–1914* (Tilburg: Stichting Zuidelijk Historisch Contact, 1977).

3. L. Deckers, *De Landbouwers van den Noord-Brabantschen zandgrond* (Eindhoven, 1912); Messing 1980; G. Knuvelder, *Vanuit Wingewesten: Een sociografie van het Zuiden* (Hilversum, 1930); L. G. J. Verberne, *Noord-Brabant in de negentiende eeuw tot omstreeks 1870* (Nijmegen, 1947); H. van Velthoven, *Noord-Brabant op weg naar groei en welvaart, 1850–1920* (Nijmegen, 1963); J. van den Zanden, *De economische ontwikkeling van de Nederlandse landbouw in de negentiende eeuw, 1800–1914* (Wageningen, 1985).

4. See for the classic statement by J. Hajnal, "European Marriage Patterns in Perspective," in D. Glass, ed., *Population in History* (London: Edward Arnold, 1965); for recent and well-researched data on eastern Brabant see the collection by G. van den Brink et al., eds., *Werk, kerk en bed in Brabant: Demografische ontwikkelingen in Oostelijk Noord-Brabant, 1700–1920* ('s Hertogenbosch: Stichting Brabantse Regionale Geschiedbeoefening, 1989). See also the literature on regional agriculture in note 3.

5. For the by now classical work on protoindustrialization see P. Kriedte et al., *Industrialisierung vor der Industrialisierung: Gewerbliche Warenproduktion auf dem land in der Formationsperiode des Kapitalismus* (Göttingen: van den Hoeck und Ruprecht, 1977). The importance of small-scale industrialization linked with the agricultural and familial cycle for developments in nineteenth-century Brabant has been known for a long time but was never theorized. See van Velthoven 1963. The work by Kriedte et al. has stimulated new intensive local research on the relationships between population, culture, and economy; see the case studies in the collection by G. van den Brink et al. (1989) and the literature cited there.

6. Van Oorschot 1982, 84.

7. Van Oorschot 1982, 1023–24.

8. Occupational statistics in the region indeed lose much of their descriptive value in the face of this fundamental fact. This is a common problem for research on peasant-worker and worker-peasant regions. For research on worker-peasantries, apart from the literature on protoindustry, see, among others, Douglas R. Holmes and Jean Quataert, "An Approach to Modern Labor: Worker Peasantries

in Historic Saxony and the Friuli Region over Three Centuries," *Comparative Studies in Society and History* 28 (1986): 191–216; Douglas R. Holmes, *Cultural Disenchantments: Worker Peasantries in Northeast Italy* (Princeton: Princeton University Press, 1989); Wanda Minge-Kalman, "Household Economy during the Peasant to Worker Transition in the Swiss Alps," *Ethnology* 17 (1978): 183–97.

9. P. A. Barentsen, "Het gezinsleven in het oosten van Noord-Brabant," *Mensch en Maatschappij* 2 (1926): 44–60, reprinted in van den Brink 1989.

10. O. Boonstra, *De waerdij van eene vroege opleiding: Een onderzoek naar de implicaties van alfabetisme op het leven van inwoners van Eindhoven en omliggende gemeenten, 1800–1920* (Wageningen: AAG Bijdragen, 1993), 263.

11. In general see the highly seminal essay by Hans Medick, "The Proto-industrial Family Economy: The Structural Function of Household and Family during the Transition from Peasant to Industrial Capitalism," *Social History* 1 (1976): 291–315; and David Levine, *Family Formation in an Age of Nascent Capitalism* (Cambridge: Cambridge University Press, 1977). For Brabant and Eindhoven: Peter Meurkens, *Bevolking, Economie en Cultuur van het Oude Kempenland* (Bergeijk: Eicha, 1985), and "Kinderrijk en katholiek: De stijging van de huwelijksvruchtbaarheid in het Kempenland, 1840–1920," in van den Brink 1989; W. Blankert, "De huwelijksstructuur in de Brabantse Kempen in de periode 1830–1859," in van den Brink 1989; O. W. A. Boonstra, "De dynamiek van het agrarisch-ambachtelijk huwelijkspatroon: Huwelijksfrequentie en huwelijksleeftijd in Eindhoven, 1800–1900," in van den Brink 1989, and *De Waardij van eene vroege opleiding* (Wageningen: AAG Bijdragen, 1993).

12. See the works by Boonstra (1989, 1993) and Meurkens (1984, 1989).

13. Boonstra 1989 and 1993.

14. Boonstra 1989 and 1993.

15. Messing 1980, 31–49; van Oorschot 1982, 1044.

16. Boonstra 1989, 99.

17. Messing 1980, 71; van Oorschot 1982, 83.

18. Messing 1980, 71.

19. See Paul Hohenberg and Lynn Lees, *The Making of Urban Europe, 1000–1950* (Cambridge: Harvard University Press, 1985), 210, 269, 271.

20. Doctor Ernst Bonebakker, who was the first educational specialist employed by the Philips social department, has been the only author on local events, as far as I know, who explicitly mentioned this fundamental and consequential characteristic of local labor market practices. E. Bonebakker, *Onderwijs en Ontspanning aan de Philips-fabrieken te Eindhoven* (Amersfoort: Patria, 1925), 4–5.

21. Van Oorschot 1982, 110–16.

22. A. Bogaart, "Industriële kinder- en vrouwenarbeid in Eindhoven tussen 1850 en 1914" (M.S. thesis, Catholic University of Nijmegen, 1980); Messing 1980, 55, 59; *Onderzoekingen* (The Hague: Directie van de Arbeid, 1911), 3:44.

23. Bogaart 1980; van Oorschot 1982, 110–16, 604–8.

24. Bogaart 1980, 58–61.

25. Bogaart 1980, 55–57; A. van der Bruggen, *De sociale toestanden in de Brabantse sigarenindustrie, 1840–1940* (M.A. thesis, Catholic University of Brabant, 1973);

van Oorschot 1982; K. Sluyterman, *Ondernemen in sigaren: Analyse van bedrijfsbeleid in vijf Nederlandse sigarenfabrieken in de perioden 1856–1865 en 1925–1934* (Tilburg: Stichting Zuidelijk Historisch Contact, 1983). German cigarmakers coped with similar shifts in locational patterns; see W. H. Schröder, *Arbeitergeschichte und Arbeiterbewegung: Industriearbeit und Organisationsverhalten im 19. und frühen 20. Jahrhundert* (Frankfurt: Campus Verlag, 1976).

26. A. Bogaart 1980, 89.

27. Van Oorschot 1982, 116–20, 599–604.

28. Bogaart 1980.

29. Messing 1980, 65–66; A. Heerding, *Geschiedenis van de N.V. Philips' Gloei-lampen Fabrieken*, vol. 1 (The Hague: Martinus Nijhoff, 1980), 279–335.

30. Heerding, vol. 2 (1986); van Oorschot 1982, 120–22, 608–14.

31. Heerding 1980 and 1986.

32. T. van der Waerden, *Geschooldheid en techniek* (Delft: Dissertatie, 1911).

33. Bogaart 1980, 61–62.

34. See for an example Ad Teulings, *Philips: Geschiedenis en praktijk van een wereldconcern* (Amsterdam: Van Gennep, 1976), 16–20.

35. Messing 1980, 101.

36. Messing 1980, 99.

37. See Messing 1980, 120.

38. Bogaart 1980, 85–86.

39. Van Oorschot 1982, 1121.

40. Bogaart 1980, 39.

41. Van Oorschot 1982, 1021.

42. Van Oorschot 1982, 492.

43. Messing 1980, 37–38.

44. Messing 1980, 7–31, 168–97.

45. Gareth Stedman Jones, *Languages of Class* (Cambridge: Cambridge University Press, 1983); Joan Scott, *Gender and the Politics of History* (New York: Basic Books, 1988).

46. See the critique on Clifford Geertz's influential "interpretive turn" by Mary Douglas, "The Self-completing Animal," *Times Literary Supplement* 8 (1975): 886–87; Roland Bonsen and Don Kalb, "Over de kunst van het interpreteren: Het Geertz-Shankman non-debat nader bezien," *Focaal* 1 (1985): 18–47; and the stimulating article by Giovanni Levi, "On Microhistory," in Peter Burke, ed., *New Perspectives on Historical Writing* (University Park: Pennsylvania State University Press, 1991).

47. Ron Aminzade, *Class, Politics, and Early Industrial Capitalism: A Study of Mid-Nineteenth-Century Toulouse, France* (Albany: SUNY Press, 1981), *Ballots and Barricades: Class Formation and Republican Politics in France, 1830–1871* (Princeton: Princeton University Press, 1993), and "Class Analysis, Politics, and French Labor History," in L. Berlanstein, ed., *Rethinking Labor History: Essays on Discourse and Class Analysis* (Urbana: University of Illinois Press, 1993); Michael Hanagan, *The Logic of Solidarity: Artisans and Industrial Workers in Three French Towns, 1871–1914* (Urbana: University of Illinois Press, 1980), and *Nascent Proletarians: Class Forma-*

tion in Post-Revolutionary France (Oxford: Basil Blackwell, 1989), and "For Reconstruction in Labor History," in Berlanstein 1993; Marc Steinberg, "The Re-making of the English Working Class?" *Theory and Society* 20, no. 2 (1991).

48. A detailed and somewhat unsystematic account is to be found in van Oorschot 1982, 1; for housing see in particular A. Otten, *Philips woningbouw, 1900–1990* (Zaltbommel: Europese Bibliotheek, 1991).

49. Van Oorschot 1982, 178.

50. Van Oorschot 1982, 1121.

51. Messing 1980, 171.

52. Otten 1991, 37.

53. Messing 1980, 175.

54. Van Oorschot 1982, 176–77.

55. See in particular Messing 1980, 168–78.

56. Messing 1980, 171.

57. Messing 1980, 171.

58. Otten 1991, 31–34.

59. Otten 1991, 31–74.

60. Otten 1991, 40.

61. A. Otten, *Vereniging Volkshuisvesting* (Zeist: Vonk, 1987), 40–44.

62. As was observed by among others the prominent socialist organizer Henry Spiekman, quoted in H. Giebels, "De Eendracht en het ontstaan van de SDAP-afdeling in Eindhoven, 1897–1904," in *Jaarboek voor de geschiedenis van socialisme en arbeidersbeweging in Nederland* (Nijmegen: SUN, 1980).

63. Van Oorschot 1982, 226.

64. Giebels 1980, 148–50; van Oorschot 1982, 227.

65. Van Oorschot 1982, 228–31.

66. Van Oorschot 1982, 228–31.

67. See van der Bruggen 1973, 73–89.

68. Van der Bruggen 1973, 104–47.

69. Giebels 1980.

70. See Giebels 1980 for all further information on De Eendracht.

71. Otten 1991, 33.

72. Van Oorschot 1982, 457.

73. Van Oorschot 1982, 461.

74. Material for this analysis of cigarmakers' conflict is derived from "De Katholieke Tabaksbewerker: Orgaan van den Nederlandschen r.k. Tabaksbewerkersbond 1906–1908" and the M.A. thesis by van der Bruggen (1973).

75. In a related manner William Reddy has drawn attention to notions of honor and independence among nineteenth-century French textile weavers in *The Rise of Market Culture* (Cambridge: Cambridge University Press, 1986).

76. Harold Benenson has rightly argued for the importance of studying such workplace-family-community overlappings for explaining workers' protest, in "The Community and Family Bases of U.S. Working Class Protest, 1880–1920: A Critique of the 'Skill Degradation' and 'Ecological Perspectives,'" *Research in Social Movements, Conflicts, and Change* 8 (1985): 109–32.

77. Bluff in historical industrial conflict has always been more important than

often recognized; see for example H. I. Dutton and J. E. King, *Ten Percent and No Surrender: The Preston Strike, 1853–1854* (Cambridge: Cambridge University Press, 1981).

78. With the recent bankruptcy of DAF Trucks (1993) a similar procession was organized though much less broadly supported.

79. Paraphrased from van der Bruggen 1973; the "Brief van de burgemeester van de gemeente Strijp d.d. 24 juni 1907 aan de commissaris van de Koningin in Noord-Brabant" is available in the Municipal Archives of Eindhoven, collection "Korrespondentiemap gemeente Strijp (1900–1908)."

80. Heerding 1986, 280–300; van Oorschot 1992, 237–41.

81. Heerding 1986, 324.

82. Heerding 1986, 295.

83. Heerding 1986, 281.

84. Heerding 1986, 288.

85. Heerding 1986, 287.

86. Heerding 1986, 289, 291.

87. This section is based on Heerding 1986, 300–307, and a restudy of Heerding's major source, *De Metaalbewerker: Orgaan van den Algemeenen Nederlandschen Metaalbewerkersbond*, vol. 1909–1912.

88. See Otten 1991, 31–52.

89. Heerding 1986, 302–7.

90. See in particular the very balanced and detailed story of the ANMB local in Eindhoven by its former secretary A. Wiecherink, in *De Metaalbewerker*, 18 May 1912.

91. *De Metaalbewerker*, 4 May 1912 and 18 May 1912.

92. *De Metaalbewerker*, 18 May 1912.

93. *De Metaalbewerker*, 18 May 1912.

94. *De Metaalbewerker*, 30 September 1911, 21 October 1911, 4 November 1911, 23 December 1911, 30 December 1911, 6 January 1912, 21 January 1912, 27 January 1912, 3 February 1912, 10 February 1912, 17 February 1912, 24 February 1912, 6 April 1912, 4 May 1912, 18 May 1912.

95. *De Metaalbewerker*, 30 September 1911.

96. *De Metaalbewerker*, 4 November 1911.

97. Heerding 1986, 305.

98. Frank Pot, *Zeggenschap over beloningssystemen* (Leiden: TNO, 1988).

99. This is indeed what both J. H. van den Griend and A. Wiecherink, former members of the local union board, concluded: *De Metaalbewerker*, 4 May 1912, 18 May 1912. Later Philips history, moreover, is certainly a confirmation of this.

100. *De Metaalbewerker*, 24 February 1912.

101. Letter from 28 December 1911 by vigar Bart de Ligt, printed in *De Metaalbewerker*, 21 January 1912.

102. *De Metaalbewerker*, 21 January 1912.

103. *De Metaalbewerker*, 18 May 1912.

104. *De Metaalbewerker*, 27 January 1912, 10 February 1912, 17 February 1912, 4 May 1912, 18 May 1912.

105. Van de Griend in *De Metaalbewerker*, 4 May 1912.

106. *De Metaalbewerker*, 27 January 1912, 13 April 1912, 4 May 1912, 18 May 1912.

107. *De Metaalbewerker*, 18 May 1912.

108. Raymond Williams, *Marxism and Literature* (Oxford: Oxford University Press, 1977).

109. Van Oorschot 1992, 460.

110. See the correspondence in Archive SDAP, file no. 1016, Eindhoven department, International Institute for Social History, Amsterdam, in particular the letters from H. J. van de Griend (21 July 1912), A. de Jong (26 November 1912), and J. Jansen (28 November 1913).

111. Otten 1991, 98.

112. See in particular the letter by H. J. van de Griend (21 July 1912), SDAP archive.

113. Letter by A. de Jong, the new SDAP local secretary at Eindhoven, to the SDAP board (26 November 1912).

5 CYCLES AND STRUCTURES OF ELECTRICAL PRODUCTION

1. A. Heerding, *Een onderneming van vele markten thuis: Geschiedenis van de Philips gloeilampenfabrieken*, vol. 2 (Leiden: Martinus Nijhof, 1986), 379–83.

2. Heerding 1986, 351–52.

3. When exactly this important phenomenon occurred for the first time is not clear. I. Blanken, writing about the context of managerial decisions in 1927, states that the female labor supply in the region "had been exhausted for years." (*De ontwikkeling van de N.V. Philips fabrieken tot electrotechnisch concern* [Leiden: Martinus Nijhof, 1992], 292.) Philips succeeded in 1923 for the last time in expanding the relative size of its female labor force. (F. Bakker Schut, *Industrie en woningbouw* [Assen: van Gorcum, 1933], 208.)

4. Heerding 1986, 345.

5. Bakker Schut 1933, 208.

6. Stoop 1992, 44.

7. See in particular Ronald Schatz, *The Electrical Workers: A History of Labor at General Electric and Westinghouse, 1923–1960* (Urbana: University of Illinois Press, 1983), chaps. 1 and 2. It is telling that the highly differentiated and heterogeneous nature of electrical industries has been noted by labor historians such as Schatz rather than by historians of industry like A. A. Bright, in *The Electrical-lamp Industry: Technological Change and Economic Development from 1800 to 1947* (New York, 1949). The labor-sociological approach to Philips by the Amsterdam sociologist Ad Teulings too uncritically assumes a unifying basis in dominated, deskilled labor. A. Teulings, *Philips: Geschiedenis en praktijk van een wereldconcern* (Amsterdam: van Gennep, 1976).

8. It is telling that its historical specialization on export to a large and differentiated set of national markets in Europe and Latin America caused such an organizational incoherence that its general management in the 1970s and 1980s under Japanese combat was unable to gain control over the organization. Large national

sales agencies had become more powerful within Philips than the vital product divisions. Marcel Metze, *Kortsluiting: Hoe Philips zijn talenten verspilde* (Nijmegen: Sun, 1991).

9. R. Milkman draws the same conclusion as to American electrical industry at large. R. Milkman, *Gender at Work: The Dynamics of Job Segregation by Sex during World War II* (Urbana: University of Illinois Press, 1987).

10. The distinction is from Althusser. For a seminal application see, among others, Michael Burawoy, *The Politics of Production* (London: Verso, 1985), and Gerald Sider, *Culture and Class in Anthropology and History* (Cambridge: Cambridge University Press, 1985).

11. The concept of production regime is borrowed from Michael Burawoy 1985.

12. Anton Philips in an interview with ILO (International Labor Organization) researchers, *Les Usines Philips* (Geneva: ILO, 1932), 16.

13. ILO 1932, 11.

14. Burawoy 1985.

15. Van Drenth 1991, 75.

16. ILO 1932, 9.

17. Van Drenth 1991.

18. This is of utmost importance but has rarely and never systematically been noted in the literature. See, however, E. Bonebakker, *Onderwijs en Ontspanning aan de Philips-fabrieken te Eindhoven* (Amersfoort: Patria, 1925), 4. Dr. Bonebakker was the head of the education department at Philips. He astutely observed: "In many families several members, fathers, sons, and daughters, work at Philips. One in a lower rank, the other in a higher function."

19. This picture also emerges from oral history.

20. Though the question has not been taken up in further research, Hilda Verwey Jonker, already in her dissertation of 1943, calculated that children earned almost 15 percent of the total income of Eindhoven families. Among her sample of 256 blue-collar "Philips families" the percentage of the children's contribution to family income amounted to as much as 47.5 percent! Hilda Verwey Jonker, *Lage Inkomens* (Assen: Van Gorcum, 1943), 180.

21. The practice of family employment at Eindhoven has been a source of considerable confusion. Eindhoven historian van Oorschot, for example, attributes complaints about "family wages" to the Catholic obsession with keeping girls out of industrial employment. Oorschot 1982, 733. The Catholic metalworkers union St. Eloy and Gerard Knuvelder, Catholic intellectual and protagonist, argued that wages at Philips were too low for breadwinners to maintain a family, and that it forced them to send their offspring to the factory. Gerard Knuvelder, *Bezuiden de Moerdijk: Problemen en verschijnselen* (Tilburg, 1929), 17; *St. Eloy: Weekblad van de Roomskatholieke metaalbewerkersbond*, 26 April 1930. This, however, had nothing to do with Catholic moralist obsessions. It was a shrewd remark on local class relationships and family relationships. Also Annemieke van Drenth in her study of Philips discourses on girls' employment at Eindhoven tends to treat Catholic objections to the factory employment of girls as exclusively morally inspired. This misses the key relationships in the locality, at the firm, and in local unskilled families.

22. On evidence for substantial wage increases at Philips from 1927 on, neces-sary to recruit grown-up males, see van Oorschot 1982, 734, where he shows a statistic suggesting a real wage rise between 1927 and 1929 of some 20 percent.

23. The ILO reported that by 1931 two-thirds of the Philips labor force had been employed for less than three years while the average age of unskilled workers had risen to over 26 years old (while 8,000 workers were still under age 18), in ILO 1932, 9.

24. See Milkman 1987 on female jobs in electrical manufacturing.

25. For the evidence see Bakker Schut 1933, and later sections of this chapter.

26. See Bakker Schut 1933, 207; van Drenth 1991, 78–80.

27. ILO 1932, 11; Stoop 1992, 44–48; van Oorschot 1982, 730–33.

28. ILO 1932, 16–21, 50–54.

29. Blanken 1992, 413.

30. ILO 1932, 12–15; Blanken 1992, 409–13; Heerding, 353–54.

31. ILO 1932, 11; Heerding 1986, 343–44.

32. *De Metaalbewerker*, 13 February 1932.

33. *De Metaalbewerker*, 7 February 1931; *St. Eloy: Weekblad van de Roomskatholieke metaalbewerkersbond*, 9 May 1931.

34. ILO 1932, 15–17.

35. See among others Joan Scott, *The Glassworkers of Carmaux* (Cambridge, Mass.: Harvard University Press, 1974).

36. Teulings 1976, 60–62. His sources, however, are unclear.

37. See section 7. Since Philips works councils played only a very subordinate role in the Philips factory regime, I treat them together with other Philips welfare practices.

38. This is still the case. See for example Peter Dicken, *Global Shift: Industrial Change in a Turbulent World* (London: Chapman, 1986), 316–56.

39. ILO 1932, 53–54.

6 THE CULTURE OF PHILIPSISM

1. Ad Otten, *Philips Woningbouw, 1900–1990* (Zaltbommel: Europese Biblio-theek, 1991); J. J. Vriend, *Bouwen als sociale daad: 50 jaar woningbouw Philips* (Eind-hoven: Philips, n.d.).

2. Otten 1991, 31–53; A. Otten, *Volkshuisvesting in Eindhoven* (Zeist: Vonk, 1987), 1–29; van Oorschot 1982, 1:167–80.

3. Heerding 1986, 276; Blanken 1992, 287.

4. Otten 1991, 67.

5. Otten 1991, 47, 57.

6. Otten 1991, 67.

7. Heerding 1986, 326.

8. This explanation occurs in Otten 1991; van Oorschot 1982; Vriend n.d.

9. Bakker Schut 1933.

10. However, Bakker Schut would have preferred a different solution than in the Eindhoven case, where so much of the housing reserve had come under the

control of a single employer. He therefore concluded that exceptional urban growth caused by the expansion of a single industry or set of industries should be realized by temporary municipal taxing of their profits. This would facilitate municipal investments in housing while at the same time secure the separation between the economy and the civic sphere.

11. Bakker Schut 1933, 208.

12. Bakker Schut 1933, 101.

13. Bakker Schut 1933, 74.

14. Bakker Schut 1933, 206.

15. Bakker Schut 1933, 81–118.

16. As an example: Bakker Schut 1933, 99.

17. Bakker Schut 1933, 99–102; ILO 1932, 28–33; see in general Milkman 1987.

18. Peter Dicken 1986, 352–53; A. Fuentes and B. Ehrenreich, *Women in the Global Factory* (Boston: South End Press, 1983); Milkman 1987.

19. Hence the strict regulation and sex segregation. See, for example, ILO 1932, 31–32; van Drenth 1991, 90–93.

20. For a contemporary estimation of this epoch-making development see, for example, Franz Fendt, *Der ungelernte Industriearbeiter* (Munich, 1936); Manuell Castells, *The Informational City* (London: Basil Blackwell, 1989), argues the end of that period since the seventies.

21. ILO 1932, 31: "Le desir d' éviter les départs volontaires a été le facteur déterminant de la politique de recrutement familial poursuivie en 1928 et 1929."

22. There is a wealth of literature exploring the intersection of family and industry, although there is a relative scarcity for the more recent periods. See, for example, the classic study by Tamara Hareven, *Family Time and Industrial Time* (London, 1982); and for a general historical perspective Tilly and Scott 1978. From the perspective of industrial regions and industrial history see Charles Sabel and Jonathan Zeitlin, "Historical Alternatives to Mass Production: Politics, Markets, and Technology in Nineteenth-Century Industrialization," *Past and Present* 108 (1985): 133–76; Michael Blim, *Made in Italy: Small-scale Industrialization and Its Consequences* (New York: Praeger, 1990). For an earlier period, the literature on protoindustry abounds with regional and branch-specific examples. See the recent review by the authors of the original synthesis: Peter Kriedtke, Hans Medick, and Jürgen Schlumbohm, "Sozialgeschichte in der Erweiterung- Proto-Industrialisierung in der Verengung?" *Geschichte und Gesellschaft* 18, no. 1 (1992): 78–87, and no. 2:231–56.

23. "Overzicht van de processen verbaal, opgemaakt in Eindhoven in de periode 1920–1940," in *25 jaar lief en leed bij de Eindhovense Politie, 1919–1945: Jubileumboek samengesteld door Hoofdinspekteur Matla* (Eindhoven, 1945). Jan Krol, "Brood en Spelen" (M.A. thesis, Nijmegen University, 1981).

24. *Roomsch Leven: Parochie Weekblad voor Eindhoven en Omgeving, 1919–1940.*

25. Van Drenth 1991, 99–100; the Catholic Youth Association (KJV) published the alarming Eindhoven report on girls' labor and girls' "souls" integrally in its journal *Dux* (1929/1930), vol. 3.

26. Both van Drenth 1991 and van Oorschot 1992 display this tendency.

27. For the emphasis on strict regulation of sexuality in southeast Brabant

socialization practices in relation to the exploitation of children's labor power, see the early article by P. A. Barentsen, "Het gezinsleven in het Oosten van Brabant," *Mensch en Maatschappij* 2 (1926): 44–60, which has recently been reprinted in G. van den Brink et al., eds., *Werk, kerk en bed in Brabant: Demografische ontwikkelingen in oostelijk Noord-Brabant, 1700–1920* ('s Hertogenbosch: Het Noordbrabants Genootschap, 1989).

28. Anton Coolen, *Het donkere licht* (Rotterdam: Nijgh en van Ditmar, 1930).

29. Coolen 1930, 111.

30. H. H. J. Maas, *Onder de gloeilamp* (Laren: A. G. Schoonderbeek, 1946).

31. Otten 1991, 103–30.

32. Otten 1991, 103; Blanken 1992, 302.

33. Indeed, this is what follows from ILO 1932, 31 (already cited).

34. Bakker Schut 1933, 144–45, shows that over 40 percent of houses built in 1928–31 was designed for "large families," again over 40 percent for "normal" families ("small" families were not provided for), and some 12 percent for skilled workers. He also produces a table in which he compares family composition and family income in three smaller quarters (Aalst, Stratum, Son), which shows that average "normal family" income (Aalst, Stratum) is less than half of "large family" earnings (72.72 guilders per week versus 36.33 guilders [Stratum] and 31.47 guilders [Aalst] per week).

35. Otten 1991, 114.

36. Bakker Schut 1933, 206; Blanken 1992, 293–96; Stoop 1992, 46.

37. Bakker Schut 1933, 203–6.

38. Blanken 1992, 294–96; Stoop 1992, 46; R. Ter Meulen and W. van Hoorn, "Psychotechniek en menselijke verhoudingen," *Grafiet* 1 (winter 1981/82): 106–56.

39. M. Simons, *Tussen turf en televisie: Acculturatieproblemen van een binnenlandse migrantengroep gedurende een aantal generaties* (Assen: van Gorcum, 1960), 22.

40. Bakker Schut 1933, 206. The ILO report mentions 700 families of which four to five members on average were employed at the plants: ILO 1932, 11. The difference in the number of families may be explained either by those who remigrated, or by the noninclusion in the figures presented by Bakker Schut of the 160 families that still arrived in 1930. Note also the difference in the average number of workers per family. The materials for the ILO report were gathered before the crisis really hit Philips. The difference in average employment numbers may point to increased employment of immigrant children in the course of the crisis (see the section on the crisis below), or may be produced by a smaller average number of children among the 160 latest arriving families. Which hypothesis is correct cannot be established on the basis of existing materials.

41. 1924 is a hypothetical date. Blanken writes that in 1927 the regional labor reserve had already been exhausted "for years." In January 1924 the number of workers at Philips for the first time exceeded the post–World-War-I record of some 6,800 workers in 1920. Blanken 1992, 292. E. Bonebakker in 1925 still observed that "of very many families" several members were working at the plants. This suggests the predominance of locally rooted workers at the time. Bonebakker 1925, 4.

42. See van Drenth 1991, 117–22; Bakker Schut 1933, 207–8. Both show rising figures of women's employment in the aftermath of the crisis.

43. For general literature on oral history see: Daniel Bertaux, ed., *Biography and Society: The Life History Approach in the Social Sciences* (Beverly Hills: Sage, 1981); Paul Thompson, *The Voice of the Past* (Oxford: Oxford University Press, 1978). For an impressive project (Lebensgeschichte und Sozialkultur im Ruhrgebiet 1930–1960), see Lutz Niethammer et al., eds., *"Die Jahre weiss man nicht, wo man die heute hinsetzen soll": Faschismus Erfahrungen im Ruhrgebiet* (Berlin: Dietz Verlag, 1983); *"Hinterher merkt man, dass es richtig war dass es Schiefgegangen ist": Nachkriegserfahrungen im Ruhrgebiet* (Berlin: Dietz Verlag, 1983); *"Wir kriegen jetzt andere Zeiten": Auf der Suche nach der Erfahrung des Volkes in Nachfaschistischen Ländern* (Berlin: Dietz Verlag, 1985).

44. Also Paul Thompson acknowledges the virtue of such a mixed approach. Thompson 1988, 165.

45. Except de Broekert, who was more of a public figure, other family names are pseudonyms.

46. This portrait is composed of data from: Archive SDAP, file no. 1016, Eindhoven letter of 21 July 1912 by H. J. van de Griend, former secretary of the local branch of the socialist party; Blanken 1992, 286–89, 297; Heerding 1986, 254, 258, 279, 326, 328, 352, 393; van Oorschot 1982, 816, 818, 825, 833, 963; Otten 1991, 70, 119, 127.

47. Although there is disagreement among historians on this, I think that Teulings 1976, 60, is right to see the Philips Association for Higher Personnel in this light. See the letter by preacher Bart de Ligt in *De Metaalbewerker*, 21 January 1912. Without giving any evidence, Philips historian Heerding denies this: 1986, 327–29.

48. More members in the family carry the same name. Though it may be confusing for the reader, I have persistently used these forenames and have not given them different pseudonyms so as to leave the impression of personal closeness and historical affinity intact.

49. I will refer to Chris (third generation) as Chris (jr.).

50. The average weekly wage for unskilled adults at Philips was about twenty-five guilders. Skilled workers could earn around forty guilders per week. Bakker Schut presents material which shows that average weekly family incomes among the large immigrant households amounted to seventy-eight guilders.

51. It is my impression that most fathers withdrew from family involvements. Gardening and quiet hobbies were very popular. See also Simons 1960.

52. For an interesting study of Philips's discourses on family life, see Krol 1981.

53. Krol 1981.

54. Krol 1981 offers an interesting study of leisure practices at Philips. See also Kalb 1991b.

55. There have been many justified criticisms of such reasoning, but at this place I want to refer to Alf Lüdtke's seminal introduction to the interesting collection of articles in *Herrschaft als soziale Praxis, Historische und Sozialanthropologische Studien* (Göttingen: Vandenhoek und Ruprecht, 1991), 9–66.

56. Otten 1991, 116–17.

57. Bakker Schut 1933, 36–37.

58. See also Bakker Schut 1933, 203–4.

59. Nevertheless, one of the people managing the formation of this new proletariat of large families, Bakker Schut, was enthusiastic about its unexpected
qualities as a loyal labor reserve. See Bakker Schut 1933, 203–4.

60. Beyen in P. Brouwers and L. Tabak, *Werken in vrijheid* (Eindhoven: Philips
persbureau, 1969), 373.

61. Van Oorschot 1982, 512.

62. For a classic love song over Dutch urbanism, see Lewis Mumford, *The
Culture of Cities* (New York: Harcourt Brace Jovanovich, 1938).

63. For discussions on the Eindhoven urban form see van Oorschot 1982, 509–
62; P. Beekman, *Eindhoven, Stadsontwikkeling, 1900–1960* (Mierlo: Beekman, 1982).

64. Van Oorschot 1982; Beekman 1982.

65. Otten 1991, 116–27.

66. Otten 1991, 121.

67. This is a point in relation to these projects which is also mentioned by
Bakker Schut 1933, 167, 171, 187–88.

68. For an account of the whole process see Otten, 1991, 116–27.

69. Housing was also a good way for shopkeepers to create a group of "forced
clients." Within the province of North Brabant, Woensel was the classic example of
this form of exploitation. Nine shopkeepers, most of them bakers, owned 313
houses out of a total housing stock of 2,655 houses in 1918. Van Oorschot 1982, 173–
8. More than one in eight households were tied to such shopkeeper-landlords.

70. Beekman, 1982.

71. Hence the great concern of the community of Woensel and Eindhoven with
"uninhabitable houses." See van Oorschot 1982, 167–74. The alliance of employers that underpinned the building association "Volkshuisvesting" (see above)
consisted partly of employers in wood-processing industries who paid relatively
high wages, like Brüning and Keunen / Mennen. Philips also prominently participated, but not in order to house unskilled workers. For them, it was generally
known in the community, it was simply impossible to build decent houses because they could never afford the necessary rent level.

72. On the concept of circuits of capital, see David Harvey, *The Urban Experience*
(Baltimore: Johns Hopkins University Press, 1985).

73. Bakker Schut 1933, 164.

74. Otten 1991, 116–21. Krol 1981 on Philips' discourses of "healthy leisure."

75. For detailed treatment of the system see Heerding 1986, 309–58; Stoop 1992,
42–105; for housing: Otten 1991; Vriend, n.d.; for leisure: C. Jansen, *60 jaar Philips
de Jongh Ontspanningsfonds* (Eindhoven: Philips de Jongh Ontspanningsfond,
1981); Krol 1981.

76. John Gaventa, *Power and Powerlessness: Quiescence and Rebellion in an Appalachian Valley* (Urbana: University of Illinois Press, 1980).

77. In particular regional Catholics felt marginalized by it. See, for example,
"Waar Brabant sterft . . . Machtsvorming in Eindhoven," in *Brabantia Nostra* 2
(1936). Philips itself, like the historians paid by the firm, tends to see it as a loose

set of contractual arrangements aimed at resolving a range of discrete social probems; see, for example, Heerding 1986, 309–58.

78. For the general debate in social policy research about the value of cultural analysis, see, for example, the discussion about the "polity centered" approach of Theda Skocpol by Alan Brinkley in the *New York Review of Books* 41, no. 10 (1994): 40–44, and the literature cited there, in particular the criticism by the feminist historian Linda Gordon in *Contention* 2 (1993): 157–87.

79. See for important reminders: Philip Corrigan and Derek Sayer, *The Great Arch: English State Formation as Cultural Revolution* (Oxford: Basil Blackwell, 1985), who connect a Durkheimian emphasis on the "conscience collective" and the state with a Marxist vision of power and social relations in their original study "English State Formation as Cultural Revoltuion"; and Michael B. Katz, *The Undeserving Poor: From the War on Poverty to the War on Welfare* (New York: Pantheon Books, 1989).

80. Corrigan and Sayer 1985.

81. See, for example, Stephen Meyer's interesting book on Ford's welfare system, *The Five-Dollar Day: Labor Management and Social Control in the Ford Motor Company, 1908–1921* (Albany: State University of New York Press, 1981).

82. Stoop 1992, 48; Philips Sociale Kalender (Eindhoven: Philips, 1953).

83. ILO 1932, 70 (trans. D.K.).

84. The relevance of those values for the Philips family is abundantly illustrated by P. J. Bouman, *Anton Philips: De Mens/ de Ondernemer* (Amsterdam: Meulenhof, 1956); and Frits Philips, *45 jaar met Philips* (Rotterdam: Ad Donker, 1976).

85. See also Heerding 1986, 309–57; ILO 1932.

86. Heerding 1986, 327; ILO 1932, 57–58, 60; Krol 1981.

87. Bonebakker 1925; van Drenth 1991, 103–17; Heerding 1986, 349; ILO 1932, 35–46; Krol 1981, 50–77; Stoop 1992, 50–52.

88. Bonebakker 1925; Krol 1981, 50–77.

89. ILO 1932, 17–27.

90. ILO 1932, 68; M. van der Steen, *Die Annie ben ik* (Baarn, 1977), is an autobiographical account of a Philips social worker at the time.

91. For Philips medical provisions, see R. Vos, *Een bedrijfsarts in het bedrijf: G. C. E. Burger als "fabrieksarts" van de N.V. Philips Gloeilampenfabrieken, 1928–1938* (Groningen: ISMW-rapport 82-SK-12); Stoop 1992, 49. For the Philips police force, see Krol 1981, 177–91.

92. ILO 1932, 68.

93. This popular aversion against house inspectors was not limited to Philips or Eindhoven. See Ali de Regt, *Arbeidersgezinnen en Beschavingsarbeid* (Meppel: Boom, 1984), 175–98.

94. ILO 1932, 58.

95. For a comprehensive treatment of women's care at Philips, see van Drenth 1991.

96. ILO 1932, 9.

97. ILO 1932, 9, 16–21.

98. ILO 1932, 16–21.

99. ILO 1932, 23. For a list of works-council issues, see Philips Corporate Archives, no. 149.1. Van Drenth 1991, 90, gives other examples of works-council engagement with "virtue."

100. This is, for example, quantitatively demonstrated by the constant high percentage of working girls in the twentieth century, low percentage of working mothers up to the late seventies, high average number of family members up to the late sixties, and low percentage of one-person households. See Stoop 1992, 59–61, and the literature cited there.

101. Production managers were more centrally guided before the start of radio set manufacturing but seem to have attained a much higher level of autonomy during the large expansions of the late twenties. In any case this is suggested by the analysis of organizational changes by Blanken 1992, 413.

102. ILO 1932, 37.

103. The words are from the interviewed son of a glassblower, who started work at age seventeen on the assembly line for television sets but is now a private driver for Philips top management. They were meant to characterize the important themes in the socialization of his adolescent children.

7 THE FRUITS OF FLEXIBLE FAMILISM

1. There has long been a lack of clarity in the figures of Philips decline since 1929. Blanken has recently presented convincing material. See Blanken 1992, 423–27.

2. Teulings 1976, 82–87, referring to the geographic study of A. de Graaf, "De industrie," in *De Nederlandse volkshuishouding tussen twee wereldoorlogen* (Utrecht, 1950).

3. *De Metaalbewerker*, 14 December 1929, 4 October 1930; *St. Eloy*, 1 December 1929.

4. *De Metaalbewerker*, 15 March 1930, 4 October 1930, 29 November 1930, 7 February 1931, 7 March 1931, 13 February 1932.

5. E. Baruch, *Grote macht in een klein land* (Amsterdam, 1955); Krol 1981, 185–91.

6. *De Metaalbewerker*, 4 October 1930.

7. *De Metaalbewerker*, 11 January 1930, 15 March 1930; van Oorschot 1982, 738.

8. Van Oorschot 1982, 738–39.

9. *St. Eloy*, 18 January 1930.

10. *St. Eloy*, 26 April 1930; Knuvelder 1929, 17.

11. *St. Eloy*, 26 April 1930.

12. Indeed, the often noted reconciliation between the Philips company and local Catholic organizations in the course of the thirties may well be explained by the end of large-scale local youth and girls employment. It took away the greatest source of Catholic moral objections to the firm's practices. In the thirties, moreover, more and more local Catholic lower middle class boys acquired clerical jobs at Philips. Instead of causing an urban invasion of "fashionable ladies" ("de dametjes," as the Philips girls used to be called), the firm now provided much-needed employment opportunities for the children of local independent and

petit bourgeois families. Together, these labor market changes form a sufficient explanation of the rapprochement of local Catholics and the electrical company. Indeed, no other good explanation has been given.

13. See for example Marja Gastelaars, *Een geregeld leven: Sociologie en sociale politiek in Nederland, 1925–1968* (Amsterdam: SUA, 1985); and the studies in J. C. H. Blom, *Crisis, bezetting en herstel: Tien studies over Nederland, 1930–1950* (Rotterdam: Rotterdam University Press, 1989); H. W. von der Dunk et al., *Wederopbouw, Welvaart en Onrust: Nederland in de jaren vijftig en zestig* (Houten: De Haan, 1986).

14. For a good analysis of the problems and the process see Blanken 1992, 381–434.

15. Blanken 1992, 413–20.

16. While everyone concerned must have known what was going on, the act itself was only talked about in such mystifying terms as mechanization and rationalization. Production speed-up may well have been the anonymous mechanism by which the replacement was effected. It stimulated labor turnover, especially of older adolescent boys, and gave managers the arguments for selection.

17. Blanken 1992, 381–409.

18. Blanken 1992, 421.

19. Blanken 1992, 421.

20. Blanken 1992, 420–27; Bouman 1956, 178–94.

21. And more complicated and interesting than Blanken, Bouman, and van Oorschot have thought. They all emphasize the importance of efficiency operations for the dismissals of 1929 and 1930, but they overlook their intimate connection with regional class structures, urban moral panic, the weakening of labor discipline, and the advent of immigrant families. By missing the whole configuration they miss theory, and vice versa.

22. Blanken 1992, 419.

23. For example Blanken 1992, 424; Otten 1991, 135.

24. Bakker Schut 1933, 88.

25. See the figures presented by Bakker Schut, which are the most detailed and reliable and the best source for all subsequent work: Bakker Schut 1933, 207–8. Otten assumes that the city of Eindhoven had 5,500 lodgers in 1929. This contradicts Bakker Schut's figures. Otten does not indicate how he arrives at that number. Bakker Schut shows that 15.57 percent of all Eindhoven inhabitants on 1 January 1930 lived "outside family relationships" (lodgers). At that date Eindhoven had 94,948 inhabitants (van Oorschot 1982, 1022) (or in another calculation 89,622; van Oorschot 1982, 705; Bakker Schut 1933, 68). This implies that the locality hosted exactly 14,783 lodgers (or 13,954 if one assumes the second population figure to be right), which is almost three times as much as Otten thinks. On 1 January 1929 the figure amounted to 9,182 (11.84 percent of 77,544 inhabitants).

26. Van Oorschot 1982, 705.

27. Note the percentage rise of females in the Philips labor force between June 1930 and January 1931, which is caused by the greater number of male lodgers, who were dismissed. The figure of 3,000 is an absolute minimum: it assumes, for example, that all 1,400 new families were founded by the bachelor-males of year before. But this was not the case, since many families were still arriving in Eind-

hoven. Moreover, the number of 3,000 provides for an additional 500 dismissals from other industries leading to departure of lodgers. This is unlikely, however, since the crisis hit textiles and cigarmaking only after 1931, while it is also true that a great many workers in those industries were rooted in local families. Philips also dismissed a large number of young, bachelor, white-collar employees, but this too happened later in 1931. As we will see, this is also true for young metalworkers, over 1,400 of whom were dismissed. Except for incidental firings of metalworker activists in 1930, mass layoffs took place only in the course of 1931.

28. Bakker Schut 1933, 206.

29. Blanken 1992, 420–23.

30. *De Metaalbewerker*, 4 October 1930.

31. *De Metaalbewerker*, 4 October 1930.

32. Blanken 1992, 409–26.

33. Blanken 1992, 422; Bakker Schut 1933, 208.

34. Blanken 1992, 423.

35. Bakker Schut 1933, 208.

36. Blanken 1992, 419.

37. *De Metaalbewerker*, 29 November 1930, 7 February 1931, 7 March 1931, 13 February 1932.

38. The socialist daily *Het Volk* not unjustifiably accused Philips of exporting its unemployment to other communities: *Het Volk*, 4 February 1931, cited in Blanken 1992, 424.

39. The central argument for the cuts in the "rationalization committee" seems to have been the high capital absorption in production. See Blanken 1992, 419. But already by 1932 the company turned out to have too much capital at its disposal. Blanken 1992, 381–88.

40. Of the 2,205 houses built by "Thuis Best" about 40 percent were designed for large families. See Bakker Schut 1933, 149. This is a crude indication of the number of large families among the Philips proletariat as a whole (another 200 large family houses, built earlier, are excluded). Thus, apart from the 554 Drents Dorp families, at least another 400 large families could have been subjected to the same reduction strategy. However, the average number of children may have been less than in Drents Dorp, while not all such houses were instantly inhabited by the households for which they were designed. But if we reckon two dismissals per family instead of four in Thuis Best houses, we still arrive at 800 layoffs.

41. Bakker Schut 1933, 203–4 (trans. D.K.).

42. Bakker Schut 1933, 196.

43. For a discussion of the comparative method, see, for example, Theda Skocpol, "Emerging Agendas and Recurrent Strategies in Historical Sociology," in Skocpol, ed., *Vision and Method in Historical Sociology* (Cambridge: Cambridge University Press, 1984), 356–92; Charles Tilly, *Big Structures, Large Processes, Huge Comparisons* (New York: Russell Sage Foundation, 1984).

44. See Stephen Meyer III, *The Five-Dollar Day: Labor Management and Social Control in the Ford Motor Company, 1908–1921* (Albany: State University of New York Press, 1981).

45. Analysts of Fordism tend to define it as modern mass production per se. See, for example, Castells 1989; Harvey 1985a, 1985b, 1989; and the review article by Bob Jessop, "Regulation Theories in Retrospect and Prospect," *Economy and Society* 19, no. 2 (1990): 154–216.

46. For relevant literature see the foregoing note and M. Piore and C. Sabel, *The Second Industrial Divide* (New York: Basic Books, 1984); C. Williams et al., "The End of Mass Production?" *Economy and Society* 16, no. 3 (1987): 405–39; C. Sabel and J. Zeitlin, "Historical Alternatives to Mass Production: Politics, Markets, and Technology in Nineteenth-Century Industrialization," *Past and Present* 108 (1985): 133–76; R. Brenner and M. Glick, "The Regulation Approach: Theory and History," *New Left Review* 144 (1991): 33–71.

47. Meyer 1981, 108.

48. Meyer 1981, 123.

49. There is a seminal interest in industrialization from the point of view of regional processes of development among critical geographers. See, for example, Michael Storper and Richard Walker, *The Capitalist Imperative: Territory, Technology, and Industrial Growth* (Oxford: Basil Blackwell, 1989).

50. Oliver Zunz, *The Changing Face of Inequality: Urbanization, Industrialization, and Immigration in Detroit, 1880–1920* (Chicago: University of Chicago Press, 1982).

51. In contrast, the historiography of Eindhoven has long been focused on the question of the centrality of "strangers" for its nineteenth-century industrialization. See, for example, F. J. M. van Puijenbroek, *Beginnen in Eindhoven* (Eindhoven: van Pierre, 1985).

52. Robert Brenner, "Agrarian Class Structure and Economic Development in Pre-Industrial Europe," *Past and Present* 70 (1976): 30–75, "The Origins of Capitalist Development: A Critique of Neo-Smithian Marxism," *New Left Review* 104 (1977): 25–92, and "The Agrarian Roots of European Capitalism," in T. H. Aston and C. H. E. Philpin, eds., *The Brenner Debate: Agrarian Class Structure and Economic Development in Pre-Industrial Europe* (Cambridge: Cambridge University Press, 1985).

53. David Brody, "The Rise and Decline of Welfare Capitalism" and "The Emergence of Mass-Production Unionism," in David Brody, *Workers in Industrial America: Essays on the Twentieth-Century Struggle* (New York: Basic Books, 1980), 49–119.

8 A DUMB GIRL AND AN EPILEPTIC *BRICOLEUR*

1. P. A. Barentsen, "Het gezinsleven in het oosten van Noord-Brabant," *Mens en Maatschappij* 2 (1926): 44–60, reproduced in the recent collection by G. van den Brink, A. van der Veen, and A. van der Woude, eds., *Werk, kerk en bed in Brabant: Demografische ontwikkelingen in oostelijk Noord-Brabant, 1700–1920* ('s Hertogenbosch: Stichting Brabantse Regionale Geschiedbeoefening, 1989).

2. Barentsen 1926, 23.

3. Edward Shorter, *The Making of the Modern Family* (New York: Basic Books, 1975).

4. For example: H. Selby, A. Murphy, and A. Lorenzen, *The Mexican Urban Household: Organizing for Self-Defense* (Austin: University of Texas Press, 1990).

5. Barentsen 1926, 27–29.

6. See in particular the work by C. van der Heijden and A. Janssens in G. van den Brink et al. 1989. At the same time it is good to take to heart the remark by Douglas Holmes that the actual variety of small-scale income practices was just not registered by authorities and therefore not present in the archives. See Douglas Holmes, *Cultural Disenchantments* (Princeton: Princeton University Press, 1989).

7. Barrington Moore Jr., *Injustice: The Social Bases of Obedience and Revolt* (New York: Sharpe, 1978); Sidney Pollard, *The Genesis of Modern Management* (Cambridge, Mass.: Harvard University Press, 1965); William Reddy, *The Rise of Market-culture: The Textile Trade and French Society, 1750–1900* (Cambridge: Cambridge University Press, 1984).

8. W. S. Whyte, *The Organization Man* (New York: Touchstone, 1957).

EPILOGUE

1. Edward Thompson, *The Poverty of Theory* (London: Merlin Press, 1978b), 231.

2. Ira Katznelson, *Marxism and the City* (Oxford: Clarendon Press, 1992), 71.

3. Mike Savage, "Class Analysis and Its Futures," *Sociological Review* 42, no. 3 (1994): 531–48.

4. For a recent and important reminder, see Jack Goody, "Culture and Its Boundaries: A European View," *Social Anthropology* 1, no. 1 (1992): 9–33.

5. Josef Ehmer, *Familienstruktur und Arbeitsorganisation im frühindustriellen Wien* (Wien: 1980).

References

PRIMARY SOURCES

Central Brabant

De Katholieke Lederbewerker (1909–13)
De Lederbewerker (1918–22)
De Leerbewerker (1908–9)
De Schoen en Lederbewerker (1913–18)
Echo van het Zuiden (1900–1911)
Gemeenteverslagen (1870–1920) Waalwijk, Loon op Zand, Oisterwijk
Municipal Archive Loon op Zand, Police notebook 1905 (Kaatsheuvel)
Vakblad voor de Schoenmakerij (1900–1905)
Verslagen van de kamer van koophandel en fabrieken te Waalwijk (1876–1920)

Eindhoven

Archive SDAP, file no. 1016, Eindhoven Department, International Institute for
    Social History, Amsterdam
Brabantia Nostra (1936)
De Katholieke Tabaksbewerker (1906–8)
De Metaalbewerker (1909–12; 1928–32)
Dux (1929–30)
Philips Sociale Kalender (Philips Company Archives)
Philips Company Archives, file no. 149.1 "Kern"
St. Eloy: Weekblad van de Roomskatholieke metaalbewerkersbond (1929–32)

SECONDARY SOURCES

Abbink, Jan, and H. Vermeulen, eds. 1992. *History and Culture: Essays on the Work
    of Eric R. Wolf.* Amsterdam: Het Spinhuis.
Abbott, Andrew. 1992. "From Causes to Events: Notes on Narrative Positivism."
    Sociological Methods and Research 20, no. 4: 428–55.
Aminzade, Ron. 1981. *Class, Politics, and Early Industrial Capitalism: A study of Mid-
    nineteenth-century Toulouse, France.* Albany: State University of New York Press.

———. 1992. "Historical Sociology and Time." *Sociological Methods and Research* 20, no. 4: 456–80.

———. 1993a. *Ballots and Barricades: Class Formation and Republican Politics in France, 1830–1871.* Princeton: Princeton University Press.

———. 1993b. "Class Analysis, Politics, and French Labor History." In *Rethinking Labor History: Essays on Discourse and Class Analysis,* ed. Lenard Berlanstein. Urbana: University of Illinois Press.

Anderson, Michael. 1971. *Family Structure in Nineteenth-Century Lancashire.* Cambridge: Cambridge University Press.

Aston, T. H., and C. H. E. Philpin, eds. 1985. *The Brenner Debate: Agrarian Class Structure and Economic Development in Pre-Industrial Europe.* Cambridge: Cambridge University Press.

Bailey, Peter. 1978. *Leisure and Class in Victorian England: Rational Recreation and the Contest for Control, 1830–1885.* London: Routledge.

Bakker Schut, F. 1933. *Industrie en Woningbouw.* Assen: van Gorcum.

Bakvis, H. 1981. *Catholic Power in the Netherlands.* Montreal: McGill–Queens University Press.

Barentsen, P. A. 1926. "Het gezinsleven in het oosten van Noord-Brabant." *Mens en Maatschappij* 2 (1926), reproduced in *Werk, kerk en bed in Brabant: Demografische ontwikkelingen in oostelijk Noord-Brabant, 1700–1920,* ed. G. van den Brink et al. 's Hertogenbosch: Stichting Brabantse Regionale Geschiedbeoefening, 1989.

Baruch, E. 1955. *Grote macht in een klein land.* Amsterdam.

Beekman, P. 1982. *Eindhoven, Stadsontwikkeling, 1900–1960.* Mierlo: Beekman.

Behr, Friedrich. 1909. *Die Wirkung der fortschreitenden Technik auf die Schuhindustrie.* Leipzig.

Benenson, Harold. 1985. "The Community and Family Bases of U.S. Working Class Protest, 1880–1920: A Critique of the 'Skill Degradation' and 'Ecological Perspectives.'" *Research in Social Movements, Conflicts, and Change* 8: 109–32.

Berlanstein, Lenard R., ed. 1993. *Rethinking Labor History: Essays on Discourse and Class Analysis.* Urbana: University of Illinois Press.

Bertaux, Daniel, ed. 1981. *Biography and Society: The Life History Approach in the Social Sciences.* Beverly Hills: Sage.

Blanken, I. 1992. *De ontwikkeling van de N.V. Philips fabrieken tot electrotechnisch concern.* Leiden: Martinus Nijhof.

Blankert, W. 1989. "De huwelijksstructuur in de Brabantse Kempen in de periode 1830–1859." In *Werk, kerk en bed in Brabant,* ed. G. van den Brink et al. 's Hertogenbosch: Stichting Brabantse Regionale Geschiedschrijving.

Blim, Michael. 1990. *Made in Italy: Small-Scale Industrialization and Its Consequences.* New York: Praeger.

Blom, J. C. H. 1981. *Verzuiling in Nederland, 1850–1925.* Amsterdam: Historisch Seminarium.

———. 1989. *Crisis, bezetting en herstel: Tien studies over Nederland, 1930–1950.* Rotterdam: Rotterdam University Press.

Bodnar, John. 1986. *Workers' World: Kinship, Community, and Protest in an Industrial Society, 1900–1940.* Baltimore: Johns Hopkins University Press.

Bogaart, A. 1980. "Industriële kinder- en vrouwenarbeid in Eindhoven tussen 1850 en 1914." M.S. thesis, Catholic University of Nijmegen.

Bonebakker, E. 1925. *Onderwijs en Ontspanning aan de Philips-fabrieken te Eindhoven.* Amersfoort: Patria.

Bonnel, Victoria. 1983. *Roots of Rebellion: Workers' Politics and Organizations in St. Petersburg and Moscow, 1900–1914.* Berkeley: University of California Press.

Bonsen, Roland, and Don Kalb. 1985. "Over de kunst van het interpreteren: Het Geertz-Shankman non-debat nader bezien." *Focaal* 1: 18–47.

Boonstra, O. 1989. "De dynamiek van het agrarisch-ambachtelijk huwelijkspatroon: Huwelijksfrequentie en huwelijksleeftijd in Eindhoven, 1800–1900." In *Werk, kerk en bed in Brabant,* ed. G. van den Brink et al. 's Hertogenbosch: Stichting Brabantse Regionale Geschiedschrijving.

———. 1993. *De waardij van eene vroege opleiding: Een onderzoek naar de implicaties van alfabetisme op het leven van inwoners van Eindhoven en omliggende gemeenten, 1800–1920.* Wageningen: AAG Bijdragen.

Boonstra, O., and A. van der Woude. 1984. "Demographic Transition in the Netherlands: A Statistical Analysis of Regional Differences in the Level and Development of the Birth Rate and of Fertility, 1850–1890." *AAG Bijdragen* 24 (1984): 1–57.

Bouman, P. J. 1956. *Anton Philips: De Mens/ De Ondernemer.* Amsterdam: Meulenhof.

Bourdieu, Pierre. 1977. *Outline of a Theory of Practice.* Cambridge: Cambridge University Press.

———. 1984. *Distinction: A Social Critique of the Judgement of Taste.* London: Routledge.

Braun, Rudolf. 1979 [1960]. *Industrialisierung und Volksleben.* Göttingen: Vandenhoeck und Ruprecht.

Braverman, Harry. 1974. *Labor and Monopoly Capital: The Degradation of Work in the Twentieth Century.* New York: Monthly Review Press.

Brekelmans, W. A. A. 1938. *Huiden, Looistoffen, Leder- en schoennijverheid: Een algemeen informatieve beschrijving.* Doetinchem: Misset.

Brenner, Robert. 1976. "Agrarian Class Structure and Economic Development in Pre-Industrial Europe." In *Past and Present* 70: 30–75.

———. 1977. "The Origins of Capitalist Development: A Critique of Neo-Smithian Marxism." *New Left Review* 104: 25–92.

———. 1985. "The Agrarian Roots of European Capitalism." In *The Brenner Debate: Agrarian Class Structure and Economic Development in Pre-Industrial Europe,* ed. T. H. Aston and C. H. E. Philpin. Cambridge: Cambridge University Press.

Brenner, R., and M. Glick. 1991. "The Regulation Approach: Theory and History." *New Left Review* 144: 33–71.

Bright, A. A. 1949. *The Electrical-lamp Industry: Technological Change and Economic Development from 1800 to 1947.* New York.

Brink, G. van den, et al., eds. 1989. *Werk, kerk en bed in Brabant: Demografische ontwikkelingen in Oostelijk Noord-Brabant, 1700–1920.* 's Hertogenbosch: Stichting Brabantse Regionale Geschiedbeoefening.

Brinkley, Alan. 1994. *New York Review of Books* 41, no. 10 (1994): 40–44.

Brody, David. 1980. *Workers in Industrial America: Essays on the Twentieth-Century Struggle.* New York: Basic Books.

Brom, Gerard. 1909. *De nieuwe kruistocht: Drankweergeschiedenis van Rooms Nederland, 1895–1907.* Helmond.

Brouwers, P., and L. Tabak. 1969. *Werken in vrijheid.* Eindhoven: Philips persbureau.

Bruggen, A. van der. 1973. *De sociale toestanden in de Brabantse sigarenindustrie, 1840–1940.* M.A. thesis, Catholic University of Brabant.

Brüggemeier, Franz Josef. 1984. *Leben vor Ort: Ruhrbergleute und Ruhrbergbau, 1889–1919.* Munich: Beck Verlag.

Brugmans, I. J. [1925] 1975. *De arbeidende klasse in Nederland in de 19e eeuw.* Utrecht: Het Spectrum.

Burawoy, Michael. 1985. *The Politics of Production: Factory Regimes under Capitalism and Socialism.* London: Verso.

———. 1989. "Marxism without Micro-Foundations." *Socialist Review* 19, no. 2: 53–86.

Burke, Peter, ed. 1991. *New Perspectives on Historical Writing.* University Park: Pennsylvania State University Press.

Calhoun, Craig. 1983. *The Question of Class Struggle.* Chicago: University of Chicago Press.

Castells, Manuell. 1983. *The City and the Grassroots.* Berkeley: University of California Press.

———. 1989. *The Informational City: Information Technology, Economic Restructuring, and the Urban-Regional Process.* Oxford: Basil Blackwell.

Clarke, John. 1979. "Capital and Culture: The Post-war Working Class Revisited." In *Working Class Culture: Studies in History and Theory*, ed. John Clarke, Chas Critcher, and Richard Johnson. London: Hutchinson.

Clarke, J., C. Critcher, and R. Johnson, eds. 1979. *Working-Class Culture.* London: Hutchinson.

Cohen, G. 1978. *Karl Marx's Theory of History: A Defence.* Oxford: Oxford University Press.

Coolen, Anton. 1930. *Het donkere licht.* Rotterdam: Nijgh en van Ditmar.

Corrigan, Philip, and Derek Sayer. 1985. *The Great Arch: English State Formation as Cultural Revolution.* Oxford: Basil Blackwell.

Costas, Ilse. 1981. "Arbeitskämpfe in der Berliner Elektroindustrie 1905 und 1906." In *Streik: Zur Geschichte des Arbeitskampfes in Deutschland während der Industrialisierung*, ed. Klaus Tenfelde and Heinrich Volkmann. Munich: Beck.

Daalder, Hans. 1971. "On Building Consociational Nations: The Cases of the Netherlands and Switzerland." *International Social Science Journal* 23: 355–70.

———. 1974. "The Consociational Democracy Theme." *World Politics* 26: 604–21.

Dawley, Alan. 1976. *Class and Community: The Industrial Revolution in Lynn.* Cambridge, Mass.: Harvard University Press.

Deckers, L. 1912. *De Landbouwers van den Noord-Brabantschen zandgrond.* Eindhoven.

Delft, L. G. A. M. van. 1949. *De schoenindustrie in Kaatsheuvel als hoofdmiddel van bestaan tussen de twee wereldoorlogen*. Den Bosch.

Dicken, Peter. 1986. *Global Shift: Industrial Change in a Turbulent World*. London: Chapman.

Directie van de Arbeid. 1909. *Gedwongen winkelnering*. The Hague.

———. 1911. *Onderzoekingen naar de toestanden in de Nederlandsche huisindustrie*. The Hague. Dl.II.

Dirks, Nicholas, Geoff Eley, and Sherry Ortner, eds. 1994. *Culture/Power/History: A Reader in Contemporary Social Theory*. Princeton: Princeton University Press.

Donker, W. N.d. *Gedenkboek voor de schoen- en lederindustrie*. Waalwijk.

Donzelot, Jacques. 1977. *La Police des Familles*. Paris: Gallimard.

Douglas, Mary. 1975. "The Self-Completing Animal." *Times Literary Supplement* 8: 886–87.

Drenth, Annemieke van. 1991. *De zorg om het Philipsmeisje: Fabrieksmeisjes in de elektrotechnische industrie in Eindhoven, 1900–1960*. Zutphen: Walburg Pers.

Dunk, H. W. von der, et al. 1986. *Wederopbouw, Welvaart en Onrust: Nederland in de jaren vijftig en zestig*. Houten: De Haan.

Dutton, H. I., and J. E. King. 1981. *Ten Percent and No Surrender: The Preston Strike, 1853–1854*. Cambridge: Cambridge University Press.

Edsforth, Ronald. 1987. *Class Conflict and Cultural Consensus: The Making of a Mass Consumer Society in Flint, Michigan*. New Brunswick: Rutgers University Press.

Eerenbeemt, H. F. J. M. van den. 1970. "Ideën rond 1900 van katholieken in Nederland over een reconstructie der maatschappij." *Sociale Wetenschappen*, no. 13: 257–84.

———. 1977. *Ontwikkelingslijnen en scharnierpunten in het Brabants industrieel bedrijf, 1777–1914*. Tilburg: Stichting Zuidelijk Historisch Contact.

Eley, Geoff. 1989. "Labor History, Social History, Alltagsgeschichte: Experience, Culture, and the Politics of the Everyday." *Journal of Modern History* 61: 297–343.

———. 1990. "Edward Thompson, Social History and Political Culture: The Making of a Working-class Public, 1780–1850." In *E. P. Thompson: Critical Perspectives*, ed. Harvey Kaye and Keith McClelland. London: Polity Press.

———. 1994. "Nations, Publics, and Political Cultures: Placing Habermas in the Nineteenth Century." In Dirks et al., eds., *Power/Culture/History*, 297–336.

Elias, Norbert. 1939. *Über den Prozess der Zivilisation: Soziogenetische und Psychogenetische Untersuchungen*. 2 vols. Frankfurt: Suhrkamp.

———. 1969. *Die höfische Gesellschaft: Eine Untersuchung zur Soziologie des Königtums und der höfischen Aristokratie*. Frankfurt: Suhrkamp.

———. 1971. *Wat is Sociologie?* Utrecht: Het Spectrum. Orig.: *Was ist Soziologie?* Munich: Juventa Verlag, 1970.

Elster, Jon. 1985. *Making Sense of Marx*. Cambridge: Cambridge University Press.

———. 1989. *Nuts and Bolts for the Social Sciences*. Cambridge: Cambridge University Press.

Fainstein, Susan, Ian Gordon, and Michael Harloe, eds. 1992. *Divided Cities: New York and London in the Contemporary World*. Oxford: Basil Blackwell.

Fantasia, Rick. 1988. *Cultures of Solidarity: Consciousness, Action, and Contemporary American Workers.* Berkeley: University of California Press.

Fendt, Franz. 1936. *Der ungelernte Industriearbeiter.* Munich.

Foster, John. 1974. *Class Struggle and the Industrial Revolution: Early Industrial Capitalism in Three English Towns.* London: Methuen.

———. 1985. "The Declassing of Language." *New Left Review* 150: 29–45.

Fuentes, A., and B. Ehrenreich. 1983. *Women in the Global Factory.* Boston: South End Press.

Gastelaars, Marja. 1985. *Een geregeld leven: Sociologie en sociale politiek in Nederland, 1925–1968.* Amsterdam: SUA.

Gaventa, John. 1980. *Power and Powerlessness: Quiescence and Rebellion in an Appalachian Valley.* Urbana: University of Illinois Press.

Geary, Dick. 1981. *European Labour Protest, 1848–1939.* London: Methuen.

Geertz, Clifford. 1973. *The Interpretation of Cultures.* New York: Basic Books.

Giddens, A., and G. Mackenzie, eds. 1982. *Social Class and the Division of Labour.* Cambridge: Cambridge University Press.

Giddens, Anthony. 1982. "Power, the Dialectic of Control and Class Structuration." In *Social Class and the Division of Labour*, ed. A. Giddens and G. Mackenzie. Cambridge: Cambridge University Press.

———. 1984. *The Constitution of Society.* Cambridge: Polity Press.

Giebels, H. 1980. "De Eendracht en het ontstaan van de SDAP-afdeling in Eindhoven, 1897–1904." In *Jaarboek voor de geschiedenis van socialisme en arbeidersbeweging in Nederland.* Nijmegen: SUN.

Gladdish, Ken. 1991. *Governing from the Centre: Politics and Policy-Making in the Netherlands.* London and The Hague: Hurst / SDU.

Godelier, Maurice. 1986. *The Mental and the Material.* London: Verso.

Goody, Jack. 1992. "Culture and Its Boundaries: A European View." *Social Anthropology* 1, no. 1: 9–33.

Gordon, Linda. 1993. *Contention* 2: 157–87.

Goudsblom, Johan. 1977. *Sociology in the Balance.* Oxford: Oxford University Press.

Goudsblom, Johan, E. L. Jones, and S. Mennel, eds. 1989. *Human History and Social Process.* Exeter: University of Exeter Press.

Graaf, A. de. 1950. "De industrie." In *De Nederlandse volkshuishouding tussen twee wereldoorlogen.* Utrecht: Het Spectrum.

Gramsci, Antonio. 1971. *Selections from The Prison Notebooks.* Edited and translated by Q. Hoare and G. Smith. New York: International Publishers.

Hajnal, John. 1965. "European Marriage Patterns in Perspective." In *Population in History*, ed. D. Glass. London: Edward Arnold.

Hanagan, Michael. 1981. *The Logic of Solidarity: Artisans and Industrial Workers in Three French Towns, 1871–1914.* Urbana: University of Illinois Press.

———. 1988. "Solidary Logics: Introduction." *Theory and Society* 17: 309–27.

———. 1989. *Nascent Proletarians: Class Formation in Post-Revolutionary France.* Oxford: Basil Blackwell.

———. 1993. "For Reconstruction in Labor History." In *Rethinking Labor History: Essays on Discourse and Class Analysis*, ed. L. Berlanstein. Urbana: University of Illinois Press.

Hareven, Tamara. 1982. *Family Time and Industrial Time*. London.

Harmsen, Ger, Jos Perry, and Floor van Gelder. 1980. *Mensenwerk: Industriële vakbonden op weg naar eenheid*. Baarn: Ambo.

Harvey, David. 1985a. *Consciousness and the Urban Experience*. Baltimore: Johns Hopkins University Press.

——. 1985b. *The Urbanization of Capital*. Baltimore: Johns Hopkins University Press.

——. 1989. *The Urban Experience*. Baltimore: Johns Hopkins University Press.

Heek, F. van. 1954. *Het geboorteniveau der Nederlandse roomskatholieken: Een demografisch sociologische studie van een geëmancipeerde minderheidsgroep*. Leiden.

Heerding, A. 1980. *Geschiedenis van de N.V. Philips' Gloeilampen Fabrieken*, vol. 1. Leiden: Martinus Nijhoff.

——. 1986. *Een onderneming van vele markten thuis: Geschiedenis van de Philips gloeilampenfabrieken*, vol. 2. Leiden: Martinus Nijhoff.

Heerma van Voss, L., and F. van Holthoon, eds. 1988. *Working Class and Popular Culture*. Amsterdam: International Institute for Social History.

Hilton, Rodney. 1973. *Bond Men Made Free*. London: Methuen.

Hobsbawm, Eric. 1984. *Workers, Worlds of Labor*. New York: Pantheon.

Hobsbawm, Eric, and Joan Scott. 1984. "Political Shoemakers." In *Workers, Worlds of Labor*, ed. Eric Hobsbawm. New York: Pantheon.

Hofstee, E. W. 1962. "De groei van de Nederlandse bevolking. Drift en koers." In *Drift en koers: Een halve eeuw sociale verandering in Nederland*, ed. A. den Hollander. Assen: van Gorcum.

——. 1981. *Korte demografische geschiedenis van Nederland van 1800 tot heden*. Haarlem: Fibula van Dishoeck.

Hohenberg, Paul, and Lynn Lees. 1985. *The Making of Urban Europe, 1000–1950*. Cambridge: Harvard University Press.

Holmes, Douglas R., and Jean Quataert. 1986. "An Approach to Modern Labor: Worker Peasantries in Historic Saxony and the Friuli Region over Three Centuries." *Comparative Studies in Society and History* 28: 191–216.

Holmes, Douglas. 1989. *Cultural Disenchantments: Worker Peasantries in Northeast Italy*. Princeton: Princeton University Press.

Huijbrechts, Marinus. 1987. "Het verloren paradijs verlaten: Een rondreis door een vervlogen verleden." In *De oplossing van Brabant: Essays en interviews ter gelegenheid van het veertig jarige bestaan van het Provinciaal Opbouworgaan Noord-Brabant (1947–1987)*, ed. G. Kruis et al. Tilburg: Provinciaal Opbouworgaan Noord-Brabant.

Hunt, Lynn, ed. 1989. *The New Cultural History*. Berkeley: University of California Press.

Hunt, Lynn. 1984. "Charles Tilly's Collective Action." In *Vision and Method in Historical Sociology*, ed. Theda Skocpol. Cambridge: Cambridge University Press.

International Labor Organization [ILO]. 1932. *Les Usines Philips*. Geneva: ILO.

Jansen, C. 1981. *60 jaar Philips de Jongh Ontspanningsfonds*. Eindhoven: Philips de Jongh Ontspanningsfonds.

Jansen, Gerrit H. 1976. *De eeuwige kroeg: Hoofdstukken uit de geschiedenis van het openbaar lokaal*. Meppel: Boom.

———. 1987. *Een roes van vrijheid: Kermis in Nederland.* Meppel: Boom.

Jay, Martin. 1984. *Marxism and Totality.* Berkeley: University of California Press.

Jessop, Bob. 1990. "Regulation Theories in Retrospect and Prospect." *Economy and Society* 19, no. 2: 216.

Johnson, Richard. 1979. "Three Problematics: Elements of a Theory of Working-Class Culture." In *Working-Class Culture,* ed. J. Clarke, C. Critcher, and R. Johnson. London: Hutchinson.

Jonge, J. A. de. 1969. *De industrialisering in Nederland tussen 1850 en 1914.* Nijmegen: Sun.

Joyce, Patrick. 1980. *Work, Society, and Politics: The Culture of the Factory in Later Victorian England.* New Brunswick: Rutgers University Press.

———. 1984a. "Labour, Capital, and Compromise: A Response to Richard Price." *Social History* 9, no. 1: 67–76.

———. 1984b. "Languages of Reciprocity and Conflict." *Social History* 9, no. 2: 225–31.

———. 1987. *The Historical Meanings of Work.* Cambridge: Cambridge University Press.

———. 1991. *Visions of the People.* Cambridge: Cambridge University Press.

Kalb, Don. 1988. *De anatomie van katholiek schoenmakers protest: Proletarisering, arbeiderskultuur en katholieke hegemonie in Midden-Brabant, 1880–1918.* M.A. thesis, Catholic University of Nymegen.

———. 1991. "Moral Production, Class Capacities, and Communal Commotion: An Illustration from Central Brabant Shoemaking." *Social History* 16: 279–99.

———. 1993. "Frameworks of Culture and Class in Historical Research." *Theory and Society* 22: 513–537.

———. 1994. "On Class, the Logic of Solidarity, and the Civilizing Process: Workers, Priests, and Alcohol in Dutch Shoemaking Communities, 1900–1920." *Social Science History* 18, no. 1: 127–52.

Kalb, Don, and Jack Burgers. 1991. "Mensen van glas: Een reportage over de laatste resten van het lampenproletariaat in de Eindhovense wijk Drents Dorp." *Intermediair* 27, no. 21: 22–31.

Kalb, Don, and Sytze Kingma, eds. 1991. *Fragmenten van Vermaak: Macht en Plezier in Moderniserend Nederland.* Amsterdam: Rodopi.

Kalb, Don, Herman Tak, and Hans Marks, eds. 1996. "Historical Anthropology: The Unwaged Debate." *Focaal,* no. 26 / 27.

Katz, Michael B. 1989. *The Undeserving Poor: From the War on Poverty to the War on Welfare.* New York: Pantheon Books.

Katznelson, Ira. 1986. "Working Class Formation: Constructing Cases and Comparisons." In *Working Class Formation: Nineteenth-Century Patterns in Western Europe and the United States,* ed. Katznelson and Zolberg. Princeton: Princeton University Press.

———. 1992. *Marxism and the City.* Oxford: Clarendon Press.

Katznelson, Ira, and Ari Zolberg, eds. 1986. *Working Class Formation: Nineteenth-Century Patterns in Western Europe and the United States.* Princeton: Princeton University Press.

Kaye, Harvey J. 1991. *The Powers of the Past*. Minneapolis: University of Minnesota Press.

Kaye, Harvey J., and Keith McClelland, eds. 1990. *E. P. Thompson: Critical Perspectives*. Cambridge: Polity Press.

Keesing, Roger. 1974. "Theories of culture." *Annual Review of Anthropology* 3: 73–97.

———. 1989. "Theories of Culture Revisited." Paper presented at annual meeting of American Anthropological Association, Washington, D.C., 1989.

Killminster, Richard. 1991. "Evaluating Elias." *Theory, Culture, and Society* 8, no. 2: 165–77.

Kleyngeld, A. 1976. "Een staking in historisch perspektief." M.A. thesis, Catholic University of Brabant, Tilburg.

Knuvelder, Gerard. 1929. *Bezuiden de Moerdijk: Problemen en verschijnselen*. Tilburg.

———. 1930. *Vanuit wingewesten: Een sociografie van het Zuiden*. Hilversum.

Kriedte, Peter, Jürgen Schlumbohm, and Hans Medick. 1977. *Industrialisierung vor der Industrialisierung: Gewerbliche Warenproduktion auf dem Land in der Formationsperiode des Kapitalismus*. Göttingen: van den Hoeck und Ruprecht. English trans.: *Industrialisation before Industrialisation*, ed. Peter Kriedte. 1981. Cambridge: Cambridge University Press.

———. 1992. "Sozialgeschichte in der Erweiterung-Proto-Industrialisierung in der Verengung?" *Geschichte und Gesellschaft* 18, no. 1: 78–87, and no. 2: 231–56.

Krol, Jan. 1981. "Brood en Spelen." M.A. thesis, Catholic University of Nijmegen.

Kuiper, C. J. 1953. *Uit het Rijk van de Arbeid: Onstaan, groei en werk van de katholieke arbeidersbeweging in Nederland*. 3 vols. Utrecht.

Lamphere, Louise. 1987. *From Working Daughters to Working Mothers: Immigrant Women in a New England Industrial Community*. Ithaca: Cornell University Press.

Larrain, Jorge. 1986. *A Reconstruction of Historical Materialism*. London: Allen and Unwin.

Levi, Giovanni. 1991. "On Microhistory." In *New Perspectives on Historical Writing*, ed. Peter Burke. University Park: Pennsylvania State University Press.

Levine, David. 1977. *Family Formation in an Age of Nascent Capitalism*. Cambridge: Cambridge University Press.

Levine, David, ed. 1984. *Proletarianization and Family History*. Orlando: Academic Press.

———. 1987. *Reproducing Families: The Political Economy of English Population History*. Cambridge: Cambridge University Press.

Lijphart, Arend. 1968. *Verzuiling, pacificatie en kentering in de Nederlandse politiek*. Amsterdam: de Bussy.

———. 1968. *The Politics of Accommodation: Pluralism and Democracy in the Netherlands*. Berkeley: University of California Press.

Lloyd, Christopher. 1993. *The Structures of History*. Oxford: Basil Blackwell.

Logan, John, and Harvey Molotch. 1987. *Urban Fortunes: The Political Economy of Place*. Berkeley: University of California Press.

Logan, J. R., and T. Swanstrom. 1990. *Beyond the City Limits: Urban Policy and*

Economic Restructuring in Comparative Perspective. Philadelphia: Temple University Press.

Lowie, Robert. 1937. *The History of Ethnological Theory*. New York: Reinhart.

Lucas, Erhard. 1976. *Arbeiterradikalismus: Zwei Formen von Radikalismus in der deutschen Arbeiterbewegung*. Frankfurt: Verlag Roter Stern.

Lüdtke, Alf. 1989. *Alltagsgeschichte: Zur Rekonstruktion historischer Erfahrungen und Lebensweisen*. Frankfurt: Campus Verlag.

———. 1992. "Practising Eigensinn: Workers beyond Domination and Resistance." *Focaal* (special issue on "Interpretations of Class," ed. Don Kalb) 19: 16–36.

———. 1993. *Eigensinn: Fabrikalltag, Arbeitererfahrungen und Politik vom Kaiserreich bis in den Faschismus*. Hamburg: Ergebnisse Verlag.

Lüdtke, Alf, ed. 1991. *Herrschaft als soziale Praxis: Historische und Sozial-anthropologische Studien*. Göttingen: Vandenhoeck und Ruprecht.

Luykx, Paul, and N. Bootsma. 1987. *De laatste tijd: Geschiedschrijving van Nederland in de 20e eeuw*. Amsterdam: Het Spectrum.

Maas, H. H. J. 1946. *Onder de gloeilamp*. Laren: A. G. Schoonderbeek.

Mandemakers, K. 1985. "De ontwikkeling van de faktor arbeid binnen de Nederlandse schoennijverheid, 1860–1910," *Jaarboek voor de geschiedenis van Bedrijf en Techniek* 2: 104–26.

Mandemakers, K., and J. van Meeuwen. 1983. *Industrial Modernization and Social Developments in the Centre of the Dutch Shoe Industry: Central Noord-Brabant, 1890–1930*. Rotterdam: Erasmus University.

Marshall, Gordon, et al. 1988. *Social Class in Modern Britain*. London: Hutchinson.

Massey, Doreen. 1984. *Spatial Divisions of Labour*. London: Macmillan.

Medick, Hans. 1976. "The Proto-industrial Family Economy: The Structural Function of Household and Family during the Transition from Peasant to Industrial Capitalism." *Social History* 1: 291–315.

Meeuwen, J. van. 1981. *Zoo rood als de roodste socialisten*. Amsterdam: SUA.

Mendels, Franklin. 1981. "Agriculture and Peasant Industry in Eighteenth-century Flanders." In *Industrialisation before Industrialisation*, ed. Peter Kriedte. Cambridge: Cambridge University Press.

Merriman, John, ed. 1979. *Consciousness and Class Experience in Nineteenth-Century Europe*. New York: Holmes and Meier.

Messing, F. A. M. 1980. *Het ontstaan van Groot Eindhoven, 1890–1920*. Tilburg: Stichting Zuidelijk Historisch Contact.

Metze, Marcel. 1991. *Kortsluiting: Hoe Philips zijn talenten verspilde*. Nijmegen: Sun.

Meurkens, Peter. 1984. *Bevolking, Economie en Cultuur van het Oude Kempenland*. Bergeijk: Eicha.

———. 1989. "Kinderrijk en katholiek: De stijging van de huwelijksvruchtbaarheid in het Kempenland, 1840–1920." In *Werk, kerk en bed in Brabant*, ed. G. van den Brink. 's Hertogenbosch: Stichting Brabantse Regionale Geschiedschrijving.

Meyer, Stephen. 1981. *The Five-Dollar Day: Labor Management and Social Control in the Ford Motor Company, 1908–1921*. Albany: State University of New York Press.

Milkman, R. 1987. *Gender at Work: The Dynamics of Job Segregation by Sex during World War II*. Urbana: University of Illinois Press.

Miller, Richard. 1984. *Analyzing Marx: Morality, Power, and History*. Princeton: Princeton University Press.

Minge-Kalman, Wanda. 1978. "Household Economy during the Peasant to Worker Transition in the Swiss Alps." *Ethnology* 17: 183–97.

Mitchell, Timothy. 1990. "Everyday Metaphors of Power." *Theory and Society* 19, no. 5: 545–78.

Montgomery, David. 1979. *Workers' Control in America: Studies in the History of Work, Technology, and Labor Struggles*. Cambridge: Cambridge University Press.

Moore, Barrington, Jr. 1978. *Injustice: The Social Bases of Obedience and Revolt*. New York: M. E. Sharpe.

Mumford, Lewis. 1938. *The Culture of Cities*. New York: Harcourt, Brace.

Moree, Marjolein. 1986. "Vrouwen en arbeidsmarktbeleid 1950–1985." In K. Schuyt, *De verdeelde samenleving: Een inleiding in de ontwikkeling van de Nederlandse verzorgingsstaat*. Leiden: Stenfert Kroese.

Nash, June. 1979. *We Eat the Mines and the Mines Eat Us*. New York: Columbia University Press.

———. 1989. *From Tank Town to High Tech: The Clash of Community and Industrial Cycles*. Albany: State University of New York Press.

Newby, H. 1979. *The Deferential Worker*. Harmondsworth: Penguin.

Newman, Katherine. 1988. *Falling from Grace: The Experience of Downward Mobility in the American Middle Class*. New York: Vintage Books.

———. 1993. *Declining Fortunes: The Withering of the American Dream*. New York: Basic Books.

Niethammer, Lutz, et al., eds. 1983. "Die Jahre weiss man nicht, wo man die heute hinsetzen soll." In *Faschismus Erfahrungen im Ruhrgebiet*. Berlin: Dietz Verlag.

———. 1983. "Hinterher merkt man, dass es richtig war dass es Schiefgegangen ist." In *Nachkriegserfahrungen im Ruhrgebiet*. Berlin: Dietz Verlag.

———. 1985. "Wir kriegen jetzt andere Zeiten." In *Auf der Suche nach der Erfahrung des Volkes in Nachfaschistischen Ländern*. Berlin: Dietz Verlag.

Nolens, W. 1965. "Van klopsteen tot zwikmachine: Een beschouwing over de industriële revolutie in de Noord-Brabantse schoenindustrie." Tilburg, unpublished manuscript.

Noordam, D. J. 1987. "De demografische ontwikkeling in West-Europa van omstreeks 1750 tot 1985." In *Van agrarische samenleving naar verzorginsstaat*, ed. H. A. Diederiks et al. Groningen: Wolters-Noordhof.

Oorschot, Jan van. 1982. *Eindhoven, een samenleving in verandering*, 2 vols. Eindhoven: gemeente Eindhoven.

Ortner, Sherry. 1984. "Theory in Anthropology since the Sixties." *Comparative Studies in Society and History* 26, no. 1: 126–66.

Otten, A. 1987. *Volkshuisvesting in Eindhoven*. Zeist: Vonk.

———. 1991. *Philips woningbouw, 1900–1990*. Zaltbommel: Europese Bibliotheek.

Oudheusden, Jan van, and Gerard Trienekens. 1993. *Een pront wijf, een mager paard en een zoon op het seminarie: Aanzetten tot een integrale geschiedschrijving van Oostelijk Noord-Brabant*. 's Hertogenbosch: Stichting Brabantse Regionale Geschiedschrijving.

Palmer, Brian. 1990. *Descent into Discourse: The Reification of Language and the Writing of Social History*. Philadelphia: Temple University Press.

Pels, Dick. 1991. "Elias and the Politics of Theory." *Theory, Culture, and Society* 8: 177–83.

Perry, Jos. 1983. *Roomsche kinine tegen roode koorts: Arbeidersbeweging en katholieke kerk in Maastricht, 1880–1920*. Amsterdam: SUA.

Philips, Frits. 1976. *45 jaar met Philips*. Rotterdam: Ad Donker.

Piore, M., and C. Sabel. 1984. *The Second Industrial Divide*. New York: Basic Books.

Pot, Frank. 1988. *Zeggenschap over beloningssystemen, 1850–1987*. Leiden: TNO.

Pred, Allan. 1990. *Making Histories and Constructing Human Geographies: The Local Transformation of Practice, Power Relations, and Consciousness*. Boulder: Westview Press.

Puijenbroek, F. J. M. van. 1985. *Beginnen in Eindhoven*. Eindhoven: Van Pierre.

Ramakers, J., and H. Righart. 1987. "Het katholicisme." In P. Luykx and N. Bootsma, *De laatste tijd*. Amsterdam: Het Spectrum.

Ranciere, Jacques. 1989. *The Nights of Labor: The Worker's Dream in Nineteenth-Century France*. Philadelphia: Temple University Press.

Rebell, Herman. 1989. "Cultural Hegemony and Class Experience: A Critical Reading of Recent Ethnological-historical Approaches." *American Ethnologist* 16, no. 1: 117–36 and no. 2: 350–65.

Reddy, William. 1984. *The Rise of Market Culture: The Textile Trade and French Society, 1750–1900*. Cambridge: Cambridge University Press.

———. 1987. *Money and Liberty in Modern Europe: A Critique of Historical Understanding*. Cambridge: Cambridge University Press.

Redfield, Robert. 1930. *Tepoztlan, a Mexican Village: A Study of Folk Life*. Chicago: Chicago University Press.

Regt, Ali de. 1984. *Arbeidersgezinnen en beschavingsarbeid: Ontwikkelingen in Nederland, 1870–1940*. Meppel: Boom.

Rehe, Carl. 1908. *Die deutsche Schuhgrossindustrie*. Jena.

Reid, Donald. 1985. *The Miners of Decazeville: A Genealogy of Deindustrialisation*. Cambridge: Cambridge University Press.

Reinalda, Bob. 1981. *Bedienden georganiseerd: Ontstaan en ontwikkeling van de vakbeweging van handels- en kantoorbedienden in Nederland van het eerste begin tot halverwege de tweede wereldoorlog*. Nijmegen: Sun.

Righart, Hans. 1986. *De katholieke zuil in Europa: Het ontstaan van verzuiling onder katholieken in Oostenrijk, Zwitserland, Belgie en Nederland*. Meppel: Boom.

Roes, Jan, ed. 1985. *Katholieke arbeidersbeweging: Studies over KAB en NKV in de economische en politieke ontwikkeling van Nederland na 1945*. Baarn: Ambo.

Roland Holst, Henriëtte. 1977. *Kapitaal en Arbeid in Nederland*. 2 vols. Nijmegen: Sun.

Roseberry, William. 1989. *Anthropologies and Histories: Essays in Culture, History, and Political Economy*. New Brunswick: Rutgers University Press.

Roth, Karl Heinz. 1974. *Die andere Arbeiterbewegung*. Munich.

Sabel, Charles, and Jonathan Zeitlin. 1985. "Historical Alternatives to Mass Production: Politics, Markets, and Technology in Nineteenth-Century Industrialisation." *Past and Present* 108: 133–76.

Samuel, Raphael. 1977. "Workshop of the World: Steam Power and Hand Technology in Mid-Victorian Britain." *History Workshop* 3: 7–72.

Sanders, Ben, and Gertjan de Groot. 1988. "Without Hope of Improvement: Casual Laborers and Bourgeois Reformers in Amsterdam, 1850–1920." In *Working Class and Popular Culture*, ed. L. Heerma van Voss and F. v. Holthoon. Amsterdam: International Institute for Social History.

Savage, Mike. 1994. "Class Analysis and Its Futures." *Sociological Review* 42, no. 3: 531–48.

Sayer, Derek. 1987. *The Violence of Abstraction*. Oxford: Basil Blackwell.

Schatz, Ronald. 1983. *The Electrical Workers: A History of Labor at General Electric and Westinghouse, 1923–1960*. Urbana: University of Illinois Press.

Schneider, Jane, and Rayna Rapp, eds. 1995. *Articulating Hidden Histories: Exploring the Influence of Eric R. Wolf*. Berkeley: University of California Press.

Schröder, W. H. 1976. *Arbeitergeschichte und Arbeiterbewegung: Industriearbeit und Organisationsverhalten im 19. und frühen 20. Jahrhundert*. Frankfurt: Campus Verlag.

Scott, Allan. 1988. *Metropolis: From the Division of Labor to Urban Form*. Berkeley: University of California Press.

Scott, James. 1985. *Weapons of the Weak: Everyday Forms of Peasant Resistance*. New Haven: Yale University Press.

———. 1990. *Domination and the Arts of Resistance: Hidden Transcripts*. New Haven: Yale University Press.

Scott, Joan. 1974. *The Glassworkers of Carmaux*. Cambridge, Mass.: Harvard University Press.

———. 1988. *Gender and the Politics of History*. New York: Basic Books.

Scott, Joan, and Louise Tilly. 1975. "Women's Work and the Family in Nineteenth-Century Europe." *Comparative Studies in Society and History* 17, no. 1: 36–64.

Scott, John, and Allan Storper. 1986. *Production, Work, Territory: The Geographical Anatomy of Industrial Capitalism*. Boston: Allen and Unwin.

Selby, H., A. Murphy, and A. Lorenzen. 1990. *The Mexican Urban Household: Organizing for Self-Defense*. Austin: University of Texas Press.

Sewell, William. 1980. *Work and Revolution in France: The Language of Labor from the Old Regime to 1848*. Cambridge: Cambridge University Press.

Shorter, Edward. 1975. *The Making of the Modern Family*. New York: Basic Books.

Sider, Gerald. 1986. *Culture and Class in Anthropology and History: A Newfoundland Illustration*. Cambridge: Cambridge University Press.

Simons, M. 1960. *Tussen turf en televisie: Acculturatieproblemen van een binnenlandse migrantengroep gedurende een aantal generaties*. Assen: van Gorcum.

Skocpol, Theda, ed. 1984. *Vision and Method in Historical Sociology*. Cambridge: Cambridge University Press.

———. 1984. "Emerging Agendas and Recurrent Strategies in Historical Sociology." In *Vision and Method in Historical Sociology*, ed. Theda Skocpol. Cambridge: Cambridge University Press.

Sluyterman, K. 1983. *Ondernemen in sigaren: Analyse van bedrijfsbeleid in vijf Nederlandse sigarenfabrieken in de perioden 1856–1865 en 1925–1934*. Tilburg: Stichting Zuidelijk Historisch Contact.

Smelser, Neil. 1959. *Social Change in the Industrial Revolution.* Chicago: Chicago University Press.

Smith, M. P., and Joe Feagin, eds. 1987. *The Capitalist City: Global Restructuring and Community Politics.* Oxford: Basil Blackwell.

Smith, Gavin. 1989. *Livelihood and Resistance: Peasants and the Politics of Law in Peru.* Berkeley: University of California Press.

Soja, Edward. 1989. *Postmodern Geographies: The Reassertion of Space in Critical Social Theory.* London: Verso.

Stedman Jones, Gareth. 1983. *Languages of Class: Studies in English Working Class History, 1832–1982.* Cambridge: Cambridge University Press.

Steen, M. van der. 1977. *Die Annie ben ik.* Baarn.

Steinberg, Marc. 1989. "The Role of Discourse in the Making of Working-class Consciousness in the Early Nineteenth Century." Paper presented at the ASA Meeting, San Francisco.

———. 1991. "The Re-making of the English Working Class?" *Theory and Society* 20, no. 2: 171–97.

Steward, Julian, et al. 1956. *The People of Puerto Rico.* Urbana: University of Illinois Press.

Stinchcombe, Arthur. 1983. *Economic Sociology.* New York: Academic Press.

Stoop, Sjef. n.d. "Fordism in the Netherlands? The Case of Philips: A Critical Test of the Concept of Fordism." Unpublished paper, Catholic University of Nijmegen.

———. 1992. *De sociale fabriek: Sociale politiek bij Philips Eindhoven, Bayer Leverkusen en Hoogovens Ijmuiden.* Leiden: Stenfert Kroese.

Storper, Michael, and Richard Walker. 1989. *The Capitalist Imperative: Territory, Technology, and Industrial Growth.* Oxford: Basil Blackwell.

Stuurman, Siep. 1983. *Verzuiling, Kapitalisme en Patriarchaat: Aspecten van de ontwikkeling van de moderne staat in Nederland.* Nijmegen: Sun.

Swaan, Abram de. 1991. *In Care of the State: Health Care, Education, and Welfare in Europe and the USA during the Modern Era.* London: Polity Press.

Taussig, Michael. 1980. *The Devil and Commodity Fetishism in South America.* Chapel Hill: University of North Carolina Press.

Ter Meulen, R., and W. van Hoorn. 1981/82. "Psychotechniek en menselijke verhoudingen." *Grafiet* 1: 106–56.

Teulings, Ad. 1976. *Philips: Geschiedenis en praktijk van een wereldconcern.* Amsterdam: Van Gennep.

Therborn, Goran. 1983. "Why Some Classes Are More Successful Than Others." *New Left Review* 138: 37–55.

Thompson, Edward P. 1963. *The Making of the English Working Class.* New York: Vintage.

———. 1971. "The Moral Economy of the English Crowd in the Eighteenth Century." *Past and Present* 50 (1971): 76–136.

———. 1974. "Patrician Society, Plebeian Culture." *Journal of Social History* (1974): 382–405.

———. 1976. *Whigs and Hunters.* New York: Pantheon Books.

———. 1978a. "Eighteenth-century English Society: Class Struggle without Class?" *Social History* 3, no. 2 (1978): 133–65.

———. 1978b. *The Poverty of Theory and Other Essays.* London: Merlin.

Thompson, Paul. 1988. *The Voice of the Past.* 2nd ed. Oxford: Oxford University Press.

Tijn, Th. van. 1977. "De algemene Nederlandsche Diamantbewerkersbond: Een succes en zijn verklaring." In *Economische ontwikkeling en sociale emancipatie,* ed. P. Geurts and F. Messing. The Hague.

Tilly, Charles. 1981. *As Sociology meets History.* New York: Academic Press.

———. 1984a. *Big Structures, Large Processes, Huge Comparisons.* New York: Russell Sage Foundation.

———. 1984b. "Demographic Origins of the European Proletariat." In *Proletarianization and Family History,* ed. David Levine. Orlando: Academic Press.

———. 1986. *The Contentious French.* Cambridge, Mass.: Harvard University Press.

———. 1988. "Solidary Logics: Conclusion." *Theory and Society* 17: 451–58.

Tilly, Louise. 1992. *Politics and Class in Milan, 1881–1901.* Oxford: Oxford University Press.

Tilly, Louise, and Joan Scott. 1978. *Women, Work, and Family.* New York: Basic Books.

Valentine, Daniel E. 1991. *Is There a Counterpoint to Culture?* Amsterdam: Center for Asian Studies.

Velthoven, H. van. 1963. *Noord-Brabant op weg naar groei en welvaart, 1850–1920.* Nijmegen.

Verberne, L. G. J. 1947. *Noord-Brabant in de negentiende eeuw tot omstreeks 1870: De sociaal-economische structuur.* Nijmegen.

Verhoeven, Cornelis. 1980. *Als een dief in de nacht.* Baarn: Ambo.

Verwey Jonker, Hilda. 1943. *Lage Inkomens.* Assen: Van Gorcum.

Vos, R. 1982. *Een bedrijfsarts in het bedrijf: G.C.E. Burger als "fabrieksarts" van de N.V. Philips Gloeilampenfabrieken, 1928–1938.* Groningen: ISMW-rapport 82-SK-12.

Vriend, J. J. n.d. *Bouwen als sociale daad: 50 jaar woningbouw Philips.* Eindhoven: Philips.

Waerden, T. van der. 1911. *Geschooldheid en techniek.* Delft: Dissertatie.

Warde, Alan. 1988. "Industrial Restructuring, Local Politics, and the Reproduction of Labour Power: Some Theoretical Considerations." *Society and Space* 6: 75–95.

———. 1989. "Conditions of Dependence: Working Class Quiescence in Lancaster in the Twentieth Century." *Lancaster Regionalism Group, Working paper 30.* Lancaster: University of Lancaster.

Waters, Chris. 1990. *British Socialists and the Politics of Popular Culture, 1884–1914.* Manchester: Manchester University Press.

Wentholt, G. J. M. 1984. *Een arbeidersbeweging en haar priesters, het einde van een relatie: Theologische vooronderstellingen en pastorale bedoelingen met betrekking tot de katholieke arbeidersbeweging in Nederland.* Nijmegen: KDC.

Williams, C., et al. 1987. "The end of mass production?" *Economy and Society* 16, no. 3: 405–39.

Williams, Raymond. 1977. *Marxism and Literature.* Oxford: Oxford University Press.

Windmuller, J., and C. de Galan. 1969. *Labor Relations in the Netherlands.* Ithaca: Cornell University Press.

Wolf, Eric. 1969. *Peasant Wars of the Twentieth Century.* New York: Harper and Row.

———. 1982. *Europe and the People without History.* Berkeley: University of California Press.

———. 1987. Interview by Jonathan Friedman. *Current Anthropology* 28, no. 1: 107–18.

———. 1990. "Facing Power: Old Insights, New Questions." *American Anthropologist* 92 (1990): 586–96.

Wood, Ellen Meiksins. 1986. *The Retreat from Class.* London: Verso.

Wood, Stephen, ed. 1982. *The Degradation of Work? Skill, Deskilling, and the Labour Process.* London: Heinemann.

Worsley, Peter. 1984. "A Landmark in Anthropology." *American Ethnologist* 11, no. 1: 174.

Wouters, Cas. 1991. *Over Minnen en Sterven.* Amsterdam: van Gennep.

Wright, Erik Olin. 1985. *Classes.* London: Verso.

Zanden, J. van den. 1985. *De economische ontwikkeling van de Nederlandse landbouw in de negentiende eeuw, 1800–1914.* Wageningen.

Zukin, Sharon. 1992. *Landscapes of Power: From Detroit to Disney World.* Berkeley: University of California Press.

Zunz, Oliver. 1982. *The Changing Face of Inequality: Urbanization, Industrialization, and Immigration in Detroit, 1880–1920.* Chicago: University of Chicago Press.

Index

Abbe, H. van, 103
Abbott, Andrew, 8, 262
AEG, 87, 130, 139
Algemene Nederlandse Metaalbe-
werkersbond, 130–131, 133, 135, 149
Aminzade, Ron, 8, 87, 110, 262
Amsterdam, 81, 102, 103, 265
Anthropology, 18, 261; conception of
culture, 19; historical anthropology
of working class identities, 13–15,
17; political economy school, 9; thick
description, 266
Antwerp, 27
Automotive industry, 143, 151, 226

Bakker Schut, F., 160
Bata, 238, 240
Beekman, Piet, 202
Berlanstein, L. R., 10
Berlin, 85, 87, 140
Bodnar, John, 88, 89
Bonebakker, Ernst, 178, 207
Boston, 268, 279
Bourdieu, Pierre, 8, 22, 260
Braun, Rudolf, 33
Braverman, Harry, 88
Breda, 103, 265
Brenner, Robert, 231, 276
Brody, David, 232
•Bruening, E., 111
Burawoy, Michael, 9, 12, 19, 90

Calhoun, Craig, 11
Capitalism, 7–11, 20, 24, 90; capital-

intensive route, 11, 268; and local
life, 90; and social and spatial unevenness, 10–11; trajectories, 84, 260,
263, 266–280; world-system, 92. *See
also* Path dependency; Paths of
accumulation
"Capital-logic" explanations, 7
Catholicism, 27, 84, 118, 137, 165, 234;
Catholic bloc, 44, 126; Catholic girls'
unions in shoemaking, 51; Catholic
labor movement, 28, 37, 39, 44, 50,
65, 83, 110, 129; and corporatism, 48,
126, 271; and demographic expansion, 29; and discourse on factory
production, 54; and employers' organizations, 126; and femininity, 166;
holy days, 75, 127; lampmakers'
guilds, 127, 129; metalworkers'
union, 129, 149, 216; as pillar of authority, 55, 75, 111; reception of, 45,
48, 129; and regional identity, 27; social Catholicism, 24, 28–29, 45, 52,
68, 69, 270; solidarity of, 1, 271;
youth movement, 166
Child labor: in cigarmaking, 102, 103
Children: as asset to employers and
parents, 33; obedience of, 91
Cigarmaking, 31, 82, 95, 101–103, 110,
116, 120, 272; corporatist ordering of,
126
Citizenship within Philips, 155, 204,
207, 211; census of, 210; and internal
labor market, 211; and social cleavages, 208–212

ization of and peasant economy, 94; key dynamic properties, 267; locational advantage, 99; locational disadvantage, 218; proletarianization in, 98; recurrent crises of underurbanization, 272, 274; registered working population, 98; service sector, 98; urban culture, 199; urbanization, 97, 105–107, 111, 142, 155, 197, 202, 277; workers' culture, 116, 243. *See also* Flexible familism

Electrical industries, 143, 151, 152, 163

Elias, Norbert, 60, 62, 77; and markets, 61–62

Embezzlement, 46, 66, 70

Enquête: Dutch government *enquête* on labor of 1880, 264

Essentialism, 1, 4, 84; and homo economicus, 5

Everyday life approach. *See* Micro perspective

Everyday politics, 21–24

Exceptionalism, 24, 26, 84, 270; and demographic transition, 31; and Philips' workers, 83

Exploitation, 234, 260; and love, 243

Factory systems: formation of, 57; work regulations, 41, 51

Family: cohesion of, 193, 194, 208; as collective resource, 188, 191, 195, 252–253; and exploitation, 234; family economy, 100, 145, 166; formation, 91; as labor reserve, 33; multiple-earner families, 91, 164, 214, 223, 232; as unit of labor recruitment, 91; whole family as alternative for young mobile workers, 170

Female labor, 91, 102; feminization of the labor force in manufacturing, 32–33

Fetishism, 5

Fixed capital, 95

Flexibility, 221, 264; flexible labor market and the family, 100, 224; and girls, 32, 135

Flexible familism, 90–91, 137, 154, 214, 228, 267, 272–277; and associated fragmentations, 106, 109, 202; and recurrent crises of urban underinvestment, 272, 274

Flexible manufacturing, 93–138 passim, 153, 200. *See also* Flexible familism

Forced shopping, 113, 119, 274

Ford Corporation, 85, 232, 276; sociological investigations, 226–227

Fordism, 143, 225, 226, 228

Foucault, Michel, 21

Garden cities movement, 157

Gender relations, 50–52, 96, 135, 234, 259–260; Catholic girls' unions, 51; and Catholicism, 166; girls as labor reserve, 32; and production regimes, 145, 146, 224, 234; sex segregation, 164

General Electric, 87, 130, 139, 143, 232

General Motors, 85, 232

Generations: relations between, 51, 52, 165, 166, 224, 234, 244, 259–260

Giddens, Anthony, 8

Glasgow, 103

Godelier, Maurice, 4, 5

Gold standard, 217

Good-Year-Welt technology, 52, 268

Gramsci, Antonio, 20, 230, 259, 280

Haarlem, 31, 93

The Hague, 177, 189

Half-watt lamp, 140

Hanagan, Michael, 63, 87, 110

Harmsen, Ger, 28

Harvey, David, 4, 90

Heerding, A., 130–131, 132

Hegemony, 2, 20–21, 85–86, 118, 165, 214; crisis of, 91, 169–170, 276; and housing, 156, 161, 163

Helmond, 31, 93

Hilton, Rodney, 5

Hilversum, 102

Hobsbawm, Eric, 13, 40, 57

Home work: in cigarmaking, 102; in
textiles, 101
Households: multiple-earner, 91, 229,
245, 273. *See also* Family; Immigrant
families
Housing, 111–113, 116, 139, 147, 154,
156, 160, 170, 204, 232, 246, 273; conflict between Philips and the city,
200; and hegemony, 156, 161, 163;
house supervisors, 208, 209; number
of inhabitants per house, 161; rents,
224

Illness, 147, 161
Immigrant families, 172, 174, 200, 214,
216, 220, 232; and layoffs, 223; selec-
tion of, 171–172. *See also* Philipsism
Industrialization of North Brabant, 27;
and feminization of the workforce,
32; and multiple-earner households,
105
Industrial unions, 147, 149
Informal economy, 70. *See also*
Popular / folk economy
Interest: concept of, 5; relation to
"meaning" and everyday politics, 22
International Labor Office, 206, 152
Intimacy, 243

Joyce, Patrick, 12–13, 87

Kaatsheuvel, 24, 38, 47, 72, 75
Katz, Michael, 205
Katznelson, Ira, 16, 259; four levels of
class, 16
Kriedte, Peter, 33
Kuiper, C., 28

Labor: control of, 130, 132, 134, 135,
144, 147, 151, 156, 160, 163, 219; crisis
of, 146, 154, 169, 227; flexibility and
whole families, 100; labor flexibility,
137, 223
Labor market, 47, 82, 231; labor processes, 52, 54, 69, 77; labor reserve,
33, 99, 107, 195, 214, 228–229, 232; la-

bor turnover, 147, 161, 163, 227; pro-
ductivity of, 147, 218, 220; short
cyclical labor, 163, 172; theory of the
crisis of labor, 215. *See also* Flexible
familism; Philipsism
Lancashire, 4
Larrain, Jorge, 4
Layoffs, 82–83, 131, 213–214, 219, 222,
276; and multiple-earner families,
223
Leerdam, 149, 175
Legitimacy, 44, 46, 58
Leiden, 31, 93
Leisure, 68–72, 139, 190, 206, 246
Liège, 107
Limburg province (Belgium), 82
"Literary turn," 1
Lloyd, Christopher, 8
Locational advantage, 31, 100, 105; and
the family labor reserve, 99
Lock-outs, 121, 122, 128
Lorraine, 89
Lowie, Robert, 20
Lüdtke, Alf, 12, 19, 21; notion of every-
day politics, 21
Lynn, 85

Maas, Henri, 168
Maastricht, 149
MacKay Stitcher, 46
Mandemakers, Kees, 45
Manufacturing: labor-intensive, 90,
100, 214, 265, 276
Markets: regulation, 53, 66, 67, 72, 264;
relations of, 77, 73, 217, 232, 264,
273–274
Marriage: age, 97; frequency of, 94; and
pressures from parental household,
96
Marx, Karl, 4, 5, 280; history and determinism, 6; notion of totality, 5; and
textile industry, 4
Materialist approaches, 61, 77; and
contingency, 6; cultural materialism,
4; and reductionism, 1, 3, 13; relational interpretivism, 261; relational

materialism, 6, 18, 20–21, 23, 259, 261; relational Marxists, 4, 6; and the theory of the civilizing process, 63

Medick, Hans, 33

Meeuwen, Jos van, 45

Mendels, Franklin, 33

Metalwire lamp, 130, 139

Meurkens, Peter, 30

Meyer, Stephen, 227, 228

Micro perspective, 19, 21, 86. *See also* Everyday politics

Mignot, A., 105, 111; and De Block, 102

Miller, Richard, 4

Mode of production, 5, 200, 225

Modernization theory, 83, 84, 244

Moral panic, 165, 169, 215

Narrativist methodologies, 8, 261; and linkages in time and space, 18, 261, 263. *See also* Path-dependency

Nederlandsche Internationale Sigaren-makers en Tabakbewerkersbond, 117

Nederlands Verbond van Vakvere-nigingen, 149

Newby, Howard, 85

New Deal, 232

New York, 140

North Brabant, 1, 24–34; as anomaly to classical theories of modernization, 24, 259; and boundaries between classes, 265; characteristic relation-ships of time and place, 263; classic descriptions of inhabitants, 25; de-mography, 25; and labor-intensive manufacturing, 31; peasant econ-omy, 93; under reformation, 26; rele-vance to Dutch republic, 26; and religion, 25; textile towns, 93; three key properties, 26; urbanization and spatial morphology, 32

Oorschot, J. van, 196

Oss, 169

Otten, Frans, 221

Pahl, Ray, 10

Particularism, 280. *See also* Path-dependency

Paternalism, 125, 139, 153, 165, 166, 169, 234

Path-dependency, 7, 10, 17–18, 90–92,' 261, 277; and key moments in a branching process, 277; multiple and interlinked trajectories, 7, 18; and particularism, 280; relations of time and space versus fixed structural determinations, 8, 261, 262–263; sequence and chronology, 8; trajec-tories of class formation, 8, 17. *See also* Capitalism; Contingency; Nar-rativist methodology

Paths of accumulation (regional), 228, 277; comparison of Eindhoven and Central Brabant, 260, 266–280. *See also* Capitalism

Peasantry: demography and family, 95, 97, 244

Peasant-workers, 33, 95–96, 137

Perry, Jos, 28

Petite bourgeoisie, 49, 56, 57, 77, 94, 112; comparison of Eindhoven and Central Brabant, 113

Petits vicaires, 47, 49, 67, 270, 271

Philips, Anton, 103, 111, 116, 144, 152, 221

Philips, Frederik, 103

Philips, Frits, 239

Philips, Gerard, 111, 128, 130–131

Philips Association for Higher Person-nel, 175

Philips Building Office, 202–203

Philips Corporation, 25, 83, 140, 142, 217; apparatuses factory, 169, 183, 184, 185, 189; commercial depart-ments, 221; employment, 103–104, 141, 213; female workforce, 104, 129, 147; glass factory, 140, 148, 150; in-dustrial school for boys, 180, 183, 204; labor force, 141; machine shop / technical departments, 130, 132, 135, 140, 148, 151, 175, 215, 221–222;

State formation, 62
Stedman Jones, Gareth, 40, 87, 109
Steinberg, Marc, 110
Stinchcombe, Arthur, 4
Stoop, Sjef, 143
Storytellers, 247, 258
Structure-action polarity, 8, 261, 263
Systematic contingency. *See* Contingency; Path-dependency

Taylorism, 143, 226
Teleology, 3, 62, 63, 84
Temperance, 46, 68–69, 71–72, 75
Teulings, Ad, 87, 88–89, 215
Textiles, 4, 10, 14, 31, 82, 101, 151, 272
Thompson, Edward P., 3, 4, 5, 9, 10, 11, 13, 40, 109, 259, 280
Tilburg, 31, 64, 67, 82, 93, 265
Tilly, Charles, 7, 40, 63, 87
Totality: structured totality, 5, 90, 92, 261. *See also* Contingency
Troelstra, Jelle, 136
Truck system, 37, 46–49, 66, 74, 269

Unemployment, 83
Union of the Cross, 71
Union rights, 56
United Shoe Machinery Company, 268, 279
Urbanization, 91, 277; and crises of urban underinvestment, 272, 274; low-level provisions in Eindhoven periphery, 108. *See also* Eindhoven

Variables paradigm, 8, 262
Vertical integration, 57, 74
Vienna, 265

Waalwijk, 32, 37, 47
Waerden, Theo van der, 104
Wages, 96, 106, 121, 124, 147, 154, 216, 237; and family relations, 164; and housing, 113, 274
Wallerstein, Immanuel, 231
Welfare: Dutch state welfare policy, 171
Wilentz, Sean, 9
Williams, Raymond, 4, 5, 260
Wolf, Eric, 1, 3, 4, 5, 90, 261
Wood, Stephen, 12
Worker-peasants, 90, 95, 96, 106, 265, 267, 272
Workers, 214; adolescents, 101, 214, 231; cigarmakers, 116, 120–121; girls, 135, 141–144; glassworkers, 140, 149, 150, 158, 173; immaturity, 84, 87; lodgers / commuters, 147, 154, 156, 161–162, 169–170, 214, 216, 219, 220, 223, 231, 276; metalworkers, 89, 130, 131, 134, 138, 140, 149, 158, 220, 223; semi-skilled, 88–89; skilled, 47, 49, 52, 67, 73, 74, 173, 215; unskilled, 87, 142, 159, 171, 274; unskilled labor as human capital, 171; white collar, 69, 73, 140, 173. *See also* Immigrant families
Workers' quiescence, 83, 84, 86, 87, 90, 91, 139, 259
Working class formation, 11, 13, 16, 87, 191; historical anthropology critique, 13
Working class identities: and absenteeism, 147, 161; and family economy, 91; historical anthropology of, 13–15, 17; and rationality of protest, 40, 57–58; struggle over, 142; workers' culture, 91, 193, 245
Working hours, 48, 218, 221
World-system theory, 263
Worsley, Peter, 7

Zeitlin, Jonathan, 12
Zolberg, Ari, 23
Zukin, Sharon, 9

DON KALB IS ASSISTANT PROFESSOR
ON THE FACULTY OF GENERAL SOCIAL SCIENCES
AT UTRECHT UNIVERSITY.

Library of Congress Cataloging-in-Publication Data
Kalb, Don.
Expanding class: Power and everyday politics in industrial communities,
The Netherlands, 1850–1950 / Don Kalb.
p.   cm. — (Comparative and international working-class history)
Includes bibliographical references (p.   ) and index.
ISBN 0-8223-2012-6 (alk. paper). — ISBN 0-8223-2022-3 (pbk. : alk. paper)
1. Working class—Netherlands—North Brabant—History.   2. Industries—Netherlands—
North Brabant—History.   3. Power (Social sciences).
I. Title.   II. Series.
HG8519.N67K35   1997
305.5'62'0949245—DC21   97-13963
                                                                          CIP